Eastern Europe, Gorbachev, and Reform

In this revised and expanded edition of her highly successful and well-received book, Karen Dawisha shows how the first five years of the Gorbachev era set the scene for the avalanche of reform that occurred throughout Eastern Europe in 1989. Communist parties lost their monopoly of power in one country after another, with multi-party systems emerging throughout the region. Wide-ranging economic changes introduced market principles and brought these countries closer to the West. Beginning with the Berlin Wall, the long-standing political, economic, and military divisions in Europe began to disappear. And even the question of German reunification emerged without a major crisis erupting in the center of Europe.

The Soviet reaction has been to welcome these changes as being in accord with the principles behind *perestroika*. The Brezhnev doctrine has finally died. But the management of Soviet relations with the new Eastern Europe neverthe-less will be full of difficulties for Gorbachev. There is great uneasiness at the prospect that a conservative backlash both in the Soviet Union and in Eastern Europe could still impede the progress of reform.

The challenges facing Gorbachev and his East European allies remain acute: to find ways to reinvigorate archaic political and economic institutions without producing an avalanche of pent-up anti-Soviet and anti-socialist pop-ular demands and to construct international relations in an undivided Europe in such a way that the Soviet Union will not be left out.

The emergence of democratic institutions and market economies in the region presents enormous opportunities also for the West. But with those opportunities also come responsibilities. The changes in Eastern Europe need support only the West can provide. At the same time changes taking place there will also produce and stimulate reforms in Western economic, political, and security relationships.

Eastern Europe, Gorbachev, and Reform addresses these historic changes and analyzes the challenges now facing new East European leaders and their Soviet and Western counterparts – challenges that will set the agenda for global politics well into the twenty-first century.

Eastern Europe, Gorbachev, and Reform

The Great Challenge

Second Edition

Karen Dawisha
University of Maryland
College Park

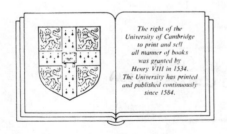

The right of the
University of Cambridge
to print and sell
all manner of books
was granted by
Henry VIII in 1534.
The University has printed
and published continuously
since 1584.

CAMBRIDGE UNIVERSITY PRESS

CAMBRIDGE

NEW YORK   PORT CHESTER   MELBOURNE   SYDNEY

Published by the Press Syndicate of the University of Cambridge
The Pitt Building, Trumpington Street, Cambridge CB2 1RP
40 West 20th Street, New York, NY 10011, USA
10 Stamford Road, Oakleigh, Melbourne 3166, Australia

© Karen Dawisha 1988, 1990

First published 1988

Second edition 1990

Printed in the United States of America

Library of Congress Cataloging-in-Publication Data
Dawisha, Karen.
Eastern Europe, Gorbachev, and reform: the great challenge
by Karen Dawisha − 2nd ed.
p. cm.
Includes bibliographical references.
ISBN 0-521-38498-2 − ISBN 0-521-38652-7 (pbk.)

1. Europe, Eastern − Foreign relations − Soviet Union. 2. Soviet
Union − Foreign relations − Europe, Eastern. 3. Europe, Eastern −
Politics and government − 1945−1989; 4. Gorbachev, Mikhail
Sergeevich, 1931− . 5. Europe − Politics and government − 1945−
I. Title.   DJK45.S65D38   1990
327'.0947 − dc20   90-1751
                                                       CIP

British Library Cataloging in Publication Data applied for

ISBN 0-521-38498-2 hardback
ISBN 0-521-38652-7 paperback

For Emile and Nadia
and Their World of Dinosaurs and Unicorns

Contents

List of Illustrations and Tables   *page* xi
Preface   xiii

Chapter 1: Introduction   I

PART ONE: THE HISTORY OF THE CHALLENGE

Chapter 2: Soviet Interests and Perspectives   9
Soviet Conceptions of Eastern Europe   11
  Slavophiles Versus Westernizers   12
  Marxism-Leninism   13
  Stalinism   15
  Impact of the War   19
  Conceptions Under Gorbachev   20
Soviet Interests in Eastern Europe   25
The Challenge to Moscow   29

**Chapter 3: East European Conceptions
and Interests**   40
East European Conceptions   40
  The Lure of the West   41
  Heirs to Autocracy?   42
East European Interests   44
History as Politics in the Bloc   47
  Memories of Greater Bulgaria   48

Romania: Latinist Aspirations Against an
    Oppressive Background   51
Hungary: The Legacy of St. Stephen   55
Czechoslovakia: Masarykism Versus Communism   59
The German Democratic Republic: History Denied   63
Poland: The West's Trojan Horse?   67

Chapter 4: The Links That Bind   81
System of Control Under Stalin   81
The Bloc System After Stalin   85
Interparty Relations   85
Military and Security Cooperation   99
Economic Leverage: Kto Kovo?   109

PART TWO: MEETING THE CHALLENGE

**Chapter 5: Beyond Coercion: Can Eastern Europe
Meet the Challenge?**   127
Durability and Change   127
    The Case of Poland   130
Viability and Transformation   132
    The Case of Czechoslovakia   134
    The Case of Hungary   136
Legitimacy and Consensus   139
    The Case of the GDR   144
Conclusion   148

Chapter 6: The East European Policy Agenda   152
Political Issues   153
    The Case of Czechoslovakia   158
Social Issues   159
    The Case of Poland   166
Economic Issues   169
Problems and Remedies   173
    The Case of Hungary   176

The Case of Poland 179
The Case of Romania 182
The Case of Bulgaria 185
The Case of Czechoslovakia 187
The Case of the GDR 191
Prospects 193

**Chapter 7: Beyond the Brezhnev Doctrine: Can
Moscow Meet the Challenge of a New Europe?** 197
Gorbachev's East European Team 198
The Emerging Debate 201
The 27th Party Congress 206
"New Thinking" and Eastern Europe 207
Democratization 208
Military Doctrine 210
Many Roads to Socialism 213
Europe as a "Common Home" 216
The Brezhnev Doctrine 218
Moscow, the German Question, and a New
European Order 222

**Chapter 8: Epilogue: Can, or Should, Europe Overcome
Its Division?** 228
Western Policy: Its Origins and Limitations 231
Alliance Cohesion: At What Cost? 238
Fostering a European Identity 241

Appendix I: Chronology of East European Events 251
Appendix II: Soviet and East European Leadership
Successions, 1945–1990 290
Appendix III: East European Communist Parties, Their
Successors, Leaders, and Memberships 296
Appendix IV: East European Elections and Major
Contenders, 1990 297
Index 300

Illustrations and Tables

Figures

4.1: Rate of growth of Soviet trade with Eastern
Europe, 1971–89   *page* 120
6.1: Average annual percentage growth of GNP   171
6.2: Percentages of East European imports by
trading partners   174
6.3: Percentages of East European exports by
trading partners   175
6.4: Soviet and East European gross and net hard-currency
debt, totals and per capita, 1988   188

Tables

4.1: Eastern Europe: gross hard-currency debt, 1971–88,
selected years   118
4.2: Soviet Union: trade with Eastern Europe, 1985–7   119
6.1: Annual percentage rates of growth of GNP, six
East European countries, 1970–88   169
6.2: Indexes of East European real GNP per capita at
adjusted factor cost, 1970 and 1975–88   170
6.3: Eastern Europe: debt indicators for 1982 and
country rankings   178

xi

Preface

In reaction to the first edition of this book, one reviewer concluded that the book kept "stumbling over the idea of reconstituting Europe, as if Europe has ever been more than a geographical expression. . . . Contrary to the impression sometimes left by this book, Europe, West and East, is not striving to unify itself" (*The Economist*, London, July 2, 1988).

Events in Eastern Europe in 1989 have provided a glorious vindication of the basic premise of the first edition – that the division of Europe was unnatural. To be sure, the ascension to power of Mikhail Gorbachev created a challenge to much of the conventional wisdom concerning the Soviet Union and Soviet leaders. New style and new substance were brought to the conduct of Soviet foreign policy. The repercussions of this new approach are only now making a significant impact on many fronts. Certainly U.S.–Soviet relations have been affected directly. It is also now being recognized that the impact on Eastern Europe of the new policy directions will be even more dramatic and far-reaching.

Many of the East European leaders who were installed and protected by Soviet power have fallen as a result of the new "openness" being proclaimed in Moscow. Opposition groups have emerged and have felt emboldened, especially as the perception continues to grow that the Cold War is grinding to an end. Dormant anti-Soviet sentiment has also made its presence felt among ethnic groups in the East-bloc countries.

Events may follow another path if a new generation of leaders can inject vitality and energy into the East European economies, expanding trade and markets. There is a great deal of untapped potential in Eastern Europe, and dramatic changes in the shape of the world of international politics and trade are still possible.

However events unfold in the Soviet bloc, the cauldron may be coming to a boil, with unpredictable consequences. I will consider this second edition a success if it helps bring to bear some historical perspective and political analysis on this turbulent and exciting region of the world. Neither policymakers nor students of international politics nor well-informed laymen can afford to underestimate the potential for change that has been unleashed in Eastern Europe by the reform campaign in the Soviet Union.

The second edition of this book is an expanded and revised version of the original, which appeared in 1988. This new edition takes account of changes up to the spring of 1990. In its preparation I wish to acknowledge the excellent editorial and research assistance of Jonathan Valdez of the University of Maryland. Also, special thanks to the staff of Cambridge University Press, including Richard Hollick, Sophia Prybylski, Linda Hollick, and all who worked diligently to get this second edition out in a timely fashion.

This second edition builds on the original, which could not have been written without the encouragement and support of the Council on Foreign Relations, whose generous assistance I readily acknowledge. The contribution of the Council can be measured in several ways. The idea for this book grew out of the John J. McCloy Study Group on Eastern Europe, which I directed at the Council in 1984–5. The group was chaired by Graham T. Allison, Jr., and co-directed with Warren Zimmermann. Members of the group included David L. Aaron, Jeremy Azrael, Robert D. Blackwill, James Chace, Arthur Cyr, Kempton Dunn, K. Scott Fisher, Charles Gati, Lincoln Gordon, Donald Green, William E. Griffith, John P. Hardt, Edward A. Hewett, Thomas L. Hughes, William G. Hyland, John Kornblum, Paul H. Kreisberg, F. Stephen Larrabee, Ivo John Lederer, Robert H. Legvold, Winston Lord, James G. Lowenstein, William Mader, J. John Montias, Zygmunt Nagorski, Jr., Matthew Nimetz, Herbert Okun, Mark Palmer, Andrew J. Pierre, Olin C. Robinson, Enid C. B. Schoettle, Marshall D. Shulman, Helmut Sonnenfeldt, Angela E. Stent, Eugene P. Trani, Richard H. Ullman, John C. Whitehead, and Charles Wolf, Jr.

The Council also organized several author's review meetings. My particular thanks to all those who attended the meetings and commented on various sections of the manuscript: John C. Campbell, Charles Gati, David Kellogg, Paul Kreisberg, F. Stephen Larrabee, Ivo John Lederer, Michael Mandelbaum, Andrew Pierre, Sarah Terry, and Warren Zimmermann. Within the Council, William Gleysteen and Gregory Treverton also provided subsequent useful comments on the original manuscript.

The University of Maryland generously facilitated the writing of the manuscript. Finally, special thanks to Michael Holdsworth at Cambridge University Press, whose enthusiastic and relentless support for the manuscript from its inception through this second edition is greatly appreciated.

KAREN DAWISHA

College Park, Maryland
April 30, 1990

I

Introduction

When Mikhail Sergeevich Gorbachev was elected general secretary of the Communist Party of the Soviet Union in March 1985, by his own admission he inherited an enormous backlog of problems. Domestically, the Soviet Union was in economic, political, and moral decline. Expenditures on the Soviet arms buildup had long exceeded the country's capability to pay for it and at the same time maintain the population's standard of living. Externally, the country faced numerous and intractable difficulties, ranging from the collapse of détente to the stalemate in the war against the Afghan resistance.

Yet when he came to power, of all the issues that urgently needed to be addressed, Gorbachev chose to emphasize as his "first commandment" the strengthening of relations with East European countries and the solution of the many difficulties which had accumulated in this area.[1] These difficulties included issues that had arisen in recent years, as well as many that appeared to be intrinsic to Soviet relations with Eastern Europe.

Facing him was a challenge which went to the very heart of socialism, for Gorbachev appeared to believe that socialism was a dynamic and transnational system capable of reforming itself not only in the USSR but also in those East European countries that have had a legacy of both fierce anti-Sovietism and strong cultural allegiance to the West. Would Gorbachev seek to improve the viability and stability of these regimes even if that would unleash societal forces which could threaten the reform movement in both Eastern Europe and the USSR? In 1956, the Hungarian uprising virtually had put an end to Khrushchev's more liberal policy of encouraging "separate paths to socialism." In 1968, the suppression of the "Prague Spring" also marked an end to more tentative Soviet reform efforts. Would the same thing happen to Gorbachev? Would untrammeled popular aspirations for change in Eastern Europe get out of control and reactivate this cycle of stagnation, reform, and repression, thereby threatening both Gorbachev's domestic policy agenda and his own political position? Or would Gorbachev seek to break this cycle by declining to use force, even if communist party rule in Eastern Europe were threatened, as it came to be in a number of countries in 1989? Breaking this apparent cycle and producing conditions which would allow reform socialism to put down real and lasting roots in Eastern Europe would be Gorbachev's greatest achievement, but also his greatest challenge. The challenge for Gorbachev, therefore, would lie in the creation of a post-imperial commonwealth of stable, allied, and friendly states within a Europe that in its new unity could once again serve as the moral compass for Western civilization. It would be a challenge no less because the reputation of socialism might be salvageable only if existing corrupt and repressive communist party regimes were allowed to collapse, to be replaced by multiparty systems in which social democratic and democratic socialist parties might become a force in the center of Europe once again.

Flowing from this challenge is a series of issues faced by the USSR, Eastern Europe, and the West. These issues, as well as the central challenge, can be analyzed only against the backdrop of the historical roots and contemporary development of the relationship between the Soviet Union and Eastern Europe, a relationship deeply affected by Eastern Europe's political and military ties with the East and its simultaneous cultural and historical links to the West. It is the all-embracing nature of this conflict between systems, values, and cultures which explains why Eastern Europe remains at the heart of the East–West rivalry. Even in an era of Soviet reform and eased U.S.–Soviet tensions, many questions about Soviet intentions in Eastern Europe remain unanswered. It is the purpose of this book to address these questions.

Part One of the book focuses on the background to the challenge presented by East European aspirations for reform. The three chapters on Soviet interests, East European responses, and

Soviet levers of influence present the political, economic, and military environment within which Soviet–East European relations have developed over the past forty-five years.

Chapter 2 addresses long-term Soviet interests in Eastern Europe and examines the historical, cultural, and ideological factors which shaped the basic Soviet conception of the region. From this chapter, the question arises whether or not any Soviet leader, including one who universally has come to be recognized as being committed to reform within his own country, could really be interested in and capable of reforming the basic structure of Soviet–East European relations. This chapter also analyzes the Soviet Union's geo-political and military stake in Eastern Europe, an interest that has been a subject of debate in the Soviet Union, leading some to conclude that the Soviet need for a massive military presence in the area has declined.

Chapter 3 then analyzes the East European reaction to Soviet power and focuses on East European interests in, and perceptions of, the Soviet Union. These perceptions are affected by the legacies of varying historical links with both East and West, links which have become part of the political landscape in the relationship between Moscow and its allies. The prospect of a reform-minded leader in the Soviet Union has elicited great excitement in the Eastern bloc; at the same time, the policy of *glasnost,* or openness, combined with increased attention to national differences between bloc states, has produced a resurgence of nationalism and of cultural traditions largely rooted in the West. The extensive changes that have occurred in Eastern Europe in general have confirmed the earlier view that greater diversity of opinion and concentration on national sovereignty would in the short run produce an outpouring of anti-Sovietism, directed not against Gorbachev personally but against past Soviet practices, against local leaders who have served Moscow or resisted change to the detriment of their own populations, and against the structure of Soviet–East European relations, which is widely perceived in Eastern Europe as being subservient to Soviet interests.

It is the structure of Soviet–East European relations that is the subject of Chapter 4. Moscow's traditional networks of political and military links have served to bind Eastern Europe to the Soviet Union in important ways. Certainly, Gorbachev has not shown himself to be interested in removing all of these links, but has sought to vitalize them and make them more dependent on bloc consensus rather than on Soviet fiat. In the realm of economic relations, both sides pursue mutual interests: Eastern Europe is dependent upon Soviet raw materials, but Moscow is eager to improve those high-technology imports from Eastern Europe necessary for restructuring the Soviet economy and improving its performance. This discussion of the interaction between Soviet and East European interests on one hand and of the links that bind the two sides on the other serves to elucidate the nature of the challenge faced by the Soviets as Eastern Europe moves through the reform era.

Part Two of the book addresses the ways in which all parties whose interests are engaged in Eastern Europe might meet the challenges ahead. Within this second part of the book, Chapter 5 examines the reactions of East European leaders to the fundamental challenges facing their regimes, while Chapter 6 addresses the short-term policy agenda in the political, social, and economic realms. The need to move beyond simple durability to viability and legitimacy has been an objective requirement for some time. Success in this realm has been slow and subject to setbacks as conservative forces at home and elsewhere in the bloc have resisted change. But with Gorbachev himself insisting that East European leaders must be responsible to their own populations, as he did during his trip to Prague in April 1987, the impetus to move beyond coercion has been provided by the Soviet leadership itself.

The debate about these fundamental issues began against the backdrop of widespread leadership changes in Eastern Europe. Such changes are bringing to the forefront a new generation who, like Gorbachev, must seek radical new solutions to the problems of nationalism, youth, religion, consumer welfare, and economic stagnation. Clearly, under certain scenarios, such changes can fundamentally strengthen socialism in Eastern Europe and thereby vindicate the risks taken. This is true particularly if more Western-oriented variants of social democracy are adopted with Soviet support. However, many other forces also are at play in the region. The dangers ahead are apparent, and they present real challenges both to the Soviet Union and to the West.

Chapter 7 addresses the prospects of the Soviet Union moving beyond the use or threat of force in Eastern Europe. It also examines the specific nature of Moscow's bilateral relations with each of the six bloc states (Poland, the German Democratic Republic, Czechoslovakia, Hungary, Romania, and Bulgaria) as they have developed since Gorbachev came to power. Gorbachev and other Soviet leaders have actively solicited reform throughout the bloc in a wide-ranging series of multilateral and bilateral meetings, but the tide of events has revealed the constraints operating on Moscow's ability to control the reform process in several bloc countries.

The final chapter examines the possible effects of changes in Soviet–East European relations on Europe and the West, analyzes Western interests in various types of change, and suggests ways in which the West can or should influence the Soviet Union to promote further reform. Of particular concern is the fact that in proposing arms reductions, economic cooperation, and expanded cultural links across a divided Europe, Gorbachev also fueled popular yearning in Eastern Europe for an end to that division.

In raising the issue of the effects of changes in the Soviet Union and Eastern Europe on a divided Europe, the final chapter returns to the questions raised at the outset of the book:

• In promoting the notion that reform in the Soviet Union can beneficially spill over and stimulate similar processes in Eastern Europe, did Gorbachev not foresee a repetition of previous upheavals, when reforms in Eastern Europe resulted not in the perfection of socialism but in its near collapse?

• In proposing changes which would produce more openness in Soviet–East European relations, did Gorbachev believe that the reputation of both socialism as a system and the USSR as the dominant partner in those relations could emerge strengthened from an open debate about the effects of four decades of stagnation and abuse?

• Finally, in calling for measures which would promote greater cooperation between Eastern and Western Europe, how optimistic was Gorbachev that East Europeans would not see this policy as a "green light" to rediscover their Western cultural orientations, and in so doing threaten to undermine Soviet geo-strategic interests in the center of Europe?

The challenges facing Gorbachev in reforming his own society are numerous and nearly intractable. Failure to achieve his objectives not only may risk Gorbachev's career but also, and more importantly, may condemn his country to more decades of waste and stagnation. But the process of reform in the Soviet Union does not carry many of the dangers inherent in that process in Eastern Europe, for in Eastern Europe there are dangers both in failing to reform and in trying to reform at all. The legitimacy of socialism, both as an ideal and as a system, depends on the success of reform, but Soviet military interests in Eastern Europe, arguably, will not in all circumstances be enhanced by reform. Indeed, the process of change and the end results of certain types of change, like the collapse of East Germany, could be seen as positively deleterious to Soviet security.

The need to proceed cautiously has been appreciated by Gorbachev and other Soviet and East European leaders. At the same time, the pace and direction of reform was also determined by the disastrous interplay between conservative leaders seeking no change and radical forces longing to open the floodgates, as occurred in Romania. The emergence of multiparty systems and market economies in Eastern Europe challenged Gorbachev to speed their introduction into the USSR, just as the near collapse of the communist party as a force in East European elections hastened its removal as a vanguard party in the USSR. The independence of East European countries from Soviet rule also strengthened the resolve of non-Russian nationalities inside the USSR to seek their own independence, threatening the very breakup of the Soviet state. The greatest challenge facing Gorbachev, therefore, remains not in promoting change but in preventing the tidewaters of accumulated desire for change amongst the East European populations from engulfing his own programs and aspirations both for their own countries and for the Soviet Union.

Note

1   *Pravda,* March 12, 1985.

Part One

The History of the Challenge

2

Soviet Interests and Perspectives

Brezhnev spoke at length about the sacrifices of the
Soviet Union in the Second World War: . . . At such a
cost, the Soviet Union had gained security, and the
guarantee of that security was the postwar division of
Europe. . . . "For us," Brezhnev went on, "the results
of the Second World War are inviolable, and we will
defend them even at the cost of risking a new war."
And then he said in so many words that they would
have undertaken the military intervention in Czechoslovakia even if such a risk had existed.—From
Czechoslovak Party Secretary Zdeněk Mlynář's eyewit-
ness account of the Moscow meeting of the Soviet and
Czechoslovak Politburos following the 1968 invasion of
Czechoslovakia.[1]

The events that are now taking place in the countries
of Eastern Europe concern the peoples and countries
of that region. . . . We have no right, moral or political, to interfere in events happening there.—Mikhail
Gorbachev to Finland's President Koivisto, Helsinki,
October 25, 1989

During the forty years which followed World War II, the establishment and maintenance of its position in Eastern Europe was
the most important goal of Soviet foreign policy. As the above
quotation from Brezhnev indicates, and as Soviet actions
showed, the Soviet Union was willing to forgo any other objective in international affairs in order to secure and promote its
influence over almost all aspects of life in those countries which

9

in 1989 constituted, along with the USSR, the member states of the Warsaw Pact: Poland, Czechoslovakia, the German Democratic Republic (GDR), Hungary, Romania, and Bulgaria.

This book focuses on Soviet policy toward Eastern Europe precisely because it is the extent of the Soviet commitment and the East-bloc states' reactions that have posed the single most continuously destabilizing aspect of international relations in the postwar period. In Soviet relations with other contiguous countries, only China has caused the Soviet Union as much concern. Afghanistan, where Soviet troops battled insurgents for a decade, was an intense problem, but it paled in comparison with Soviet costs and commitments in Eastern Europe since 1945. Eastern Europe is also seen in Moscow as being more important than any other noncontiguous area or country, such as the Middle East, or any pro-Soviet Third World regime, including Vietnam and Cuba. Other socialist countries, pro-Soviet regimes, non-ruling communist parties, and national liberation movements similarly recede toward the periphery of Soviet interests when compared with Eastern Europe. The nature of the Soviet–East European relationship is qualitatively more intense and substantial than are Soviet relations with any other country, and despite the enormous changes taking place in Eastern Europe, there is little prospect of change in Soviet priorities for the foreseeable future. If anything, the crises and transformations occurring there have increased the intensity of Soviet activities, while also changing their nature.

Many in both the East and West have long believed that Eastern Europe was a crisis waiting to happen, because of the interplay between entrenched Soviet commitments and the resultant difficulties which indigenous regimes experienced in securing the support of their own populations. This interplay had wider repercussions because local populations not infrequently looked to the West for encouragement, both as an exemplar in the fields of democracy and human rights and as an active supporter in the process of encouraging these regimes to be more accountable to local aspirations – a process that in the past has impinged directly on Soviet interests. In addition, Western leaders long calculated not only that the Soviet Union would resist any Western attempt to reduce its military control of Eastern

Europe but also that to maintain control Moscow would be prepared to take actions which risked escalation to nuclear war. Whether or not the Soviets would have sacrificed their own existence in the defense of Eastern Europe is not the point. Rather, Soviet military doctrine depended on the West and the East Europeans believing that the defense of the Soviet homeland rested on the maintenance of military vigilance in Eastern Europe. Even with the extensive changes which have taken place in Soviet military thinking, Eastern Europe remains an area of great national security concern for Moscow.

Why have the Soviets attached so much importance to the protection of their position in Eastern Europe? An answer to this question requires a consideration of Soviet conceptions of Eastern Europe, as well as an analysis of Soviet interests in that region.

Soviet Conceptions of Eastern Europe

The historical, cultural, and ideological influences which have combined to shape contemporary Soviet views of Eastern Europe are important to consider not only because for centuries Russia, a large and militarily powerful country, has had a love–hate relationship with the region but also because since the time of Lenin its leaders have espoused an ideology which takes the historical process extremely seriously. They have derived their legitimacy from being agents and vanguards of a historical process which, they have maintained, will culminate in the establishment of a communist society. Even with the ascendancy of Mikhail Gorbachev, elements of this forward-looking vision remain. In the past, Soviet leaders also have derived authority from being at the head of a community of "fraternal peoples" who, in the words of the program approved at the 27th Congress of the Communist Party of the Soviet Union (CPSU) in 1986, have "common historical destinies."[2] Despite clear Soviet acquiescence in the emergence of multiparty systems in Eastern Europe in 1989, Moscow still sought to maintain unity amongst the remaining communists. At a bloc meeting called in Varna, Bulgaria, in September 1989, for example, the official communiqué called for greater "interaction, solidarity, and unanimity of the

Central Committees in the socialist countries."[3] The views of Soviet leaders are important, therefore, both because they do in fact seek to shape the destinies of the East Europeans and because their success or failure in this effort affects their own party's stature with the Soviet population.

Slavophiles Versus Westernizers. The Soviet conception of Eastern Europe also has roots in the contradictory and complex Russian views of Europe as a whole. Dating from the 1830s, Russian intellectual life was influenced strongly by the debate between the Slavophiles and Westernizers. Although the split between the two groups was not as clear-cut as is sometimes presented, the Westernizers nevertheless did seek to introduce "enlightened" Western ideas and political institutions into Russia against the objections of most Slavophiles. The latter, in their determination to defend Russian traditions and in their conviction of the moral superiority of the Russians over European peoples, turned their backs on the "contagion" of Western civilization.

As for the non-Germanic countries of northeastern and southeastern Europe, the gap between Russia's Westernizers and Slavophiles was not always so large. Neither group, for example, saw this geographic area as a separate entity in the middle of Europe; both saw Europe as divided between a Latin or Germanic West and a Slavic East. However, although the Slavophiles saw the two forces or cultures as being implacably opposed, the Westernizers sought the merger of the Slavic East with the West. Both groups neglected the minority nationalities of the area (the Hungarians and the Romanians), with the little that was written about them being essentially negative. The Hungarians in particular were seen by the Slavophiles as enemies of Russia and Slavdom and were considered as a nation to be a "proud, militant, wild, and cruel Asiatic horde."[4] Both Westernizers and Slavophiles also were rather ambivalent about the Czechs and Slovaks, having had less contact with them than with other Slavs to the north and south. There was widespread pan-Slavic sentiment in both groups toward the Balkan states, particularly in the second half of the nineteenth century, when these countries began emerging from Ottoman rule. And in the north, both groups were consumed by "the Polish question."

On the issue of Polish independence and reunification, Russian opinion in the nineteenth century, as in the twentieth, was both more divided and more impassioned. To both the Slavophiles and the non-Slavophile right, the Polish question was intimately connected to Catholicism. This grouping would not have quarreled with the judgment of the Russian nationalist poet Fyodor Tiutchev, who branded Poland as the "Judas of Slavdom."[5] Seeing the Poles as having betrayed their Slavdom, these Russians also held Catholicism responsible for the decline of Poland – an extremely enduring perception that again emerged not only during the 1980–1 Polish crisis but also since then, including since Gorbachev came to power.[6]

Liberal thought in Russia was less inclined to pinpoint Catholicism as the root of Polish problems. Leading liberal thinkers and political agitators Alexander Herzen and Mikhail Bakunin were at different times supporters of Polish independence. But this group, like all other Russians then and since, resented continued Polish attempts to deny their cultural and ethnic links with the Russians. Even Paul Miliukov, regarded by some as the last pre-Revolutionary Westernizer, expressed his annoyance at the extreme Russophobia of Polish nationalists who, he believed, had "presented themselves to European public opinion as defenders of Europe from Russian 'barbarism' – in the past, present, and future."[7]

Marxism-Leninism. Eurocentric by nature, once Marxism took root on Russian soil, it should have resolved these differences over Eastern Europe decisively in favor of the Westernizers. Marx and Engels both believed Europe to be the natural home of the eventual socialist revolution, not only because they saw in it an economic system close to collapse but also because they believed that culturally and educationally the European proletariat was best equipped to build a new social order on the ruins of the old. Admittedly, in the introduction to the first Russian edition of the *Communist Manifesto* they conceded the possibility that the small peasant commune (*obshchina*) in rural Russia might be capable of making a direct transition to socialism, but nowhere did they conceive it possible that this sleepy Russian giant would ever, or could ever, be the beacon for socialism in Europe. Nor did they see the non-Germanic nations of Central Europe as standard-bearers. On the contrary, they regarded them uniformly to be part of the "East," riven by national and anti-feudal insurrections. Their only hope, echoing Herzen, and in a foretaste of Lenin, was that as a result of these volcanic upheavals, the lava would flow from East to West.

It took first Lenin and then Stalin to change the center of gravity toward Muscovy. Lenin's major theoretical contributions came before the revolution in *What Is To Be Done?* and *Imperialism, The Highest Stage of Capitalism.* In the former tract, he set the stage for the break with the social democratic traditions dominant in Central Europe by declaring that "the working class, by their own efforts, are capable only of trade union consciousness." What was required was a highly centralized vanguard party composed of full-time revolutionaries, many from the ranks of the progressive intelligentsia. The party would educate and mobilize the working class in preparation for the revolution, but also act as an agent for the proletariat in organizing and executing the takeover. This tract was criticized both at the time and subsequently as the prime example of Lenin's own inability to shake off the Russian autocratic and anti-popular impulses he was trying to overthrow. At this stage, however, he did not see Russia as a natural or likely setting for the first socialist revolution. In *Imperialism,* he repeatedly stated that true socialism could be established only in Europe, where capitalism was most developed. But capitalism there, he believed, had been able to postpone its demise by expanding into underdeveloped countries in search of cheap labor, raw materials, and additional markets. Only by depriving Europe of its new lifeline to the colonies, therefore, could capitalism be sufficiently weakened to allow the proletariat and its vanguard to rise up and overthrow the bourgeois state.

After 1917, Lenin maintained that the revolution in Russia had helped to weaken capitalism in several ways: It had been a blow to European capitalists, who had significant investments in Russian banking and industry; it served as a beacon of hope, a symbol of socialism to the working classes and left-wing intelligentsia of Europe; and it also was seen as an important home base, safe haven, hideout, and arms cache all rolled into one for European revolution. Thus, to the extent that the European communists were asked to subordinate their own struggle to the defense of the Russian Revolution, it was primarily because they conceived of it as both the ideological avant-garde and the material rear guard of their own revolutions.

For Lenin, as for Marx and Engels before him, Europe meant Germany and the countries to its west. Indeed, the Baltic states and the new nations of Eastern Europe (especially hostile Poland) were seen by him as a "hindrance to our revolution because they separate Soviet Russia from revolutionary Germany."[8] The war between Poland and the new Soviet republic in 1920–1 further reinforced this view. Only Hungary, where communists seized power for a short time in 1919, was consistently portrayed as part of the European revolutionary process.

By the time of Lenin's death in 1924, much had been done to establish Russian hegemony over the international communist movement; nevertheless, the object of this exercise, in Lenin's eyes, was to better coordinate all revolutionary forces in order to achieve the more speedy collapse of capitalism *in Europe*. Thus, Lenin saw his major role on the one hand as "keeping the revolution warm" for Europe, while on the other hand working feverishly to raise the cultural and political consciousness of the Russian people so that the revolution would not be distorted out of all proportion while in a "holding pattern" over Moscow. However, even Lenin had occasion to doubt that this would be possible and to wonder if the Bolsheviks themselves were not gradually falling under the influence of those autocratic reflexes of centuries of tsarist rule. In his report to the 11th Party Congress in 1922, Lenin despaired:

> The economic power in the hands of the proletarian state of Russia is quite adequate to ensure the transition to communism. What then is lacking? Obviously what is lacking is culture among the . . . communists. If we take Moscow with its 4,700 communists in responsible positions, and if we take that huge bureaucratic machine, that gigantic heap, we must ask: who is directing whom? . . . The communists are not directing; they are being directed.[9]

Stalinism. Stalin did not suffer from any similar doubts about where the capital of the international communist movement should be. Faced with the failure of the European revolution and the rise of fascism and militant ultranationalism in Germany and other European states, many of them in Eastern Europe, Stalin ruled under conditions that allowed, and some would say necessitated, a totally different conception of Central Europe.

Stalin never conceived of Russia as having a place *in* Europe, or even as being an extension of European culture and civilization. He did not adhere to the Leninist view that the revolution risked being weighed down by Russian culture. On the contrary, he extolled "Russian" values and constantly denigrated the corruption and consumerism that he believed were rife among the European bourgeoisie and proletariat alike, seeing little of value that the Russians could extract from Europe. (He thought more highly of the United States, exhorting Communist Party members in Moscow, for example, to combine "Russian revolutionary sweep" with "American efficiency" in order to achieve the proper Leninist style of work.[10]) Equally, he eschewed the notion that the USSR was merely a staging post for the implantation of socialism in its natural home – Germany. On the contrary, although he conceded that Germany may have been the heartland of socialism in the 1840s when Marx and Engels wrote the *Communist Manifesto,* Stalin felt that by the beginning of the twentieth century, "because Russia was the only country in which there existed a real force capable of resolving the contradiction of imperialism in a revolutionary way . . . the center of the revolutionary movement was bound to shift to Russia."[11]

Out of this rejection of Europe as the natural center of the proletarian revolution came the development of "socialism in one country," which marked the final ascendancy of Slavophile reflexes vis-à-vis Europe. No longer was Europe seen as verging on the brink of collapse; it was militarily strong and threatening. The only way the USSR could meet the challenge, according to Stalin, was to establish the necessary military, industrial, and agricultural autarky to repel the attack. Hitler's promulgation of his militarist, expansionist, and anti-Slav views convinced Stalin that Germany was preparing to renew the war against Russia left unfinished by Napoleon. Stalin sought to rally the rest of Europe, but the immobility of some European leaders in the face of fascism and the open sympathy of others, including those in

Croatia, Bulgaria, Romania, Hungary, Slovakia, and among the Sudeten Germans of Bohemia and Moravia, convinced him that while publicly they may not have employed the same racist rhetoric as Hitler, nevertheless privately they too shared the Führer's basic hostility toward communism and Russia.

The Nazi–Soviet Pact of 1939 not only stalled for time in trying to prevent a Nazi invasion but also marked the birth of "national Bolshevism" as a mirror image of Hitler's domestic and foreign policies. The lands between the two powers were invaded and cynically annexed. And in the Russian heartland, Stalin's call went out not only to protect socialism but also increasingly to defend a great civilization, a great culture, and a great people. The strength of ultrapatriotism and ultranationalism was such during this period that, in the words of the Soviet historian Konstantin F. Shteppa, "a new Slavophilism negating Western influence extolled Chernyshevsky, Lenin, and Stalin at the expense of Marx himself."[12] While the new Slavophilism did embrace all Slavs, it glorified primarily the virtues of the Russians.

If "socialism in one country" evolved in the decade and a half before the outbreak of World War II, the experience of the war, when Russia saw itself standing alone against fascism, even further lowered the esteem in which Europe (and the West in general) was held by Stalin and all the Soviet leaders who rose through the ranks during that period. It was Europe that had given birth to fascism, but it was Russia that had buried it. Thus, the Communist Party line drew the consistent distinction between "the decisive role of the USSR, . . . its consistent, honest policy in international relations with the members of the anti-Hitler coalition, and on the other hand, the perfidious, mercenary, and treacherous policy of the Anglo-American imperialists in this war."[13]

This perceived failure of Russia's allies to come to its aid when it was under attack sowed the seeds in Stalin's mind for the continued chauvinistic elevation of Russia as the natural and permanent center of the postwar international communist system and the simultaneous denigration of all things European, including certain aspects of Marxism. Such was Stalin's power that by 1949, in his "On the Article of Engels: 'The External Policy of Russian

Tsarism,'" he was able to condemn Marx and Engels openly for
their negative appraisal of Russian foreign policy *under the tsar!*[14]
Stalin and his influential party secretary for culture, Andrei
Zhdanov, also enunciated the famous "two-camp" doctrine,
which both reflected and strengthened the postwar division of the
world into two great power blocs. In ideology, this led to the
rigorous fight against "cosmopolitanism," in which party officials
were warned against "blackening the past of the Great Russian
people and understating its role in world history." The exhorta-
tion continued:

> Experience proves that any undervaluation of the role
> and significance of the Russian people in world history
> is directly tied in with admiration for foreign lands.
> Nihilism in the evaluation of the great achievements of
> Russian culture and the culture of the other peoples of
> the USSR is the reverse side of fawning before the
> bourgeois culture of the West.[15]

Such views came to the fore at a time when the Soviet Union
was developing its own infrastructure in Eastern Europe. Soviet
leaders perceived the politics of that region as having been dominated over the previous twenty years by anti-Slav fascists, Rus-
sophobic nationalists, "bourgeois deviationist" social democrats,
and communists who all too often, as in the case of Poland, had
come under the influence of cosmopolitanism, an anti-Semitic
euphemism for the large numbers of Jews among the ranks of
local communists.

Even those East European leaders who had studied in Moscow and were pro-Soviet by inclination were reluctant to accept
Stalin's rigid and xenophobic assessment of the superiority of
Russian culture and the concomitant evils of cooperating with
the West. For example, Jakub Berman was a lifelong communist
who had spent the war in the USSR, returning to Poland in 1944
and becoming the secretary in charge of ideology for the ruling
Polish United Workers' Party in 1948. As such, he might have
been expected to have enthusiastically endorsed at least the anti-
Western aspects of Zhdanovism. However, he has testified that
in 1948 the Polish leadership attempted to "tone down" the most
excessive aspects of the policy:

> We knew by then that it was inevitable, but we tried to
> lend it a more European character. It was an attempt

> to defend . . . our cultural ties with Western Europe,
> . . . and not to allow ourselves at any price to become
> walled up in only one part of the world.[16]

Such attempts to soften the blow of the two-camp doctrine on cultural policy only further convinced Stalin and Zhdanov of the necessity of imposing total control over this politically unreliable region. For example, having been threatened by Zhdanov not to start "throwing your weight around,"[17] since "in Moscow we know better how to apply Marxism-Leninism," Berman, in an act paralleled throughout Eastern Europe, fell in line, parroting Zhdanov in a speech by declaring at a party conference devoted to cultural affairs in May 1949:

> We must inspire disgust for art which is laden with
> formalist cynicism and lack of ideals, for decadent
> capitalist art, for American cosmopolitanism; we must
> be passionate and ruthless in combating fascist trends;
> we must above all combat reactionary Catholic
> trends.[18]

Impact of the War. Many of the more chauvinistic excesses inherent in the postwar Soviet conception of Europe died with Stalin. It was no longer so permissible to extol the virtues of the Russians as a people, particularly now that socialism had at last spread to parts of Europe, and in particular to the eastern sector of divided Germany. Nevertheless, although millions of East Europeans had also perished during the war, it was the 20 million Soviet dead whose sacrifice was the basis for the deep conviction that the peoples of Eastern Europe were in eternal *debt* to the Red Army. It is a further feature of Soviet political culture that future generations of Soviet citizens and leaders have the sacred *duty* to ensure that the gains of World War II are permanently guaranteed. This dual sense of debt and duty is captured in the single Russian word *dolg,* whose invocation has a special meaning for a nation that lost a whole generation of fathers, brothers, and sons.

Perhaps equally important as a key to the formation of contemporary political culture, and equally unfathomable in the West, was that these sacrifices were made in the darkest days of Stalinism, when virtually every family had been personally affected either by forced collectivization or by political purges which together killed, starved, or imprisoned upward of 50 million people. Yet, in the face of near defeat, when Stalin appealed to his "brothers and sisters" to save Mother Russia, they gave him everything. In so doing, the system whose foundations previously had been tenuous became more firmly established.

Memories of the war and the lessons derived from it remained vivid in the Soviet Union, despite the vilification of Stalin. As with the Jewish attitude to the Holocaust, so with the attitude amongst many Soviet citizens toward the war: The loss will not, and must not, be forgotten, and the gains made as a result of the war will never be surrendered in Eastern Europe in general and in Germany in particular. This was amply demonstrated in official statements issued by the Soviet leadership to mark the end of World War II, including the joint Communist Party and government declaration on the fortieth anniversary, which contained the following typical, and no doubt heartfelt, passage:

> The war forced on the Soviet Union the loss of twenty million of its sons and daughters. No family remained unsinged by the flames of war. Our pain and sorrow will never subside; the grief of soldiers' widows, mothers and orphans is inconsolable. The harsh and instructive lessons of the war cannot be forgotten. . . . The historic Yalta and Potsdam agreements [dividing Europe] . . . have been dependably serving the Europeans' security interests and deterring militaristic and revivalist ambitions for forty years. *All attempts to encroach on these agreements are doomed to failure.*[19]

For that section of the Soviet population which continued to adhere to these views even after Gorbachev came to power, the changes which were taking place in Central Europe were particularly hard to take.

Conceptions Under Gorbachev. When General Secretary Gorbachev spoke before the 19th Soviet Party Conference in June 1988, he admitted that "world socialism is living through a difficult and crucial period."[20] Not only were major political and economic reforms being announced and implemented inside the Soviet Union, but fundamental changes were also being sought, both within other East European states and in the mechanisms binding Moscow to its bloc allies. At the core of this effort was the realization on the part of most within the Soviet leadership that the ability to reform socialism – rather than to set into motion changes which might produce its collapse – depended on establishing its prestige and legitimacy amongst populations in those countries ruled by communist parties.

In order to succeed, Gorbachev and his supporters clearly felt it necessary to remove those "accretions of the past" which had slowed economic and social development, violated universal humanitarian principles, and consequently blackened the reputation of socialism as a system capable of harnessing human intellectual and spiritual potential to the full. For this reason, Gorbachev appeared to have decided that he needed change in Eastern Europe just as surely as he needed it in the Soviet Union. He needed it because within the Soviet bloc each country was uniquely tied to the other. There was the universal perception that Moscow had leverage in Eastern Europe and could set in motion changes if it so chose; failure to reform therefore would have been interpreted either as a sign of lack of will by Moscow or as proof that some East European leaders did not believe that Gorbachev had the political clout to enact the necessary changes. While it is highly unlikely that Gorbachev anticipated, much less stage-managed, the multitude of changes which occurred in Eastern Europe in 1989, nevertheless his public statements calling the changes a "logical outcome" of pent-up needs and characterizing them as being "in the same mainstream as our *perestroika*" would seem to suggest that he sought to promote the impression that the transformations were fully approved by Moscow.[21]

The changes which took place in Eastern Europe in 1989 brought the region back into Europe. This could have been welcomed by the Soviet leadership only to the extent that it had the same objectives for the Soviet Union. Gorbachev clearly sought from early in his rule to bring the Soviet Union closer to Europe. And from mid-1988 onward, this objective coincided with the realization that Eastern Europe also would have to be reintegrated with Europe if "Europe as a common home" were to be built.

But the opportunity to create a pan-European community,

while eagerly sought by the Westernizers in the Gorbachev circle, also threatened to increase the movement toward independence in the Baltic states and simultaneously create a backlash from Russian nationalists. There exist both internationalist and xenophobic trends within contemporary Russian national thought, as well as both pro- and anti-imperial tendencies.

Gorbachev's desire to end Russia's isolation from Europe is supported by those Russian nationalist intellectuals who see themselves as internationalist and anti-imperial, insofar as they advocate the integration of the Soviet Union into the international system on the basis of equality with other states. They would promote Russian patriotism, while rejecting the chauvinistic and xenophobic overtones inherent in much of the Russian nationalist tradition. The respected academician and Russian cultural historian Dmitrii Likhachev, who was named by Gorbachev to be head of the Soviet Cultural Foundation and who is a deputy to the Congress of Peoples' Deputies, made the distinction that "for me, patriotism is the love of one's country, while nationalism is the hatred of other peoples."[22] A paternalistic attitude toward other nations, including those inside and outside Soviet boundaries, however, also informs this strand of Russian nationalist thought: "The Russian people must never lose their moral authority among other peoples. . . . Only by being aware of our world responsibility can we, the Russians, preserve our position of leadership in our country."[23]

While elements of this wing of Russian nationalism have been co-opted by Gorbachev, nevertheless there are certain of his policies with which even they disagree. In particular, they oppose his idea that the Soviet Union should become part of a "common European home." If such a policy were to be pursued on the basis of equality and purely at the interstate level, that would be one thing; but they are concerned that a "common European home" signifies a reorientation in Russian political culture. That this is precisely what Gorbachev and his supporters have in mind is indicated by their repeated references to Russia's debt to European ideals, as in the following statement by Vladimir Lukin, then in the Foreign Ministry's Planning and Assessments Department and later chief of Gorbachev's own planning staff: "By Europe," he wrote,

we should understand not only the geopolitical phenomenon, but also a definite method as to how to live, think, communicate with other people. . . . The "common European home" is the home of a civilization of which we have been on the periphery for a long time. The processes that are going on today in our country and in a number of socialist countries in Eastern Europe have besides everything else a similar historical dimension – the dimension of movement towards a return to Europe in the civilized meaning of the word.[24]

Another trend is still more chauvinistic and nationalistic in its approach, seeing the USSR as having a rightful place of preeminence in international affairs, either because of the supremacy of its Marxist-Leninist ideology or because of its historical legacy. Although there is much that divides these two subgroups, they have in common a shared view of the intrinsic greatness of the Soviet Union, believing past errors to be the responsibility of imported ideas and non-Russian individuals or nations (especially Jews). This tendency opposes Gorbachev's restructuring of foreign policy, lamenting as did one poster at a popular rally that *Imperiya nasha rushetsya* ("Our empire is falling apart"). Thus, Nina Andreeva, the Leningrad teacher made famous by her attacks on *perestroika,* and the Christian mathematician and academician Igor Shafarevich agree at least on the point that it has been Russia and the Russians who have incurred the greatest losses in the development of the USSR's Great Power status: It was Russia that shouldered the burden for the defeat of fascism; it was Russian raw materials that powered economic development in Eastern Europe; it was Russia that lost the most young soldiers in Afghanistan.[25] While this group is willing to accept that mistakes have been made in the past (although not on the whole by Russians, in their view), nevertheless the basic external and expansionist orientation of Soviet foreign policy is supported by them. On this point, the group finds common cause with those conservative elements within the country and the Communist Party who fear that Gorbachev's foreign policy orientation will weaken the one area – the military – in which the USSR has enjoyed parity with the West. For this reason, the views of this group are often published in Soviet military publications like *Krasnaya zvezda.*

The third trend is amongst those xenophobic and isolationist Russian nationalists who want to withdraw Russia from world affairs and who fear that Gorbachev's foreign (and domestic) policy is going to produce a "catastrophe" for the Russian nation. On the whole, the group is both right-wing and anti-Bolshevik, seeing Marxism-Leninism as an alien ideology imposed by outsiders and resulting in the desecration of Russian culture and the devastation of the Russian countryside. This group is also anti-Western and anti-Gorbachev, seeing *perestroika* and *glasnost* as vehicles for the subversion of Russia by foreigners and Jews whose aim, according to one allegation, is to "legalize unemployment, prostitution, heavy metalists, rockers, hippies and the rest of the punks."[26] For them, Gorbachev's call for "pluralism of views" is an invitation to dilute the purity of Russian culture with imported Western ideas. They watched with horror as the emergence of multiparty systems in Eastern Europe produced similar calls in the December 1989 meeting of the Soviet Congress of Peoples' Deputies. Their battle cry throughout has been that there can be no "pluralism of morality."[27]

A not insignificant section of leading Russian writers and intellectuals would agree with the sentiment expressed by Yurii Bondarev, a member of the board of the Russian Writers' Union, that Gorbachev's foreign economic policy will increase "the danger of our country being turned into a colony of multinational corporations."[28] Many have looked at the experience of Eastern Europe and concluded that the wide-ranging changes in laws governing foreign investment have not produced the economic miracles anticipated. Speaking at the Congress of Peoples' Deputies, the writer Valentin Rasputin echoed these sentiments, calling on Gorbachev to jettison his attempts to secure foreign investment in Russian economic development, and charging that foreign participation in Russian joint stock companies is "ruinous for the country and excessively destructive for nature, but probably profitable for foreign firms."[29]

Old tendencies and debates thus have come to the surface seeking to influence the formulation of Soviet foreign policy toward Eastern Europe. While Gorbachev's conception of the region is politically the dominant one, nevertheless his efforts to redefine Soviet interests in the area are made against the backdrop of resistance from conservative and Russian nationalist forces.

Soviet Interests in Eastern Europe

Elements of history, culture, and ideology combined in 1945 to shape Soviet policy toward Eastern Europe in the postwar era. That policy has undergone many changes since then, but it has always been motivated by core Soviet interests, interests determined by geography as much as by ideology and power politics. And these interests, although subject to varying analyses by different Soviet leaders, have all played their part in driving Soviet policy towards Eastern Europe in the last forty-five years.

The primary Soviet interest has stemmed from the geographic vulnerability of the Russian and Ukrainian heartland to attack through the plains and valleys of Czechoslovakia and Poland. Stalin had a clear interest in securing this territory to protect the Soviet Union from further incursions. Churchill's initial support for granting Moscow a modified *cordon sanitaire* in Europe, later sanctified amongst the Allies at the Yalta Conference, lent credence to the Soviet view that steps had to be taken to prevent those routes from being used by any future aggressor.

Second, the Soviet takeover of Eastern Europe served to suppress all the overt and latent conflicts in that region between states, nationalities, ethnic groups, and religions, all of which had served as kindling for the flames of wars that had regularly engulfed Russia in both the pre- and post-Revolutionary periods. No Western governments mourned the passing or displacement of Nazi sympathizers in Germany, Bulgaria, Romania, Slovakia, or Hungary when the Red Army took over. It is well to remember, however, that from the Soviet viewpoint, both Poland and Czechoslovakia, about whose fate the West ostensibly had been much more concerned, also had been extremely troublesome neighbors in the interwar period. Tomáš Masaryk, the first president of Czechoslovakia, had supported White Russian efforts to topple Lenin, and the Poles had openly engaged the Red Army in 1920. Thus, the Soviet presence in Eastern Europe was designed to act not only as a defensive glacis protecting Soviet territory from future Western, and particularly German, expansion but also as a stabilizer, ensuring that local rivalries could not be used by the West or escalate independently to threaten the security of either the Soviet Union's borders or its political system.

General Secretary Gorbachev initially appeared to reaffirm this interpretation of Soviet interests in Eastern Europe during his April 1987 visit to Czechoslovakia. On that occasion, he forthrightly stated:

> Socialism has marked a crucial turn in the centuries-old history of this part of the world. From time immemorial, wars have been milestones here. The routing of fascism and the victory of socialist revolution in East European countries brought about a new situation on the continent. A powerful force arose here which set itself the aim of breaking the continuous chain of military conflicts. It is precisely to Socialism that Europe is indebted for the fact that over four decades its peoples have known no wars.[30]

In this respect alone, Moscow met with some success, although each new crisis reawakened these latent hostilities and threatened Soviet control. For example, neither the 1968 revival of reform in Czechoslovakia (popularly known as the Prague Spring) nor the Solidarity movement in Poland in 1980–1 was or could have been confined to those two countries alone. Both spread and reverberated, to awaken new hopes and aggravate old wounds. Ukrainian nationalism, anti-Semitism, Czech and Slovak rivalries, and even Romanian–Hungarian animosities reemerged in 1968. In 1980–1 the increased authority and activity of the Catholic Church against the Polish regime created additional difficulties for the Soviet Union in Catholic Lithuania and elsewhere. These difficulties were increased by the widespread, though never substantiated, belief amongst many East Europeans that the Soviet Union was somehow involved through Bulgaria in the assassination attempt on Pope John Paul II in May 1981. Historical hatreds between the Poles, Germans, and Czechs also contributed during the Polish crisis to a lack of sympathy with Poland's economic plight among her more prosperous and disciplined neighbors. And both crises fanned popular hostility to the Soviet Union. Indeed, one of the unintended effects of the Soviet suppression of other forms of nationalism was the reinforcement of a separate *East European* identity whose major defining characteristic was the fact that most East Europeans came to dislike the Soviets more than they disliked each other or the Germans, the other traditional objects of fear and contempt. Crises in Eastern Europe thus have had the capacity to spread, like peat fires, via buried, but still smoldering, networks of subterranean rivalries and break through at different times, long after the original crisis has subsided, threatening already fragile political structures. As a result, the weakening of Russophobia and rival nationalisms was always a major Soviet interest in the area.

Third, the existence of allied socialist regimes in Eastern Europe also may have been desired by some in the Soviet leadership to seal more completely the Soviet border from Western Europe. Western-style democracy and standards of human rights always have spread into Russia via its western borders, smuggled in by students, intellectuals, and travelers returning from the Baltic states, Poland, Bohemia, and lands west. Once inside Russia, these infectious ideas have provided an alternative cultural model, simultaneously attracting split loyalties amongst the Russian intelligentsia and weakening the hold of central authority. Yurii Andropov, while head of the Soviet Committee for State Security (KGB), admitted as much in a speech celebrating the fiftieth anniversary of the organization's founding, by stating that "the situation today on our borders is altogether different from what it used to be. We now share common borders . . . with fraternal socialist countries. . . ."[31]

Fourth, while Eastern Europe may have been viewed by some in Moscow as a sealant, it was viewed by others as a major source for innovative ideas about the improvement of socialism. Although the division between East and West in Europe may have been more or less complete militarily, it had long been recognized that in other spheres the USSR could not extinguish all Western influences, even if it so wished. As a result, East European countries have tended to be more open, freer societies than the Soviet Union. They have acted concurrently as a filter for the more negative Western influences and as an intermediary for the transmission of ideas and culture between East and West. They also have served as a laboratory for the experimental reform of Soviet-style systems. For a variety of political, bureaucratic, and even cultural reasons, reforms not always initially acceptable in the USSR often have developed first in Eastern Europe, with the

Soviet leadership and the intelligentsia monitoring the progress of such reforms both for their compatibility with Soviet-style socialism and for their applicability to the USSR itself.[32]

Gorbachev has been more forthcoming than some of his predecessors in calling on his party to learn from the positive experiences of East European reformers. Speaking at the 27th Party Congress in February 1986, he emphasized the need "to understand the processes of protecting democracy, management methods, and personnel policy on the basis of several countries rather than of one country [the USSR]. A considerate and respectful attitude to each other's experience and the employment of this experience in practice are a huge potential of the socialist world."[33]

Soviet analysts also viewed attempts to reform socialism abroad as interacting with internal political struggles. It is for this reason that the changes in Eastern Europe were so closely monitored in the USSR. As one analyst stated in writing about Poland when the roundtable talks between the communist government and Solidarity were just beginning in the summer of 1988:

> Any serious failure of Polish renewal plays into the
> hands of [Soviet] conservative forces who won't fail to
> use it as a trump card against [Soviet] *perestroika*. . . .
> [Conversely] each of Poland's major successes in over-
> coming the presently complicated "stalemate" situation
> means success for the supporters of radical reform in
> our country, too, just as the favorable developments in
> the Soviet Union are the most reliable support and
> best political background for the efforts of our
> allies.[34]

Finally, Eastern Europe has been important to the Soviet Union because the ideological legitimacy of Soviet-style socialism was on the line there, more so than in underdeveloped socialist countries like Cuba and Vietnam. During Moscow's decade-long occupation of Afghanistan, for example, the Soviets continually maintained their willingness to restore Afghanistan's nonaligned status in the context of an international settlement. However much Moscow's proposals for increased power sharing fell short of Western demands and expectations, the point never-

theless was that the proposals far exceeded the level of independence allowed to the East Europeans before Gorbachev came to
power. This disparity arose from the fact that a substantial set-
back for socialism in the Third World could be justified ideologically as an example of a basically semi-feudal society not sufficiently developed to make the transition directly to socialism
without going through the bourgeois phase.

For decades, Soviet leaders calculated that no such excuse could
be mustered if socialism were to collapse in Eastern Europe. They
were particularly keen to "protect socialism" in those countries,
such as the GDR, Hungary, Czechoslovakia, and Poland, whose
levels of economic development were as high as, or higher than,
that of the Soviet Union. Until far-reaching reforms took root in
Moscow, it was believed there that the collapse of Soviet-style
socialism would have the most serious implications for the legitimacy of communist rule in the Soviet Union itself, exposing the
fallibility of the central core of Soviet ideology – namely, the
irreversibility of the historical process and the universal applicability and scientific nature of Marxism-Leninism. Moreover,
the emergence of a revised "Eurocommunism" in an East European country traditionally was seen as being equally destabilizing
for Soviet control in the bloc and inside the USSR, particularly
among those Russian intellectuals, Ukrainians, and Baltic peoples
who also feel the pull toward Europe. Clearly, the move toward
independence in the Baltic states gained momentum and encouragement from similar movements in Eastern Europe in 1989. To
the extent, therefore, that Moscow has defined its international
prestige and status in terms of its leadership of a unified and
growing socialist community, it has a very considerable interest in
ensuring the stability of socialist regimes and the maintenance of
Soviet influence.

The Challenge to Moscow

Despite the preeminence of Soviet interests in Eastern Europe,
the relationship between Moscow and Eastern Europe has never
been a simple one-way street. It is not solely the viability of East
European regimes that is at stake; the Soviet system, too, is
challenged in fundamental, if quite different, ways by its connec-

tion with this region which lies, but does not rest, between East and West.

As discussed previously in this chapter, some Soviets have seen Eastern Europe as a barrier to the spread of Western ideals eastward, just as, conversely, Poland served in previous eras to stem the tide of Russian Orthodoxy westward. But Eastern Europe never has been nor could be an impermeable iron curtain. It always has absorbed influences from one side and transmitted them in altered form to the other.

Even in the centuries before the advent of communist rule, the area acted less as a defensive glacis than as a catalyst for the subversion of central authority. Thus, just as Prague's Hussite rebellion of the fifteenth century and Saxony's Lutheran Reformation of the sixteenth both divided and weakened the Roman Catholic world, so too in the post-1945 era have strong religious, nationalistic, and social democratic impulses throughout Eastern Europe divided and weakened the Soviet-ruled communist world. This has occurred despite the repeated pledges of pro-Moscow East European elites that, to quote Poland's General Wojciech Jaruzelski in 1981, they have no intention of allowing their countries to be used by the West as a Trojan horse, attacking the socialist camp from within.[35]

Many East Europeans, in seeking to explain Moscow's original motives in imposing a system that was essentially alien to Eastern Europe, underscored the relevance of a tract written in 1863 by Alexander Herzen. Seeking to explain Russia's motives for participating in yet another partition of Poland, which put to rest once again that country's dreams of national unity and freedom, Herzen wrote:

> Why does the government not want to give up Po-
> land? Because it realizes that when Poland is free
> Russia will be free. . . . [Russia] believes that by
> crushing the Polish movement, it suppresses any move-
> ment of the kind in Russia.[36]

Echoes of Herzen's words reverberated through every crisis in Eastern Europe until 1989. The vital interests the Soviets had at stake were acutely perceived, sometimes too late, by the Hungarians in 1956, the Czechoslovaks in 1968, and the Poles in 1980–

1, all of whom would have had to agree with an assessment by the Polish weekly, *Polityka,* after the imposition of martial law in December 1981: "The socialist community is politically interested in maintaining the socialist system in all its members, for otherwise it may face disintegration."[37] Put another way, it was the USSR that was most interested in maintaining socialism in each allied state, for otherwise the bloc would collapse, jeopardizing the security Moscow derived from the Warsaw Pact and the legitimacy it gained from being the source of an ideology that was espoused transnationally. The veteran *Izvestiya* commentator Aleksandr Bovin could not have put it more crisply when he stated that in Eastern Europe, "not only security is at stake, but ideology as well."[38]

As the Russian Empire learned in the nineteenth century, however, so did the Soviet Union at the end of the twentieth: The elimination of, or strong control over, state institutions in Eastern Europe does not prevent the continued existence of the nation. The forms of national expression can to some extent be controlled through the suppression of both free speech and rival organizations like the Church and the trade unions, but its content cannot be artificially manufactured. Indeed, as those communist authorities who were toppled in the last six months of 1989 discovered, the more it is suppressed or supplanted by artificial versions, the more virulent and extreme becomes a nation's opposition to these rival and imposed state institutions.

All Soviet leaders, including Gorbachev, came to appreciate that unless this central question of regional viability was addressed more satisfactorily, the appeal of Marxism-Leninism could only decline both in Eastern Europe and in the USSR. The attractiveness of Marxism-Leninism would additionally be diminished so long as it was the West and not the Soviet Union that set the standards of consumer welfare, technological prowess, and human rights that were sought throughout the bloc. Pointedly choosing Hungary as the site for a speech recognizing this challenge, Gorbachev bluntly admitted that unless the most thoroughgoing reforms were adopted, the Soviet Union would be unable to "place the immense reserves and opportunities of socialism at the service of the working people." Further recognizing the totality of the challenge that the system faced, he called for the "practical strengthening of socialism in all spheres – economic, political, and spiritual."[39]

This theme continued to be developed and expanded by Gorbachev. Speaking at the Sorbonne in July 1989, the Soviet leader clearly connected the processes of *perestroika* in domestic and foreign policy with ideas central to the French Revolution. In attempting to reintegrate the Soviet bloc back into the Europe which gave birth to those concepts of freedom and justice, Gorbachev espoused, then and subsequently, a firm commitment to the absolute concept of freedom of choice for nation-states.[40] Even after communist parties had lost power because of the changes which swept the region in 1989, he reaffirmed the principle, telling the CPSU Central Committee that "the Soviet Union is building its relations with East European countries . . . on a single position of respect for sovereignty, non-interference and recognition of freedom of choice. We proceed from the fact that any nation has the right to decide its fate itself, including the choice of a system, ways, the pace and methods of its development."[41]

If there is any chance of East European states freely choosing socialism, as Gorbachev obviously hopes, the challenge will be particularly acute in Poland, Czechoslovakia, East Germany, and Hungary – the four countries whose standards of living were higher than that of the Soviet Union before the war and who therefore feel most sharply that being allied with the Soviet Union has held them back. These four countries, like Romania and the Slovene sectors of Yugoslavia, and even more than Bulgaria, Albania, and the remainder of Yugoslavia, have a cultural and intellectual tradition that has linked them with, and attracted them to, Western Europe. As a result, while the state institutions have been co-opted by the East, these nations always have resided spiritually in the West. This disjunction between a Western-oriented nation and an Eastern-oriented state has been particularly marked in Poland, East Germany, Czechoslovakia, Romania, and Hungary. In all of these countries, to varying degrees and at different times, this tension between East and West, between state and nation, contributed to the widespread popular rebellion and the inward collapse or implosion of central authority which characterized politics in the region in 1989. This dual threat of rebellion and implosion remains present and challenging, not only to Soviet influence in the area but also to the West and to broader security in Europe.

The seriousness of the challenge was demonstrated time and again in the era preceding Gorbachev's rise to power, whether in 1953 in East Germany, in 1956 in Hungary, in 1968 in Czechoslovakia, or in 1980–1 in Poland. Although the circumstances varied in each of these crises, all exhibited the same downward spiral in which the Soviets promoted their own interests at the expense of the East European regimes, which themselves became more unstable as a result of their acquiescence. The failure to build domestic bases of support made the regimes particularly vulnerable both to popular pressures and to external, particularly Western, pressures. These circumstances produced crises that the regimes either were too weak to manage alone or were disinclined to suppress because of widespread, if latent, nationalistic and anti-Soviet tendencies in the leadership. The Soviets, having perceived a marked increase in threats to their security, took steps in each case that involved extensive political and sometimes military interference. Such measures, which temporarily may have ameliorated the immediate situation, did not improve the long-term viability of the regimes and indeed exacerbated the root cause of Soviet concern – namely, the continuing existence of anti-Sovietism and virulent nationalism throughout Eastern Europe.

This cyclical pattern of "two steps forward, one step back" also held dangers for European security. Much self-congratulatory rhetoric was issued by all sides on the anniversaries of the Yalta and Potsdam agreements and the anniversaries of the establishment of the North Atlantic Treaty Organization (NATO, founded in 1949) and the Warsaw Treaty Organization (the Warsaw Pact, founded in 1955). Indeed, if security is defined narrowly as the absence of war, then many congratulations were in order, particularly in the nuclear age. After all, while the greater stability of the bloc system had not eliminated crises in Eastern Europe, it had contained their effects. In consequence, while Leonid Brezhnev could claim in 1968 that the Soviets would have invaded Czechoslovakia even at the risk of a third world war, in fact the Soviets could, and did, calculate that the chances of a war breaking out were negligible.[42] So, too, with the Polish crisis in 1980–1; the Soviet leadership risked sanctions and censure, but could estimate with some accuracy that the West would not go to war over Poland.[43] Yet it was by no means clear that calculations of nonescalation were made so easily in the first postwar decade. The 1948 Berlin crisis carried grave risks of escalation, and in 1956 the Hungarians waited in vain for the West to back up its rhetoric with action. Berlin often has been seen as the Achilles' heel of security systems in Europe, the one issue over which the West would go to war.[44] In fact, Nikita Khrushchev's success in constructing the Berlin Wall in 1961 without Western military countermeasures ushered in an era in which the West adopted this strict and narrow definition of European security. The absence of war henceforth would be the governing criterion by which the state of European security would be judged. It was not until well after the invasion of Czechoslovakia that a more satisfactory definition would be sought.

After 1968, leaders on both sides of the European divide came to realize that despite the absence of war, there remained fundamental sources of insecurity which, if left unattended, not only would not go away, but would become more dangerous over time. Thus, the signatories of the 1975 Helsinki Final Act of the Conference on Security and Cooperation in Europe recognized the need to address both the security of states and the security of peoples. The broadening of this concept of security has been of fundamental importance to the East Europeans, who previously had had good reason to believe that the security of Europe was being constructed at their expense. There has been a greater awareness in the 1980s than ever before that Europe is a single entity and that its division is unnatural and should be eliminated. This feeling has grown on both sides of the European divide. It first became evident during the 1983–4 campaign to stop the deployment of Soviet and American intermediate-range missiles in Europe, when parallel peace movements against deployment sprang up in Eastern and Western Europe.[45]

East European states have become active in asserting their role in promoting a fundamental broadening of the notion of European security. While this is to be welcomed by all who have sought an improved situation in Eastern Europe, it is not without its dangers. Whereas previously, popular apathy and acquiescence supported regime and bloc stability in Eastern Europe, then conversely, the popular pursuit of European identity can also increase instability to the extent that such a pursuit is regarded by conservative opinion in Moscow as a threat to traditional Soviet conceptions of, and interests in, Eastern Europe. This threat is not diminished when East European leaders themselves begin to voice popular aspirations, effectively pursuing national interests at the expense of collectivist bloc goals. And although Gorbachev's great tolerance of bloc diversity decreased the risk of Soviet intervention as bloc states realigned their internal politics in 1989, the risk of crises generated by conflicts within or between East European states or by miscalculation, misperception, and nonsynchronization of policies did not similarly decrease.

There have been many occasions during the past millennium when East Europeans have risked, and sometimes precipitated, the destruction of the prevailing global order for the sake of national independence. Who is to say that this might not happen again? Indeed, why should the people of Eastern Europe sacrifice more for the survival of the planet than their Soviet or American counterparts? It is this sense of Eastern Europe as a "crisis waiting to happen" that presents a challenge. This challenge is acute not just in Eastern Europe but also in the USSR. In a political memorandum prepared for Gorbachev by his top advisors, they implored him not to overlook "the lessons of Eastern Europe and China." In both regions, the "weariness and apathy" of society ultimately produced "aggression against the party." The concern his advisors legitimately expressed was that if such a conflict broke out in the USSR, "in view of the country's size, its multinational composition, and specific Russian characteristics, this conflict may take forms beside which Tiananmen Square and Romania would pale in significance."[46] In both Eastern Europe and the Soviet Union, not only are persistent problems between elites and society threatening a revolution of rising expectations, but, in addition, interbloc and intrabloc shifts always risk a backlash by either the Soviet Union or the United States, both of which have their own misgivings (discussed further in Chapters

7 and 8) about eliminating the bloc system in Europe. In 1988, the political agenda in the region included only the reform of socialism within a largely unchanged bloc system. By 1990, the agenda had changed to include the emergence of a reunified Germany potentially neither anchored to any bloc nor demilitarized. In this way, Eastern Europe has served both as a victim of prevailing notions of European security and as a potential challenge to those notions.

For centuries, trends in Eastern Europe have served as a litmus test for the ebb and flow of the competition between Eastern and Western cultures and values. With the advent of a reform-minded and Westernizing leader in Moscow, the competition has entered a qualitatively new round and can no longer be considered a mere atavistic continuation of previous cycles. Under Gorbachev, there is reason to believe that the outcome of the competition for Eastern Europe has become, in Kafka's terms, "a drumbeat sounding into the world beyond."[47] The dilemma of how to achieve change in Eastern Europe against the backdrop of competing conceptions and interests presents an acute challenge. But with the crashing down of the Berlin Wall and other less tangible symbols of East–West divide, that challenge has finally exploded onto the Soviet conscience and the East European consciousness.

Notes

1   Zdeněk Mlynář, *Night Frost in Prague: The End of Humane Socialism* (London: C. Hurst & Co., 1980), pp. 239–41.
2   "Programme of the Communist Party of the Soviet Union. A New Edition, Approved by Twenty-Seventh Party Congress," *Information Bulletin,* Vol. 24, No. 9, 1986 (Moscow: Novosti Press Agency Publishing House), p. 72.
3   Bulgarian Telegraphic Agency (BTA), September 30, 1989. Hungary refused to sign the communiqué, citing among other reasons the lack of *glasnost* at the meeting.
4   Nicholas V. Riasanovsky, *Russia and the West in the Teaching of the Slavophiles* (Cambridge, Mass.: Harvard University Press, 1952), p. 110. I am grateful to Itzhak Brudny of Princeton University for comments on this section.
5   Andrzej Walicki, *The Slavophile Controversy* (Oxford: Clarendon Press, 1975), p. 220.

6 Soviet analyses of the 1980–1 Polish crisis are extensively discussed in Sidney I. Ploss, *Moscow and the Polish Crisis* (Boulder, Colo.: Westview Press, 1986). Although attacks on the Catholic Church in the Soviet press have subsided since Gorbachev came to power, one interesting exception was provided by a *Krasnaya zvezda* article on May 5, 1987. Timed to appear during the same week that Gorbachev and Jaruzelski signed a significant bilateral agreement improving political and cultural relations, the article pointedly maintained that "the influence [of the Church] is not harmless, as some would like to argue."

7 Paul Miliukov, *Political Memoirs, 1905–1917* (Ann Arbor: University of Michigan Press), pp. 213–14.

8 *Izvestiya*, December 25, 1918.

9 Vladimir I. Lenin, *Selected Works in Three Volumes* (Moscow: Progress Publishers, 1971), Vol. 3, p. 695.

10 Josef V. Stalin, "The Foundations of Leninism," in *The Essential Stalin* (London: Croom Helm, 1973), p. 184.

11 *Ibid.,* pp. 95–7.

12 Konstantin F. Shteppa, *Russian Historians and the Soviet State* (New Brunswick: Rutgers University Press, 1962), p. 147.

13 [Editorial], "Zadachi sovetskikh istorikov v oblasti novoi i noveishei istorii," *Voprosy istorii*, No. 3, 1949, p. 7.

14 "Zadachi sovetskikh," pp. 3–4, in referring to the article, states: "In this article of genius, J. V. Stalin with complete persuasiveness, showed the mistaken views of Engels in the 1840s with regard to the external policy of Russia. . . . Stalin showed that the role of the last stronghold of reaction . . . more and more was transferred from Russia to the imperialistic bourgeois states of Western Europe. . . ."

15 "Protiv ob″ektivizma v istoricheskoi nauke," *Voprosy istorii*, No. 12, 1948, p. 11.

16 From the interview with Berman in Teresa Toranska, *"Them": Stalin's Polish Puppets* (New York: Harper & Row, 1987), p. 291.

17 *Ibid.,* p. 284.

18 *Ibid.,* p. 291.

19 "Address by the CPSU Central Committee, the Presidium of the USSR Supreme Soviet and the USSR Council of Ministers to the Peoples, Parliaments and Governments of all Nations on the Fortieth Anniversary of the Ending of World War II," *Pravda*, May 10, 1985 (emphasis added).

20 CPSU Central Committee report delivered by M. S. Gorbachev at the 19th All-Union CPSU Conference, Moscow, June 28, 1988, *Pravda*, June 29, 1988.

21 M. S. Gorbachev's speech at the December 9 CPSU Central Committee Plenum, *Pravda*, December 10, 1989.

22 *Le Nouvel Observateur*, May 8–14, 1987, p. 36. This view of patriotism was essentially repeated in an unsigned editorial, reportedly written by Party Secretary Aleksandr Yakovlev, and entitled "Principles of Perestroika,"

which appeared in *Pravda* on April 5, 1988, in response to an earlier attack on *perestroika* by Nina Andreeva, cited below. The tendency amongst Gorbachev's supporters to press for more internationalism, as well as a renewed commitment to democratic and socialist ideals, is typified in articles by the group of Moscow liberal intellectuals like the economist Gavril Popov, the historians Yurii Afanas'yev and Roy Medvedev, the journalist Fyodor Bur'latskii, and the human rights activist Andrei Sakharov, all of whom were elected to the Congress of Peoples' Deputies.

23   Dmitrii Likhachev, "Beden ne tot, u kogo malo, a tot, komu malo," *Druzhba narodov,* No. 6, 1988, p. 224.

24   *Moscow News,* No. 38, September 25–October 2, 1988.

25   Nina Andreeva's first letter, entitled "I Cannot Forsake Principles," appeared in *Sovetskaya Rossiya,* March 13, 1988. Igor Shafarevich's article, which was published along with a rebuttal by Roy Medvedev, appeared in *Moscow News,* No. 24, 1988. Andreeva and Shafarevich also agreed in their assignation of blame for Stalinism to the influence of imported (mainly Jewish) ideas. This view was originally espoused by V. Kozhinov in the article "The Truth and Justice," which appeared in *Nash Sovremennik,* No. 4, 1988.

26   I. Pavlov, "Letter in Response to Article by Boris Berman," *Moscow News,* No. 26, July 3–10, 1988.

27   Valentin Rasputin, the Russian nationalist writer, speaking at the Congress of Peoples' Deputies, Moscow Television Service, June 6, 1989, Foreign Broadcast Information Service, *Soviet Daily Report (FBIS-SOV),* June 7, 1989, p. 24.

28   The first Bondarev quotation is taken from his speech at the 19th Party Conference, as reported by *Moscow News,* July 1988. The charge and others similar to it were considered serious enough to be the subject of a specific rebuttal by Gorbachev at the CPSU Central Committee plenum on July 29, 1988 (*Pravda,* July 30, 1988). The second Bondarev quotation is from his speech at a meeting of the secretariat of the board of the RSFSR Writers' Union, held in Ryazan, as reported in *Literaturnaya Rossiya,* No. 43, October 28, 1988, pp. 2–9. The fact that the meeting was apparently devoted to a concerted attack on Gorbachev's policies and that Yegor Ligachev, Gorbachev's conservative rival on the Politburo, also paid a visit to Ryazan turned the affair into a major political debate. The liberal journal *Ogonyok* censured the meeting (No. 52, 1988, pp. 13–15), and *Kommunist* published an unsigned editorial ("Old Myths and New Fears," No. 17, November 1988, pp. 23–6) criticizing this group in the harshest terms yet used.

29   Moscow Television Service, in Russian, June 6, 1989, *FBIS-SOV,* June 8, 1989, pp. 22–3.

30   *Pravda,* April 11, 1987.

31   *Pravda,* December 21, 1967.

32   For elaboration of the notion that Eastern Europe acts as a laboratory

for innovation of Soviet-style systems, see Zvi Y. Gitelman, *The Diffusion of Political Innovation from Eastern Europe to the Soviet Union* (Beverly Hills: Sage Publications, 1972).

33 *Pravda,* February 26, 1986.

34 Marina Pavlova-Silvanskaya, *Moscow News,* No. 29, July 7, 1988.

35 Jaruzelski's speech to the Polish Sejm, accepting the post of chairman of the Council of Ministers, *Trybuna Ludu,* February 13, 1981.

36 Quoted in Ploss, *op. cit.,* p. x.

37 *Polityka,* January 22, 1983.

38 As quoted by Joseph Kraft, *The New Yorker,* January 13, 1983.

39 Speech by Mikhail Gorbachev, TASS, in English, June 9, 1986.

40 *Pravda,* July 6, 1989.

41 *Pravda,* December 10, 1989.

42 See Karen Dawisha, *The Kremlin and the Prague Spring* (Berkeley: University of California Press, 1985).

43 See Ploss, *op. cit.,* p. 18.

44 See Avi Shlaim, *The United States and the Berlin Blockade, 1948–49: A Study in Crisis Decision-making* (Berkeley: University of California Press, 1983).

45 See Robert English, "Eastern Europe's Doves," *Foreign Policy,* Fall 1984, and A. Ross Johnson, *The Impact of Eastern Europe on Soviet Policy Toward Western Europe* (Santa Monica, Calif.: The Rand Corporation, R-3332-AF, March 1986), pp. 25–61.

46 According to a "political note" drafted by Gorbachev aides urging him to break with conservatives and to transform the party in radical ways. The note was excerpted in *Le Monde,* January 31, 1990.

47 Quoted by Frederick V. Grunfeld, *Prophets Without Honor: A Background to Freud, Kafka, Einstein and Their World* (New York: Holt, Rinehart & Winston, 1979), p. 190.

3

East European Conceptions and Interests

What does Europe mean to a Hungarian, a Czech, a
Pole: For thousands of years their nations have be-
longed to a part of Europe rooted in Roman Christianity. They have participated in every period of its
history. For them the word "Europe" does not represent a phenomenon of geography but a spiritual notion synonymous with the West. The moment
Hungary is no longer European – that is, no longer
Western – it is driven from its destiny, beyond its own
history: it loses the essence of its identity.[1]

East European Conceptions

This view, expressed so eloquently by the émigré Czech writer
Milan Kundera, strikes a sympathetic chord with all those in the
West who have roots in Eastern Europe or who count themselves fortunate to have traveled to that area and made friends
there. It is impossible not to be impressed by the richness of
culture and historical tradition binding the peoples of Europe
together despite its division after 1945. It is also difficult not to be
struck by a sense of loss – of great social and political potential
still unfulfilled.

For decades, all East European leaders – whether those of
Poland, East Germany, Czechoslovakia, Hungary, Romania, or
Bulgaria – protested that their countries had made great strides
since the war. They claimed to provide a more equal distribution
of wealth and a higher standard of living for the peasantry and
the working classes than was the case before the advent of socialism. Moreover, we were told that drug addiction, violent

crime, unemployment, and homelessness, all of which are present to differing extents in the West's industrial centers, were virtually unknown in Eastern Europe during this period. Indeed, Western statistics supported their claim that until the late 1970s, when all East-bloc countries went into economic decline, in terms of many key social indicators, such as public expenditure per capita, infant mortality, or daily consumption of protein and calories, several of these countries (including the USSR) ranked among the world's top ten.[2] To a certain degree, therefore, it was audacious for anyone in the West to have believed that a Western system could have served as an exemplar for the region.

The Lure of the West. Yet it was not Westerners, but the East Europeans themselves, who held up the notion, the very idea, of "the West" as the destination in their widespread process of spiritual migration. It was not just Americans or West Europeans but also and even primarily the East Europeans themselves who regarded their region as having been "driven from its destiny." Their view was that while the 1917 Russian Revolution gave rise to an indigenous form of socialism in the Soviet Union, Marxism-Leninism was largely exogenous to Eastern Europe and therefore had greater difficulty establishing itself there.

Of course, both social democracy and Marxism had deep roots in Central Europe, and communist parties gained many adherents throughout the region in the mid-1930s and during the war, not least because of their important role in the anti-fascist resistance movements. In the Balkans, the communist regimes established after the war in Albania and Yugoslavia were headed by two men, Enver Hoxha and Josip Broz Tito, respectively, who not only took power without direct Soviet military assistance but also subsequently maintained it in the face of Soviet hostility. Moreover, in 1946, in further testimony to the strength of indigenous communists, the Communist Party of Czechoslovakia secured a rather remarkable 36 percent of the vote, the largest percentage for any party in that election – the only postwar election in Eastern Europe considered by Western observers not to have been rigged by the Soviets or by local communists.

The preexistence of strong leftist movements did not always ease the introduction of Marxism-Leninism, however. On the contrary, in some cases it made the process more difficult, because the local and independent socialists and communists first had to be purged before pro-Moscow factions could be securely installed. It is unlikely that socialism of the Marxist-Leninist variant would have been established or could have been maintained without, as the Soviets themselves were fond of admitting, the "tremendous role" of the Soviet Union in creating the necessary "key conditions."[3]

Heirs to Autocracy? Any student of Central European history and literature knows that in addition to the area's Western and social democratic orientation, there have been many dark decades (sometimes stretching into whole centuries) about which the best that can be said, to paraphrase Kafka, is that the oppressive rulers generally knew their own limitations, and, less through excess than inefficiency, were intermittently overthrown. Periods of independence from Tatar, Ottoman, Russian, or Teutonic rule too often produced not cultural revival but internecine rivalry, inviting further intervention. The oldest surviving account of Central Europe, written in Arabic by a Moorish Jew in 965 A.D. after a visit to the area by the Khalif of Cordoba, stated prophetically: "In general, the Slavs are violent, and inclined to aggression. If not for the disharmony amongst them, caused by the multiplication of factions and by their fragmentation into clans, no people could match their strength."[4]

The Soviets themselves have been the primary promulgators of the view that the Red Army, acting as an "accelerator" of the historical process, did all of Europe a service at the end of World War II by putting an end, "once and for all" (according to Moscow), to the region's legacy of fascism, feudalism, and violent nationalism. The Soviet view has not been that Eastern Europe was "cut off from its own history," but, on the contrary, that it was "saved" from it; further, the Soviets have argued that by 1945, Eastern Europe was ripe for change, having reached the limits of its political capabilities. They necessarily have regarded despotism and exploitation as the leitmotifs of the previous decades, if not centuries, of East European history. Accordingly, Soviet and official East European accounts have taken great pride in the social and economic transformations that they believe would not have occurred without the socialist "revolutions from above." Even though contemporary Soviet accounts admit that distortions in the construction of socialism have taken place in Eastern Europe, there still has not been any basic revision in the view that the region was dominated by autocracy prior to 1945.[5]

Western analysts are not unanimous on the issue whether or not democratic systems would have emerged in Eastern Europe if the Yalta agreement had not given Stalin virtually free rein there. No doubt most would agree that, far from accelerating Eastern Europe's development, the imposition of Soviet-style governments sent these countries' political and economic systems sharply into reverse, particularly in the first postwar decade. Nevertheless, Western scholars remain divided between those who believe that without a communist takeover, some countries (particularly those in southeastern Europe) were headed for more decades of autocracy, and those who maintain that Western democratic traditions had sufficiently deep roots to flourish even in the Balkans, and especially in northeastern Europe. Making an exception of Poland and the Czech lands of Czechoslovakia, where democracy gained a tenuous foothold in the interwar period, most historians would certainly not object to the assessment offered by the British historian Hugh Seton-Watson in 1951 that on the eve of the socialist takeover, after centuries of autocracy and ultranationalism, "the social structure of Eastern Europe more closely resembled that of Russia, or even of Asiatic countries, than that of France, Britain, or Germany." Moreover, although the intelligentsia was developed and eager "to be accepted as equals by their Western colleagues," the teaching in village schools "all too often degenerated to the three R's plus a training in national hatred."[6]

While such analyses as Seton-Watson's may tend toward the conclusion that historical development facilitated the establishment of Soviet control, it should be borne in mind that this is not the view of the population in Central Europe, who on the whole have maintained that neither autocracy nor a pro-Russian orientation was the dominant theme of the presocialist period. Rather, they have tended to stress periods of national independence and cultural ties with Europe as being far more characteristic of their presocialist evolution. Thus, a fundamental problem always has been manifest in the political culture of these states, insofar as there has never been any consensus between the communist leaders and the people regarding whether or not they are indeed "beyond" their history. The absence of consensus has represented a major challenge both to the viability of the regimes and to the ability of indigenous elites to legitimize their rule and define national interests. The failure of local communists to address popular sentiments on this issue was a key reason why they fell from power in the 1989 electoral and popular revolts which eliminated their monopoly of power.

East European Interests

Given the record of Soviet behavior in Eastern Europe, it is not surprising that indigenous interests often have been at odds with those of Moscow. Even the most loyal bloc leader chafed, for example, at the notion that one of his country's major roles should be to serve as a defensive glacis for the USSR. Consequently, there were many points of divergence between Moscow and even its staunchest bloc allies.

Just as the Soviet Union sought after the war to establish a *cordon sanitaire* as protection against any future security threats emanating from the West, it also was in the interest of the countries of Central Europe to seek security guarantees against their historically hostile neighbors. With the demilitarization and division of Germany, confluence was achieved between certain Soviet and East European objectives, but Moscow had no interest in protecting Eastern Europe from the other traditional source of insecurity – namely, Russia itself. Thus, the Soviet control of Eastern Europe, designed ostensibly to promote greater security for the Soviet Union and Eastern Europe alike, became from the moment of its inception the major source of insecurity in Eastern Europe. Indeed, the most elementary interest of any state – the defense of its borders – was violated in Eastern Europe, insofar as the region's value as a *place d'armes* and theater of forward military operations for the Soviet army relied on the openness of East European borders to troop movements from the east. Even the Soviets themselves came to realize that "in the eyes of the population of the East European countries, the Soviet Union was gradually changing from the liberator from fascism to an oppressor."[7]

East European leaders were tied into this system initially through their total political dependence on Moscow. The personal involvement of Stalin and his secret police in ordering and supervising the extensive purges of national communists (who were, by implication, potentially independent and anti-Soviet in their inclinations) during the late 1940s and early 1950s made it clear to the remaining leaders that loyalty to Moscow was a higher value than loyalty to their own indigenous communist inheritance. In this way, narrow personal interests took precedence over national interests.

The ultimate willingness of subsequent Soviet leaders to use force to maintain their position "for time everlasting" (to use the final words of the secret Moscow protocol signed under duress by the Czechoslovak leadership only days after the Soviet invasion of their country in 1968)[8] demonstrated why even the most outspoken among East European intellectuals pessimistically came to conclude, like Hungary's George Konrád, that "it is impossible to alter the Yalta system from inside by means of dynamic uncontrolled mass movements."[9] Nikita Khrushchev, general secretary of the Soviet Communist Party from 1953 until 1964, may have been sincere when he assured a visiting Egyptian delegation in 1961 that the Soviets did not export revolution, because "people cannot be driven into paradise with a stick,"[10] but from the perspective of many in Eastern Europe, that had been precisely the Soviet intention after the war.

Thus, a dual mechanism of extensive purges and threatened invasion was developed by the Soviets to blunt both popular aspirations for change in Eastern Europe and indigenous support for increased independence from Soviet control. The flaw in this strategy was that by promoting defeatism and hopelessness, the Soviets also prevented local regimes from achieving legitimacy and gravely diminished their efforts to achieve political and economic development.

It is important to emphasize that Soviet control of Eastern Europe simply would have collapsed if there had not been crucial points of convergence between Soviet and East European interests and objectives, as well as Soviet sensitivity to the political costs of more intrusive efforts to control events. Agreement with, or at least acquiescence to, Soviet-defined interests and objectives was strongest at the elite level in Eastern Europe, among what the Soviets euphemistically called "realistic circles." Such agreement was based, in the military sphere, on the view that as long as NATO existed, there would be a need for a counterbalancing military organization. Politically, it was also accepted that the influence of the socialist bloc in the international arena was immeasurably enhanced when the leaders of the bloc's individual states spoke with a single voice. Because members of the bloc shared a common, if sometimes begrudging, commitment to the strengthening of socialism internationally, the need to maintain unity emerged as a de facto constraint on open defiance of agreed bloc policy, which Moscow played a major, if not always singular, role in establishing.

Nevertheless, this was the system that was imposed on Eastern Europe after 1945. East European interests in the maintenance of that system were more complex and contradictory than those of the Soviet Union. There were the personal interests of the elites, whose decisions were motivated both by the desire to stay in power (or, in previous days, alive) and by the belief that somehow they were serving their countries' interests by preventing unnamed "worse alternatives," in the form of even more direct Soviet control.[11] Secondly, the interests of the nation, whether expressed by individual leaders, church authorities, or the population at large, came to be viewed as, by definition, contrary to the more repressive aspects of Soviet control. There also were the interests of the East European states, whose fundamental role in safeguarding territory and defending borders was undercut and denied by the "higher" demands of both Soviet security and the maintenance of socialism. And, finally, there were the interests of socialism itself, whose ability to put down roots and gain adherents was limited by continued Soviet control of ideological innovation in the bloc.

To be sure, East European regimes did seek to strengthen the basis of their domestic support. And although no regime met Western standards of human rights and democratic freedoms, beginning in the 1960s many responded to popular pressures by improving housing, importing more consumer goods, and even allowing more foreign travel. However, the emergence of a strong neoconservative political mood imposed by Moscow following the 1968 invasion of Czechoslovakia and the subsequent crises which gripped bloc regimes as a result of their political inability to reform their economies effectively set limits on the gains that could be made. The moral and distributive capabilities of these systems had been exhausted; they were reaching a dead end. As a result, in the 1970s, at the height of the so-called policy of "normalization," most East European regimes externally appeared to be less prone to crisis and collapse than they had been in the first years of communist power. However, in fact, by draining these countries' spiritual and material reserves, bloc leaders laid the basis for the extensive transformations away from communist power which began with the Solidarity movement in Poland in 1980–1 and emerged fully formed in 1989.

While Gorbachev clearly was sensitive to East European interests, the fundamental and intrinsic asymmetry of the relationship still diminished the legitimacy of any regime, the popularity of any leader, and the authority of any state which maintained a strong alliance with the USSR. As a result, not only was the reputation of socialism harmed, but so too was the stability of this region undermined, thereby also effectively ensuring that the Soviet Union's own ideological and security interests were constantly being threatened in the region. It is this paradox that Gorbachev has been addressing since coming to power.

History as Politics in the Bloc

No account of East European conceptions and interests would be complete without a closer look at the ways in which the different historical self-perceptions of each of these diverse countries have affected their emergence into the modern era. It is too often assumed in the West that the high degree of uniformity among East European political systems betokens a similar uniformity in political cultures. Although there are certain similarities, there are other differences that are equally important, if not more important. These derive from acute national historical sensitivities that are sometimes difficult to comprehend in the

West, where there is a tendency to stress the future at the expense of the past. In Eastern Europe, people exhibit a keen historical consciousness, and all leaders seek to present themselves as guardians of their nations' most cherished bygone eras. At the same time, the question of which episodes in each nation's history should be vilified, glorified, forgotten, or suppressed is of central importance, both in the efforts of the indigenous communist authorities to legitimize their rule and in Moscow's previous attempts to portray the past history of these countries – especially their historical links with the West – in a less than favorable light. These are the common themes and issues addressed in the following sections on the various countries.

Memories of Greater Bulgaria. Of all the countries in the Soviet bloc, the nation that at the outset of the communist era most closely accorded with the description provided by Hugh Seton-Watson in this chapter's first section was Bulgaria. When the Ottoman Empire, riven by internal weakness, granted Bulgaria independence in 1878, it left a dual legacy of underdevelopment and fierce nationalism. The structure of Ottoman rule being what it was, nationalism had not grown primarily in the universities in Bulgaria as it had throughout eastern Central Europe during the eighteenth century, when the philosophy of the French Revolution caught hold. Nor was the Orthodox Church a particular vehicle of radicalism, as both the Protestant and Catholic churches in Czechoslovakia, Germany, and Poland had been. In those countries, the Reformation and Counter-Reformation on the one hand and the struggle between Orthodox and Latin Christianity on the other produced an extremely politicized clergy and intelligentsia and eventually pitted whole nations against each other. In Bulgaria, however, the structure of Ottoman rule combined with the influence of Eastern Orthodoxy to produce a nationalism that was not the preserve of the intelligentsia, clergy, or urban population; rather, nationalism emerged from Bulgaria's largely peasant population, from whose ranks rose most of the leaders of Bulgaria in the postindependence period, including the communists.[12]

The readiness of Russia to support national aspirations for Macedonian inclusion in a greater Bulgaria in the 1878 San Stefano Treaty also set the pattern for the widespread perception that the two Slavic and Orthodox states had a community of interests in the Balkans. Bulgaria, which had lost most of Macedonia during the second round of the Balkan wars, continued to claim all of the area and, in pursuit of its claim, fought both world wars on the losing side. In World War II, however, although the Bulgarians declared war on Britain and America, they refused to join Hitler in fighting the Russians, who were still favorably perceived as their nineteenth-century liberators.

After 1945, most of Macedonia was federated with Yugoslavia, but Bulgarian claims continued – despite the fact that both Bulgaria and Yugoslavia were then allied in the Soviet bloc. Bulgaria proposed the formation of a South Slav federation incorporating Bulgaria, Yugoslavia, and Macedonia, which, according to Sofia's plans, was to be independent and inclusive of those portions of Greece also claimed by Bulgaria. But this plan was vigorously resisted by Stalin, who saw it as an attempt to place nationalism above socialism. It also would have strengthened Tito's hand in dealing with Moscow, which even at that time, before the formal break between the two countries, Stalin was keen to avoid.[13]

The improvement of relations between Yugoslavia and Bulgaria was prevented by Yugoslav concerns over the repression of Macedonian culture in Bulgaria and claims that Sofia denied the very existence of a distinct Macedonian language and culture, choosing to treat this group as ethnic Bulgars. Although the Macedonian issue gradually became taboo in the Bulgarian press, the nation's leadership, under the active supervision of General Secretary Todor Zhivkov and his daughter Lyudmila, presided over a reawakening of specifically Bulgarian nationalism in the 1980s. Thus, the current Bulgarian state was portrayed as the direct descendent of the first Bulgarian empire, which had thrived from the seventh to the eleventh centuries and had included Macedonia. The 1,300th anniversary of its foundation was celebrated with a lavish display of nationalism in 1981, as was in 1985 the 800th anniversary of its reestablishment after an interregnum of Byzantine control.

Unlike the peoples of eastern Central Europe, the Bulgarians had no prior history of subjugation to Russia; in fact, historically, they had sought Russian protection against stronger rulers in Constantinople, Belgrade, and Vienna. The Soviets might have been expected, therefore, to view Zhivkov's attempt to "perfect socialist culture on the basis of preceding national traditions" as increasing the domestic popularity and legitimacy of the regime, while also emphasizing the close historical bonds between the two countries. But the Soviets expressed serious reservations about the 1981 celebrations, and during his first visit to Sofia in October 1985, Gorbachev made a pointed reference to a "few sharp edges" in the relationship. This reference, combined with the sudden postponement of the "Day of Bulgaria," originally scheduled to occur during the visit, seemed to be a further indication that Moscow viewed the Soviet formula of "national in form, socialist in content" as having been essentially reversed by the Bulgarians.

Zhivkov appeared unwilling to back down too far from his policy of relying on Bulgarian national pride. His pride in Bulgaria's achievements had been evident during the visit to Sofia of British Foreign Secretary Sir Geoffrey Howe in February 1985. Zhivkov was reliably reported to have told Howe that Bulgaria was the first colony in the history of the world that was economically more advanced than its imperial center. At the 13th Congress of the Bulgarian Communist Party in April 1986, after Gorbachev had come to power in Moscow, he went out of his way to remark as follows in the closing paragraphs of his speech:

> The Bulgarian people have always been famous for their patriotism. But while in the past our forebears were patriots of their impoverished homeland, plundered by nations and foreigners alike and barely able to make ends meet, all the more justified and all the more strong is our filial love for present-day socialist Bulgaria! . . .
> The Bulgarian people are not alone in the building of socialism in our country. They march shoulder to shoulder with and rely on the mighty support of the Soviet Union, on the other socialist countries. We, in turn, make a contribution to their development. . . .
> This is unity of socialist patriotism and internationalism indeed.[14]

Even while Zhivkov's power was slipping away, he attempted to play the card of nationalism to shore up his position. Beginning in May 1989, Bulgarian authorities began the forced expulsion of those Turkish Bulgarians who had refused to accept cultural assimilation with the Bulgar majority. Claiming that any Moslems who still lived in the country were descendents of Bulgarians forcibly converted to Islam in the centuries of Ottoman rule before the emancipation of Bulgaria in 1878, the authorities argued that there were no more Turks left in Bulgaria. Human-rights demonstrations erupted, resulting in scores of deaths and in mass population movements across the Turkish border. In the ensuing three months, over 310,000 Turkish Bulgarians crossed the border into Turkey, prompting international pressure – including from Moscow – on Zhivkov to moderate his nationalist stance.

The Bulgarians, like other bloc allies, had to walk a tightrope between ideological allegiances dictated from abroad and national preferences designed to shore up the viability of the regime at home. Nevertheless, despite pressure from Moscow, many Bulgarians consider the postwar alliance with the Soviet Union to have fulfilled more of their national aspirations than was the case for any other period since the Bulgarian empire was overrun by the Ottomans at the end of the fourteenth century. Moscow likewise came to consider Bulgaria to be a model of socialist development and both an ideological and national barrier to the spread of disaffection from neighboring Yugoslavia and Romania. For these reasons, although the replacement of Todor Zhivkov in November 1989 was accompanied in Bulgaria by an outpouring of scorn for the thirty-five years of excesses which he had inflicted upon the population, there was less anti-Sovietism in the official and popular reactions than in almost any other East-bloc country.

Romania: Latinist Aspirations Against an Oppressive Background. Of all the countries of Eastern Europe, it is perhaps most difficult to calculate Romania's conception of the gains and losses derived from the postwar division of Europe. Its eastern provinces of Bessarabia and northern Bukovina were annexed by the Soviets in June 1940, at roughly the same time that Moscow took over Latvia, Lithuania, and Estonia. However, after the war the Soviets ceded to Romania large portions of Transylvania which had been governed by the Hungarians during the war but had been controlled by Romania in the interwar period. This territory is settled by a substantial Magyar, or ethnic Hungarian, population, the survivors of centuries of Hungarian control. The Hungarian–Romanian border, drawn without much demographic sensitivity, was guaranteed by the Soviet Union and marked a substantial gain for Romanian national interests, which in this case were promoted against Hungary.

With a longer historical perspective, one also sees that of all the nationalities and nation-states of Central Europe, only since the postwar period have the Romanians emerged from a centuries-old pattern of feudalism and autocracy. Yet they also emerged with a strong sense that independence would allow them to cultivate their long-standing links with Western culture.

Benefiting from the natural protection provided by the Danube, the Transylvanian Alps, and the Carpathian mountains, the native Romanians alone amongst the Balkan peoples had been able to maintain their Latin-based language and culture by withdrawing to the mountains when the Huns and other eastern tribes swept through in the third century (the period that marked the end of Roman rule and the stability it had brought to the Balkans). For the next thousand years they had been able to develop relatively independently because of a confluence of geography and fortune. They also split into two major groups, the first consisting of Romanians who were under the political and cultural influence of a minority Magyar elite in the area to the northwest of the Transylvanian Alps, and the second consisting of Romanians who mixed with Tatars and Slavs in Wallachia and Moldavia, located in the northeast and the south of modern-day Romania.

The two groups had quite different historical antecedents. Although Transylvania was subject to Ottoman authority during the fifteenth, sixteenth, and seventeenth centuries, it was effectively a semiautonomous principality ruled by Hungarian princes. In the seventeenth century, Transylvania, along with Hungary, was absorbed into the Austro-Hungarian Empire, thereby extending its association and involvement with Central and Western

Europe. More than the Romanians in Wallachia and Moldavia, they were influenced by the 1848 revolutions in France and elsewhere. In addition, the Habsburg decision to encourage their conversion from Orthodoxy to Roman Catholicism led to the revival of their Roman heritage and the replacement of the Cyrillic alphabet with the Latin.

In the fifteen hundred years that elapsed between the fall of the Roman Empire and the emergence of a Romanian state in 1878, the Romanians in Wallachia and Moldavia figured little in world affairs. They were on the trade routes of neither ancient Araby nor medieval Europe. They avoided conquest by Charlemagne, but then did not reap the full benefits of the Enlightenment a millennium later. Although converted to Christianity, they did not participate in the Crusades, nor were they affected by the disputes of the Reformation and Counter-Reformation period, having by that time become tributaries of the Ottomans.

The Romanians in Wallachia and Moldavia managed to avoid direct incorporation into the Ottoman Empire longer than any other part of the Balkans, with the exception of Montenegro on the Dalmatian coast. But unlike Montenegro, which avoided absorption by fierce rebellion, the Romanians in the Danubian Principalities (as they were then known) maintained independence from the Ottomans so long as the Sultan received his tribute. Local boyars and Greek civil servants of the Ottoman state could buy titles and jurisdiction, recouping the cost by savage taxation. As a result, although the area was nominally independent, its status was achieved only through the perpetuation of backwardness and poverty amongst the peasant population and the stimulation of corruption and despotism in the ruling groups. Nevertheless, the local Greek rulers did introduce French as the official court language, and Romanian students and the nascent intelligentsia flocked to France, where they, like their cohorts in Transylvania, derived inspiration from French philosophy and culture.

While the ruling elite may have studied French language and literature, they largely circumvented the liberal provisions of the 1866 Romanian Constitution and kept power in the hands of the landed aristocracy. Peasant rebellions were ruthlessly suppressed, and the small urban and primarily Jewish middle class was subject to intense official and unofficial discrimination, as were Hungarian and German minorities in Transylvania when they came under Romanian control in the interwar period. Romania's activism in foreign affairs during the interwar period, particularly as a member of the doomed anti-Soviet alliance with Yugoslavia and Czechoslovakia known as the Little Entente, belied the oppressiveness of domestic life and served as a precursor for postwar trends in domestic and foreign policy.[15]

In the decade and a half between the communist takeover and Romania's break with Moscow, the Western and Latin roots of Romanian culture were suppressed. The alphabet was Slavicized, as were all geographic place names. History was completely rewritten to emphasize only areas of Soviet–Romanian empathy and to delete sources of tension, such as the Soviet occupation of Bessarabia. But beginning at the time of the Sino–Soviet split, first General Secretary Gheorghe Gheorghiu-Dej and then his successor, Nicolae Ceauşescu, increased their distance from the Soviet line in crucial domestic and foreign policies. They refused to participate in the bloc-wide division of labor that would have consigned Romania to being the underdeveloped breadbasket of the bloc, and they further refused to accept Soviet hegemony in ideological or political matters, even withdrawing from the integrated military command of the Warsaw Pact. The Western orientation of the culture was once again stressed, the language was once again Latinized, and Romanian nationalism served as a valuable tool in the promotion of the regime's goals. However, those goals did not greatly enhance popular welfare or widen popular participation in decision-making. Therefore, while the "pull toward the West" may have been a major pillar of official regime policy, it was more illusory than real in the sphere of domestic policy.[16]

The emergence of a more active and Western-oriented Romanian foreign policy in the early 1960s thus did not represent a qualitative break from the past. By choosing a maverick role, while also serving as a bridge between both East and West and East and East, first Gheorghiu-Dej and then Ceauşescu were able to play a role on the world stage and in intrabloc affairs disproportionate to their country's demographic, economic, and military standing. Although this role was shaped in defiance of

Soviet wishes, whatever success Romania had as a mediator nevertheless was attributable at least in part to the duality of its Western heritage and access to Kremlin leaders. Furthermore, with the changes in Soviet foreign policy under Gorbachev, Romanian positions on issues such as European arms control frequently became bloc policy, thereby reducing still further the threat of Romanian defiance.

The domestic corruption and abuse of the Ceauşescu regime came to overshadow whatever role Romania played internationally, however. Those who assumed leadership after the violent national revolt which overthrew him and his family in December 1989 quickly moved to reassure both East and West that Romania's traditional role in the center of Europe would be reasserted. Thus, the first communiqué issued by Ion Iliescu, who emerged as a leader of the National Salvation Front, promised both "to observe commitments with the Warsaw Pact" and "to direct the entire foreign policy to united Europe."[17] With the simultaneous announcement that Romania would abandon the leading role previously reserved for its Communist Party and drop all pretenses of being called a socialist society, authorities clearly were responding to widespread bitterness that the Ceauşescu family had been able to use the trappings of socialism to perpetuate tyranny – a fact that would not make the reestablishment of intersocietal relations with the Soviet Union any easier. Clearly, the new regime hoped to reestablish Romania's presocialist orientation towards Europe, and the most that Soviet diplomacy could hope for at that stage was that a new Little Entente would not emerge.

Hungary: The Legacy of St. Stephen. In the introduction to his history of Hungary, the Oxford historian C. A. Macartney observed that ever since the Magyars entered the mid-Danube basin and settled there in the ninth century, there had been a competition between East and West:

> These two elements – Europe and Asia – strove for mastery, and neither ever achieved it quite completely. The horsemen, when they arrived, were usually the stronger in the field and some of them carried their conquests across the Danube and as far as the western

forests, but in time they always weakened, their empires collapsed and Europe reasserted itself.[18]
The reassertion of this European identity was responsible, according to Macartney, for the 1956 Hungarian uprising against
Soviet rule. But with the failure of the uprising, he concluded in
the last sentence of his book, "the Hungarian people remained
the prisoners of that East on which they had turned their backs
when Árpád led them across the Carpathians, more than 1,000
years ago."[19]

The 1956 Soviet invasion of Hungary put an end to any illusions that Hungary or other bloc states may have had about the
extent to which they could freely choose between East and West
in their military and political allegiances, but the Hungarian
perception of Russia as an oppressor rather than liberator did
not begin in the communist period. Unlike the Romanians, who
had developed a positive evaluation of the Russians because of
their role both in reducing Ottoman control and in spurring the
emergence of a united Romanian state administered along
French lines in the 1830s, the Hungarians remembered only that
it was Russian troops who had suppressed the 1849 revolution.

At that time, the Habsburg Empire was aflame with unrest
spreading from the 1848 revolutionary events in France, and in
these conditions Hungary sought independence from Vienna's
rule. No other foreign powers came to the aid of Hungary, but
Tsar Nicholas I, concerned – like all Russian leaders, then and
now – that such disaffection would spread to Poland and from
Poland to Russia, offered his assistance to Austria's Francis
Joseph I. Two Russian armies entered Hungary, and at the end of
a brief and bloody campaign the Russian commander Paskievich
was able to report to the king that "Hungary lies at the feet of
Your Majesty."[20] The fact that the Hungarian army fought
alongside Hitler's troops in the Ukraine during World War II
only underlined the fact that by the beginning of the communist
period, Hungary's lack of empathy towards Russia was recipro-
cated.

The most negative Hungarian view, shared by many other
intellectuals in Eastern Europe, was summarized by the Hungarian author George Konrád, when he wrote that in order for
the Soviets to gain the respect and voluntary support of the

Hungarians, "Moscow would have to become a center of civilization capable of offering its partners more than obsolete technology."[21] To be sure, he found many "European" aspects in Russian culture and reformist sympathies in Soviet politics, but these were subservient, in his view, to the more negative and traditional elements, forcing him to the following conclusion in the early 1980s:

> When the colonizer is no more advanced economically and culturally than the colonized, it becomes necessary to draw up the weapons again and again as a sure argument for the perpetuation of dependence. . . .
>
> If Hungarian tourists could drive around in the Soviet Union, roaming wherever they wished; if they could eat in inexpensive restaurants, find bargains in Soviet shops, and make friends with frank and open Soviet citizens; if the Soviet artistic avant-garde occupied a prominent place in the world of the arts; if it were worth learning Russian because you could learn something about the world from Russian newspapers; if Hungarians returned from their visit feeling they had seen an interesting and expressive society – then fraternal sentiments would be aroused spontaneously and the unpleasant memory of two suppressed revolutions (1849 and 1956) would fade before the realization that here is a neighbor worth visiting.[22]

There are, however, at least two other aspects of Hungarian political culture that arguably have shaped and defined attitudes towards incorporation into the Soviet bloc. One is the fact, as pointed out by the Hungarian-born British scholar George Schöpflin, that in the past the Hungarians had in fact tolerated and to a certain extent flourished under foreign domination.[23] The period after the 1867 *Ausgleich,* or compromise, between Vienna and Budapest laid the foundations for the view that because Hungary was such a small state, it was acceptable to be within the ambit of a great power. While the Hungarians found it easier to accept the tutelage of the Austrians than that of the Soviets, this attitude nevertheless was a factor in facilitating the eventual, if begrudging, Hungarian acceptance of Soviet control after the failure of the 1956 uprising.

Acceptance was also aided by a second aspect of Hungarian political culture: the central concern that the Hungarian nation should be represented by a continuously existing Hungarian state. Hungarians living within the boundaries of the current Hungarian state, much diminished as it was after the war, considered themselves responsible both for the well-being of Hungarians living elsewhere and for the cultivation of conditions that would eliminate or moderate threats to the welfare of all the Hungarian inhabitants of the Carpathian basin, which in the eleventh century constituted the Crownlands of St. Stephen, the territory governed by Stephen, the first Christian king of Hungary. Thus, Hungarians judged Romanian policy not by the barometer of Ceauşescu's independence from the Soviet Union but rather by his poor treatment of the 1.7 million Hungarians living in Transylvania. Equally, in 1968, the Czechoslovak reform movement was monitored in Budapest as much for its impact on the Hungarian minority in Slovakia as for its possible effects on Hungary's own recently enacted New Economic Mechanism.

These four elements – identification as a Western society, toleration of foreign domination, concern for the survival of the state, and promotion of the welfare of the Hungarian diaspora – have been the cornerstones of Hungarian political culture in the modern era. They explain why General Secretary János Kádár took the lead in the mid-1980s, along with East Germany's General Secretary Erich Honecker, in proposing that the small states of Europe should act in concert to maintain détente. It also explains why, after the experience of 1956, Hungary settled down to thirty years of relative stability and apparent loyalty to the external aims of the Warsaw Pact: So long as the ruling Hungarian Socialist Workers' Party was the protector of the nation, and so long as Hungarians saw incremental improvements in their standard of living and quality of life, the government could expect enhancement of the legitimacy that it had gradually built up during Kádár's thirty years in power.

It was, however, the failure of the government to achieve economic improvements which eroded Kádár's tenuous hold on power. Thus, despite the relative abundance of food and consumer durables and the access to unencumbered travel abroad, the popularity of the regime slipped dramatically in the 1980s. The pressure for change was fueled by the knowledge that accumulated foreign debts (which gave Hungary the worst per capita debt in the bloc) were going to force future economic austerity and that with Gorbachev in power in Moscow the chance to demand a real change in the system was at hand. Consequently, not only did Kádár lose his position, but the ruling Hungarian Socialist Workers' Party (HSWP), facing almost certain defeat in the multiparty elections that were announced, changed its name and program. In so doing, the new party – called simply the Hungarian Socialist Party – brought itself closer into line with the electoral policies of many of the more than thirty parties which emerged during that period. A European orientation was once again emphasized, thereby redressing the balance in favor of Moscow which had characterized the HSWP line, with clear nationalist sentiments expressed – nationalism which during that phase was directed less against Moscow than against President Nicolae Ceauşescu's harsh suppression of the Hungarian minority in Romania. Acceptance of foreign domination would not quickly or easily reappear as part of Hungarian political culture, but the other three elements clearly were reinforced after the demise of the HSWP's monopoly in 1989.

Czechoslovakia: Masarykism Versus Communism. Many of the other East European countries have based their popular or unofficial political cultures on events that occurred decades or even centuries ago. That has not been true in Czechoslovakia, however. The nation entered into its communist phase following only a ten-year interval between the Munich Agreement of 1938 that incorporated the country into the Third Reich and the communist take-over of 1948. Before 1938, under the republic's founder and first president, Tomáš Masaryk, Czechoslovakia had enjoyed twenty years of open, democratic, and libertarian government that were unrivaled anywhere in Eastern or Central Europe at the time.[24] Over twenty political parties represented all persuasions, nationalities, and religions during that period of the First Republic, with the Social Democrats occupying a key position. That period of liberal democratic rule had an obvious and major impact on popular perceptions in the postwar era.

Such perceptions can be examined more closely in Czechoslovakia than elsewhere in Eastern Europe because public-opinion researchers were able to carry out polls in the immediate postwar period and again during and after the 1968 Prague Spring. Such polls showed striking support for the general aims of the First Republic and, most significantly, indicated that its popularity as "the most glorious period in Czech history" (the phrase used in the polls) increased over time.[25] Thus, when the poll was first taken in 1946, only 8 percent of all Czechs (the poll was not taken in Slovakia) considered the First Republic to have been their most glorious era, with the Hussite wars (19 percent), the reign of King Charles IV (17 percent), the current time of 1945–6 (16 percent), and the age of St. Wenceslas (8 percent) all scoring as high or higher. After twenty years of official socialization in the communist system, during which Masaryk and the period of the First Republic were particularly vilified, the popularity of the interwar period had risen to first place. When the poll was taken in October 1968, 39 percent identified the First Republic as the most glorious period, followed by the age of Jan Hus (1369–1415), the reign of Charles IV (1346–78), and the period after January 1968 (which was chosen by 21 percent of the respondents). Remarkably, only 3 percent of the respondents named the period between 1948 and 1968 as the most glorious.

In Slovakia, where the poll was taken in 1968, the responses also showed the extent of support for the period since January 1968 (36 percent) and more limited backing for the two decades since February 1948 (16 percent). They further revealed that while the Masaryk period was chosen by more respondents (17 percent) than the period since 1948, the First Republic nevertheless clearly held more positive connotations for the Czechs than for the Slovaks.

The popular and extensive idealization of Masaryk's legacy always has been a direct challenge to the ruling Communist Party. Masaryk's name came to be synonymous with a democratic government, absence of censorship, strong civic awareness, participation in groups such as the Sokol movement (which imbued civic-mindedness and national consciousness among the country's youth), and the preeminence of middle-class values and intellectual discourse.

Masaryk also became a symbol – albeit of a different kind – to those who sought to tarnish his image. For example, in 1968, an anonymous poison-pen letter written to and subsequently published by Edward Goldstücker, chairman of the Czechoslovak Writers' Union, revealed the way in which the conservatives would have liked Masaryk to be portrayed: "The road to our convictions as Communists was filled with want, hunger, suffering, unemployment, and imprisonment during the First Republic. . . . We couldn't give our own children dry bread for lunch during the period of Masaryk's humanism, . . . a time when a dangerous hyena like you could study at universities."[26]

In 1968, when the campaign by a briefly uncensored press to rehabilitate Masaryk reached its height, the Soviets also became involved in the controversy. They saw Masaryk as a symbol of bourgeois and social democracy, which they recognized as having deep roots in Czechoslovakia. They also saw him as a committed anti-Bolshevik, someone who had rallied his forces to help the White Russians in their attempts to overturn the Russian Revolution. One of the myriad charges leveled against Czechoslovaks by the Soviets in the lengthy official *Pravda* editorial announcing and justifying the August 21, 1968, invasion was that the Czechoslovak Communist Party had taken an "uncritical, nonclass approach to some pages of the country's history." As an example, *Pravda* used "the recent revival of the cult of Masaryk, who was always a sworn enemy of the Communist movement and was an instigator of the intervention against Soviet Russia and at whose instructions the Czechoslovak Communist Party was persecuted."[27]

Although the Soviet invasion ended the open glorification of the Masaryk period, there is no reason to believe that the period was forgotten after 1968, as was suggested by the annual lighting of candles at his grave. This was particularly true in the Czech lands of Bohemia and Moravia, whose influence in the federal system waned after Gustáv Husák, a Slovak, became general secretary in 1969.

The Slovaks had quite a different historical development. They had been under strict Magyar control until 1918 and consequently did not put down the democratic roots that sprouted in the Czech lands after 1918. The Slovaks considered themselves to have been treated as second-class citizens during the First

Republic, a perception nourished by Hitler, who established an independent fascist Slovak state at the same time that the Czech lands became a protectorate ruled by Sudeten Germans. Separatist leanings by the Slovaks have not been evident since the war. However, distinctly different historical experiences have fueled mutual antagonism and have interfered with the legitimation of communist rule.

The one encumbrance to this legitimation that was absent in both the Czech lands and Slovakia before 1948 was an open hostility to Russia and converse adulation of the West. On the contrary, especially in the Czech lands, the decade immediately preceding the February 1948 communist takeover saw bitter disillusionment with the West as a result of the Munich Agreement, the bifurcation of Czechoslovakia, and the occupation of the Czech lands by German troops. Russian troops entering Prague in 1945 were treated as genuine liberators, and the fact that they withdrew along with American troops in the following year created a more favorable impression of Soviet intentions than was being created elsewhere.

Under these circumstances, it can be understood how Alexander Dubček, the general secretary of the Czechoslovak Communist Party during 1968, might genuinely have found it impossible to believe, when he was informed on the night of August 20–1, 1968, that the Soviets were at that moment invading his country. As was the case for many of his countrymen, pan-Slavism and a pro-Russian orientation had shaped his political outlook during the war, and in contrast to the situation for the people of Hungary or Poland, there had been no historical memories of Russian suppression of Czechoslovak independence. The worst excesses of the Stalin period in Czechoslovakia were seen as having been directed by conservatives in the Czechoslovak Communist Party, with the extent of direct Soviet participation only gradually becoming known in the 1950s and 1960s. And the fact that Antonín Novotný, the head of the Czechoslovak Communist Party until 1968, was far more conservative than his Soviet counterpart Nikita Khrushchev and had resisted de-Stalinization to the last made even liberals focus more on the mistakes of their own party rather than on the Soviets. The invasion, of course, changed all that.

When the troops of the Soviet Union, Poland, East Germany,

Hungary, and Bulgaria invaded Czechoslovakia, a major transformation occurred in the political culture of the entire Czechoslovak population. It ended the brief interlude of liberalization in which Dubček had presided over the lifting of media censorship, the introduction of multicandidate elections for Communist Party posts, the revival of noncommunist political associations, and the open debate about past excesses and future hopes for a "socialism with a human face."[28] The intervention, more than any other act, transformed the Czechoslovak conception of the Soviet Union and ended any hopes that the Soviets might have had about friendship between the two peoples. Brezhnev is credited with having told the Czechoslovak leadership that the transitory alienation of one or two generations of Czechoslovak citizens was an acceptable price to pay for the maintenance of socialism,[29] but memories in Central Europe are much longer than one or two generations. With the final admission by Warsaw Pact leaders, in December 1989, that the invasion had been a moral and political mistake, there finally appeared to be a realization that coercion alone cannot implant socialism, a fact of which Lenin himself appeared acutely aware when he cautioned his more zealous party comrades that "a fist in a dispute over principle is the most senseless argument."[30]

The German Democratic Republic: History Denied. Of all the nations of Eastern and Central Europe, Germany has presented the greatest challenge to both East and West, whether united in a single state, as it was before 1945, or divided, as it was thereafter between, first, two zones of occupation, and then two states: the Western-oriented Federal Republic of Germany (FRG) and the Eastern-oriented German Democratic Republic (GDR). Historically, Germany has challenged the West through its search for acceptance, whether in culture, arts, science, or military prowess, and has challenged the East in its quest for preeminence. Since the rise of the German Empire of 1871, both East and West have been obsessed with the question of how to deal with this powerful and revisionist state that lies in the very center of Europe.

While some historians view Hitler as a typically "German" phenomenon, pursuing conventional German objectives by highly unconventional means,[31] most see the period 1933–45 as a qualitative break from any previous cycle of German history. Here was someone who built a police and military machine dedicated to the wholesale destruction of all peoples who were not of the Aryan race. The brutality of the methods used, their systematic and extensive nature, and the choice of enemies from within (the Jews) and from without (the Slavs, gypsies, and peoples from other occupied countries) created a universal consensus among both victims and witnesses after the war that while the German nation may not have been responsible for these atrocities, nevertheless they were carried out by Germans. At the very least, guilt was assigned to the German people for not rejecting fascism. As a result, the perception of Germany was transformed after the war from being a *problem* of coping with the growth of German power to a *question* of how to prevent this power from ever again exerting itself.

After 1945, the two German states existed side by side, initially in mutual nonrecognition, and then gradually, after 1969, in conditions of coexistence and increased cooperation. Each created its own economic miracle in the heart of Europe, expanding to the maximum the capabilities of the two competing systems implanted after the war. Seeking to cast off the mantles of German nationalism and of Hitler's revanchism, the ruling Socialist Unity Party (SED) in East Germany initially identified itself as the most stalwart supporter of Soviet policies and objectives in Central Europe.

The GDR emerged from isolation and deprivation to become economically the most successful country in Eastern Europe, with figures for per capita gross national product (GNP), infant mortality, and mean life expectancy much better than elsewhere in the bloc or in many West European nations. For example, in the early 1980s the GDR had a per capita GNP between $7,000 and $10,000, depending on the method of calculation. Moreover, U.S. government figures recorded a 1984 economic growth rate of 3 percent, infant mortality of 10 per 1,000, and life expectancy of 68.8 years for men and 74.7 years for women. Comparable figures for the FRG were $10,670 GNP per capita, a growth rate of 2.7 percent, infant mortality of 11 per 1,000, and life expectancy of 67.2 years for men and 73.4 years for women.[32]

Other figures might portray the GDR in a less favorable light, but the point here is to demonstrate that the GDR could no longer be dismissed as "the state that ought not to be."[33] Domestically, regionally, and internationally it had evolved from being the most dependent on Soviet goodwill to being the most prominent East European state in the international arena, capable of trading its own activism in supporting Soviet policy in the Third World for a major role in shaping bloc policy in Central Europe.

This is not to say, however, that the greater viability of the East German regime resolved "the German question." Rather, it elevated the regime's stature and allowed a more robust East German leadership to formulate its own views somewhat more independently of Soviet control.

Under these circumstances, the East German regime set out on a risky and delicate course. Using its apparently greater political stability and economic performance as a safety net, the regime maintained all its commitments to the Soviet bloc while incrementally improving contacts with the Federal Republic. The GDR also became much more active in co-opting German history in the service of the legitimacy of the regime. It sought to dispel the notion that the FRG rather than the GDR was the successor to the glories of Frederick the Great (1740–86) and Otto von Bismarck (1862–90), whose memories were officially resurrected in the GDR. Moreover, not only were the roots of socialism on German soil assiduously traced back to the Middle Ages, but the regime also rehabilitated Martin Luther, calling him one of the "greatest sons of the German people."[34]

While the East Germans may have decided that the best defense was a good offense in dealing with the challenge of being between East and West, problems still remained. It is important to emphasize here that East Germany was not strictly between East and West. West Berlin's existence as an island of the West inside the East had an enormous practical and emotional impact on all parties, not least the East Germans. While the 1971 Four Powers Agreement on Berlin may have regulated and stabilized the situation there, it also powerfully reminded the East and West Germans alike that, natural or unnatural, the division of Germany was considered by many to be a fair price to pay for stability in Europe.

If stability meant that Germany would be "driven from its destiny," to quote Kundera again, then for many this was a more than acceptable price to pay. After all, most East Europeans, including both official and dissident sources, were concerned with what Europe meant to a Hungarian, a Pole, or a Czech – not a German. The perception was always strong that Germans saw Europe, or more particularly Eastern Europe, as a space into which Germany could expand, as happened after 1938, and the East Europeans had no particular desire to let them attempt this again. Like the Soviets, the East Europeans were not sympathetic to the notion of German reunification. Non-German dissident or underground tracts coming out of Eastern Europe or from émigré sources did not put reunification on their list of priorities, nor did any of the official, but anti-Soviet, sources in Eastern Europe in the 1950s and 1960s, such as Hungary's one-time prime minister, Imre Nagy, or Tito, Ceauşescu, or Dubček, ever espouse the cause of German reunification. On the contrary, despite the Soviet Union's constant and arguably cynical use of the threat of German revanchism as a means of bolstering bloc unity, the division of Germany and the Soviet guarantee of its permanence constituted one of the big successes for Soviet policy in the bloc.

The unfolding of Mikhail Gorbachev's East European policy in 1988–9, which included wide-ranging declarations in Yugoslavia, Finland, and Western Europe, signaled that Moscow would no longer insist on slavish devotion to previous norms in its relations with bloc states. This policy was accompanied by the emergence of democratization and economic reforms in the Soviet Union which if not adopted elsewhere in Eastern Europe would isolate recalcitrant regimes. West Germany, meanwhile, was continuing to promote its special relationship with the GDR, giving the FRG unusual leverage in the GDR's internal affairs. And finally, in 1988 the GDR, which previously had enjoyed a healthier economy than its allies, suffered severe setbacks. Although its GNP per capita had grown steadily between 1975 and 1987, at the approximate rate of 2.5 percent per annum, in 1988 the figures showed a *negative* growth rate of about 2 percent, making it the most stagnant country in the bloc.[35]

The decline in the fortunes of the East German regime was

accompanied by increased West German interest in the future of Germany. In a bold statement, viewed as controversial at the time, West Germany's president, Richard von Weizsaecker, bluntly observed: "Experience teaches us that a question does not cease to exist simply because nobody has an answer to it."[36]

The collapse of rule by the Socialist Unity Party in East Germany and the lifting of all remaining travel restrictions between the two Germanys which began in November 1989 with the opening of the Berlin Wall brought to the fore renewed and urgent debate about "the German question." However, as to the nature of the question and its solution, there seemed no clearer consensus as Europe moved into the 1990s than there had been in previous decades (see Chapters 7 and 8 for further discussion of the German question).[37]

All past and current debates about the German question put more strain on the weaker and politically more fragile of the two Germanys – the GDR. This was made apparent by the popular demonstrations in the country which erupted in the fall of 1989, exposing both the unpopularity of the existing East German leadership and the longings of a substantial portion of the population for reunification. Western-oriented parties, led by the Christian Democrats, were swept to power in the March 1990 elections, which confirmed a popular yearning for a united Germany.

Poland: The West's Trojan Horse? Concerning Poland, which enjoyed an independent existence until the eighteenth century and established close cultural and religious ties with Catholic Europe, there is great reluctance to dismiss its postwar predicament as being a result of historical predestination. On the contrary, historians have become fascinated with Poland as with no other country in Eastern Europe, including Czechoslovakia. Most do not see it as just another of *The Lands Between,* to use Alan Palmer's felicitous book title. Rather, many, like Norman Davies, see Poland as *God's Playground,* as "the repository of the ideas and values which can outlast any number of military and political catastrophes . . . as an enduring symbol of moral purpose in European life."[38] This view sees the centuries of rule by the *liberum veto* – in which every nobleman had the absolute right to veto any assembly measure – as a blessing that checked the rise of absolutism. It also considers the rule of Jan Sobieski (1674–96), who defeated the Turks at Vienna and thereby saved Europe and Christendom from the advance of Islam, as the exemplar of Polish aspirations and capabilities. The assessment of Sobieski's rule contained in *The Cambridge History of Poland* is typical of this genre:

> Polish life found a form, both European and national, which included communion with the whole nation, friendliness toward the poor and oppressed, candour towards everyone and tolerance towards foreigners. . . . Bright and imperishable in the firmament and on the horizon of the nation, shines the star of Sobieski.[39]

If the autocracy of previous centuries facilitated the rise elsewhere in Eastern Europe of a Leninist credo imbued with centralism, did Poland's quite different past offer up nothing to ease the way for Soviet control? Might it not be that the very tradition of rule by the whole of the nobility (or *szlachta*) using the paralyzing device of the *liberum veto* was Poland's greatest gift to more willful neighbors? By the middle of the seventeenth century, the Polish assembly, the Sejm, was paralyzed by competition within the *szlachta,* whose collective ethic had produced anarchy. Unable to raise armies for lack of taxes or to change the constitution because of vested interests, these competing magnates pursued their local interests at the expense of the state. As a result, the "paradoxical philosophy of anarchy," as its devotees called it, was nurtured and passed down over the centuries as the jewel of Poland in its age of "Golden Freedom."

The Poles have always seen their best defense not in absolutism but, to quote the French political theorist Jean-Jacques Rousseau's advice to them, in "indigestibility." At the same time, however, the absence of a strong central authority in Poland certainly helped neighboring countries exert their influence, and often, with the aid of self-serving members of the nobility, Poland was partitioned. As French philosopher Montesquieu once observed in writing on the "inconveniency" of the *liberum veto,* "the independence of individuals is the end aimed at by the laws of Poland, and from thence results the oppression of the whole."[40]

It is not surprising, seen from this perspective, that in the

eighteenth century the Russians became the champions of Poland's *liberum veto* and its "Golden Freedom." Not wishing to
import these principles, but rather to exploit them, the Russians,
along with the Austrians and Germans, were able to manipulate
the Polish system to their will from that time onward. Then, as
later, the question was posed whether Poland's reputation for
anarchy, romanticism, and idealism was such a disservice to
Moscow's aims as is commonly believed, and whether or not
Poland was in fact "beyond its history."[41] This was precisely the
question asked during the height of Solidarity's influence in
1980–1, when the debate raged whether or not the philosophy of
anarchy was a disservice to Poland. Many voices were raised
within Solidarity itself, imploring the trade-union organization
not to exercise its veto over the running of the country.[42] Authorities also expressed concern about a return to the pattern of
the eighteenth century, when various "lone wolf" magnates pursued their interests at the expense of a state so weak that it went
"into hiding." Thus, in one of his first defenses of martial law,
General Wojciech Jaruzelski told a Central Committee plenum of
the ruling Polish United Workers' Party in February 1982 that in
the days of Solidarity:

> The spirit of *Liberum Veto* triumphed, the times of
> lone wolves returned. Many times, openly and loudly,
> we have warned against the danger. The authorities
> announced that they would not hesitate to use the
> constitutional measures of defending the state if this
> were inevitable. . . . We did not remain in hiding.[43]

It has also been argued that the strong nationalism of Poles
and their desire for an independent state led them to adopt a
more pragmatic approach to their incorporation into the Soviet
bloc. The Polish fear of partition and constant concern for the
very survival of the state have been dominant themes in Polish
political culture. The fact that a Polish state emerged after 1945
to take control of the Polish nation was used rather successfully
by communist authorities to justify both the emergence of an
uncharacteristically strong state and the alliance with the Soviet
Union, with the latter in particular being portrayed as a guarantee against any future German revanchist claims on Polish territory. Thus, upon becoming chairman of the Council of Minis-

ters in February 1981, Jaruzelski delivered a speech threatening harsh measures and reaffirming Poland's alliance with the USSR. Repeating phrases used by every Polish leader since 1945, he justified Poland's special relationship with the Soviet Union not primarily from Poland's adherence to socialism but rather "from Polish raison d'état, the bitter experiences from which history did not spare us."[44] He went on to talk about the "period when we lost and then recovered our independence" and to say that "all Poles are responsible for the fate of Poland," not, by implication, as a socialist state but "for its existence as a sovereign and independent state within the borders between the Bug, the Odra, and the Lusatian Nysa." As for the alliance with the Soviet Union, he maintained that Poland would never forget "how the battle for its present borders was fought, and who was always our staunch ally in this context."

While these arguments were used to establish a modicum of legitimacy for Poland's Soviet and socialist orientation, this is not to suggest that equal or even greater forces were not operating to undermine that legitimacy. One of the strongest of these was a deep and abiding Russophobia. In Poland, this view stemmed from centuries of struggle between Polish Catholicism and Russian Orthodoxy, as well as from territorial disputes in which the union between Poland and Catholic Lithuania was challenged and ultimately severed by Russia. Since the days of both Peter the Great and Catherine the Great, Russia's expansion westward came into conflict with Poland's Jagiellonian legacy of territorial claims to the east. From the seventeenth century until the present day, therefore, Russia has acted to contain Poland and prevent it from reestablishing a presence "beyond the Bug."

Russophobia also worked to diminish the acceptance of Marxism-Leninism by the Polish population. Because of the long-standing disputes between the Polish and Russian sections of the Second International, which carried over into debates between Lenin and the Polish Bundists, the Bolsheviks regarded the Polish Communist Party as unduly influenced by social democracy and nationalism, a perception that was enhanced by the Polish–Soviet war of 1920.[45] Consequently, the party was dissolved by order of the Comintern, and it was reconstituted pri-

marily from Polish Jews residing in the Soviet Union during
World War II. The fact that it was this group of Moscow-trained
Poles, known initially as the Lublin Committee, who took
over after 1945 only further reinforced the view that Marxism-
Leninism was a foreign ideology, imposed by a power whose
interests both historically and in the recent past had been opposed to Poland's.

The Poles' hatred of Russians and their cynicism about Soviet
intentions were reinforced by the experiences of World War II,
when, for Poland, Hitler was not the only aggressor. The Soviet
counterinvasion of Poland in September 1939, the probable Soviet responsibility for the massacre in the Katyn woods of almost
the entire Polish officer corps, and the slowness with which the
Soviets liberated Warsaw (first allowing indigenous resistance to
be crushed) are all deeply felt and widely discussed in Poland. For
example, on the thirty-seventh anniversary of the outbreak of
the war, one of the Polish bishops declared from the pulpit in a
sermon full of anti-Soviet innuendo:

> In August 1939, an infamous Ribbentrop–Molotov
> pact was signed, that meant the fourth partition, pre-
> planned by Hitler and Stalin. . . . And we know how
> Molotov triumphantly said "the bastard of the Ver-
> sailles Treaty has disappeared from the earth's surface."
> We all remember that, and the Nation remembers and
> waits for the grievance to be repaid. . . . We remember
> those who were killed, we remember concentration
> camps, we remember removals, we remember Katyn.[46]

Given the history of antagonism and conflict between the two
countries, it is not surprising that in survey after survey, when-
ever Poles have been asked with which nations Poland has had
the friendliest relations, the Soviet Union always has scored at or
near the bottom.[47]

In addition to Russophobia, the strong nationalism of the
Poles has been of great detriment to the establishment of a firm
basis for Soviet-style socialism. Nationalism has expressed itself,
of course, against the Soviet Union, and Russophobia is therefore a component of it, but it is also a broader notion in Poland.
Nationalism entails an attachment to the idea of Poland, to its
culture, history, and traditions, and to its distinctiveness from

both of the other competing and dominant cultures of the region – Russian and German.

This is not to say, however, that Polish nationalism is grounded in a belief in the uniqueness of its culture. On the contrary, two major connections are made by Poles, both of which undermine their political ties to Moscow: One is the connection to Catholicism, and the other is the cultural link to the West. When considering the role of Catholicism in Poland, it is vital to recall that Poles view Catholicism not just as a religion but as a credo that sets them apart and protects them from alien beliefs imposed by occupying powers. And they see the Catholic Church not just as the rock of Peter but also as the rock of the nation – that institution which survived to represent the nation when the institutions of the state succumbed to foreign partition.

Since the beginning of communist rule, therefore, the Church has stood as the protector of the Polish nation. The former Polish Primate, Cardinal Stefan Wyszyński, declared on more than one occasion that "next to God is Poland. For us, next to God, our first love is Poland. After God one must above all remain faithful to one's homeland, to the Polish national culture."[48] Delivered in a West European country where Church and state coexist, such a statement would not in any way have been notable, but in a communist country it was an open challenge to the authorities' patriotism and to the official ideology of Marxism-Leninism. Wyszyński maintained that "only the Church in Poland stands in defense of the Nation. While the political needs of the state may change, the Nation endures."[49] As for Catholicism representing a challenge to the legitimacy of communism, the number of quotations one could cite is almost endless. One that captures the Polish sense of the historic centrality and worldwide importance of their struggle against this "anti-Gospel" was provided by Cardinal Karol Wojtyła before he became pope:

> We are now standing in the face of the greatest
> historical confrontation humanity has gone through.
> We are now facing the final confrontation between the
> Church and the anti-Church, the Gospel versus the
> anti-Gospel. . . . It is a trial not only of our nation and

the Church, but in a sense a test of 2,000 years of culture and Christian civilization with all its consequences for human dignity, individual rights, human rights, and the rights of nations.[50]

It goes without saying that the Polish use of Catholicism as an instrument of both nationalism and faith created enormous problems for the Sovietization of the country. It meant above all that the communist regime was unable to forge a new culture with new historical roots. The fight between the Church and the regime for the "correct" interpretation of historical events took on enormous significance and was manifested in the uncontrolled burgeoning of semiofficial publications during and since the Solidarity period.

It also led to numerous demands for the regime to allow the rewriting of history textbooks. In February 1981, the government agreed to the proposal made by the universities for "the speediest possible preparation of new history textbooks containing historical truth, particular attention being paid to the most recent history of Poland."[51] Private farmers in Poland, who traditionally have represented a stronghold of Catholicism, similarly demanded and obtained from the government during the Solidarity period a commitment for "the fullest possible presentation of historical truth in teaching history."[52]

The Soviets were blunt and direct in their reaction. In an open letter to the Polish leadership, the Central Committee of the Soviet Communist Party charged that "counterrevolutionary forces have been actively spreading all sorts of anti-Soviet fabrications aimed at canceling out the results of the work done by our parties, at revising nationalistic, anti-Soviet sentiments among various sections of Polish society." The letter went on to warn: "The extremely serious danger which is hanging over socialism in Poland is a threat also to the very existence of the independent Polish state."[53] One cannot help but compare this Soviet warning with the nineteenth-century lament of Pope Pius IX: "The Poles seek Poland above all, not the Kingdom of God, and that is why they have no Poland."[54]

If Polish nationalism has been supported by the role of the Church, it also has been popularly defined as being intrinsically Western in orientation. Far from dying out after Poland's political and military integration with the East, the determination of the Polish people to maintain and strengthen their cultural ties with the West was reinforced tenfold after being brought under Soviet sway. Thus, the first of the "basic values" contained in the Solidarity Course of Action declared Polish culture to be a merger between European culture and Catholicism.[55]

In reaction, even indigenous communist authorities sought closer ties with the West as a way of legitimizing their rule. For example, a speech by the Polish foreign minister in 1986 imploring Europe not to turn its back on Poland was not only or even primarily motivated by economic dictates; rather, he feared that in turning its back on Poland, Europe would only further delegitimize a new set of leaders who had little support among the population after the declaration of martial law in December 1981. Thus, speaking to the assembled deputies of the Sejm, he said:

> Regaining its rightful place, Poland has given proof
> that it can be relied upon in Europe and the world as
> a strong and stable country, and that without such a
> country there will be no equal and lasting security and
> détente in Europe. . . .
>
> Citizen deputies, Poland, an inseparable part of
> Europe, feels jointly responsible for its civilization,
> heritage, and cultural identity. . . .
>
> Poland needs France, France needs Poland. . . . The
> traditions of many centuries of Polish–French ties
> oblige us to restore their former shape and extent.
> Poland is aware of their general European dimensions.
> Everything which takes place between Poland and
> France has a significant meaning for the whole of
> Europe, for the creation of an appropriate climate for
> agreement and cooperation, for the halting of the
> division of Europe.[56]

All of these factors combined to form a peculiarly Polish predicament. The largest country of Eastern Europe, the land link between Russia and Germany, the single most vital geographic buffer against any future Western incursions onto Russian soil — for all these reasons and many more Poland always emerged as the most important Soviet ally in Eastern Europe. But despite Jaruzelski's assurances to the contrary, Poland was also the most likely candidate to play the Trojan horse of the socialist community – not the nation that stands between East and West, but rather the one that is the West in the East. That was the challenge of Poland, a challenge that was always present below the surface and always threatening to erupt.

Soviet recognition of the need to overcome, or at least diminish, the age-old Russophobia of the Poles was at the heart of the bilateral declaration signed by Mikhail Gorbachev and Wojciech Jaruzelski in April 1987. The two sides agreed to undertake a series of joint projects in the fields of social science, history, economics, and journalism designed to bridge the gap between the theory and practice of relations between the two countries. Indicating the extent to which history had indeed injected itself into the bilateral relationship, the two leaders stated that "history must not be the subject of ideological speculations and the cause of the kindling of nationalist passions." They called for joint historical studies containing "no blank spots," in which "all the episodes, dramatic ones included, must be objectively and clearly interpreted."[57]

Progress on eliminating such "blank spots" was slow, however, with the Poles growing increasingly frustrated with the slow pace at which the Soviets were releasing archival information. But in any case, most Poles had long since made up their minds how all the many blank spots were going to be filled in. By April 1989, when communist and Solidarity negotiators signed a roundtable agreement to legalize Solidarity and establish an electoral procedure to govern the country's first free elections in over forty years, the damage had already been done. In the June elections, the ruling Polish United Workers' Party suffered a humiliating defeat when candidates endorsed by Solidarity won 260 of the 261 seats they were allowed to contest. With that result, the writing was on the wall regarding all the changes which began to take place in the bloc in the months which followed.

Gorbachev's leadership is undoubtedly appreciated in Poland, as elsewhere in the bloc. It is highly unlikely, however, that he intends to sever the ties that bind Poland and all the countries of Eastern Europe to the USSR. While he may be more sensitive to the need to transform the basis of the relationship, a strong community of allied states nevertheless is still a preeminent Soviet goal. As such, it is unlikely that the intrinsic conflict between certain core Soviet and East European interests will easily subside. Indeed as East European countries seek to fashion their own relationships with the West, generalized competition and conflict between them can be expected to increase. They will have to contend also with greatly increased Soviet activism in its own dealings with Europe and the United States. East European leaders, therefore, themselves may seek a structure among former Soviet-bloc allies that facilitates entry into the international community. Only in this way might the web of interactions and controls (the subject of the next chapter) be maintained – this time to promote independence rather than to constrain it.

Notes

1 Milan Kundera, "The Tragedy of Central Europe," *New York Review of Books,* April 26, 1984, p. 33.

2 George T. Kurian, *The New Book of World Rankings* (New York: Facts on File Publications, 1984). Figures presented by Nicholas Eberstadt demonstrate the decline in public health and life expectancy which accompanied the economic downturn of the late 1970s. See his "Health and Mortality in Eastern Europe, 1965 to 1985," in 101st Congress, Joint Economic Committee, *Pressures for Reform in the East European Economies* (Washington, D.C.: U.S. Government Printing Office, 1989), Vol. 1, pp. 97–120.

3 A. A. Gromyko and B. N. Ponomarev, eds., *Soviet Foreign Policy, 1945–1980* (Moscow: Progress Publishers, 1981), Vol. 2, p. 17.

4 Quoted in Norman Davies, *God's Playground: A History of Poland* (New York: Columbia University Press, 1984), Vol. 1, p. 3.

5 A more muted, but fundamentally similar, analysis appeared in a paper delivered by a top Gorbachev advisor, Academician Oleg Bogomolov, director of the Soviet Academy of Sciences' Institute of Economics of the World Socialist System. The paper, delivered in July 1988 and published in the May–August 1988 issue of *Problems of Communism,* continued to uphold the standard negative appraisal of the presocialist period, even though it contained sweeping indictments of "deformations" caused by the implantation of Stalinist "administrative-command systems of power."

6 Hugh Seton-Watson, *The East European Revolution* (New York: Praeger, 1951), pp. 12–13.

7 According to a typed text of thirty-seven pages, entitled "The Concept of an All-European House and the German Question," which purport-

edly was written as a background paper by Soviet aides for Mikhail Gorbachev's trip to Bonn in June 1989, a copy of which was given to the author.

8   Quoted from the text in Zdeněk Mlynář, *Night Frost in Prague: The End of Humane Socialism* (London: C. Hurst & Co., 1980), p. 286.

9   George Konrád, interviewed by Richard Falk and Mary Kaldor, "The Post-Yalta Debate," *World Policy Journal*, Vol. 2, No. 3, Summer 1985, p. 456.

10 As quoted in Karen Dawisha, *Soviet Foreign Policy Towards Egypt* (London: Macmillan, 1979), p. 26.

11 Every one of the postwar leaders of Poland interviewed by Teresa Toranska in her book *"Them": Stalin's Polish Puppets* (New York: Harper & Row, 1987) cited these two reasons as justification for their actions during the Stalinist period.

12 For further details, see Stephen Runciman, *A History of the First Bulgarian Empire* (London: G. Bell & Son, 1930); C. E. Black, *The Establishment of Constitutional Government in Bulgaria* (Princeton University Press, 1943); Nissan Oren, *Bulgarian Communism, The Road to Power 1934–44* (New York: Columbia University Press, 1971); Robert Lee Wolff, *The Balkans in Our Times* (Cambridge, Mass.: Harvard University Press, 1974); Merein Macdermott, *A History of Bulgaria, 1393–1885* (New York: Praeger, 1962); and John R. Lampe and Marvin R. Jackson, *Balkan Economic History, 1550–1950* (Bloomington: Indiana University Press, 1982).

13 For a more detailed account of postwar Bulgarian policies, including proposals for a South Slav federation, see J. F. Brown, *Bulgaria Under Communist Rule* (New York: Praeger, 1970); and François Fejtö, *Histoire des démocraties populaires: l'ère de Staline, 1945–1952* (Paris: Éditions du Seuil, 1952), pp. 196–200.

14 *Rabotnichesko delo*, April 3, 1986, as contained in *Information Bulletin, Documents of the Communist and Workers' Parties*, Vol. 24, No. 9, May 1986, p. 36.

15 For more on presocialist Romanian development, see Henry L. Roberts, *Rumania* (New Haven, Conn.: Yale University Press, 1951); David Mitrany, *The Land and Peasant in Rumania: The War and Agrarian Reform 1917–1921* (London: H. Milford, 1930); R. W. Seton-Watson, *History of the Roumanians: From Roman Times to the Completion of Unity* (Cambridge University Press, 1934).

16 For more on socialist Romania, see Robert R. King, *History of the Romanian Communist Party* (Stanford, Calif.: Hoover Institution Press, 1980); Kenneth Jowitt, *Revolutionary Breakthroughs and National Development, The Case of Romania, 1944–1965* (Berkeley: University of California Press, 1971); John M. Montias, *Economic Development in Communist Rumania* (Cambridge, Mass.: M.I.T. Press, 1967); Stephen Fischer-Galati, *The New Rumania: From People's Democracy to Socialist Republic* (Baltimore, Md.: Johns Hopkins University Press, 1969); and Ghiţa Ionescu, *Communism in Rumania, 1944–1962* (Oxford University Press, 1964).

17 *New York Times*, December 24, 1989.

18 C. A. Macartney, *Hungary* (Edinburgh University Press, 1962), pp. 3–4.
19 *Ibid.*, p. 243.
20 *Ibid.*, p. 163.
21 George Konrád, *Anti-Politics* (New York: Harcourt Brace Jovanovich, 1984), pp. 75–6.
22 *Ibid.*, p. 76.
23 See Schöpflin's thoughtful piece "Hungary: An Uneasy Stability" in Archie Brown and Jack Gray, eds., *Political Culture and Political Change in Communist States,* 2nd ed. (London: Macmillan, 1979), p. 132.
24 For more on this period and also on its influence on contemporary political culture, see R. W. Seton-Watson, *A History of the Czechs and Slovaks* (London: 1943; reprinted by Arden Library, 1980); Victor S. Mamatey and Radomir Luza, eds., *A History of the Czechoslovak Republic, 1918–1943* (Princeton University Press, 1973); and David W. Paul, "Nationalism, Pluralism and Schweikism in Czechoslovakia's Political Culture," unpublished Ph.D. thesis, Princeton University, 1973.
25 More complete figures are given in the excellent article by Archie Brown and Gordon Wightman, "Czechoslovakia: Revival and Retreat," in Brown and Gray, *op. cit.,* pp. 159–97; Jaroslaw A. Piekalkiewicz and Barry Bede, *Public Opinion Polling in Czechoslovakia, 1968–69: Results and Analysis of Surveys Conducted during the Dubček Era* (New York: Irvington, 1972); and Ithiel de Sola Pool, "Public Opinion in Czechoslovakia," *Public Opinion Quarterly,* Vol. 24, Spring 1970, pp. 10–25.
26 *Rudé právo,* June 23, 1968.
27 *Pravda,* August 22, 1968.
28 Of the large number of works on the origins and nature of the Prague Spring, the best remain H. Gordon Skilling, *Czechoslovakia's Interrupted Revolution* (Princeton University Press, 1976); Galia Golan, *The Czechoslovak Reform Movement* (Cambridge University Press, 1971); Galia Golan, *Reform Rule in Czechoslovakia: The Dubček Era, 1968–1969* (Cambridge University Press, 1973); V. V. Kusin, *The Intellectual Origins of the Prague Spring* (Cambridge University Press, 1977); V. V. Kusin, *Political Grouping in the Czechoslovak Reform Movement* (New York: Columbia University Press, 1972); and Alex Pravda, *Reform and Change in the Czechoslovak Political System: January–August 1968* (London: Sage Research Paper, 1975).
29 This and other Soviet calculations in the invasion of Czechoslovakia are discussed in Karen Dawisha, *The Kremlin and the Prague Spring* (Berkeley: University of California Press, 1985).
30 As quoted in Sidney I. Ploss, *Moscow and the Polish Crisis* (Boulder, Colo.: Westview Press, 1986), p. 18.
31 Notably A. J. P. Taylor, *Origins of the Second World War* (New York: Atheneum, 1983).
32 Central Intelligence Agency, *The World Factbook 1986,* June 1986, CR WF 86-001, pp. 89–92. The GNP figures used by the CIA have been disputed by some Western economists as being too high. Two independent calculations completed by Thad Alton and Paul Marer concluded that for

the early 1980s, when the data for these studies were collected, GNP levels for European countries in the Council for Mutual Economic Assistance (CMEA) should be calculated at between 65 and 85 percent of the CIA figures. In other words, the CIA figure of approximately $10,000 per capita GNP for East Germany would yield an approximate result, using Marer's methodology, of $7,000 per capita GNP in 1984, while Alton's figure would be in excess of $8,500. Whichever method is used, it is important to emphasize that none of these measures is meant to show the standard of living in Eastern Europe as compared with the West, since such figures do not indicate the vast differential between spending on consumer goods and services in Eastern and Western countries. For these alternate figures, see Thad P. Alton, "East European GNP's: Origins of Product, Final Uses, Rates of Growth, and International Comparisons," and Paul Marer, "Alternative Estimates of the Dollar GNP and Growth Rates of the CMEA Countries," both contained in 99th Congress, Joint Economic Committee, *East European Economies: Slow Growth in the 1980s* (Washington, D.C.: U.S. Government Printing Office, 1985), Vol. 1, pp. 133–94.

33 Ernst Richtert, *Das zweite Deutschland: Ein Staat der nicht sein darf* (Guetersloh: 1964), as quoted in Ronald D. Asmus, "Between East and West: Domestic Determinants of G.D.R. Foreign Policy," paper presented on March 6, 1985, to the John J. McCloy Study Group on Eastern Europe, Council on Foreign Relations, New York.

34 See Ronald D. Asmus, "The G.D.R. and Martin Luther," *Survey*, Vol. 28, No. 3, Autumn 1984, pp. 124–56.

35 Thad Alton, "East European GNP's, Domestic Final Uses of Gross Product, Rates of Growth, and International Comparisons," in 101st Congress, *Pressures for Reform in the East European Economies* (Washington, D.C.: U.S. Government Printing Office, 1989), Vol. 1, p. 82.

36 *Die Zeit*, September 30, 1983, as quoted in N. Edwina Moreton, "The German Question in the 1980s," in N. Edwina Moreton, ed., *Germany Between East and West* (London: Royal Institute for International Affairs, 1987).

37 For an excellent analysis and explication of the issue, see Anne-Marie Burley, "The Once and Future German Question," *Foreign Affairs*, Vol. 68, No. 5, Winter 1989–90, pp. 65–84.

38 Norman Davies, *op. cit.*, Vol. 2, p. 642.

39 *The Cambridge History of Poland* (New York: Octagon, 1971), Vol. 1, pp. 555–556.

40 Charles Louis de Secondat, Baron de Montesquieu, *The Spirit of Laws* (Berkeley: University of California Press, 1977), p. 201.

41 Variations on this theme are discussed by George Kolankiewicz and Ray Taras, "Poland: Socialism for Everyman?" in Brown and Gray, *op. cit.*, pp. 116–117; and Adam Bromke, *Poland's Politics: Idealism vs. Realism* (Cambridge, Mass.: Harvard University Press, 1967).

42 References to Solidarity's veto power can be found, for example, in the account by a leading Polish sociologist who supported and worked for

Solidarity, Jadwiga Staniszkis, in *Poland's Self-Limiting Revolution* (Princeton University Press, 1984).

43 As quoted by government spokesman Jerzy Urban, June 6, 1986, Foreign Broadcast Information Service, *East European Daily Report* (*FBIS-EEU*), June 9, 1986, G4.

44 Jaruzelski's speech to the Sejm, February 12, 1981, *Trybuna Ludu*, February 13, 1981.

45 See the excellent article by James McCann on the theme of contending Soviet and Polish accounts of their clash in 1920, "Beyond the Bug, Soviet Historiography of the Soviet–Polish War of 1920," *Soviet Studies*, Vol. 36, No. 4, October 1984, pp. 475–93.

46 Bishop Ignacy Tokarczuk of Przemyśl, as quoted in a well-documented paper by Robert Zuzowski, La Trobe University, Victoria, Australia, "The Dissenting Intelligentsia and the Church in Contemporary Poland," presented at Australasian Political Studies Association Conference, Brisbane, August 1986.

47 Some of these surveys are cited by Kolankiewicz and Taras, *op. cit.*, p. 106.

48 Wyszyński, speaking in 1974, is quoted by M. Dobbs, K. S. Karol, and D. Trevisan, *Poland: Solidarity, Walesa* (Oxford: Pergamon Press, 1982), p. 32.

49 Stefan Wyszyński, *Prymat Czlowieka w ladzie spolecznym* (London: Odnowa, 1976), p. 196, quoted by Zuzowski, *op. cit.*

50 Karol Wojtyła in 1976, as quoted by James Oram, *The People's Pope* (Sydney: Bay Books, 1979), p. 148.

51 "Agreement between the Inter-Ministerial Commission and the Inter University Coordinating Commission in Łódź," *Sztander Młodych*, February 19, 1981, quoted in *Communist Affairs, Documents and Analysis*, Vol. 1, No. 1, January 1982, p. 228.

52 "Protocol of Agreement between the Government Commission and the Strike Committee Acting on Behalf of the National Founding Committee of the Trade Union of Private Farmers," *Słowo Powszechne*, March 10, 1981, quoted in *Communist Affairs, Documents and Analysis*, Vol. 1, No. 1, January 1982, p. 258.

53 *Pravda*, June 12, 1981.

54 Quoted in Adam Piekarski, *The Church in Poland* (Warsaw: Interpress Publishers, 1978), p. 57.

55 "Independent Self-governing Trade Union Solidarity: Course of Action in the Country's Present Situation – Theses for Discussion," April 17, 1981, in *Communist Affairs, Documents and Analysis*, Vol. 1, No. 1, January 1982, p. 234.

56 Speech by Foreign Minister Orzechowski at January 19, 1986, Sejm session, Warsaw Domestic Service, January 29, 1986, *FBIS-EEU*, pp. G2–8.

57 *Pravda*, April 22, 1987. The issues involved are analyzed by Elizabeth Kridl Valkenier, "Filling in Blank Spots: Soviet–Polish History and Polish Renewal," *The Harriman Institute Forum*, Vol. 2, No. 12, December 1989.

4

The Links That Bind

System of Control Under Stalin

Many of the controversies within the field of Soviet and East European studies focus on the nature of Stalinism as a system, both as it affected politics and daily life within the USSR and as it was exported to the bloc countries in the period 1945–53. As regards Eastern Europe, interest is focused primarily on the extent of Soviet control. One group sees the distinctive features of Stalin's rule in Eastern Europe in the cult of personality, the arbitrary nature of Moscow's rule, and the role of terror and purges. Another group views this period's importance less in the transient features that died with Stalin than in the foundations for a total system of control that survived him.[1]

The two positions, however, surely are not mutually exclusive. The period 1945–53 was marked both by arbitrary practices that were criticized by the Soviets themselves after 1953 and by the foundations that were laid for a socialist-bloc system. Soviet tolerance for diversity increased somewhat after 1953, but the extensive if still imperfect system of control laid down in the Stalinist period survived. Although the Warsaw Pact was not formed until 1955, most of the other levers used by the Soviets to influence events in Eastern Europe have their roots in this period.

Because of de-Stalinization, and also because of the greater cohesion of the bloc and the improved standing of the East European states vis-à-vis the Soviet Union in subsequent years, the nature and extent of Soviet control were altered. Yet despite the generally greater level of tolerance for change and reform exhibited by successive post-Stalin leaderships, one cannot overlook the fact that it was Stalin's successors who took the decisions to build the Berlin Wall and to invade Hungary and Czechoslovakia. Thus, it is difficult to disagree with the verdict of Soviet historian Roy Medvedev that while socialism "does not generate lawlessness, . . . we know that socialism in itself is no guarantee against lawlessness and the abuse of power." Moreover, despite the substantial changes made in the means used by the USSR to exert influence in Eastern Europe, it is also impossible, even as the Soviet Union has moved into the Gorbachev era, to fault Medvedev's earlier conclusion that "not everything connected with Stalinism is behind us, by no means everything."[2]

While many authors have written about Stalinism as a domestic system, fewer have analyzed the essential features of Stalinism in international relations. What were these features, and to what methods did the Soviets resort during this initial period from 1945 to 1953? One can identify three core elements of Stalinism as a form of international relations. The first was the imposition of a single political model. Although Stalinism evolved over a period of two decades in the USSR, only with its uniform implantation throughout Eastern Europe was it possible to observe, as émigré Polish economist Włodzimierz Brus pointed out, the essential features of this Stalinist model.[3] Its core and distinctive features as transmitted to Eastern Europe in the period 1945–53 were as follows: the cult of personality; arbitrary rule by the leadership, with all organizations being mere transmission belts for this rule; widespread use of terror and ritualistic purges as a means of controlling all sections of the populace; and the subordination of all cultural, economic, and societal transactions to the needs of the state. The wholesale implantation of this model under Stalin's direct supervision marked a qualitative departure from the Leninist pattern.[4] Few East European communist leaders either could or chose to resist the importation of the model. Yugoslavia's Tito was one leader who, in resisting, was able to avoid the worst excesses of Stalinism for his country. Poland's Władysław Gomułka was another who resisted, only to become a victim of the 1930s-style Soviet purges that cast their shadow over Eastern Europe in the late 1940s. After Stalin's death, Gomułka was rehabilitated and elected to head the ruling Polish United Workers' Party. At that time, he offered the following cogent analysis of the "revolution from above" and the cult of personality that had been exported to Eastern Europe:

> The cult of personality is a certain system which prevailed in the Soviet Union and which was grafted to probably all Communist parties. . . .
>
> The essence of this system consisted in the fact that an individual, hierarchic ladder of cults was created. . . . In the bloc of socialist states it was Stalin who stood at the top of this hierarchic ladder of cults. All those who stood on lower rungs of the ladder bowed their heads before him. . . . The First Secretaries of the Central Committees of the Parties of the various countries who sat on the second rung of the ladder of the cult of personality, in turn donned the robes of infallibility and wisdom. But their cult radiated only on the territory of the countries where they stood at the top of the national cult ladder. This cult could be called only a reflected brilliance, a borrowed light. It shone as the moon does.[5]

The second crucial element of Stalinism as a system of international relations was the denial of the independent, sovereign, and equal status of any of the bloc states. While bilateral treaties signed after the war gave the appearance of an emerging interstate system, in fact Stalin did not view his relations with the bloc as being in the domain of *international* politics. Rather, he saw relations with these countries as an extension of *domestic* Soviet politics. Hence, all normal mechanisms and channels for interstate relations were poorly developed and even deformed under Stalin, with the Soviet Foreign Ministry used not to develop a system of interstate relations but to serve as a vehicle for the personal extension of Stalin's rule. It was "natural" that someone like Andrei Vyshinskii, the chief prosecutor in the 1930s show trials, should become the deputy foreign minister, in which capacity he oversaw similar trials in Eastern Europe. Moreover, Soviet advisors and embassy officials were placed in key directing positions in each state, often running the countries like constituent republics of the USSR. Soviet ambassadors summoned East European leaders to the embassy for instructions and consulta-

tions at a moment's notice. Soviet advisors were placed throughout the military and security apparatus of each state, thereby
informally but effectively controlling it. Thus, according to Edward Ochab, the former general secretary of the ruling Polish
United Workers' Party, "the Soviet advisors were more often
than not the ones who had the final say in a number of ministries, and especially in organs of the Ministry of Public Security."[6] And in countries such as Poland, the minister of defense
and many senior officers either were Soviet citizens or had dual
citizenship.

The third element of Stalinism in international relations was
the emphasis on bilateral relations at the expense of multilateral
channels. Subordinate to Moscow, the socialist states were prevented from developing substantial links with each other. Hopes
of postwar cooperation among the bloc states were dashed as
Stalin moved to divide and rule by firmly rebuking any independent attempts to seek closer intra–East European links, such as
the efforts for greater Polish–Czechoslovak cooperation and the
proposed union of Balkan states. The Soviets did create several
multilateral organizations during this period. Most notably, the
Cominform was established in 1947, ostensibly for the exchange
of views and experiences, but actually as an instrument of Soviet
ideological control, as the Yugoslavs discovered the following
year when the Cominform was used to rally the bloc against
them. In addition, the Council for Mutual Economic Assistance
(CMEA, also called Comecon) was formed in 1949 as a counterpart to Marshall Plan assistance, but was supportive of autarkic
development. However, the purposes of these organizations
were almost entirely subordinated to Soviet interests.

These, then, were the major features of Stalinism in international relations: export of the cult of personality under the guise
of the revolution from above; denial of the independence, sovereignty, and equality of East European states, which instead
were subordinated to Soviet interests; and isolation of East European states from each other. The means used included direct
interference by Stalin, control by Soviet emissaries, emplacement
of Soviet liaison officers in key political positions in the security
services and in the military, and, of course, extensive cooperation
by pro-Moscow factions within the East European communist

elites. As discussed in the following sections, by no means were all these mechanisms abandoned by Moscow after 1953, but the Soviets did come to rely increasingly on interparty relations and compliance by East European elites themselves.

The Bloc System After Stalin

De-Stalinization put a halt to many arbitrary practices in Eastern Europe. Although the threat of force would remain, Stalin's successors virtually eliminated the direct and overt Soviet supervision of all the key ministries in every bloc capital. De-Stalinization also produced a greater emphasis on multilateral diplomacy, with the formation of the Warsaw Pact in 1955 and the invigoration of the CMEA. First Georgii Malenkov and then Nikita Khrushchev presided over a "New Course" in intrabloc relations, promising an end to the excesses of Stalinism and a respect for "different paths to socialism."

Khrushchev was accused in 1964 by the neo-Stalinist right of almost "throwing out the baby with the bath water" in his rush to remove the more unacceptable levers of control.[7] But whatever the inclinations of a hard-line core in the Soviet leadership, by 1964 Stalinist methods had become unacceptable except as a last resort. The Soviets had to evolve more subtle and less obtrusive methods and formulae for maintaining control on a more "normal" basis. In particular, they developed interparty relations as a core mechanism for building a bloc consensus supporting Soviet interests.

Interparty Relations

Of all these methods and formulae, after Stalin's death the system of relationships between the ruling communist parties became the linchpin of the Soviet Union's hegemonic position in the bloc. With the dissolution of the Cominform in 1956 and the challenge from both Chinese communism and Eurocommunism in the 1960s and 1970s, some authors predicted that Warsaw Pact institutions would replace the communist parties as the key conduits of communication and influence in bloc affairs.[8] However, in a book on party–military relations, General Aleksei Yepishev, the long-time head of the military's Main Political Administration, emphasized the centrality of the party in intrabloc relations. Calling it "the chief factor" that strengthened the unity and cohesion of the socialist community, he quoted Soviet Communist Party leader Leonid Brezhnev to the same effect:

> The fundamental core of our close collaboration, its living spirit and its directing organizational force is, of course, the unbreakable militant union of *communist parties of the socialist countries,* the unity of their world outlook, the unity of their aims, the unity of their will.[9]

The importance to Soviet interests of maintaining the ties between ruling communist parties was emphasized by every general secretary, including Gorbachev, until those parties began to fall from power in 1989. These relations were based on the acceptance in Eastern Europe of three key principles, largely defined by the Soviet Union. The first was *socialist internationalism,* which clearly reemerged after 1968 as the so-called Brezhnev Doctrine, or the doctrine of limited sovereignty. Before then, the Soviets, having renounced the Stalinist dictum that "he is an internationalist who steadfastly promotes the strengthening of the Soviet state," protested their loyalty to the principle of full equality between socialist states. But challenges to that principle by the Chinese, Albanians, Romanians, and Czechoslovaks in the mid-1960s led to a fundamental redefinition. After the invasion of Czechoslovakia, internationalism came to mean the acknowledgment that the socialist bloc's greatest strength lay in its *class*-based unity. Sovereign states, therefore, had to subordinate their separate national interests to the historically more progressive interests of socialism. Because the Soviet Union was deemed the most experienced in the construction of socialism, the principle in practice limited the independence of East Europeans far more than that of the Soviets.

Collective loyalty to socialist internationalism facilitated and legitimized the continued development throughout the bloc of formal and informal mechanisms which in fact greatly constrained state sovereignty. The mechanisms included the whole network of continual high-level consultations, exchanges, and negotiations between the Soviets and the leaders of all the East-bloc communist parties. Interparty agreements between Moscow and the "East European five" (the German Democratic Republic, Czechoslovakia, Poland, Hungary, and Bulgaria, but not Romania, Yugoslavia, or Albania) provided for crisscrossing party networks that resulted both in the Soviet training of bloc personnel and in close Soviet monitoring of bloc events. It was this key party connection that was the most effective means of day-to-day influence, coordination, and consultation in the bloc.

Moscow also used socialist internationalism to promote the notion that although it may have been the senior partner, the common duty of all states was to maintain the unity of the alliance. The management and prevention of crisis in any single bloc state thus became the collective responsibility of the entire bloc. While bilateral channels were the primary mechanisms for crisis management, Moscow also relied on multilateral bloc forums to obtain a consensus on how to manage particular crises and on how to prevent a crisis from spreading. In both the Czechoslovak and Polish crises, the Soviets used formal and informal multilateral meetings to cope with challenges.

Since coming to power, Gorbachev gradually has moved away from the restrictive definition of socialist internationalism. Thus, in a major speech delivered on the seventieth anniversary of the October Revolution, Gorbachev outlined his view of this core principle. He reaffirmed Khrushchev's formula of different roads to socialism, stating that "all parties are fully and irreversibly independent. We said that as long ago as the 20th Congress. True, it took time to free ourselves of the old habits. Now, however, this is an immutable reality." Going on to discuss the practice of socialist internationalism, he singled out the need for "unconditional and total equality, the responsibility of the ruling party for the affairs of its own state, . . . a serious attitude toward what has been achieved and tried out by friends, [and] voluntary and varied cooperation." The broadening of the definition of socialist internationalism, however, by no means symbolized its demise as a cornerstone of intrabloc relations. On the contrary, Gorbachev emphasized that "we also know what damage can be done by a weakening of the internationalist principle in mutual relations of socialist states, by deviation from the principles of mutual benefit and mutual aid. . . ."[10]

It was not until 1988 that strong official signals began coming from Moscow indicating that the Soviet Union would no longer adhere to socialist internationalism as a principle governing its relations with other parties. An important mutual declaration with the Yugoslavs in March 1988 affirmed the principles of the independence and sovereignty of every state, the "inalienable right" of all parties "to make decisions on the choice of paths of social development" and the "impermissibility of interference in internal affairs under any pretext whatsoever."[11] In his speech to the 19th Party Conference in June 1988, Gorbachev also emphasized that "the imposition from outside by any means – not to mention military means – of a social system, way of life, or policy constitutes the dangerous armor of past years."[12] Many of his top foreign-policy advisors, including Nikolai Shishlin and Georgii Korniyenko, both key Central Committee aides, stated quite explicitly when challenged by Western reporters that "we think a state's sovereignty must not be limited by anything or anyone, whatever its nature. . . . We've given up the Brezhnev principle of limited sovereignty."[13]

In the midst of the far-reaching changes which swept Eastern Europe in the autumn of 1989, at a time when the West was watching very carefully to see if Moscow would try to stabilize the situation there by reasserting its traditional interests, the Soviet leadership distanced itself even further from the old principle of socialist internationalism. In a significant declaration signed with Finland in October 1989, the Soviet side committed itself to the principle that "there can be no justification for any use of force: whether by one military-political alliance against another, or within such alliances." It went on to lay out the principles which effectively would replace socialist internationalism as the norm governing relations between socialist countries: "freedom of sociopolitical choice, deideologizing and humanizing of relations among states, subordination of foreign-political activity to international law, and supremacy of universal human interests and values."[14] These principles were reaffirmed by Gorbachev at the first CPSU Central Committee plenum held after leadership changes had taken place in the GDR, Poland, Czechoslovakia, and Bulgaria, thereby indicating Moscow's acceptance of the need to build relations with other communist parties (many of them by that time virtually non-ruling) on a new basis. The complete absence of any mention of socialist internationalism from any of these statements was a clear indication of Soviet recognition that they could no longer depend upon the "class loyalty" of fraternal parties to provide an automatic entrée to positions of influence in Eastern Europe.[15]

The second key principle was *democratic centralism*. This principle had guided the internal workings and structures of communist parties since it was first enunciated by Lenin, who insisted that all fraternal parties within the Third International (also called the Communist International, or Comintern) adopt it as their key organizing concept. Communist parties thereafter copied the Soviet experience, giving them the same pyramidal top-to-bottom structure and creating within all parties the same powerful full-time corps of party cadres to control the weaker, democratically elected bodies of party members. It was this distinctive style of inner-party organization which historically distinguished communist parties from other socialist or social democratic groups. It was also the key to their success as both underground and ruling parties, since the structures of social democratic or other traditional political parties were not as well suited to the organizational demands of either of these situations. The imposition of Soviet-style socialism in Eastern Europe, therefore, naturally was accompanied by the imposition of this principle on the newly formed Marxist-Leninist parties, thereby ensuring that each communist party in Eastern Europe was organized to maximize central control first by indigenous party leaders and then, through fidelity to socialist internationalism, by Moscow. In combination, the two principles provided the Soviet Communist Party with immense opportunities for gaining information and exerting influence down to the lowest societal level in each of the East European communist parties.

If democratic centralism provided vertical control, it was the third principle, that of *the leading role of the communist party*, which ensured horizontal control. The relationship between the ruling communist party and other coalition parties, government ministries, state organs, or mass organizations was governed by the rule that they were free to carry out their prescribed functions only so long as they recognized that it was the communist party to which they were ultimately responsible.

Such a principle, which was enshrined in the constitutions of all bloc states, gave communist parties the exclusive right to organize in every place of work and to maintain full-time party staff within all offices, educational institutions, social organizations, military and police units, and publishing houses. It gave the party an enormous capability to eavesdrop on the whole society without having to break the law. They could control all activities, supervise personnel, censor the news media, and do much more without ever having to write elaborate legal codes allowing it – everything was covered by the simple constitutional formula making each of these parties "the leading and guiding force in the construction of socialism."

That was why the debate about the repeal of this article was so high on the agenda of opposition forces throughout the Soviet bloc beginning in 1989. Without the cover of a constitutional monopoly, communist parties really had only two choices: They could return to the days of illegality and underground work, for which most of their officials no longer had the stomach, having become accustomed to a life of limousines and summer homes, or they could compete with other parties for power in open, democratic elections. As the summer 1989 elections in Poland showed, however, the latter option would be suicidal for these parties unless they succeeded in distancing themselves from the four decades of privilege and abuse. Several parties, as in Hungary, Poland, and the GDR, changed their names and platforms to signal a break with the past (see Appendix III); some, as in Romania and again in East Germany, prosecuted their former leaders in an attempt to saddle them with the entire burden for the system that had been created. Others, as in Czechoslovakia, engaged in a revolving-door strategy of purging the current leadership and bringing back to power communists who themselves had been victims of earlier purges. And still others, as in Poland and Bulgaria, tried to impress the population with their realism, openness, and moderation, hoping that somehow they would be able to maintain some influence.

Whatever strategies were pursued by the parties, almost universally throughout the bloc individual communists pursued in overwhelming numbers a single strategy – they resigned. Even the careerists who had flocked into these parties when membership had been necessary for promotion and perks quickly left as soon as the winds of change began blowing. Only the Bulgarian Communist Party, which refused to rename itself at an extraordinary congress in January 1990, did not suffer mass defections from its ranks. In all the other East European countries, the strategy of renaming the communist parties and attempting to dissociate them from the past four decades of misrule could not stem mass resignations, in Hungary, Poland, and Romania to less than 10 percent of their previous levels.

All of this was noted in Moscow, where Gorbachev himself came under liberal pressure to follow the East European example. His response initially was to point to the CPSU as the sole "consolidating and unifying force" capable of keeping the Soviet Union together in a time of nationalist and separatist challenges.[16] While the principles which had guided Soviet Communist Party relations with Eastern Europe had been challenged and changed thoroughly by the end of 1989, therefore, two of them – the leading role of the party and democratic centralism – were still in force within the Soviet Union. But even in the USSR these principles were being challenged and were subjects of heated debate at the February 1990 CPSU Central Committee plenum.

In addition to these three principles, there were three mechanisms which were developed to ensure that non-party organizations remained strictly within the confines of the leading role of the party. The first was the *parallel party bureaucracy,* whose functions mirrored those of the government machinery and whose officials oversaw the operation of all such organs. With the exceptions of Romania, Yugoslavia, and Albania, it was the "Eighth Department for State Administration" within each East European party apparat which supervised the workings of the police, judiciary, defense, and intelligence services. The secretaries in charge of these departments in Eastern Europe worked closely with the relevant government minister or party secretary in Moscow.

The second mechanism for maintaining the party's leading role was the *nomenklatura* system, which enabled the central party apparat in each country to control appointments to all key positions in the party and government. Again, the Soviets exercised a guiding hand over the *nomenklatura* process in Eastern Europe through their own Central Committee. Many examples can be found of Soviet involvement in the selection, promotion, and demotion of East European party leaders, particularly in the pre-Gorbachev era. For example, in July 1956, Soviet Minister Anastas Mikoyan, upon arriving in Budapest, went directly to a Central Committee meeting that was already in session and demanded the removal of Hungarian Communist Party leader Mátyás Rákosi. On this occasion, the Soviets passed over János Kádár (who was to become general secretary in November 1956) and chose Ernő Gerő instead.

Following the Soviet invasion of Czechoslovakia in 1968, the Soviet ambassador tried to form a quisling "Workers' and Peasants' Government" to replace the party leadership. When this failed, Alexander Dubček was allowed to stay on, but only after signing the Moscow Protocol, thereby agreeing to "discharge from their posts those individuals whose further activities would not conform to the needs of consolidating the leading role of the working class and the Communist Party."[17] Dubček was himself "discharged" the next year at the beginning of the purge that eventually led to the expulsion of half the entire membership of the Czechoslovak Communist Party and the reassertion of a Soviet role in the selection of leading personnel.

Soviet influence was not always exercised solely to prevent reform. De-Stalinization in Eastern Europe delivered the *coup de grace* to many hard-liners. In 1970, when the political climate in Central Europe changed, East Germany's Walter Ulbricht was removed when he proved to be an obstacle to Moscow's policy of détente with West Germany. And in Poland that same year, the Soviets did not intervene to prevent Gomułka's replacement by the more moderate Edward Gierek. What was important to Moscow, then, was not that an East European leader be right-wing or left-wing, but that he be chosen in consultation with Moscow and that he be capable of changing his outlook should opinion change in the Kremlin.

Soviet influence in the selection of leaders was not limited to party positions. Through the East European parties, Moscow also maintained control in other fields. Certainly, for example, no key appointment in the security field would be made without Soviet approval. This point was highlighted at the post-invasion negotiations in Moscow between the Soviets and the Czechoslovaks. Brezhnev, who had been lecturing the Czechoslovak leadership on how supportive he personally had been of Dubček's leadership in the early months of 1968, reminded the Czechoslovaks that in January 1968 he had asked Dubček: "Do you want to relieve the Interior Minister? You maintained at the time that this was not necessary. . . . And then I suddenly find out that you are replacing the Minister of Interior, the Defense Minister, . . . and the Secretaries of the Central Committee. . . ."[18] The point here, as far as Brezhnev was concerned, was not that the Soviets necessarily would have chosen hard-line candidates, since Brezhnev had personally approved Novotný's replacement by Dubček. Rather, the issue was that while a *Czechoslovak* leader had replaced government and party elites, a *Soviet* party leader, believing it his right to participate in the selection, had made it clear that Moscow would not sanction a complete loss of control over that process.

Leadership selection did not in every case go Moscow's way, however. During the 1956 crisis in Poland, Khrushchev was so alarmed at the prospect of a Polish leader unapproved by Moscow taking power that he led a top-level political-military delegation to Warsaw in a last-ditch effort to forestall the election of Gomułka. Presented with a *fait accompli*, Khrushchev is said to have remarked that "we shed our blood for this country, and they're trying to sell it out to the Americans and Zionists."[19] The Polish transcript of the plenum electing Gomułka noted more dryly that "the Russian visitors were . . . interested in our proposals for the composition of the leadership. . . . They pointed out that . . . in spite of our ties we had not informed our Soviet comrades."[20] However, Gomułka came to enjoy Soviet support, which was vital in protecting him from an attempted coup in 1968 by ultranationalists headed by Minister of Interior Mieczysław Moczar.

There have been other examples of successful East European resistance to Soviet pressure to influence succession. The Bulgarians are said to have promoted Bulgarian leader Todor

Zhivkov's daughter, Lyudmila, to a full position on the Polit-buro in 1979 despite Soviet protests that she would support the further flowering of Bulgarian nationalism. Extensive public knowledge of the dispute also fueled the widespread rumor in Bulgaria that the KGB was responsible for her premature death the following year. In Romania, once Ceauşescu's own person-ality cult was established, the CPSU effectively lost its leverage over succession issues there. As a consequence, whatever influ-ence Moscow had over succession had to be exercised outside the interparty channel. In Czechoslovakia, the selection of Miloš Jakeš as general secretary to replace Gustáv Husák in December 1987 did not have an obvious Soviet hand, although he was well known to Soviet leaders. However, while it would appear to be the case that Soviet interference became less overt beginning in the 1980s, there nevertheless was clear Soviet involvement in the selection of every general secretary who came to power up to 1985, with the possible exception of Stanisław Kania, whose ten-ure as Poland's general secretary (1980–1) was in any case very short. Similarly, it was the rule rather than the exception that candidates known to be acceptable to Moscow would be chosen for other key posts in the party, security, and military hierar-chies.

That was the legacy that Gorbachev inherited. Clearly, when Gorbachev came to power in 1985 he had no intention of presid-ing over the collapse of Soviet influence in the bloc, as appeared might happen in 1989. But his protestations that communist parties had to be responsible to their own people began to be taken seriously in Eastern Europe, with the result that within four years an entire generation of leaders had been swept from power, leaders who had looked first to Moscow and only then to their own domestic bases in the formulation of policies. To replace them came a new breed of communists, many of whom had suffered personally as a result of defiance of Moscow (such as Alexander Dubček, who returned from twenty years of internal exile to become president of the Czechoslovak National Assem-bly), and some of whom were the sons and daughters of commu-nists who had fought in Spain in the 1930s and later fought against fascism and Stalinism in their own countries. Gregor Gysi, elected head of the newly renamed Socialist Unity Party–

Party of Democratic Socialism in the GDR to replace Egon Krenz in December 1989, was a lawyer who had spent recent years defending reformers and dissidents. His father had been a member of the German Communist Party prior to World War II and had fled to France. Ion Iliescu, who was named the provisional president of Romania following the bloody uprising that toppled the Ceauşescu regime in December 1989, previously had been demoted for openly criticizing regime policies. He was the son of a founder of Romania's small, prewar underground Communist Party.

The speed with which all these new party leaders announced their desire both to establish close relations with Europe and to formulate policies in line with national conditions was a clear indication of the political distance they thought it necessary to keep from Moscow. In the initial statements delivered by the Solidarity government in Poland, the Civic Forum in Czechoslovakia, the Democratic Forum in Hungary, and the National Salvation Front in Romania, all endorsed a strong pro-European platform.

Nevertheless, there are many indications that the withdrawal of Moscow's support for remaining hard-liners had been crucial to the emergence of opposition to the existing leadership. This was certainly true in Czechoslovakia, where Gorbachev's visit in April 1987 set the stage for the fall of Gustáv Husák, even though liberals there were prevented from taking power by the interim leadership of Miloš Jakeš. In Poland, it was Gorbachev's telephone call from Moscow to Mieczysław Rakowski, leader of the Polish United Workers' Party, on August 22, 1989, urging the party to accept a minority position in a new government headed by Solidarity, which marked the beginning of the post-communist period in Eastern Europe.

In East Germany, Gorbachev's visit there in the first week of October 1989 was the precursor for the removal of Erich Honecker, who reportedly appealed without success for Soviet support in putting down the mass demonstrations in Leipzig, Dresden, and Berlin which ultimately toppled him. An East German diplomat reported that in his meeting with the SED Politburo, Gorbachev did not try to prescribe what the East Germans should do; however, "he made it very clear that the spectacle of thousands of people running away from the country and of violence being the only way to keep them in was not helping him in his own difficult situation."[21] Kurt Hager, seventy-seven-year-old chief ideologist, returned from the Soviet Union a week later, calling for "necessary renovations."[22] Three days later, Honecker was replaced at an emergency Politburo meeting. His successor, Egon Krenz, flew to Moscow two weeks later to endorse Soviet-style *perestroika*.

This pattern of close involvement and consultation was repeated elsewhere in the bloc. In Bulgaria, the emergency Central Committee plenum which elected Petar Mladenov as the replacement to Todor Zhivkov had been preceded by Mladenov's stopover visit to Moscow on his return from China. In Romania, the speed with which the National Salvation Front emerged, announced its platform, and selected Iliescu as its leader led many to look for preplanning of the succession events. The fact that Iliescu was personally known to Gorbachev from their days as students at Moscow State University supported the contention that the Soviets had managed through all the years of poor relations with the Ceaușescu regime nevertheless to court some within the disfranchised elite. In Czechoslovakia, once it became clear that the Jakeš regime could stay in power only by using force against massive peaceful demonstrations, Moscow exerted pressure to bring down the government. However, the Soviets certainly were not involved in the selection of Václav Havel as interim president. The transition from Krenz to Gysi in East Germany was another transition which did not bear any sign of Soviet involvement. In Hungary, too, Imre Pozsgay, an avowed social democrat without any ties to, or apparent affinity for, the USSR, emerged as the presidential candidate of the new Hungarian Socialist Party (this party being the heir to the Hungarian Socialist Workers' Party, which was disbanded in October 1989) without Soviet reaction or resistance. This was an indication that if in the late 1980s the rule of Soviet involvement in leadership selection had begun to be more often breached than observed, by the beginning of the 1990s and a new era of democratic elections that rule had virtually ceased to exist altogether.

Not all the new communist officials in Eastern Europe chose to distance themselves from Moscow, however. All continued to support the existence of the Warsaw Pact and other treaty obligations. And some, seeing their own popularity slide at home, were concerned that Moscow might abandon them in favor of improved relations with the more important emerging social democratic parties in the region. In Poland, for example, faced with declining support in public-opinion polls, in which the Polish United Workers' Party (PUWP) earned the confidence of only 11 percent of the population, compared with 66 percent for Solidarity,[23] the PUWP leadership pursued a policy of relying more on the link with Moscow in an effort to avoid being left out of the emerging relationship between Moscow and the Solidarity-led government. Realizing the popularity of Gorbachev's leadership, Mieczysław Rakowski, first secretary of the PUWP Central Committee, sought to shore up sagging ratings at home by presenting Moscow as being supportive of the PUWP efforts to reform. Thus, after meeting Gorbachev in Moscow in October, Rakowski told journalists that "we can rely on the support of the CPSU in our efforts to adapt the party to the situation in which Poland now finds itself, and in the cause of creating a new look for the Party. In general, we can continue to lean, as it were, on the East Slav wall."[24] In the past, communist parties had been kept alive by a Soviet military presence; now some of them hoped to remain viable by riding on the coattails of Gorbachev's personal popularity. Even this tactic failed, however, in Poland, where both the PUWP and Rakowski's leadership of it were rejected by rank-and-file members, who decided at the end of January 1990 to split into two parties.

The third mechanism for ensuring party supremacy involved the *party committees* located within all ministries, government offices, and mass associations. Each committee had a full-time staff whose task was both to supervise the work of the office to which it was attached and, in accordance with the principle of democratic centralism, to report on the workings of that office to the party committee at the next highest echelon. Thus, the desire of Solidarity to establish an independent trade union challenged this key principle precisely because Solidarity refused to recognize the party's leading role and expose its internal operations accordingly.

The principle of the leading role of the party also applied to

East European military establishments, all of which had, at every level, party cells that were under the control of the central party secretariat and their own country's Main Political Administration (MPA). These organs were then subject to numerous co-optation agreements with their Soviet counterparts, including the Soviet MPA. The Soviet MPA is subordinate both to the Soviet Ministry of Defense and to the CPSU Central Committee. Its purpose in Eastern Europe was to monitor bloc armies constantly for signs of anti-Sovietism and, in the words of General Yepishev, its former head, "to strengthen the military unity of the socialist armies . . . and educate the fighters in the spirit of socialist internationalism."[25]

The constitutional amendments deleting the "leading role of the party" which were widely debated and passed throughout Eastern Europe in the winter of 1989 led to the dismantling of party committees in the workplaces. With that development, the Soviets lost a major capability to monitor social unrest in these countries. More importantly, oaths being taken by the new wave of political and military leaders no longer required fealty to the party and to the goals of socialism. In many of the countries, party organizations were banned not only from the armed forces but also from units of the border guards, the armed agencies of the Ministries of Internal Affairs, and other security and intelligence agencies. With that, Moscow clearly lost a major mechanism for control in Eastern Europe.

In short, through these three key principles – socialist internationalism, democratic centralism, and the leading role of the communist parties – the CPSU had succeeded in establishing a series of binding relationships and mechanisms (the parallel party bureaucracy, the *nomenklatura,* and cells within non-party organizations) for alliance management that was totally without equal in the West. It was a system that underwent substantial change after Stalin's death; under Stalin, interparty relations had been moribund and subject to whimsical control by Stalin and his emissaries and ambassadorial viceroys. Brezhnev relied heavily on this system, but as his own leadership began to stagnate, so too did this system fall into disrepair.

Beginning in 1985, the Soviets put great emphasis on increasing the number and substance of interparty agreements and affiliations at all levels. Gorbachev and many other top-level Politburo and Central Committee members asserted the need to revitalize such connections, with the result that unprecedented numbers of visits and exchanges occurred in the first years of Gorbachev's tenure.

At the same time, he and other members of the Politburo began to emphasize that such meetings did not represent a new Soviet bid to exert control. As Politburo Secretary Yegor Ligachev stressed during a visit to Hungary in April 1987,

> every country looks for solutions independently, not as in the past. It is not true that Moscow's conductor's baton, or Moscow's hand is in everything. . . . Every nation has a right to its own way.[26]

The Soviets' insistence that they had forsaken strict methods of control only strengthened the requirement for a more active diplomacy in achieving consensus among the various communist parties. Undoubtedly, Gorbachev's ambitious objectives in bringing about changes in Eastern Europe could not be attained without greater attention to bloc requirements and sensitivities, which in turn could best be gleaned by enhanced cooperation in the interparty sphere. The increased numbers of visits by Gorbachev, Foreign Minister Shevardnadze, and Party Secretaries Yakovlev and Medvedev to Eastern Europe in the turbulent last six months of 1989 showed the Soviet desire not to turn its back on Eastern Europe, but to support positive trends and diminish the potential for destabilization. Multilateral meetings of bloc ideology secretaries, such as those held in Varna and Berlin in September 1989, also attested that while intergovernmental relations may have begun to displace the interparty connection as the crucial link in the Soviet bloc system, nevertheless both the Soviets and their allies in the East European communist parties, in the words of the Varna declaration, "expressed the firm will of their parties to strengthen their cohesion even more [and] to continue actively developing comprehensive cooperation and interaction in the international arena in the interests of the cause of socialism and peace."[27]

Military and Security Cooperation

Soviet control of Eastern Europe always has been exercised against the backdrop of the threat of force. But the use of force, while excellent for the control of territory, is both inefficient and counterproductive for the control of people. A major dilemma facing the Soviets has been that the Warsaw Pact and the other bilateral military relationships in the bloc had to be designed to present a credible military threat to NATO without giving East European armies, individually or collectively, the ability to defy the Soviet Union.

The dilemma became pressing when, only a year after formation of the Warsaw Pact in 1955, crises rocked Hungary and Poland. In both cases, important sections of the military establishments of those countries showed themselves willing to resist any use of force by Soviet troops and to side with the local population. Hungarian resistance was brutally suppressed by the Soviet invasion, and the Hungarian military had to be completely rebuilt. In Poland in 1956, Soviet force was forestalled once it became clear that Polish forces would take the side of the "native" faction of the Polish United Workers' Party in supporting the election of Gomułka as general secretary, irrespective of the wishes of the Soviet leadership and Soviet officers in command of Polish troops. The only account of these events to come out of Poland at the time, a smuggled tape of a PUWP meeting, was replete with references to resistance by the military and security forces:

> The security office of Warsaw supported as one the side of progress. [Applause.] The Internal Security Corps also took the side of progress. [Applause.] In these dramatic days, the Internal Security Corps not only protected the Central Committee but it also occupied the premises of the Polish radio. . . .
> The attitude the troops adopted you all know. When orders were issued to staff and political officers, they answered simply that these orders would be ignored.[28]

Polish independence from Moscow benefited thereafter from uncertainty about the ultimate loyalty of the Polish military.

In Romania, whose leaders succeeded in securing total withdrawal of Soviet forces in 1958, the military was openly committed to following the Yugoslav example of total national defense, which also was adopted by Albania. Claiming that their doctrine of popular resistance had its roots in the medieval struggle of Vlad the Impaler against the invading Turkish infidels, Romania's President Nicolae Ceauşescu tried to legitimize his own rule by building a military beyond Moscow's control.

These examples were, however, more in the category of exceptions that prove the rule, for throughout Eastern Europe, Moscow had been able to use the security services and the military as major levers of influence. Over time, structures and measures had been developed by the Soviets to suit these purposes. In the field of intelligence gathering, ever since the signing of the 1955 treaty establishing the Warsaw Pact, the East European regimes had accepted the Soviet argument that successful intelligence and counterintelligence against NATO required the fullest possible cooperation between the Soviets and their East European allies. Since it is Eastern Europe that borders on the West, its regimes have acted as hosts to Soviet employees of the Committee for State Security (KGB) and the military's Main Intelligence Directorate (GRU). The substantial monitoring facilities along the entire border between Eastern and Western Europe have been operated primarily by the Soviets, and while they were placed there ostensibly to monitor NATO activities, their capability to receive, control, and interdict similar communications within East European countries had been established and accepted, however reluctantly, by the East European leaders.

Thus, in the event of war or in case of an East European crisis in which there would be a threat of a Soviet invasion, since the mid-1960s it had been assumed that Moscow had the ability to eavesdrop on, and jam, all high-level communications between and within East European regimes. Resistance to Soviet military moves was thereby made even more futile. The acceptance of the need for cooperation in fact ensured far greater Soviet access to bloc intelligence files than vice versa. It also legitimized the presence in all bloc capitals of Soviet intelligence offices, whose employees monitored the activities of the host Ministries of Interior and Defense. Although a systematic Soviet presence in non-Soviet Warsaw Pact units was curtailed after 1956, East European officers have maintained that the sizes of the Soviet military and intelligence missions in host commands have increased dramatically at times of crisis. Such a phenomenon was observed by indigenous officers both in Czechoslovakia in 1968 and in Poland in 1980–1. Moreover, this presence often was maintained long after the political crisis abated, allowing Soviet military officers time to evaluate loyalty and performance. For example, an émigré Czech officer reported that during 1969 maneuvers, a Czech division was directly subordinated to Soviet command.[29]

Such actions would have been difficult without the active cooperation of key elites in the East European intelligence community. Such cooperation had been guaranteed not only by Soviet participation in the selection, training, and promotion of key officials but also by maintaining a network of "two-check employees" who were also in the pay of Moscow. Such employees were estimated in 1968 by one Czech official with access to the files to include one-third of the entire apparat of the Prague central office of the Ministry of Interior.[30] Certainly, during the Prague Spring, despite the liberal credentials of Josef Pavel, who was appointed Minister of Interior without Soviet knowledge or approval, the whole carefully constructed system of liaison officers, monitoring stations, pro-Soviet deputy ministers, and two-check employees frustrated the efforts of the Dubček leadership to liberalize the system. The existence of this network explains why, on more than one occasion, Dubček was awakened by calls from Soviet leaders angrily complaining of some activity or publication about which Dubček himself had not yet been informed.

While the Soviets have been able to monitor events very closely in Eastern Europe through their intelligence networks, de-Stalinization has meant that for some time the KGB has not been able, by itself, to put an end to any incipient reform movement. When it became clear in Czechoslovakia during 1968, for example, that these various "organs of state administration" were themselves unwilling, or unable, to take those "administrative actions" repeatedly and publicly urged upon them by Moscow, military force had to be used. During the 1980–1 Polish crisis, the outcome was different precisely because the secret police remained loyal to Moscow and were willing to use force against the local population under the direction of top Polish generals. While their reasons for doing so may indeed have been to avert "the worse alternatives" of a Soviet invasion or a civil war, such action nevertheless served Soviet objectives without requiring direct and overwhelming involvement of either the Soviet military or the KGB. And amid the swirl of rumors which accompanied the sweeping changes in Eastern Europe in 1989, one that was notably absent was any mention of KGB involvement to promote or prevent any particular outcome. While Soviet embassies throughout the area appeared to have increased their staffs in an effort to monitor the hectic events, there appeared to be few reports of the kind that normally are rife in Eastern Europe regarding Moscow's "hidden hand." To be sure, liberals throughout the bloc feared that if Gorbachev lost power, Moscow conservatives would move quickly to rebuild old networks. Soviet military units also maintained a low profile. In the GDR, Soviet forces were put on alert for the brief period in November when local militia and Interior Ministry offices were being overrun. And in Prague, Soviet diplomats told senior party officials that if the Czechoslovak army moved on the capital, it might be blocked. In neither the GDR nor Czechoslovakia, however, did Soviet troops leave their bases.

Moscow also has sought to gain influence through the selection of up-and-coming officers. The top military and intelligence elites in Eastern Europe typically have received part of their training in the USSR. The purpose of such training has been to inculcate pro-Soviet feelings among the officers, but also, as émigré interviews have revealed, to recruit officers as agents for the USSR. Officers who sign such "cooperation agreements" should not, according to one émigré, "be thought of as regular agents who cooperate with the Soviets on a daily basis. Rather, they form a network which the Soviets may tap when the need arises."[31] In addition to this covert link, there have been constant open exchanges at all levels between general staffs and at the field level between Soviet officers from the western military districts and corresponding East European units. The exception has always been Romania, whose officer corps has been entirely native-trained, having been purged by Ceauşescu in the late 1960s of those who had spent time in the USSR.

The political loyalty and morale of East European military establishments also have been assessed by the MPA of the Soviet army and navy. The MPA's function has been to assess, for example, the effects of political and economic reforms on the morale of Warsaw Pact armies. Although such reforms might nominally have been considered the internal affair of any East European state, the moment the MPA decided that the reform might affect the morale and reliability of the military, the reform ceased to be a purely internal affair. An MPA delegation would be sent to assess the extent to which the contagion had spread to the military. Joint communiqués issued on these occasions always made the inevitable references to the fact that while "subversion is at the forefront of imperialism's efforts to weaken the unity and cohesion of the Warsaw Pact, such attempts are doomed to failure, since the solidarity of the socialist armies in the face of these latest provocations has never been higher."[32] In this way, domestic reforms that otherwise would have been internal matters became the concern of the Soviet Union and the whole bloc. The ability of the MPA to exercise political influence within Warsaw Pact military forces depended, however, on the willingness of East European communist parties and military establishments to sign agreements providing such access. The virtual collapse of constitutional provisions giving communists the right to organize within most East European armed forces put an end to most of those agreements, thereby depriving the USSR of an important mechanism of control.

Because the East European forces traditionally were relatively well armed to fulfill their role against NATO, the Soviets could not count on assurances of loyalty alone. They had to create a structure that although viable against the West, would be ineffective without Soviet control. To do this, they had to make the East European armies subordinate to the Soviet-designed Warsaw Pact, and despite cosmetic changes introduced in 1969, that structure remained largely unchanged. All pact armies except Romania's were supplied solely with Soviet equipment. Unlike their West European counterparts in NATO, none of the East European members of the Warsaw Pact had a substantial or independent defense industry. Except for Polish shipbuilding, Czech and Hungarian small-arms manufacture, East German electronics and optics, and the limited production of Soviet tanks under license, Eastern Europe was totally dependent on Soviet weapons.

Of course, this meant that the Soviet Union alone bore the heavy economic burden of research, development, and production of all new weapons systems. The East Europeans had a defense budget that paid for their armed forces and equipment, but the burden of military spending on these economies was significantly less than on the USSR. Figures varied from state to state according to the method of calculation, but in general the East Europeans spent 6 percent of their gross national product (GNP) on defense, compared with 12–15 percent in the USSR. In an echo of NATO debates, Soviet efforts to encourage greater "burden sharing" were never particularly successful. Only the German Democratic Republic increased defense spending as a percentage of GNP by more than 1 percent in the period 1965–82, and figures for non-Soviet Warsaw Pact countries as a whole suggest a decline over this period from 6.1 percent of GNP on defense spending (using current dollars) in 1965 to 5.9 percent in 1982.[33] In addition, all East European armed forces cut their budgets for military procurement in the 1980s, with expenditures for defense procurement declining on average 2.7 percent during the 1981–6 period, even though GNP showed a modest gain of 1.5 percent throughout the bloc during the same period.[34] Apparently, the East Europeans, cognizant of the primacy of Soviet security objectives during this period, expected greater economic sacrifice from Moscow in return.

Turning to military doctrine, no military academy or defense establishment in Eastern Europe could debate or develop any military doctrine independent of the Soviet Union. Of course, debates over tactics took place within the context of the Warsaw Pact. With the exception of Romania, however, no sustained official dialogue occurred in any bloc country over the crucial issue of defense against invasion by any aggressor, east or west. Émigré Czechoslovak officers have testified that resistance to a Soviet-planned reorganization gave rise to calls for an independent military doctrine. At a meeting in 1965, Czechoslovak officers "stood up and told General K that the whole [reorganization] was all nonsense [because] the Czechoslovak army did not use its own doctrine." Participants challenged the "impossible tasks" implied in Czechoslovakia's military mission and went on to criticize, according to one source, the whole unequal relationship between Czechoslovakia and the Soviet Union in the Warsaw Pact.[35] This criticism flared up again in 1968, when the Gottwald Military Academy in Prague produced a draft document calling for total territorial defense. It was immediately suppressed by the Czechoslovak party leadership, who recognized that the Soviets would regard such a debate as additional grounds for intervention.

Furthermore, all the C[3] functions – command, control, and communications – of individual armies had been integrated within the Warsaw Pact structure, a structure that Western analysts believed would come under the direct control of the USSR Ministry of Defense in time of war. As noted earlier, it was most unlikely that East European Ministries of Defense could have mobilized their forces without Soviet knowledge, and as the Czechoslovak and Polish crises showed, the Soviets had the capability to jam indigenous military communications. In any case, since East European stocks of spare parts and reserve war matériel were kept deliberately low, local motivation to mobilize against the USSR would have been dulled by knowledge of indigenous limitations. The status-of-forces agreements governing the movements of Soviet forces in the various bloc countries allowed Soviet troops to be mobilized and deployed within bloc countries without the prior approval of host governments. In some cases, they were even allowed to enter urban centers without prior approval, thereby affording the Soviet military privileges and capabilities that the host armies themselves did not enjoy.

For these reasons and others, the military in all the East European countries (except Romania) proved to be a very reliable instrument of ultimate Soviet control. In Poland, it can be argued that the military showed itself to be more steadfast in the face of a threat to the regime than did the ruling Polish United Workers' Party, although the question of its ultimate loyalty in the face of a Soviet invasion remained moot. Equally, in Czechoslovakia, even in the face of invasion, resistance, and the internment of popular national leaders, the troops of the Czechoslovak army obeyed the orders of their commanders and remained in their barracks. Whether they could have done otherwise, or even wanted to do otherwise, was not the issue. Rather, the point is that the Soviet use of indigenous military establishments as levers of control survived most, although not all, of the difficult tests to which it was subjected. The leaders of the East European armies themselves would have been the first to recognize the limits of their independence, with General Jaruzelski in 1980 pointedly underlining for any Poles who thought otherwise that in all areas of Warsaw Pact collaboration, the Soviet Union played a "basic and priceless role."[36]

It was by no means clear in advance what role Mikhail Gorbachev intended for the Warsaw Pact and for military and security cooperation within the bloc as he moved to implement far-reaching reforms. Clearly, the emergence of a new military doctrine in the Soviet Union emphasizing defense as opposed to offense and sufficiency as opposed to continuous arms buildup had implications for the importance of Eastern Europe as a zone for forward and offensive Soviet operations in the event of war. As the redefinition of the role of Eastern Europe in protecting Soviet territory began, the way was open for extensive agreements on conventional arms reductions which would produce a pullback of Soviet forces and reduce their ability to serve as instruments of control in Eastern Europe. Gorbachev's announcement before the United Nations General Assembly in December 1988 that the USSR would cut 500,000 troops from its armed forces and withdraw units from Eastern Europe was followed a year later by further Soviet proposals to cut military expenditures and negotiate a total ban on all foreign bases by the year 2000. These proposals in Moscow fueled cuts in defense expenditures in Eastern Europe, as bloc leaders took the opportunity to free up scarce resources by making cuts averaging 10 percent in military budgets for 1989–90. Moreover, the changes which took place in the region in 1989 further decreased the likelihood that the Soviet military presence could survive the upheavals unscathed. Indeed, the first act of the new Czechoslovak foreign minister, Jiří Dienstbier, was to announce that the 1968 agreement allowing Soviet troops to be stationed in Czechoslovakia was "invalid" because it was made under pressure, and he called for talks with Moscow that could lead to their with-drawal. That action followed on the heels of calls in both Poland and Hungary for revisions in the formal arrangements governing those countries' membership in the Warsaw Pact, with Hungarian Socialist Party leader Resző Nyers stating that "sovereignty, the right of self-defense, and securing independence" would have to be emphasized more strongly "also in the Warsaw Pact."³⁷

The Soviet reaction was to convene more multilateral meetings of Warsaw Pact groups, such as the Political Consultative Committee, the Committee of Foreign Ministers, and the Committee of Defense Ministers. This appeared to be in line with proposals that Moscow began to float suggesting that the Warsaw Pact's functions should be expanded and revised to deemphasize its military function and upgrade its political coordination role.

Moscow was concerned that as communist parties in Eastern Europe lost their importance, so too would the interparty link decline as Moscow's key conduit for gathering information and building influence within the bloc. Consequently, calls began to be made for the establishment of a permanent headquarters for the Warsaw Pact which would "allow systemization of all the multiform and multilevel ties that already exist" but which used to go "through the network of communications between the ruling Communist parties." "Today," one influential piece observed, "the situation is rapidly changing. . . . Such developments cannot help but undercut the effectiveness and reliability of cooperation between [Warsaw Pact] members through a communication network based on the ruling Communist parties. The [Warsaw Pact] clearly needs much more politically neutral structures for the dialogue between its members."³⁸

With the decline in the interparty connection, therefore, Moscow hoped to replace it with increased reliance on a newly politicized Warsaw Pact structure to maintain stability and cohesion in the bloc. There appeared universal willingness amongst even the most radical East European leaders to attend more meetings of bloc foreign and defense ministers. Even the Political Consultative Committee meeting in Bucharest in July 1989 produced more declarations on a wider range of foreign and domestic policy issues than had previously been the case. However, initial elite and popular reactions within Eastern Europe to the formation of a permanent political headquarters were negative, indicating that Moscow would have great difficulties in gaining acceptance for any qualitatively new structures.

Economic Leverage: Kto Kovo?

In this discussion of levers of control, the one obvious mechanism that has not been considered is the network of multilateral and bilateral economic links that bind the bloc together. This lever is best considered separately because it has undergone the most systematic transformation in the postwar period and presents the best current and future prospects for reverse leverage by the East Europeans on Moscow. The Soviet Union may be the largest bloc economy in total output, but in terms of GNP per capita, most of the East European countries are at a higher level of economic development. Moreover, while East European populations maintain that affiliation with Moscow has held them back, the Soviets believe that East European progress often has been achieved only through massive Soviet assistance, provided to the detriment of the Soviet economy. It would be difficult to find many other historical examples of imperial "centers" that were more impoverished than their "colonies," and the question often had been raised in the West whether or not the Soviet Union would eventually seek to divest itself of the "burdens of empire." It is for this reason that the issue is raised *kto kovo* or, in other words, who is controlling whom in the complex web of economic interactions within the Soviet–East European relationship?

It should be said at the outset that the Soviets have never conceived of themselves as being imperialists in Eastern Europe. Looking through the prism of their own ideology, they have maintained that only capitalist states are motivated to structure their foreign policies in the service of empire building. According to Lenin's theory of imperialism, this is because the inner workings of capitalism inevitably lead businesses and banks to expand abroad under the protective shield which empires can best provide in the search for markets, raw materials, cheap labor, and investment opportunities. The Soviet view of imperialism may indeed offer an important insight into the motives behind the European scramble for territory in Asia and Africa in the second half of the nineteenth century. Its problem as a theory is that it simply does not provide a full explanation of the widespread historical phenomenon of territorial aggrandizement, of which Soviet behavior in the wake of World War II is but one example.

Some of the reasons for the extent of Soviet interest in Eastern Europe were presented in Chapter 2, but economic interests were not listed among them. This was not out of any deference to the Soviet argument, but because the desire to derive economic advantages from Eastern Europe has never figured as a major motivation for either the establishment or maintenance of Soviet control. This does not mean that the Soviet Union has not derived economic benefits from different countries of Eastern Europe at different times. Indeed, in the immediate postwar period, the dual system of reparations and tribute extracted by Moscow from vanquished and victorious alike amongst the East-bloc countries brought considerable advantages to the war-ravaged Soviet economy and held back East European recovery. Paul Marer has estimated that between 1945 and 1953, "the size of the uncompensated flow of resources from Eastern Europe to the Soviet Union was approximately equivalent to the flow of resources from the United States to Western Europe under the Marshall Plan – roughly on the order of $14 billion."[39] But this was a by-product, not a cause, of the Soviet advance.

A further argument that is often forwarded is that whatever their original intentions, once the Soviets gained control of Eastern Europe they structured the economies and the bilateral and multilateral trading relationships to their benefit. It is certainly true that, with few exceptions, the East European economies were essentially patterned on the Soviet model, with each country's external economic links being dominated by trade with Moscow. But while this may have been to the benefit of Soviet political and military control of the bloc, it was not always to the benefit of the Soviet economy.

Several Western studies have concluded that Moscow used what amounted to Soviet subsidies in order to achieve and maintain East European economic structures. One such study argued that "the Soviet Union has transferred resources equivalent to almost $80 billion in 1980 dollars during the decade 1971–1980."[40] Similar but slightly less dramatic conclusions were reached in a study conducted by the Rand Corporation for the U.S. Department of Defense. That study calculated that Soviet trade subsidies to East European CMEA members amounted to an annual average of $4.63 billion (rising from 0.39 billion in 1971 to 16.48 billion current U.S. dollars in 1980).[41] Moreover, the Soviets ran significant trade surpluses (amounting to implicit trade credits) with Eastern Europe during much of the same period. The Rand study concluded that the cost to the Soviet Union of maintaining its total position in Eastern Europe was roughly 2 percent of its GNP per annum. These figures applied only to the 1970s, for which the relevant studies were conducted, and represented a burden on the Soviet economy approximately five times greater than was borne by the U.S. economy for all of its overseas commitments during the same period.[42]

These conclusions have been criticized on several grounds, however. First of all, conclusions reached using 1970s data appear to have reflected an aberration, caused in part by the favorable prices East Europeans paid for Soviet oil. CMEA pricing mechanisms were changed in 1975 so that the price of oil would be altered annually (instead of every five years), according to a five-year rolling price average. This formula worked against the USSR as long as prices increased, even though it was more sensitive to the rapid and acute oil price increases than the previous method had been. However, in the mid-1980s, when prices collapsed, it was the East Europeans who complained that the system of five-year rolling averages worked against them. Subsidies have been automatic products of intra-CMEA price determinations, with opportunity costs benefiting both the Soviets and the East Europeans alternately according to the direction of price movements in international markets.

Leaving oil and other raw materials aside, calculating the possible subsidies on manufactured goods becomes even more difficult. Unlike raw materials, whose dollar values can be accurately fixed, manufactured goods produced in and primarily for the CMEA countries do not have values that can be so strictly computed. The studies assuming a high Soviet subsidy of Eastern Europe calculate the automatic superiority of Western goods, for example, and conclude that the Soviets therefore are subsidizing Eastern Europe by buying their poorer-quality products. But as Paul Marer and others have argued, "there must be many instances where the East European products are as, or even more, suitable to Soviet conditions than the most modern Western counterparts."[43]

Nevertheless, even Marer admits that the USSR provided a net cumulative subsidy to CMEA countries amounting to $14 billion during the 1971–8 period.[44] In other words, even according to more conservative estimates, during the 1970s the Soviets put back into Eastern Europe much of what they had taken out in the 1945–53 period. During the remainder of the 1950s and 1960s, as well as during the first half of the 1980s, the positive and negative aspects of trade fell much more evenly on the two sides, although the size of the Soviet economy and Soviet predominance in determining pricing mechanisms and other CMEA structures worked to the advantage of Moscow.

Apart from the question of subsidies, it is nevertheless true that heavy East European reliance on Soviet raw materials and energy has bred dependence. Moreover, because the Soviets could switch raw-materials exports to the West in exchange for hard-currency goods, while the East Europeans on the whole could not, the Soviets were in a stronger bargaining position vis-à-vis the East Europeans. The question thus arises: In what ways, if any, have the Soviets used their economic position to achieve changes in Eastern Europe? First of all, it would appear that benefits and subsidies in the trading relationship have been distributed to some extent according to political loyalty, with Romania emerging as the only CMEA country that did not receive a net subsidy from the Soviet Union during the 1970s.[45] Moreover, it has been argued that the Soviets paid higher than world prices for East European manufactured goods in the 1960s in order to foster specialization patterns, or a division of labor, within the CMEA that East European leaders had been reluctant to accept at the 1961 CMEA summit.[46]

Whatever views Western analysts may have, the issues of economic leverage, burdens, exploitation, and subsidies have been very troublesome in the Soviet–East European relationship. The East Europeans uniformly have felt held back and constrained by the tie with Moscow, and the Soviets have considered the East Europeans to be ungrateful. In every crisis, these issues have come quickly to the surface, along with charges and counter-charges about the use of Soviet economic leverage to obtain political compliance. Thus, the Czechoslovaks in 1968 charged Moscow with using nondelivery of a quarterly wheat shipment as a form of minatory diplomacy. Not only did the Soviets deny this, but at the time of the invasion they harshly rebuked the Czechoslovak leadership and press for suggesting that Soviet–Czechoslovak economic relations worked to Moscow's advantage:

> The press indirectly, and sometimes even directly, linked the exaggerated shortcomings in Czechoslovak economic development to Czechoslovakia's economic relations with the Soviet Union. The trade between the ČSR [Czechoslovak Socialist Republic] and the USSR was pictured in a disadvantageous light. . . .
>
> If Czechoslovakia had had to purchase all these commodities [raw materials and manufactured goods delivered in the 1956–68 period] for free currency, it would have been forced to spend about $3,500,000,000. . . .
>
> Needless to say, if the Soviet Union switched over to a purely commercial basis in its trade with Czecho-slovakia . . . this obviously would not benefit Czecho-slovakia's economy.[47]

During the 1980–1 Polish crisis, the Soviet Central Committee angrily demanded an end to the revival in Poland of "nationalistic, anti-Soviet sentiments." It charged:

> These slanderers and liars stop at nothing. They even claim that the Soviet Union "plunders" Poland. And this is being said notwithstanding the fact that the Soviet Union has given and continues to give enormous additional material to Poland at this difficult time. This is being said about a country which, by its

supply of oil, gas, ore, and cotton at prices from 33 to
50 percent lower than world prices, actually nourishes
the main branches of Polish industry.[48]

And the Soviet refusal to sell oil to Romania at concessionary
prices during the period of acute energy shortage in the early
1980s certainly did (and appears to have been intended to) bring
home to the Romanian population the consequences of
Ceauşescu's defiance of Moscow.

It is difficult to find clear evidence of any pattern, either of the
Soviets' punitively withholding subsidies or of their using emergency aid as a lever of control in times of crisis. What is clearer is
that the importance of such subsidies in the total package of
instruments used by the USSR to exert pressure on Eastern
Europe has been waning. Increasingly, Moscow has sought a
more stable basis for this type of cooperation and has not
favored the overt use of economic mechanisms as a means of
maintaining control in times of crisis.

It was perhaps out of a realization of the high cost to the
Soviet economy of maintaining "uneconomic" and highly rigid
centralized planning structures in Eastern Europe that the Soviets, in the mid-1960s, waived their previous objections to purely economic reforms in the bloc. Provided that such reforms
were aimed at improving the working of the socialist economy,
and not at dismantling it, Moscow on the whole welcomed such
changes.

The two types of reforms that were allowed included the
partial devolution of economic decisions to enterprises and the
introduction of a strictly regulated market mechanism.
Włodzimierz Brus, formerly a professor at Warsaw University,
and a participant in many bloc conferences on economic reform,
has written of his experience:

> . . . not much proof of Soviet attempts to block
> economic reforms in the strict sense can be seen,
> particularly in what I call the "second wave" of re-
> forms (from the early 1960s), when the initial fears of
> the inevitably "subversive" political implications of
> economic reform subsided, and the ideological reserva-
> tions against "market socialism" . . . lost some of their
> political urgency. Consequently, it seems that the (gen-

erally) unsuccessful reform attempts so far can scarcely be regarded as a result of Soviet pressure or the single case of relative success (Hungary) as a hard-won and exceptional concession.[49]

Rather than insisting on uniformity of domestic economic structures, the Soviets for some time tried to maintain the bloc's economic cohesion by fostering greater integration, or "drawing together" (*sblizhenie,* as it was called). At the 25th Soviet Party Congress in 1976, Brezhnev stirred up a political controversy by declaring that the "process of a gradual drawing together of socialist countries is now operating quite definitely as an objective law" and by following this statement with a denunciation of "national exclusiveness" on the part of unnamed socialist countries.[50] East European regimes recognized Moscow's primacy in formulating doctrine and were constantly fearful of the implications for their own maneuverability of the "discovery" of yet another "objective law" by Kremlin leaders. As a result, the following years saw greater East European intransigence in implementing any of Moscow's proposals for coordination of the planning process or for a summit of CMEA heads of state. Moscow was forced to eliminate any mention of "objective laws" in the report to the 1981 Congress, with Brezhnev virtually issuing an apology: "It was said at the past congress that a process of convergence of the socialist states was taking place. That process is continuing. But it does not obliterate the specific national features . . . of the socialist countries. We should see the variety of forms in their social life and economic organization for what it really is – a wealth of ways and methods of establishing the socialist way of life."[51]

As regards coordination in the drawing up of five-year plans, Brezhnev was slightly more bold: Although he refrained from any reference to the word "law," he did attempt to invoke the equally universal and worrisome word "life" when he said that "life is setting us the task of supplementing coordination of our plans with coordination of economic policy as a whole. Also being put on the order of the day are such issues as aligning the structures of economic mechanisms, further extending direct ties between ministries, amalgamations, and enterprises participating in cooperation, and establishing joint firms." On the basis of all these "major problems" that required solution, Brezhnev proposed in a rather more reluctant way that "perhaps it would be useful for the leaders of the fraternal countries to discuss them collectively in the near future."[52]

Brezhnev did not live to see such a meeting. It was only in June 1984 that the Soviet leaders succeeded in convening a summit of CMEA heads of state – the first such summit since 1971. A comparison of the speeches given by the East European delegates on the one hand and by the Soviets on the other indicated a major divergence of views on the issue of *sblizhenie*. The Soviets made frequent reference to it, calling particularly for plan coordination in the field of science and technology. They also proposed that all member-states' economies develop apace (the notion of leveling out, or *vyravnivanie*), indicating that Moscow had become interested in sharing with the East Europeans the burden of aid to Cuba, Vietnam, and Mongolia. These three countries were also full members of CMEA, but were aided disproportionately by the USSR. Afghanistan, Ethiopia, and other pro-Soviet regimes were not full members of the CMEA, although some had observer status, and therefore Moscow could not automatically expect "burden sharing" from its generally very reluctant East European allies.

The East European speeches at the summit were notable for the almost complete lack of reference to either of these two notions. Instead, they were replete with calls for greater cooperation on the basis of mutual interests. Showing the growth of East European influence in the past decades, the final statement contained a carefully constructed amalgam of the two views (where concessions to Eastern Europe are presented in brackets as [EE] and concessions to Moscow are presented as [SU]):

> The correctness and timeliness of the collectively
> worked-out course [EE – no more "life teaches" or
> "objective law"] aimed at the deepening of cooperation [EE] and the development of socialist economic
> integration [SU], which have become important factors in the all-around progress of each of the fraternal
> countries [EE – by putting individual progress above
> the progress of the whole bloc] and the drawing
> together of their levels of economic development [SU],

have been confirmed. The principles of socialist internationalism [SU], respect for state sovereignty, independence, and national interests [EE], complete
equality [EE], mutual advantage [EE], and comradely
mutual assistance [SU – the phrase has not been
favored by the East Europeans ever since it was used
to justify Soviet intervention in Czechoslovakia] . . .
have been firmly established.[53]

Of course, it would be wrong to suppose that on every issue
and on every occasion East European views were united against
the Soviet Union, either before 1985 or since Gorbachev came to
power. There are widespread and fundamental differences in economic interests among East European countries, which themselves have varying levels of development, product concentra-
tions, and economic structures. However, the massive
fluctuations in world oil prices which began in the 1970s and
continued into the 1980s clearly created tensions between the
Soviet Union and most of Eastern Europe.

Both sides have an interest in limiting the negative consequences of tension. The East Europeans have sought to diversify
the sources of their energy supply by increasing their trade with
Middle Eastern oil-producing countries, but their capability to
do so has been limited by their low hard-currency reserves,
which in any case they have preferred to use on higher-priority
purchases from the West.

The Soviets, for their part, have been openly displeased with
the quality of goods which the East Europeans have been sending them to pay off energy and raw-materials debts. The 1984
CMEA summit and several of Gorbachev's speeches since then
have referred to this situation specifically, not calling for any
revision in price structure but instead talking about an increase in
East European involvement in Soviet raw-materials and energy
production. A particularly forthright passage of the final document, an apparent concession to Soviet displeasure, bluntly
stated:

In order to create economic conditions ensuring . . .
deliveries from the Soviet Union . . . of raw materials
and energy, . . . the interested countries . . . will gradually and consistently develop their structure of pro-

Table 4.1. *Eastern Europe: gross hard-currency debt, 1971–88,*
selected years (*billion U.S. dollars*)

Country	1971	1975	1980	1981	1982	1984	1987	1988
Bulgaria	0.7	2.6	3.5	3.0	2.8	2.2	6.1	7.8
Czechoslovakia	0.5	1.1	4.9	4.5	4.0	3.6	5.9	6.7
East Germany	1.4	5.4	14.1	14.9	13.1	12.4	20.4	20.7
Hungary	1.1	3.1	9.1	8.7	7.7	8.8	17.7	19.3
Poland	1.1	8.0	25.0	25.5	24.8	26.8	39.2	39.2
Romania	1.2	2.9	9.4	10.2	9.8	7.1	4.9	1.9
Total	6.1	23.2	66.1	66.8	62.3	60.9	94.3	95.6

Source: CIA, Directorate of Intelligence, *Handbook of Economic Statistics*, 1987, 1988; *PlanEcon Report*, Vol. 5, No. 42–3, November 3, 1989, p. 53.

duction . . . with the aim of supplying the Soviet Union with products that it needs – in particular, foodstuffs, manufactured consumer goods, some types of building materials, and machinery and equipment that is of high quality and meets world technical standards.[54]

Throughout the 1970s, East European imports of hard-currency goods from the West vastly increased, without, however, commensurate growth in East European exports. An anomalous situation therefore emerged: In the wake of East European disappointment with the risks and adverse outcomes of a decade of trading with the West (gross hard-currency debt accrued during this period is presented in Table 4.1), they once again turned to the Soviet Union for increased trade. But with the changes in world market prices and alterations in the price mechanism, trading with Moscow was not as advantageous for the East Europeans as it once had been. Clearly, Moscow did not wish to be used as a dumping ground for inferior East European manufactures, particularly in exchange for raw materials which could earn hard currency.

Moreover, Gorbachev's efforts to restructure both the Soviet economy and the basis of Soviet–East European trade produced disruptions that the Soviets hoped would be short-term. Plans for establishing transnational joint enterprises foundered on lack of data, an antiquated pricing and currency system, and a fre-

Table 4.2. *Soviet Union: trade with Eastern
Europe, 1985–7 (million rubles)*

Category and country	1985	1986	1987
Exports	34,022	35,895	34,370
Bulgaria	6,456	6,752	6,276
Czechoslovakia	6,830	6,947	6,777
East Germany	7,670	7,884	7,636
Hungary	4,577	4,678	4,600
Poland	6,532	6,814	6,542
Romania	1,957	2,823	2,539
Imports	33,075	33,290	34,308
Bulgaria	6,056	6,191	6,552
Czechoslovakia	6,632	6,556	6,907
East Germany	7,592	7,128	7,093
Hungary	4,892	4,873	5,080
Poland	5,600	6,127	6,329
Romania	2,303	2,415	2,347
Balance	947	2,605	62
Bulgaria	400	561	−275
Czechoslovakia	198	391	−130
East Germany	78	752	543
Hungary	−315	−195	−480
Poland	931	686	213
Romania	−346	408	192

Source: USSR, *Foreign Trade*, quarterly indexes and annual reports.

quent absence of political will by both Soviet and East European
bureaucrats. The result was the open admission by the CMEA
secretary general that "we are somewhat worried about the delay
in making agreements for production, specialization, and cooperation."[55]

Such worry appeared justified when, despite Soviet insistence
both that the debt crisis of the early 1980s not be repeated and
that Eastern Europe assist the Soviet Union in modernizing its
industrial base, official statistics showed that Soviet imports
from the three most advanced East European economies – East
Germany, Czechoslovakia, and Hungary – actually decreased in
1986, as shown in Table 4.2. Imports from East Germany, the

Figure 4.1.   Rate of growth of Soviet trade with Eastern
Europe, 1971–89. Source: USSR, *Foreign Trade,* quarterly
indexes and annual reports.

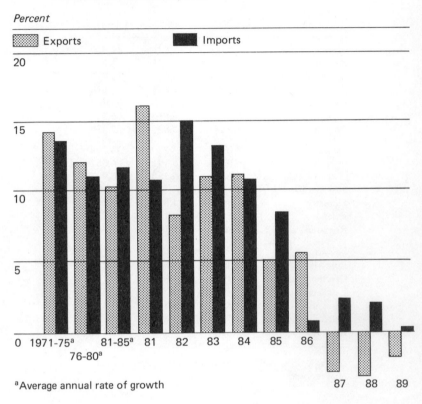

Percent

Exports   Imports

[a]Average annual rate of growth

bloc's technological leader, fell by over 6 percent, measured
against a decline in GDR total exports of only 3 percent.[56] Clearly, it was a major Soviet concern to arrest the decline in the
growth rate of its imports from Eastern Europe; as is shown in
Figure 4.1, the rate of increase in such imports steadily declined
after 1982. In response, Moscow tried to negotiate improved
trading agreements both with state agencies and with individual
enterprises in Eastern Europe. But when this did not greatly
improve the flow of imports, the Soviets moved to decrease their
trade surpluses with these countries. As a result, as shown in
Figure 4.1, in 1987, 1988 and 1989 the Soviets exported less to the

bloc than they had in the previous year. This effort to balance their trade with Eastern Europe in fact produced by 1989 a considerable Soviet trade deficit with all socialist countries totaling over 1.2 billion "transferable" rubles.[57] Such an imbalance, however, was offset by East European debt to the USSR. As of November 1989, Poland owed 5 billion rubles, followed by 622 million from Hungary, 433 million from Bulgaria, 394 million from Yugoslavia, 127 million from Albania, and 110 million from the GDR.[58] Unfortunately, the two countries that had the greatest trade surplus with the USSR also were least indebted – Czechoslovakia and Hungary. These irregularities are going to do little to decrease the debate between the USSR and Eastern Europe about who benefits most (or least) from their economic interaction.

However, the USSR remains the single greatest market for East European exports, as well as the single greatest source of East European imports, including strategic raw materials. Thus, while the USSR is dependent on East European trade in certain commodities not easily substituted for elsewhere, an asymmetry of dependence places the East European countries at a disadvantage vis-à-vis the Soviet Union. The greater efficiency of East European economies only partially compensates for Soviet advantages, including the sheer size of the economy and the historical development of bloc economic institutions that favor the Soviet Union. While these institutions have begun to atrophy in recent years, both sides are likely to continue high levels of trade with each other, at least until such time as their economies are strong enough to be fully reintegrated into the world economic system. Given the enormous problems all these economies face, this is likely to be some time away.

Notes

1 The former group is best exemplified in the writings of Robert C. Tucker, including his *Stalinism, Essays in Historical Interpretation* (New York: Norton, 1977). In that collection, Włodzimierz Brus and H. Gordon Skilling share Tucker's view of Stalinism as a peculiar form of Soviet communism. The opposite view is taken by Leszek Kołakowski and

Mihailo Marković in the same volume. Another major advocate of the latter view is Zbigniew Brzezinski, *The Soviet Bloc, Unity and Conflict* (Cambridge, Mass.: Harvard University Press, 1967).

2 Roy A. Medvedev, *Let History Judge: The Origins and Consequences of Stalinism* (New York: Knopf, 1972), p. 566.

3 Włodzimierz Brus, "Stalinism and the 'Peoples' Democracies'," in Tucker, *op. cit.*, p. 239.

4 Two books which chronicle and analyze Stalin's personal role in formulating policies toward Eastern Europe, as well as the factional disputes which also broke out within the Soviet elite, are William O. McCagg, Jr., *Stalin Embattled, 1943–48* (Detroit, Mich.: Wayne State University Press, 1978), and Gavriel D. Ra'anan, *International Policy Formation in the USSR* (Hamden, Conn.: Archon Books, 1983).

5 As quoted in Brzezinski, *op. cit.*, p. 65.

6 As interviewed by Teresa Toranska, *"Them": Stalin's Polish Puppets* (New York: Harper & Row, 1987), p. 49; details of the role of Soviet embassy staff in Yugoslavia and elsewhere in Eastern Europe are presented in Brzezinski, *op. cit.*, pp. 112–25, and in Vladimir Dedijer, *Tito* (New York: Simon & Schuster, 1953), pp. 329–32.

7 See Roy Medvedev's *Political Diary*, as reprinted in Stephen Cohen, ed., *An End to Silence* (New York: Norton, 1982).

8 See, for example, Christopher D. Jones, *Soviet Influence in Eastern Europe: Political Autonomy and the Warsaw Pact* (New York: Praeger, 1981).

9 A. A. Yepishev, *Partiya i Armiya* (Moscow: Voennizdat, 1980), p. 345 (emphasis in original).

10 Gorbachev speech to Great October Socialist Revolution meeting, Moscow Television Service, in Russian, November 2, 1987, Foreign Broadcast Information Service, *Soviet Daily Report (FBIS-SOV)*, November 3, 1987, pp. 59–60.

11 *Pravda*, March 19, 1988.

12 "CPSU Central Committee report delivered by Mikhail Sergeevich Gorbachev at the 19th All-Union CPSU Conference," Moscow Television Service, in Russian, June 28, 1988, *FBIS-SOV*, June 29, 1988, p. 12.

13 The statement was made by Korniyenko during a debate in Italy, as reported by ANSA, Rome, September 16, 1988, *FBIS-SOV*, September 19, 1988, p. 76. Shishlin also categorically denied that Soviet troops would be used in Eastern Europe if the Gorbachev leadership deemed socialism to be collapsing: Public Broadcasting System (PBS), *Global Rivals*, Part IV, October 11, 1988.

14 *Pravda*, October 27, 1989.

15 Gorbachev's speech at the December 9 CPSU Central Committee plenum appeared in *Pravda*, December 10, 1989.

16 *Pravda*, December 10, 1989.

17 "The Moscow Protocol," in Robin Remington, ed., *Winter in Prague, Documents on Czechoslovak Communism in Crisis* (Cambridge, Mass.: M.I.T. Press, 1969), p. 379. For more details, see Karen Dawisha, *The*

Kremlin and the Prague Spring (Berkeley: University of California Press, 1984), pp. 341–66.

18 Zdeněk Mlynář, *Night Frost in Prague: The End of Humane Socialism* (London: C. Hurst & Co., 1980), p. 298.

19 Quoted in Jones, *op. cit.*, p. 29.

20 *Ibid.*

21 *New York Times*, November 19, 1989.

22 *Pravda*, October 14, 1989; *Moscow News*, in English, October 15, 1989.

23 OBOP Center for Public Opinion Research, *Gazeta Wyborcza*, October 20, 1989, Foreign Broadcast Information Service, *East European Daily Report (FBIS-EEU)*, November 2, 1989, p. 74.

24 Moscow Television Service, in Russian, October 11, 1989, *FBIS-SOV*, October 12, 1989.

25 Yepishev, *op. cit.*, p. 346.

26 Budapest Television Service (BTS), in Hungarian, April 26, 1987, *FBIS-EEU*, April 27, 1987, p. F6.

27 *Pravda*, September 30, 1989.

28 Radio Szczecin and Gdańsk account of Gdańsk meeting of party activists, October 26, 1956, quoted by Brzezinski, *op. cit.*, p. 256.

29 Alexander Alexiev and A. Ross Johnson, *East European Military Reliability, an Émigré-based Assessment* (Santa Monica, Calif.: The Rand Corporation, 1986), R-3480, p. 55.

30 Zdeněk Mlynář, as interviewed by and quoted in Dawisha, *op. cit.*, p. 53.

31 Alexiev and Johnson, *op. cit.*, p. 58.

32 See Karen Dawisha, "Soviet Security and the Role of the Military: The 1968 Czechoslovak Crisis," *British Journal of Political Science*, Vol. 10, No. 3, 1980, pp. 341–63.

33 Figures derived from T. P. Alton et al., "East European Defense Expenditures, 1965–1982," in 99th Congress, Joint Economic Committee, *East European Economies: Slow Growth in the 1980s* (Washington, D.C.: U.S. Government Printing Office, 1985), Vol. 1, pp. 478–9, and Karen Dawisha and Philip Hanson, eds., *Soviet–East European Dilemmas: Coercion, Competition and Consent* (London: Heinemann, for the Royal Institute of International Relations, 1981), pp. 221–2.

34 Figures derived from John P. Hardt and Richard F. Kaufman, "Introduction," 101st Congress, Joint Economic Committee, *Pressures for Reform in the East European Economies* (Washington, D.C.: U.S. Government Printing Office, 1989), Vol. 1, p. xiii.

35 Alexiev and Johnson, *op. cit.*, p. 53.

36 Wojciech Jaruzelski, "25 lat w służbie pokoju i socjalizmu," *Wojsko Ludowe*, No. 5, 1980, p. 8.

37 Radio Budapest, October 15, 1989, quoted in Vladimir Kusin, "A Soviet Proposal to Make the Warsaw Pact into a New Cominform," Radio Free Europe, *Eastern Europe Background Report*, No. 196, October 20, 1989.

38 An article by two strategy experts at the USA Institute was widely circulated in both East and West, appearing in Soviet publications such as

New Times and also in the West (*Mediterranean Quarterly,* inaugural issue, Fall 1989).

39 Paul Marer, "Has Eastern Europe Become a Liability to the Soviet Union? (III) – The Economic Aspect," in Charles Gati, ed., *The International Politics of Eastern Europe* (New York: Praeger, 1976), p. 61.

40 As quoted by Paul Marer, "The Political Economy of Soviet Relations with Eastern Europe," in Sarah Meiklejohn Terry, ed., *Soviet Policy in Eastern Europe* (New Haven: Yale University Press, 1984), p. 174.

41 Charles Wolf, Jr., et al., *The Costs of the Soviet Empire* (Santa Monica, Calif.: The Rand Corporation, 1983), R-3073/1-NA, prepared for the Director of Net Assessment, Office of the Secretary of Defense, p. 28.

42 Figures supplied by Charles Wolf and extrapolated from *ibid.*

43 Paul Marer, "The Political Economy of Soviet Relations with Eastern Europe," in Terry, *op. cit.,* p. 177. Also see Raymond Dietz, "Advantages and Disadvantages in Soviet Trade with Eastern Europe: The Pricing Dimension," in 99th Congress, *op. cit.,* Vol. 2, 1986, pp. 263–302.

44 *Ibid.,* p. 179.

45 *Ibid.*

46 See Edward Hewett, *Foreign Trade Prices in the Council for Mutual Economic Assistance* (Cambridge University Press, 1974).

47 *Pravda,* August 22, 1968.

48 *Pravda,* June 12, 1981.

49 Włodzimierz Brus, "Economic Reforms as an Issue in Soviet–East European Relations," in Dawisha and Hanson, *op. cit.,* p. 85.

50 L. I. Brezhnev, *Report of the CPSU Central Committee and the Immediate Tasks of the Party in Home and Foreign Policy* (Moscow: Novosti Press Agency Publishing House, 1976), p. 9.

51 L. I. Brezhnev, *Report of the Central Committee of the CPSU to the XXVI Congress of the Communist Party of the Soviet Union and the Immediate Tasks of the Party in Home and Foreign Policy* (Moscow: Novosti Press Agency Publishing House, 1981), p. 17.

52 *Ibid.,* p. 13.

53 *Pravda,* June 16, 1984.

54 *Ibid.*

55 *Népszabadság,* May 1, 1987, *FBIS-SOV,* May 12, 1987, p. BB1.

56 Marek Misiak, "'The Seven' in 1986," *Życie Gospodarcze,* No. 14, April 5, 1987, pp. 12–13.

57 *PlanEcon Report* (Washington, D.C.), Vol. 6, Nos. 7–8, February 21, 1990, p. 29.

58 *Izvestiya,* March 2, 1990.

Part Two

Meeting the Challenge

5

Beyond Coercion: Can Eastern Europe Meet the Challenge?

Durability and Change

Whatever else one may conclude about the changes which swept Eastern Europe after Gorbachev came to power, it is necessary to underline the fact that in the preceding forty years these regimes had proved to be much more durable than many had predicted. Moreover, the area as a whole had receded as a source of major global crises. This is not to say that events in this region had ceased to be major causes of East–West tension; the Polish crisis in 1980–1 showed that that was not the case. Rather, it is to suggest that as East European leaders prepared to mark a half century of rule, they did so with the false confidence that their regimes had passed the test of durability and were more stable entering the second half-century of rule than they had been entering the first.

Not only had Soviet-style systems proved more durable than expected, but the tenure of East European communist party leaders also had been longer than might have been predicted, given the considerable internal and external challenges these leaders often faced. Thus, for the twenty-three general secretaries who served in Eastern Europe between 1945 and 1989 (excluding those in Albania and Yugoslavia), the average tenure was in excess of a decade. Similar patterns are found for other key positions, particularly in the post-Stalin period. (A complete listing of East European leaders appears in Appendix II.) From the point of view of durability, therefore, the East European regimes compared very favorably with other systems, democratic and nondemocratic alike.

It is, however, one thing to assert that a system is durable and that its leaders remain in office for long periods, but quite another to maintain that those systems were as a consequence either viable or legitimate. The sources of a regime's durability are in some cases the very causes of its illegitimacy, and the consequences of the longevity of a nation's leadership often detract from a government's viability.

First, as concerns regime durability, Soviet-style systems were established and maintained in Eastern Europe as a result of the use or threat of Soviet military power. Fully one-third of the East European general secretaries who ruled in the 1945–89 period came to power or left it as a direct consequence of Soviet military actions or threats. In the postwar period, this could be compared only with the frequency of U.S. direct and indirect intervention to achieve regime changes in the Caribbean and in Central and South America.[1] The Soviets, therefore, proved willing to sacrifice individual leaders' chances of establishing indigenous bases for legitimate support in order to ensure the durability of systems which served Moscow's interests.

Even where military force was not used, the rules of the succession game in Eastern Europe demanded advice and consent in Moscow. The failure to receive Moscow's imprimatur on key leadership changes often was a source of crisis in itself. For example, in 1956, the Poles' unilateral election of Władysław Gomułka as general secretary provoked the unannounced arrival in Warsaw of Khrushchev and almost the entire Soviet Politburo, who nonetheless failed to reverse the decision.[2] Several similar occurrences marred Soviet–Czechoslovak relations throughout 1968, when the Czechoslovaks tried unsuccessfully to wrest control of the succession process from Soviet interference.[3] And the Soviets appeared to have played a crucial role in the replacement of Stanisław Kania with Wojciech Jaruzelski as Poland's general secretary in October 1981.[4]

The difficulty for those East European leaders who came to power "at the barrel of a gun" was that, having essentially been imposed by Moscow at a time of turmoil, their ability to stabilize the internal situation by peaceful means was hampered greatly by the universal perception that they were "Moscow's men." Efforts to establish a genuine rapport with the population, which would have aided in legitimizing the regime, were made impossible in the short term by the fact that the population was systematically excluded from the succession process. Western-style multiparty elections, of course, were lacking throughout Eastern Europe until 1990, although party-controlled multicandidate elections for secondary positions became increasingly common in the mid-1980s. The essential source of instability was not only the one-party system but also the subversion of even this system by Soviet interference.

Only after considerable meritorious achievements on the part of the imposed East European leaders – including the establishment of some independence from Soviet direction – was there any chance that a nation's leaders could overcome the circumstances of their succession. János Kádár, whose first speech appealing for Hungarian support in 1956 was apparently taped on Soviet territory, was one such example of a leader who eventually succeeded in establishing his own indigenous base of support. However, Kádár squandered that support by staying on too long and refusing to allow a younger generation of leaders to succeed him. Gustáv Husák, who was designated as general secretary of the Communist Party of Czechoslovakia (CPCz) first by the Soviets and only subsequently by his own party, failed to make this transition despite Czechoslovakia's undoubted economic success, largely because he continued to be an unquestioning supporter of hard-line positions.

Conversely, leaders who managed to come to power in the face of Soviet opposition automatically accrued enormous reserves of support from their own population that they could either build upon or squander. Tito's ability to transform Yugoslavia from a war-torn and economically underdeveloped state into a semi-industrialized modern society with a major position in world politics was aided greatly by reserves of political capital stemming from his defiance of Soviet control.

Romania's Nicolae Ceaușescu, on the other hand, received an initial boost of popularity for defying the USSR, but failed to transform it into a viable strategy for economic and political development. He also surrounded himself with family members who possessed even fewer qualifications for rule, including his imperious wife, the self-styled "Comrade Academician Doctor Engineer Elena Ceaușescu."[5] By the end of the second decade of

Ceauşescu's rule, his regime was in shambles and economically was more dependent on the Soviet Union than it had been for years. The violent uprising which overthrew the regime in December 1989 illustrated the essential fact that durability without legitimacy cannot be sustained indefinitely. In the absence of external changes, the population had little hope of succeeding in any revolt; but when the glacial changes of the 1960s and 1970s turned into the flood of the 1980s, even a regime as immune to outside influence as Ceauşescu's succumbed.

The Case of Poland. Even if Soviet interference proved to be a major source of instability within these regimes, the solution for local leaders, as the Poles learned, did not necessarily rest in distancing themselves from Moscow. First of all, many if not most East European leaders regarded Soviet interest in key decisions such as succession not as "unwarranted interference in domestic affairs" but as "comradely interest in the affairs of a member of the Warsaw Treaty Organization." Both phrases were used by the Soviets in denying the former and asserting the latter when putting pressure on General Secretary Kania and other Polish United Workers' Party (PUWP) leaders to protest the fact that, among other things, "alien elements, who openly advocate opportunist views, take up posts of leaders [while] experienced functionaries dedicated to the cause of the Party and having an unblemished reputation and moral qualities are being dismissed."[6] While Kania was trying to resist Soviet pressure, two other groups were not – domestic hard-liners and leaders in neighboring Czechoslovakia and East Germany concerned about the spillover effects of Solidarity.

In Poland, the first group was represented in mid-1981 by, among others, Polish United Workers' Party Secretaries Tadeusz Grabski and Stefan Olszowski. Both had been denounced in Poland as "men who present themselves to our neighbors as being the only force capable of guaranteeing the durability of our alliances and of the state system."[7] Furthermore, according to Polish sources, the fact that neither had been ousted from the PUWP Central Committee during its March 29–30 plenum was a direct result of a telephone call from Brezhnev to Kania during a recess in the proceedings.[8]

When indigenous leaders sought to distance themselves from Moscow, as occurred to some extent during the Polish crisis, such efforts always raised fears among Soviet leaders. They, in turn, escalated tensions by unleashing a campaign which featured charges of "anti-Sovietism," "antisocialism," "nationalist revivals," "revisionism," "remnants of the bourgeois past," "opportunism," and so forth. Examples from the Soviet press campaign during the Polish crisis illustrate this point:

> Antisocialist, counterrevolutionary elements have held an anti-Soviet orgy at a Warsaw cemetery.[9]

> We would like to make special mention of the fact that in recent months counterrevolutionary forces have been aimed at cancelling out the results of the work done by our Parties, at reviving nationalistic, anti-Soviet sentiments among various sections of Polish society.[10]

> The socialist foundations of Polish society are being eroded under the flag of the so-called "renewal."[11]

> The representatives of the fraternal Parties re-affirmed their solidarity with the Communists and all patriots of socialist Poland in their struggle against the antipopular forces of counterrevolution and anarchy.[12]

Thus, we have the paradoxical situation in which the Soviet Union was at the same time the major source of both elite durability and societal instability in these regimes. In Poland, as elsewhere in the bloc, Soviet-style systems would not have been maintained without Soviet presence and pressure. But at the same time, it was precisely this unequal relationship which prevented those systems from making the transition from being an exogenous species to being an indigenous species. Soviet and East European leaders could ensure that the species endured, but only the East European people could guarantee that it would take root and evolve.

Once Soviet leaders realized that even the strongest system of power would eventually collapse without an internal foundation, the way was open for the changes which took place in 1989. The speed with which regimes crumbled surprised many, but if seen against the backdrop of the complete failure of local communist parties to build bases of support independent of Moscow, then it is not so surprising. Throughout Eastern Europe, a new generation of communist party leaders struggled to reshape their parties, giving them new names and new images in a desperate bid to save them from eradication in multiparty elections (the new names, leaders, and membership figures are presented in Appendix III). But the legacy they inherited remained: Although individual leaders who in the past had been communists might enjoy popular support, the system of power put in place by Moscow could not survive a democratic revolution. Whether or not democracy, so long desired and yet so fragile, would establish itself quickly enough to prevent the reemergence in the region of nationalist and authoritarian movements remained to be seen.

Viability and Transformation

The foregoing discussion serves to highlight the tension between durability and viability, as well as the problems East European regimes faced in establishing and maintaining a legitimate base of support in light of overwhelming internal divisions and often overriding Soviet ideological and security concerns. As was stated at the beginning of the preceding section, there is no necessary link between durability and viability, or between the longevity of the leadership and the legitimacy of the regime.

Indeed, the debate in the Soviet Union spurred by Gorbachev's succession showed that longevity often can be an invitation to corruption, inertia, backsliding, and all the other sins said to have been visited upon the Soviet system by the stagnation of the Brezhnev years – sins that the Soviets themselves admitted were exported in varying degrees to Eastern Europe. The viability of regimes in Eastern Europe, therefore, was adversely affected both by direct Soviet interference and by Soviet insistence on adherence to a model of socialism that, as Gorbachev conceded, was in danger of failing to "place the immense reserves and opportunities of socialism at the service of the working people."[13]

Many challenges faced these regimes in overcoming systemic

and external constraints, however. There were several reasons why East European regimes largely failed in their attempts to move from durability to viability. One was that the specific circumstances surrounding the creation and maintenance of these regimes prevented them from developing homeostatic mechanisms for adjusting to change. Centrally planned economies, irrespective of their advantages in terms of creating a stable domestic marketplace, cannot plan for disruption in external trading relations, and systematically they respond poorly to sharp reversals. This was proved during the late 1970s and early 1980s, when the East European regimes almost all suffered economic crises brought about both by very unfavorable external economic conditions (oil price rises, economic sanctions, further restrictions on high-technology trade, etc.) and by internal economic failures (the most notable being the slow movement towards the introduction of more efficient, intensive forms of development).

The same was true in the political realm, where leaders resisted the introduction of mechanisms that would ensure a continuous, incremental, and nondisruptive generational turnover at the elite level. All top-level positions in the party and government apparatus carried with them a contradictory promise: As long as things were going smoothly, tenure was safeguarded, but if anything went wrong, no sinecure was safe.

The possibility that leadership stability might produce wider political stagnation and lay the groundwork for a reactive crisis was therefore enormous in all the Soviet-style systems. The recognition of this fact throughout the bloc produced a gradual move to limit tenure for top party officials (generally to two terms of five years each) and introduce elections to achieve turnover in government and legislative bodies. Multicandidate parliamentary elections within the framework of existing communist party states in Hungary and Poland in 1988 and 1989 were accompanied by a Soviet-initiated move to introduce mandatory retirement ages and limit the length of time any one person could serve in a top party or government position. By routinizing procedures for periodic replacement of elites and admission of new generations, such measures were aimed at reducing the fragile rigidity of the existing system without its complete overhaul. The moves toward multiparty elections in Eastern Europe, however, signaled that more radical measures would be adopted to solve this problem.

Another important reason why regimes often proved to be brittle was that they paid insufficient attention to addressing and absorbing lessons from previous crises. By blaming all crises on "imperialist subversion," regimes sought to avoid any debate which would reflect negatively on the fundamental causes of instability. In this way, successive East German regimes suppressed any debate on the 1953 uprising. And in Hungary, soon after coming to power, Kádár arrested a group of intellectuals who, under the pseudonym "Hungaricus," had published a pamphlet on the lessons of the 1956 uprising.[14]

The Case of Czechoslovakia. The Czechoslovaks published a document at their 14th Party Congress in 1971 designed to draw appropriate lessons from the "crisis development" in their party, but the document also was designed to end debate rather than spur it.[15] In particular, although it recognized that the political and economic stagnation of the Novotný era (1953–68) was partially responsible for producing the pent-up frustrations that exploded in 1968, the document made no attempt to deal with the substantial changes that had either occurred or been proposed in the course of the Prague Spring. The lid was simply put on the debate, and all those who had participated in any way in the 1968 events were purged from their positions. Nearly half of the membership of the CPCz was purged (under the supervision of Miloš Jakeš, who headed the Central Control and Auditing Commission), along with similar proportions in the armed forces, government ministries, news media, and academic circles. Most were reassigned to menial jobs in the service sector.

Czechoslovak party leader Gustáv Husák failed to open the way for any kind of national reconciliation, as had occurred in Hungary when Kádár had declared that "despotism is not a socialist phenomenon," and "he who is not against us is with us."[16] Husák's failure alienated an enormous pool of skilled and talented workers who could have been put at the country's service, had the "normalization" strategy evolved differently. The situation in Czechoslovakia had been so poorly managed by

Husák that in a statement issued on the seventeenth anniversary of the 1968 Soviet invasion, the dissident group known as Charter 77, established to monitor Czechoslovakia's compliance with the Helsinki accords, reserved the harshest criticism not for the Soviets but rather for Czechoslovak leaders. Indeed, hope and inspiration were derived from Gorbachev's recent accession:

We cannot . . . fail to note the interest with which people follow new developments in the Soviet Union, how they listen to and read the speeches of Mikhail Gorbachev and compare his formulae with the deadly motionlessness in Czechoslovakia. The most experienced [among us] note that Soviet speeches are censored in our press. . . .

Without giving in to hasty illusions, we wish to express a certain measure of hope that the current social motion in the Soviet Union might evolve into a wider impulse. . . .[17]

Until early November 1989, CPCz officials were holding resolutely to the line that "there is nothing we have to change in our assessment of the 1968 crisis."[18] But when Hungary and Poland officially apologized for their part in the invasion of Czechoslovakia, thereby increasing popular sentiment for a reevaluation, the pressure was on both Czechoslovak and Soviet officials to fall in line. The chief ideologist of the CPCz was summoned to Moscow in mid-November for talks with his Soviet counterpart, Vadim Medvedev. Only after his return was it revealed that the two had discussed the "histories of Czechoslovakia and the USSR, including 1968." It was agreed that "without a thorough analysis of the past, it is not possible to set clear intentions and objectives for the future."[19]

This news spurred on students who had been beaten brutally at a rally on November 17. Two days later, Civic Forum was founded and immediately began organizing pro-democracy demonstrations. On November 24, those leaders, headed by Miloš Jakeš, who had been responsible for purging the party and imposing harsh "normalization" measures on the population in the wake of the 1968 invasion were forced to resign. That same night, Alexander Dubček, who had lived under virtual house arrest for twenty years since losing his position as the general secretary of the party during the fateful months of the Prague Spring, returned to Prague and addressed an ecstatic crowd of a quarter of a million citizens. Less than two weeks later, the new general secretary and prime minister, Karel Urbánek and Ladislav Adamec, flew to Moscow for a Warsaw Pact meeting which officially apologized for the 1968 invasion, calling it "an intervention in the internal affairs" of Czechoslovakia and a violation of "the norms of relations between sovereign governments."[20]

In the twenty years since the invasion, much effort had been spent finding scapegoats for the events which took place, but in the meantime the failure to deal with the real causes and consequences of the suppression of the reform movement made it impossible for a truly viable leadership to emerge. As a result, the CPCz itself, a party which had received the largest number of votes of any party in free postwar elections, was almost irreparably damaged, making it practically impossible to foresee the circumstances under which it could govern with popular consent.

The Case of Hungary. In Hungary, it took the regime thirty years to acknowledge the need for an open debate on the causes and consequences of the 1956 Hungarian uprising. As János Berecz, a secretary of the ruling Hungarian Socialist Workers' Party (HSWP) Central Committee, stated, "we will probably be dealing more and more with the lessons of 1956 during the next few years. We have spoken little about these lessons in recent years because we wanted to clear away the waste, we wanted to heal the wounds, we wanted to eliminate from people's lives the suspicion, the mistrust, the constant feeling of political danger."[21]

Berecz's views appeared to acknowledge the force of arguments circulating among Hungarian intellectuals decrying the "hopelessness," "cynicism," "helplessness," and "nihilism" of a nation prevented from "living its own history" by the "forced compromise" imposed after 1956.[22] Hungarian officials like Berecz may have come to recognize the need for debate, but they certainly did not concede that the stability achieved since 1956 had necessitated, in the words of Sándor Fekete, a "dismal acceptance of reality." This view was shared by some of the most radical intellectuals imprisoned after 1956, including Fekete, who issued a cynical challenge of these intellectuals' position:

If there is no difference between a dismal acceptance
of reality and a struggle to the death, . . . we Hungarians and especially we intellectuals should not hesitate, we should die for liberty!

Don't hesitate! . . . As long as we are rotting here in
the distant Eastern reaches of the world, let us behave
in an Eastern way; let us make a Lebanon out of
Hungary, . . . let the boredom of Politburo meetings
be shattered by the sound of guns as in Aden, let us
kill each other, as in Afghanistan or Cambodia; long
live death, Hungarians have a great time in the grave,
let's go on to the new ruins and the new gallows!
Don't worry, the catastrophe won't be total in any
case, because the smart and clever people will once
again escape to safety in time.[23]

Fekete rejected both "servile acceptance of reality" and "deathly
adventurism" in favor of a third way – the path of reform, a path
that had been implemented in Hungary "at a time when in other
quarters [the USSR] even stagnation was not called by its true
name."[24]

Despite the heated debates over reform or revolution which
characterized the political scene in Hungary in the mid-1980s, a
real reassessment of the 1956 uprising had to await the political
passing of those installed in its wake. The ouster of János Kádár
as HSWP general secretary in the summer of 1988 and his removal as president almost a year later allowed reexamination of
these events. In May 1989 it was announced that the remains of
Imre Nagy, the prime minister who had headed the reform
movement in 1956 and who had been executed under Kádár's
direction in 1958, would be moved from an unmarked grave to an
official resting place. The communiqué stated that he had fought
for the country's "salvation" in October 1956, blaming his failure
on a lack of support from the party and coalition partners in the
government. It also said that he "erred in his judgment of the
international conditions and of the consequences of his foreign
policy," while refusing to compromise. The HSWP's desire to
associate itself with a reformist course was seen in its acceptance
of the "legacy" of reforms proposed in 1953–4 during Nagy's
first term as prime minister.[25]

The pressure for political reassessment also was seen in the Hungarian decision to drop the term "people's" from the country's official name, proclaiming itself simply the Republic of Hungary on the thirty-third anniversary of the 1956 uprising. The new state, it was said, would be one in which the values of "bourgeois democracy and democratic socialism" would apply equally. At the same time, the 1956 events were characterized officially as a "popular uprising and national independence action."[26] This, together with the renaming of the HSWP to the Hungarian Socialist Party (HSP), and the abandonment of Marxist-Leninist ideology and organizational principles in favor of a "Europeanized, Western-style socialist party," indicated the seriousness of efforts to distance the party from its Stalinist past.[27]

Individual leaders, too, recognized the need to disavow past affiliations to ensure their political survival. Thus, when HSP Presidium member Imre Pozsgay was asked if he was still a communist, his response was unequivocal: "I am a Hungarian, a socialist, and I like social democracy."[28]

Faced with an uphill struggle to gain votes in the first free parliamentary elections, virtually all parties and politicians scrambled to protest their abhorrence of past Soviet and HSWP practices. In the face of anti-Hungarian policies pursued in neighboring Romania before Ceauşescu's demise, leaders also scrambled to capitalize on the wave of nationalist sentiment which swept the country, with the acting president of the new republic, a former ambassador to the Soviet Union, Mátyás Szürös, claiming that "the new Republic feels responsibility for the fate of the Magyars [Hungarians] who live outside" its borders.[29]

This emphasis on national independence also was reflected in relations with the Soviet Union. In January 1990, Hungary officially announced its request for the complete withdrawal of Soviet troops. At a press conference in Vienna called during East–West talks on reducing conventional armed forces in Europe, the Hungarian state secretary for foreign affairs announced that "there are no reasons, be it of a political, military, security or arms control character, that would justify the stationing of foreign troops on the territory of Hungary. Accordingly," he continued, "the Hungarian government, fully supported by the Parliament and the public, persistently strives for the complete withdrawal this year – or by 1991 at the latest – of Soviet troops stationed in our country."[30] In Hungary, as elsewhere in the bloc, it had become clear that association with Moscow was a handicap in the transformation of these regimes from mere durability to real viability.

Legitimacy and Consensus

Unlike the concepts of durability and viability, legitimacy implies the presence of a consensual relationship between the governed and the governors. It is not necessarily dependent upon free elections to leadership positions – the mechanism used in the West to endow elites with legitimacy – but it does imply that consent is freely given and that the state sees its obligation primarily as acting in the best interests of its own citizens.

In Eastern Europe, as in the Soviet Union, the state, acting in accordance with Marxist-Leninist doctrine, shifted the balance between individual and collective interests in favor of the latter. This in itself is no basis for denying the legitimacy of East European regimes, provided that such a balance was freely adopted and supported by the vast majority of the population. In those countries of the Soviet bloc with their own indigenous revolutions, such as the USSR, Yugoslavia, and Albania, the adoption of laws and practices that emphasized the primacy of collective over individual rights was no bar to legitimation, although the violation of these laws to further, and arbitrarily, limit individual freedoms did, of course, lead to the erosion of regime legitimacy.

The other regimes in Eastern Europe were in a more difficult situation, since not even the Soviets would argue that the establishment of communist rule was a wholly or even primarily indigenous affair. As a result, these regimes were faced with a dilemma: They could flout the requirement for legitimacy as some kind of Western bourgeois notion that had no basis in the higher consideration of "socialist legality," or they could attempt to overcome the circumstances of their regimes' origins and seek gradually to win acceptance from the population through meritorious behavior.

This dilemma had sparked continuous debate in Eastern Europe since the inception of communist rule, including an interesting debate in the mid-1980s that reflected the growing recognition both of individual rights and of the inadequacy of existing mechanisms for regime legitimation. The debate, which was most prominent in Poland and Hungary, accepted the contention that legitimacy is "rightly considered a condition of lasting and stable power."[31] Quoting Talleyrand, Josef Bayer, a senior member of the HSWP's Social Science Institute, wrote that "with bayonets much can be done, only it is impossible to sit on them."[32] Bayer insisted that for socialist countries to be called legitimate, they first had to establish a political order worthy of popular support and then had to develop political structures and mechanisms that would permit and encourage the "autonomous, spontaneous, and organic reproduction of legitimacy from below."

East European debate on this issue most often focused on the "legitimacy reserves" of the socialist system. These reserves were said to include the intrinsic fairness of the ideals embodied in socialism and the widespread acceptance of these ideals by the populations living in the Soviet bloc. There was, moreover, constant reference to the "reform capacity of society."[33] This notion – that the "enormous reserves of socialism" (a favorite term of Gorbachev's) could be mobilized for the improvement of society's capacity to fulfill these socialist ideals – represented both an admission that "developed socialism" still was in need of considerable development and a conviction that reform, as Kádár often said, was socialism's "natural state." In this view, it was stasis and stagnation that were the aberrant forms. Speaking at the 13th Congress of the HSWP in March 1985, Kádár reiterated this theme, saying that the reform process in Hungary, at least, had become irreversible and intrinsic to the natural process of renewal in socialism. Reassuring those who feared the collapse of reform after his own passing, he told the delegates that while stagnation was the result of "subjective errors" in leadership, reform and dynamism were intrinsic to socialism: "There are no magicians and wizards here."[34]

Whether or not socialism's inherent "legitimacy reserves" were going to be accepted by the populations in Eastern Europe depended on the success of the strategies pursued by the regimes for transforming socialism's potential into a real basis for governance. Clearly, measures that improved the economic welfare of a country's citizens could not but contribute to the regime's quest for legitimacy. The steady growth of GNPs in almost all East European countries up to 1970 (with the notable exception of Czechoslovakia in the period before the Prague Spring) and the more rapid expansion in consumer welfare that occurred in the early and middle 1970s put several East European countries among the world's most developed states, using any number of economic and social indicators. This growth allowed the regimes to contend that socialism had proved its ability to allocate resources efficiently and to harness the human and material reserves of the country in the service of the people.

In order for economic progress to succeed as a strategy for legitimizing these regimes, however, the results of that growth must be perceived by the populations as being distributed among all citizens on the basis of the socialist principle "to each according to his work." After all, these were not capitalist countries in which the principle of "equal opportunity" was used to justify both unearned income and unequal distribution of wealth. In socialist countries, the legitimacy of the regimes depended upon more strict adherence to egalitarian principles. Therefore, while economic growth was important for system maintenance, it was not in itself a sufficient condition for legitimacy. This was shown in Poland, where despite the impressive growth rate achieved throughout the 1970s, the excesses and corruption associated with the period when Edward Gierek was general secretary of the ruling Polish United Workers' Party (1970–80) greatly contributed to the 1980–1 crisis. Economic growth may have delayed its onset, but as all the Soviet-bloc leaders came to appreciate, growth alone did not prevent societal crisis in Poland, nor would it in their own countries. And, of course, if the economies ceased to grow altogether, as happened throughout Eastern Europe in the 1980s, then all chances of building legitimacy on the basis of economic performance were dashed.

Another difficult challenge faced by East European communist leaders lay in addressing the politically explosive issue of the extent to which they were heirs to and guardians of their nations' pre-communist heritages. As discussed in previous chapters, the official ideology of these states and the unofficial constraints imposed by their alliance with Moscow denied these regimes the most potent mechanism for legitimation of state authority. The protection of a nation's heritage and the promotion of its well-being are the most common sources of any state's legitimacy. East European regimes, however, were constrained from building on nationalism as a source of legitimacy by the Marxist view of nationalism as a retrograde force used only by bourgeois states to oppress the proletariat. Its continued existence in Eastern Europe was, therefore, officially condemned as a "remnant of the bourgeois past" that officials hoped would die out as socialism progressed.

Those East European communist leaders who were loyal to Moscow were also constrained from using nationalism as a source of legitimation because it often manifested itself in Russophobia. Throughout the bloc, major efforts had been made over the past forty-five years to socialize the population to accept, if not embrace, the Soviet Union as the preeminent ally. However, given the speed with which anti-Sovietism and Russophobia reemerged once freedom of expression was allowed, one wonders how much traditional attitudes had changed since the time when Czesław Miłosz, the Polish writer who defected in the early 1950s after a short period as a communist official, penned the following bitter and cynical remarks:

> Official safety valves are probably insufficient channels for feelings of national pride if most Estonians, Lithuanians, Latvians, Poles, Czechs, Hungarians, or Romanians would willingly cut the throat of any available Russian were they not restrained by fear. Even Party cadres, one suspects, would not renounce such a pleasant prospect. One can only complain of the backwardness of these nations and hope that socialist upbringing will enlighten them. But it would be a mistake to deny . . . that such hatred exists even in nations which have undergone a longer period of careful education.[35]

After coming to power, Gorbachev attempted to address and

correct some of these long-standing tensions. He often spoke openly about them when traveling in Eastern Europe. For example, during a 1986 visit to Poland he admitted that "wars, violence, and seizures of territory" in the history of Russian–Polish relations had "poisoned the minds of the peoples and aroused mutual hostility in them."[36]

To a certain extent, Gorbachev succeeded. The 1989 events which toppled existing regimes were characterized neither by acts of violence against Soviet installations or property (as in all previous East European uprisings in 1953, 1956, and 1968, and at various times in Poland) nor by widespread expressions of hostility towards the USSR. Anti-Sovietism was limited because of Gorbachev's personal popularity and the recognition that it was precisely because of Soviet *perestroika* that changes were sweeping Eastern Europe. Throughout the region there was enormous interest in the Soviet Union, which for the first time was seen as a factor for increasing domestic democratization and decreasing international tensions, rather than vice versa.

Nevertheless, there remained a generalized feeling that Russians as a people would resist Westernization, that dedicated Soviet Marxist-Leninists might yet force a halt to Gorbachev's "deideologization" campaign, and that the Soviet military-security apparatus could still move to prevent the complete disintegration of its empire, internal and external. Seeing the harsh reaction, even by Gorbachev, to secessionist sentiments in the Baltic states, and fearing that escalation of ethnic strife on the Soviet Union's perimeter might imperil *perestroika* and even endanger Gorbachev's tenure, the generation of East European leaders who came to power in 1989 moved swiftly to institutionalize their gains and rid their countries of Soviet influence while they could. Calls appeared in Czechoslovakia, Poland, and Hungary for total withdrawal of Soviet forces. Czechoslovak authorities openly admitted they feared that if Gorbachev were substantially weakened or overthrown by a coup d'état in Moscow led by hard-liners, "supporters of the old regime" in Prague, who were said still to be prevalent in the bureaucracy and army and who were accused of "trying to build a conspiracy network for the future," could stage a comeback by relying on the support of local Soviet forces.[37] It was precisely such concerns throughout the bloc which fueled the continuation of deep anti-Sovietism and strengthened the conviction of noncommunist leaders that the legitimacy of their new systems would depend upon wresting immediate and major concessions from Moscow, even if it weakened Gorbachev in the process.

The Case of the GDR. As the East European state with the best record of economic performance and the worst of virulent nationalism, the GDR is a case that deserves closer scrutiny. Because the GDR was carved out of the truncated eastern provinces of Hitler's Reich, the East German authorities initially were not able to draw on the German roots of the state in their own quest for legitimacy. The oppressive measures imposed before and after the 1953 uprising (when widespread protests against such measures led to a Soviet-declared state of siege throughout East Germany that resulted in over 25,000 arrests and scores of executions) did little to assure the population that the authorities were seeking to enhance the legitimacy of the regime by popular support. Until the establishment of inter-German relations in the 1970s, the GDR was also denied de jure recognition in the West, thereby removing another source of legitimacy. In the absence of both domestic and external sources of support, the GDR under Walter Ulbricht made staunch support for hard-line Soviet positions the raison d'être for his regime. But in May 1971, Ulbricht was swept aside in the first of the changes brought about by *Ostpolitik* and détente.

In the years after taking power, Erich Honecker pursued a delicate and balanced policy designed to demonstrate his country's loyalty to Moscow while systematically and incrementally increasing its cultural and economic ties with West Germany. Without massive West German subsidies of the East German economy in the form of credits, visa and toll payments, construction assistance, private transfers, trade, and other forms of assistance, the GDR's position as the second largest bloc economy and the eighth largest world economy would have been seriously eroded. Western estimates of East Germany's average annual intake in the 1980–5 period refer to a figure of $1 billion, excluding tariff-free access to the Common Market. Less tangibly, but no less important from the standpoint of regime legitimacy, was the development of person-to-person contacts between East and West Germans and the easing of emigration restrictions for pensioners and divided families — a remarkable *volte-face* for a country in which the Berlin Wall had been built less than two decades previously. In 1987, 12 percent of the East German working-age population received short-term visas to go to the FRG, compared with 0.6 percent in 1985. This was an increase from 66,000 to 1.2 million visits. In return, the West German government guaranteed further billion-deutsche-mark bank loans to the GDR and agreed to increase its lump-sum payments for transit and road taxes between the FRG and West Berlin to the annual figure of 915 million deutsche marks.[38] Without such extensive subsidization of the GDR economy, the economic slide which began to be visible after 1987 would have produced austerity conditions much more quickly.

By the end of the 1970s, a number of events conspired to erode Honecker's efforts to construct a legitimate basis for rule. Foremost was the decline of détente, both in Europe and between Moscow and Washington. The Soviet deployment of SS-20 medium-range ballistic missiles and the subsequent "two-track" NATO decision to counterdeploy the Pershing II and cruise missiles unless arms-control talks succeeded had the effect of reluctantly pitting the two German states against each other.

Détente had been of vital importance to Honecker in bolstering the legitimacy of the East German regime. When the Soviets announced in 1983 that a further round of Soviet missiles would be deployed — this time on East German and Czechoslovak soil — if NATO deployment of intermediate-range nuclear missiles proceeded, Honecker appealed to the Kohl government "in the name of the German people" not to allow a "palisade of missiles" to be erected between the two Germanys.[39] One can judge the East German reaction to the breakdown of talks in Geneva by Honecker's statement in November 1983 that while the leadership will do "what has to be done," nevertheless, "these measures . . . did not evoke jubilation in our country."[40]

In a move designed to limit the damage of missile deployment, Honecker announced his plans to be the first East German leader to visit West Germany. The goal of the visit was to signal mutual German determination to construct an island of détente in Central Europe, a "coalition of reason" in an implied sea of irrationality. Honecker's concerns were shared by the Hungarians, and less openly by the Bulgarians.

However, in September 1984 it was announced that Honecker's trip had been "postponed." Clearly, he had miscalculated the limits of tolerance in Moscow. Two months later, in the keynote speech on the anniversary of the October Revolution, Andrei Gromyko, who was foreign minister at the time, presented the harshest rebuke of Honecker's policy to date. He warned "revanchists" [the West Germans] and "semi-revanchists" [the East Germans] "of all stripes, wherever they are" [in either Bonn or East Berlin] that "the German Reich [not just Hitler's Third Reich, but any hope for a unified German state] burned to the ground in the fire of the Second World War. There is no return to it, nor will there be."[41]

The postponement of Honecker's visit appeared to signal the determination of at least some Soviet leaders to maintain the strictest possible ideological *Abgrenzung* (strict definition) of East German policy. However, the strength of the German economies and the tenacity of the German leaders allowed for greater maneuverability than might otherwise have been the case. Thus, although the visit did not immediately go ahead, other lower-level contacts were maintained and expanded. Moreover, as Gorbachev increased his criticism of the economic, political, and foreign-policy mistakes of his predecessors, Honecker emerged after the first two years of Gorbachev's rule looking stronger and more in charge than ever before. Speaking before the 11th Congress of the Socialist Unity Party in April 1986, Honecker appeared to be little damaged by the events of the previous four years, eliminating the statutory praise for the Soviet model (despite Gorbachev's presence on the podium) and declaring that the GDR had evolved into a "politically stable and economically efficient socialist state."[42] This process was capped in the summer of 1987 when Honecker at last visited the Federal Republic, and he provided further impetus, both in his speeches and by his mere presence, for improved economic and political relations.

It became increasingly difficult, however, for Honecker to stay in power in the face of rising internal and external pressures.

First, the economic crisis produced direct and indirect difficulties for Honecker's rule. In particular, the economic causes and consequences of the crisis led to the imposition of a harsh austerity program to deal with East Germany's debt-repayment problems. Although it did not immediately produce domestic unrest, it amounted to a partial renunciation of a key pillar of Honecker's social contract with his own people, and, as such, it laid the groundwork for the events which swept him from power in 1989.

In addition, this collapse posed a second threat to Honecker's domestic popularity, by causing widespread fear that the fruits of the inter-German relationship would wither. These involved not just economic benefits and hundreds of thousands of cross-border visits but also tens of thousands of East German emigrations, as well as unencumbered telephone, postal, and telegraph services and East German cooperation in the transmission of West German television to all parts of East Germany.[43]

The deterioration of the economic situation led the regime to search for new sources of legitimacy. That process led to the rediscovery of the regime's German roots. During the 1970s, East German historians had traced the roots of socialism on German soil back to the Middle Ages, but had also rehabilitated such previously reviled figures as Frederick the Great and Martin Luther. In this manner, they had sought to rebuild pride in previous German cultural and political contributions and lay legitimate claim to being a natural successor regime.

The limited rapprochement reached with the East German Lutheran Church was indicative of the success of these attempts.[44] The regime's interest in co-opting the Lutheran Church as a pillar for its own legitimacy obliged it to turn a blind eye to the gradual, quiet, and always nonviolent emergence of the Lutheran Church as a meeting place for otherwise disfranchised elements of socialist society: writers and artists, students, environmentalists, and others. Weekly peace vigils began to be held; the Lutheran Church gradually emerged as an organized countrywide force; and when in October and November 1989 demonstrations broke out surrounding the massive flight to the West of more than 80,000 East German citizens, mainly young people, the Lutheran Church was able to organize peaceful candlelight marches of 500,000 citizens in Dresden, Leipzig, and East Berlin.

It had been Mikhail Gorbachev who had brought home to Honecker the message that it was no longer enough to be faithful to an abstract ideology, that real legitimacy could come about only by obtaining popular support and consensus. According to Kurt Mayer, one of the three Leipzig Communist Party leaders who broke with Honecker over the use of force to suppress demonstrators, "Gorbachev said a very crucial thing, that a leadership that isolates itself from its people will no longer enjoy the right to exist." Significantly, in his meetings with East German leaders in October 1989, Gorbachev also stated that "it was up to each Communist Party to find a way to renew itself." As Mayer said, "that gave us a lot of courage."[45]

Conclusion

For years, Eastern Europe rested between East and West, both geographically and politically. Soviet and Western conceptions of legitimacy differed as much as the bases of their two systems. Western critics who agreed with émigré Hungarian writer Paul Ignotus that the East Europeans had "many freedoms if not freedom itself"[46] nevertheless denied the fundamental legitimacy of these regimes. Soviet leaders traditionally did not see the granting of individual freedom as a prerequisite for the legitimacy of socialist rule; to them, legitimacy was based on adherence to Marxism-Leninism. Yet, as this chapter has shown, until Gorbachev came to power, the East European regimes were under great pressure to be loyal to both definitions. There were continual debates about democracy and reform in Eastern Europe, at the heart of which were these questions: Can such measures be introduced without eroding the Marxist-Leninist basis of the regime? Can the regime maintain support among the population without such changes?

The tension between these questions, which reflected the two competing conceptions of legitimacy, became more apparent in the Soviet Union after Gorbachev accelerated his calls for democratization following the January 1987 CPSU Central Committee plenum. In Eastern Europe, by the summer of 1989, the contradiction between the two questions had been resolved essentially in favor of the latter, with socialism being so broadly redefined as to mean only the most generalized commitment to state-supported welfare and assistance programs. In some countries, such as Poland and Hungary, this transition was achieved peacefully, if accompanied by much debate and negotiation. But throughout the rest of the region, aged leaders hung on to the bitter end, more fond of the benefits they received from their positions than of the ideas that originally motivated them to join their parties decades earlier. Some, like Jakeš and Krenz, were fully aware of the catastrophic state to which their societies had descended. Others, like Ceauşescu, Honecker, and Zhivkov, gave orders to the last for repression and brutality, never really appreciating that the time for such measures had long since passed, hopefully never to return.

Whether or not individual leaders realized that they had lost all credibility with their own populations, the real victim was the idea of socialism itself. In the minds of the electorate who voted freely for the first time in 1989, socialism had become synonymous with corruption, decay, and both moral and economic poverty. For this reason, not only communists but also politically untainted social democrats were swept aside, thereby diminishing the chances of social democratic policies being adopted in the post-communist period.

Notes

1 See Jan Triska, ed., *Dominant Powers and Subordinate States* (Durham, N.C.: Duke University Press, 1986), and Edy Kaufman, *Superpowers and Their Spheres of Influence* (London: Croom Helm, 1976).

2 As detailed in Zbigniew Brzezinski, *The Soviet Bloc* (Cambridge, Mass.: Harvard University Press, 1967), p. 256.

3 See Karen Dawisha, *The Kremlin and the Prague Spring* (Berkeley: University of California Press, 1984).

4 See Sydney I. Ploss, *Moscow and the Polish Crisis* (Boulder, Colo.: Westview Press, 1986), pp. 130–3.

5 See the April 1986 Romanian Central Committee plenum documents, Joint Publication Research Service, *East Europe Review* (JPRS, *EER*), June 9, 1986, p. 36.

6 From the "Open Letter to the Central Committee of the Polish United

Workers' Party from the CPSU Central Committee," as published in *Pravda*, June 12, 1981.

7   "Open Letter from Stefan Bratkowski," chairman of the Polish Journalists' Association, *Le Monde*, March 25, 1981.

8   *New York Times*, April 14, 1981.

9   *Pravda*, April 1981, protesting the Polish decision to allow a meeting at a Warsaw cemetery in which participants made claims of Soviet responsibility for the massacre of Polish officers in the Katyn forest during World War II.

10 "Open Letter to the Central Committee," *Pravda*, June 12, 1981.

11 *Pravda*, October 13, 1981, criticizing Kania's policy of reconciliation with the Church and Solidarity in the name of renewal.

12 *Pravda*, November 5, 1981, following a Moscow meeting of bloc secretaries for international and ideological affairs that apparently urged the Poles to take more resolute measures against Solidarity.

13 Gorbachev speech to Hungarian workers, TASS, in English, June 9, 1986, as quoted in Radio Free Europe (RFE), *Soviet/East European Report*, Vol. 3, No. 26, June 20, 1986.

14 "Hungaricus" [pseudonym], *On a Few Lessons of the Hungarian National-Democratic Revolution* (Brussels: Imre Nagy Institute for Political Research, 1959); Bill Lomax, *Hungary 1956* (London: Allison & Busby, 1976), pp. 182–92.

15 See Vladimir Kusin, *From Dubček to Charter 77: A Study of "Normalization" in Czechoslovakia, 1968–1978* (New York: St. Martin's Press, 1978).

16 *Pravda*, December 26, 1961.

17 RFE, *Czechoslovakia Situation Report*, No. 15, September 24, 1985, pp. 5–6.

18 Ideology Secretary Ján Fojtík, on Czechoslovak television, November 13, 1989, RFE, *Czechoslovakia Situation Report*, No. 24, December 8, 1989, p. 10.

19 *Rudé právo*, November 18, 1989, quoted in *ibid*.

20 *Pravda*, December 5, 1989.

21 Text of speech to the Hungarian Communist Youth League, November 15, 1985, in *Magyar Ifjúság*, December 6, 1985, JPRS, *EER*, March 3, 1986, p. 111.

22 The quotations are from Steven Koppany, "Hungarian Opposition Groups Hold Meeting to Discuss Nation's Future," *RAD Background Report/24 (Hungary)*, Radio Free Europe Research, February 13, 1986, and *Hungary Situation Report 9/86*, Radio Free Europe Research, Vol. 11, No. 36, September 5, 1986, pp. 9–11.

23 Sándor Fekete, writing in *Új Tükör*, March 9, 1986, as translated in JPRS, *EER*, May 12, 1986, p. 80.

24 *Ibid.*, p. 81.

25 See the HSWP communiqué, Budapest Domestic Service, in Hungarian, May 31, 1989, Foreign Broadcast Information Service, *East European Daily Report (FBIS-EEU)*, June 1, 1989, p. 41.

26 Budapest Domestic Service, in Hungarian, October 23, 1989, *FBIS-EEU*, October 24, 1989, pp. 56–7.

27 News conference by Imre Pozsgay, Budapest, September 28, 1989, Reuters, September 28, 1989.

28 *Der Standard* (Vienna), October 2, 1989.

29 Budapest Television Service, in Hungarian, October 23, 1989, *FBIS-EEU*, October 24, 1989, p. 56.

30 *Washington Post*, January 19, 1990.

31 Josef Bayer, "Legitimacy and Consensus," *Társadalmi Szemle*, No. 12, December 1985, pp. 83–8, as translated in JPRS, *EER*, March 6, 1986, pp. 89–96.

32 *Ibid.*

33 *Ibid.*

34 Kádár's speech before the 13th Congress of the Hungarian Socialist Workers' Party, March 25, 1985, *FBIS-EEU*, March 27, 1985, p. F16.

35 Czesław Miłosz, *The Captive Mind* (New York: Knopf, 1953), p. 245.

36 As quoted in the *Washington Post*, July 3, 1986. The Soviet news media did not report these remarks.

37 Civic Forum Chief of Staff Ján Urban, as quoted in the *Washington Post*, January 19, 1990.

38 Figures from Irwin L. Collier, Jr., "Cost Cutting and Macroeconomic Adjustment: The GDR in the 1980s," 101st Congress, *Pressures for Reform in the East European Economies* (Washington, D.C.: U.S. Government Printing Office, 1989), Vol. 2, p. 286.

39 Quoted in Ronald D. Asmus, *East Berlin and Moscow: The Documentation of a Dispute*, Radio Free Europe Occasional Papers, No. 1 (Munich: Radio Free Europe, 1985), p. 8.

40 Speech by Erich Honecker delivered at the SED's seventh Central Committee plenum, November 26–7, 1983, *Neues Deutschland*, November 26–7, 1983, quoted in Asmus, *op. cit.*, p. 19.

41 *Pravda*, November 6, 1984.

42 "SED Central Committee Report to the 11th SED Congress," East Berlin Domestic Service, in German, April 17, 1986, *FBIS-EEU*, April 21, 1986, E17.

43 When an East German study revealed that the highest level of emigration applications came from Dresden, the only area unable to pick up airborne West German television signals, the East Germans obligingly laid a cable. As a result, all areas of East Germany were able to receive West German television.

44 See Ronald D. Asmus, "The GDR and Martin Luther," *Survey*, Vol. 28, No. 3, Autumn 1984, pp. 124–56.

45 *Washington Post*, January 14, 1990.

46 Quoted in François Fejtö, *A History of the People's Democracies* (London: Penguin, 1974), p. 169.

6

The East European Policy Agenda

The East European states entered the 1990s having made progress in certain areas, but with many goals still unmet. If nothing else, the spirit of *glasnost* in the Soviet Union allowed Soviet and East European leaders and theorists to say in public what previously could be said only in private, namely, in the words of a leading Soviet economist, that "in many scientific and technological fields, capitalism has gone far ahead of us and has essentially exceeded socialism."[1]

The challenge to socialism in Eastern Europe which erupted in 1989 was wide-reaching and deeply rooted. It was a challenge presented, of course, both by Western policies and by the lure of Western institutions. But it was also, and indeed primarily, one that emanated from the people of Eastern Europe; they may genuinely have embraced the egalitarian principles of socialism, but at the same time they rejected all that had been done in the name of those principles that smacked of corruption, repression, illegality, bureaucratism, and inefficiency.

Following Mikhail Gorbachev's condemnation of those same excesses in the Soviet Union, the East European leaders who had come to power before him were no longer able to count on Soviet support in covering up their own problems. In the first three years of his rule, Gorbachev may have been undecided about the extent to which reform should be encouraged or allowed in Eastern Europe. Nevertheless, even in the absence of specific Soviet pressures, the force of example sharpened the policy debates in Eastern Europe and stimulated popular aspirations for genuine change. In 1988, therefore, when many clear signals came from the Kremlin regarding the desirability of change, reform was already at the top of the East European policy agenda in the key political, social, and economic fields.

Political Issues

The major issues on the political agenda in Eastern Europe prior to 1989 were succession, democratization, and governance. Looking at succession first, it was clear before 1989 that many East European problems simply would not be resolved until this issue was settled. The leaders of four of the six East European states (all but Poland and Czechoslovakia) had been born at the time of the Bolshevik Revolution and had been in power more than twenty-five years. In most of these countries there had been few changes since the early 1970s in any of the leading Politburo and government positions, where the average age was in the mid-sixties, and none had made public any plans for succession following the death of the general secretary. Only in Hungary was a deputy general secretary, Károly Németh, named, and even there it was widely assumed that Németh would serve only as a caretaker while other political forces jockeyed for power, much as Konstantin Chernenko did in the year between the death in 1984 of Soviet General Secretary Yurii Andropov and the selection in 1985 of Mikhail Gorbachev. And in the end, when Kádár was pushed aside in May 1988, he was replaced not by Németh but by Károly Grósz and then by a four-member collegium headed by the "father" of Hungarian economic reform, Reszö Nyers. So even in the one country which had established a mechanism for succession, that mechanism did not function.

The poor record of Western sovietology in forecasting succession in the USSR during the 1982–5 period suggested that it would not be wise to attempt to forecast the outcomes of any of the East European succession struggles. And, indeed, when the successions occurred, even the communist party leaders who emerged were, on the whole, unlikely. Gregor Gysi in East Germany, Ion Iliescu in Romania, Marián Calfa in Czechoslovakia, and Petar Mladenov in Bulgaria all had come to power by atypical means. That is to say, few of them had held a position in the party elite in the period immediately prior to taking over the leadership. The speed with which the changes took place was also unexpected, with change in one country having a domino effect elsewhere, and with Gorbachev, if anything, accelerating this process throughout the bloc. And finally, the rapidity with which the communist monopoly of power was overthrown was also striking. An entire generation of communist elites had virtually grown old waiting for Zhivkov, Ceaușescu, Honecker, Kádár, and Husák to pass from the scene, only to find in the months following those successions that it was already too late – the possibility of reforming those systems while maintaining the "leading role" of their communist parties was practically nil.

One of the most important issues facing new leaders was *political* reform of the system, at the center of which was the question of the democratization of public life. This issue, which had been the object of deep and divisive debate in Eastern Europe for some time, was undoubtedly put back on top of the policy agenda by Gorbachev's own call for thoroughgoing electoral reform, a reform that led to the convening in June 1989 of the newly established Congress of People's Deputies. That Congress elected a Supreme Soviet, the first permanent legislative body in Moscow since the Duma was dissolved by the tsar.

The example set in Moscow stimulated the political debate in Eastern Europe, where ideas about parliaments and multiparty systems had lain dormant since the 1946–8 period. Once the democratization debate in Moscow gave the green light to political reforms elsewhere, Hungary was the first to move. As a result of limited electoral reforms, three Central Committee members were ousted from their seats in Parliament following 1986 elections. HSWP Secretary János Berecz presciently concluded from those results that "the Party will in the future not be able to work as it has so far."[2]

In Poland two years later, a round-table agreement between the ruling Polish United Workers' Party and Solidarity produced elections to a bicameral legislature. The result was devastating for the communists. In the Senate, where a completely free election had taken place, Solidarity won 99 of the 100 seats. Senior PUWP candidates ran uncontested for seats in the other chamber, the Sejm. But there, too, they met with the most stunning defeats, when many of them failed to receive the necessary 50 percent of the valid votes. In several cases, party candidates received less than 5 percent of the total ballots. As a result, the PUWP was unable to form a government. In August, the two parties normally allied with the PUWP deserted, making it theoretically possible for Solidarity to form a government totally without communist involvement. Negotiations became tense and acrimonious and threatened to break down altogether. In the meantime, Romania tried to strengthen the hand of Polish hard-liners by proposing "joint action" with other socialist states to prevent such a "disaster" in Poland. The deadlock was broken when Gorbachev made a forty-minute telephone call to the communist leadership urging them to join a Solidarity-led government under Prime Minister Tadeusz Mazowiecki.[3] That was the first instance in which the communist monopoly of power was broken in Eastern Europe, and it was widely perceived as having been facilitated by Gorbachev.

After that, events gained momentum. Lech Wałęsa in Poland, Václav Havel in Czechoslovakia, and other leaders in dissident circles began to talk openly about the inevitability of changes along Hungarian, Soviet, and Polish lines. The decision of the Hungarians in September 1989 to hold elections the following year on a completely free and open multiparty basis was accompanied by the decision of the Hungarian Socialist Workers' Party to dissolve itself, with a majority of its more liberal membership reemerging as the Hungarian Socialist Party. It was these rather orderly transitions along the road to democracy in Hungary, the Soviet Union, and Poland and the accompanying demise of the HSWP in Hungary which set the stage for the collapse of communist rule and the virtual deluge of democratization in the GDR, Czechoslovakia, and Romania in November and December 1989.

The surge of democracy, however, produced neither quick nor satisfactory solutions to the crisis of governance which still plagued the region even though the old communist leaders had been swept from power. The East European challenge was not merely to replace old leaders with new; there was also the challenge of constructing an entirely new system – a system based on governance and laws, rather than on power and decrees, a system which would structure citizens' relationships to society, to the state, and to their work in fundamentally different ways. The East European events were not simply the equivalent of a coup d'état in which elite in-groups and out-groups simply changed places without substantially affecting the structure of the society; every aspect of East European life would be touched by the chain reaction which was set off in 1989.

This chain reaction would energize the entire reconstruction process, rather than produce revolutionary fissures, only if it could be harnessed by the emergence of true governance. The impediments to this emergence were enormous: East European leaders did not have the luxury of starting all over again "from scratch." There was no wealth to squander if mistakes were made, as there had been in some of the rich African countries in the postindependence period. On the contrary, one of the most delicate and incendiary challenges which these new East European governments faced was in preparing their populations for the fact that economic conditions, at least in the short term, would be even more austere in the new Eastern Europe than they had been in the old. Moreover, these leaders were not emerging in some sleepy part of the world where no one would notice if civil war broke out. East Germany was not Benin (a state in western Africa whose renunciation of adherence to Marxism-Leninism had gone largely unreported in the capitalist world). Not only were East European transmutations being watched under a global microscope, but outside interests were directly and indirectly active in trying to shape the emerging governmental structures.

The emergence of true governance was further constrained by the fact that not only economically but also politically the new leaders did not start with a *tabula rasa*. Top communists may have left the scene, but the *nomenklatura* system they had created remained. New noncommunist ministers took power, but all too often they had to battle an entrenched communist-controlled bureaucracy that may have lost the battle of the streets but had every intention of winning the battle of the corridors.

In all the East European countries, new leaders had to rely on this system to keep essential government functions going, but they risked losing all popular support unless they moved decisively against it. In Poland, for example, roughly a million office holders owed their livelihood to a system whose only guiding principle had been political loyalty to the Leninist machine.[4] The enormous resistance of this *apparat* to the implementation of market reforms prompted the government to move forward the date for local government elections. Dismantling these *nomenklatura* systems and replacing them with a genuine civil service based on Weberian meritocratic principles would be an enormous challenge for new governments, not least because of the lack of qualified individuals who had not been compromised under the communist regimes.

This dilemma was particularly acute in Romania, where the National Salvation Front under Ion Iliescu was criticized for including so many communists amongst its ranks. In defense, Iliescu pointed out that the old Communist Party had included over 4 million individuals, with virtually the entire educated stratum of society being members. Under the harsh conditions of the Romanian dictatorship, no alternative groups had been able to emerge; there had been no possibility for the development of a loyal opposition, as had existed for some time in Hungary. Not to use communists and former communists, in Romania and elsewhere, would simply deprive new governments of an enormous pool of potential talent. To rely on them too strongly, however, would undermine popular support. The response generally was to seek noncommunist participants in the government even before elections were conducted.

Communist-dominated *apparats*, however, remained in power to a greater or lesser extent throughout the region even after noncommunists had entered the governments and even after the communist right to exercise a monopoly of power had been excised from all constitutions. They not only remained in an excellent position to move back into power if democratic experiments should fail but also took actions designed to enervate these experiments, reducing their moral vigor, lowering their physical horizons, and thereby increasing their chances of failing. At the very time when new leaders needed a synergy between societal supports and governmental institutions to make qualitative transformations, these bureaucracies created enormous friction in an effort to brake progress. Until new personnel could be trained, there was no easy or quick answer to the problem, with this and other challenges to governance appearing intractable in the short term.

The Case of Czechoslovakia. Within Eastern Europe there are roughly three types of elites. Czechoslovakia is one country in which all three groups have existed, without, however, coexisting. The first group consists of those loyal and staunch communists who, we must assume, would choose to live in a socialist system if, as they say, they had it to do all over again. This group ruled throughout the region until 1989. The second group consists of a rather substantial stratum of professionally qualified but ideologically disengaged officials who have sought high party and state positions in order to receive the perks of life at the top of the *nomenklatura* ladder. This group still exists, but their loyalties have shifted away from the communists. The third group is composed of the expert, culturally sophisticated intelligentsia elite. From their ranks rose many of the economic reforms, political demands, and cultural programs designed to serve indigenous national requirements and forge closer links with Western Europe than Moscow had previously encouraged.

In Czechoslovakia, a significant portion of the third elite group was expelled from the party in 1969–70 and existed only in opposition. Rule in the country was therefore based primarily on a coalition between the first and second groups. This problem, which was also repeated in the GDR, Romania, and Bulgaria, produced both ideological orthodoxy and far-reaching corruption, along with a deadening of intellectual life – all in the name of the policy of "normalization."

The regime's political agenda came to be dominated by relations with this very large third group, which constituted almost one-half of the 1970 membership of the entire Communist Party of Czechoslovakia. (Further details on the numbers purged are on p. 162.) This group was not a subsection of the Central Committee, simply waiting for the demise of the *ancien régime* so that they could come to power under reform-minded Soviet sponsorship. Having been expelled from the party, they existed both outside and, therefore, against the party. The members of this group, who remained politically active joined other dissidents like Václav Havel to form Charter 77. It was out of Charter 77 that the nationwide movement Civic Forum emerged in 1989 to wrest power from the Communist Party. As long as the loyalties of the middle group of careerists remained solidly behind the new Civic Forum leadership, there was little chance of the Communist Party reemerging. But marked resistance to radical reform shown by the bureaucracies in the USSR, Poland, and elsewhere suggested that this group would continue to look out for its own interests.

Social Issues

Among the social issues at the top of the East European agenda in the mid-1980s were generational change and relations with the intelligentsia and the churches. In many fields of relations between the regime and society, Eastern Europe is a tapestry of varying yet interwoven threads. Thus, although conclusions reached for one country may not apply entirely to another, there are enough common features to make a comparative study possible.

Turning first to the issue of *generational change,* it is important to emphasize that whereas most Western countries do not have ministries of youth affairs (as they generally regard the normal life-style of young people to be outside the bounds of state authority, much less control), such definitely was not the case in Soviet-bloc countries. There, responsibility for the socialization of young people was always entrusted to one of the most high-ranking party officials, and considerable attention was paid to molding the next generation into worthy citizens.

The problem which increasingly confronted the East European regimes in this area was that the population under forty years of age had no direct negative experience of Western culture or politics. Their elders had lived first through the economic collapse of the 1920s and 1930s and then through the rise of fascism and the war. Many were therefore able to appreciate the Soviet Union's positive role in Hitler's defeat. But the generation born in the 1950s and 1960s became politically aware during the decade of détente, when anti-fascist rhetoric subsided and more direct contacts with the West emerged. They therefore developed a very different view of the relative benefits of Russian and Western influence in their region.

Most people considered Western pop culture and fashion to be the most attractive aspect of Western influence amongst Eastern-bloc youth. However, equally worrisome to the regimes was the massive yet largely unofficial importation of home computers. Studies showed that computer science was the only branch of industry that Soviet-bloc youth were genuinely interested in entering. The regimes were concerned that young people were growing up with the view that Soviet-bloc technology could not match the West. As the creator of the Ondra microcomputer in Czechoslovakia lamented:

> In Czechoslovakia there are at present several tens of thousands of Western-made microcomputers, and each summer their number increases by about 10,000. With these computers comes not only technology but also ideology. . . . Children might soon begin to believe that Western technology represents the peak and that our technology is obsolete and bad. . . .
>
> One of these days I will record on the tape for you what the children say and how they laugh when they see how we are unable to meet our plans for computer production, how they laugh when [the casings on] our computers [have] to be opened periodically to prevent them from burning out. . . . We must look at it from the political point of view, because in 10 years' time it will be too late to change our children. By then they will want to change us.[5]

Of further concern to East European leaders was the fact that the expansion of contacts with the West coincided with a slow-down in economic performance and generational succession throughout Eastern Europe: The increased cost of living that resulted from economic stagnation coincided with decreased opportunities for advancement within the party. As a result, East European leaders expressed concern over their difficulty in recruiting the best graduates into party positions. This problem was particularly acute both in Poland, where in the aftermath of the Solidarity crisis the party further lost support, and in Hungary, where jobs in the more lucrative and expanding private sector lured young professionals away. In Czechoslovakia, on the other hand, recruitment patterns among the young did not suffer, mainly because the party spurned young Czech intellectuals and university graduates, preferring instead to rebuild the party from working-class stock, with a preponderance of new Slovak members.

A primary concern, of course, was that the next generation would be more contemptuous of the Soviet Union than their elders. And as the quality of life and professional opportunities declined, the fear often was expressed in the East European press that a whole generation of young people was growing up without any stake in the socialist system and also without any great appreciation for the balance between its benefits and its natural and imposed restrictions – including the alliance with the Soviet Union. As Hungarian Socialist Workers' Party Secretary János Berecz frankly admitted:

> Some young people do not understand the signifi-
> cance of Hungarian–Soviet friendship. . . . Young
> people do not have the decisive experience of fraternal
> relations that we do, and they must therefore follow
> another emotional and intellectual path of whole-
> hearted acceptance of this friendship.[6]

Other aspects of regime–society linkages were no less worrisome for East European leaders in the middle and late 1980s. In the crucial role of relations with the intelligentsia and the churches, many regimes' efforts were complicated by the fact that both groups were organized and enjoyed considerable support in the West. Moreover, both groups set themselves up as the guardians of these states' history, as the conscience of the nation against "internationalist" obligations, as the "David" of individual rights against the "Goliath" of collective responsibility.

Nations that had given birth to Jan Hus, Martin Luther, and the tradition of the Black Madonna (an icon from the monastery in Częstochowa, Poland, historically invoked as the Polish nation's spiritual shield against foreign invasion) were not easily going to surrender this heritage to a vision of the future that required as its first commandment the vilification of everything that had been part of the pre-communist period. Neither would these regimes be able to establish their place in Europe and as part of Europe – an objective repeated over and over again by the leaders of Poland, the German Democratic Republic, Hungary, Romania, and also, in the past, Czechoslovakia – unless they reached a *modus vivendi* with the intelligentsia and organized religion, who, more than any other groups in these societies, bound them both to their European past and to their European future.

East European regimes pursued varying strategies for dealing with the two groups. The first, of course, was violent and complete *suppression and confrontation,* as occurred throughout the bloc during the entire Stalin period and sporadically in different countries and against different groups subsequently. For example, in early 1968, the delicate balance between the Polish United Workers' Party and the intellectuals collapsed, partly under the weight of charges by right-wing nationalists within the party that the country, including its ruling party and security services, was being taken over by Jews. Thousands of Jews were forced out of the country that year, accepting invitations to emigrate that they could not refuse.

The following year in Prague, the new Husák regime began an even more thoroughgoing purge of reform-minded intellectuals from the Communist Party. Approximately one-third of the CPCz membership of 1.5 million was expelled, with the burden falling on Czechs with higher education and positions of responsibility in the party (about 90 percent of all casualties). Moreover, thousands of scientists lost their positions, along with 900 university professors. Two-thirds of the membership of the Czechoslovak Writers' Union were expelled, and twenty-one scientific institutes were closed altogether. As if to make sure that they never again rose to dominate public life, the government not only reassigned this group (an estimated 1 million people in a total population of 15 million) to manual labor but also passed laws preventing the children of these outcasts from having any access to higher education.[7]

The CPCz also turned against the Catholic Church after 1969 – a situation that became so bad that Slovak Party Secretary Vasil Bil'ak suggested that the Catholic Church in Czechoslovakia might have to sever its connection with the Vatican as a precondition for "normalizing" Church–state relations. Despite efforts by the regime to contain Catholicism, especially in Slovakia, in 1985 the 1,100th anniversary of the death of St. Methodius produced a crowd of between 100,000 and 200,000 (composed mainly of Slovaks), even though the regime refused to allow a papal visit.

In Romania, the Catholic Church also failed to reach an accommodation with the regime. However, Nicolae Ceaușescu's simultaneous tolerance of Orthodoxy (professed by 70 percent of the population at the last poll in 1948) and stifling of Catholicism suggested that his actions had less to do with concern over Vatican interference than with the regime's suppression of its Hungarian minority, who form the vast majority of the Catholic population.

The second strategy, and the one most widely practiced by communist regimes up to the end of the 1980s, was *uneasy coexistence*. In none of the East European states was the communist revolution made for either the intelligentsia or the churches. On the contrary, both were normally considered to be implacable enemies of proletarian power. However, no East European regime could face a concerted onslaught by these two groups without serious damage to its authority within the country at large. Most regimes, therefore, came to realize that, at least in the short term, there was no alternative to some form of accommodation with both groups.

The cat-and-mouse pattern that existed throughout Eastern Europe involved legal and bureaucratic restrictions on the part of the state authorities, who periodically took extreme measures against a dissident or group of believers in order to assert their authority. On the other side, intellectuals and believers regularly made use of contacts with Western human-rights and religious organizations to bring pressure to bear on the authorities, in the hope of incrementally improving their situation.

This was the pattern followed in the GDR following the ouster of Walter Ulbricht in 1971. He had presided over the building of the Berlin Wall to prevent the flight of East Germany's skilled workers and intelligentsia, but then failed to construct a viable cultural policy that would accommodate them. When Erich Honecker succeeded Ulbricht, he paid greater attention to cultural policy, declaring at the 8th SED Congress that no restrictions would be placed on any artist or writer whose work proceeded from the basic tenets of socialism. That led to great expectations of cultural liberalism, but such expectations were not always met. In particular, writers, singers, and philosophers who maintained their own adherence to socialism, while questioning the regime's deviations, were subjected to arrest and harassment. Gregor Gysi, who succeeded Egon Krenz as chairman of the Socialist Unity Party–Party of Democratic Socialism in November 1989, had acted as a defense lawyer for several such cases.

The third method for dealing with the challenge from the intelligentsia and the churches was *co-optation*, to which East European governments increasingly resorted in the late 1980s. This strategy represented both an admission of failure and a sign of maturity – failure insofar as the state recognized that it could rule but could not govern without the support of these groups, and maturity in the acknowledgment that progress could best be made through dialogue. It also would not have occurred had these regimes not felt that the best way to meet their internationalist obligations, particularly under the new conditions which prevailed once Gorbachev came to power, was to become more sensitive to their national constituencies.

Of all the bloc countries, only Romania was free of such obligations – at least in the cultural domain. Barriers to the co-optation of indigenous elites could have been removed, particularly as the regime sought to use the intelligentsia to bolster and rediscover its Western origins. Romania's foreign-policy orientation between East and West ostensibly made it more sensitive than other bloc states to pressure on human-rights issues. As a result, there should have been little open suppression of either dissidents or believers. The key problem in Romania was the cult of personality surrounding the Ceauşescu family, which made any real dialogue between the state and either the intelligentsia or the churches impossible.

In Hungary, Church–state relations became less troubled following the 1974 death of Cardinal József Mindszenty, who had preferred imprisonment to cooperation. With the accession of László Lékai as Primate of Hungary in 1976, the Church both supported the regime's national and social programs and became more active in forming them, leading János Kádár at one point to comment that "without exception the churches are loyal to our system. . . . Is it possible that by doing this the churches may be prolonging their existence? It may be so. . . . It could be said that this is a compromise. . . . But we learn from Lenin that any compromise which advances our revolutionary course is acceptable."[8] By 1983, Bishop Cserhat, secretary of the Hungarian Conference of Bishops, went so far as to urge further Church–state collaboration in the creation of a generation of men and women who would embody both the ideals of communism and the teachings of the Church.[9] The process of co-optation culminated in June 1985 when three priests were elected to the Hungarian Parliament.

This policy of Church–state accord was replicated in the area of regime–intelligentsia relations. Although more restrictions existed in Hungary than in the West, and more subjects – such as the alliance with the Soviet Union – were taboo for official public discussion, there nevertheless was no law on censorship in Hungary, and there were no political restrictions on travel abroad or on contacts with foreigners, even when Kádár was still in power. This created a much freer environment in Hungary than elsewhere in the bloc, as witnessed by the Budapest Cultural Forum held in 1985 – an event that brought together major cultural figures from East and West for free-ranging and almost entirely unrestricted discussions of world literary and political trends.

In Bulgaria, a lackluster relationship between the regime and the cultural world was transformed in the 1970s under the auspices of General Secretary Todor Zhivkov's daughter, Lyudmila Zhivkova, who as the Politburo member in charge of culture presided over the rediscovery of Bulgarian history. The Bulgarian Academy of Sciences produced a fourteen-volume *History of Bulgaria* under her direction, and Bulgarian art flourished as never before. Zhivkova personally supervised the lavish preparations for the 1,300th anniversary of Bulgarian statehood in 1981. Although she died shortly before the celebrations took place, they were not suspended, and the official revival of Bulgarian nationalism continued, although not without Soviet displeasure.

The popularity of the Bulgarian nationalist revival amongst the Slav majority led in the late 1980s to its use by Zhivkov as a tool for staying in power. Beginning in 1985, all ethnic Turks were forced to adopt Slav names, with the census taken in that year omitting, for the first time, any mention of the Turkish minority. Not only was the use of the Turkish language suppressed, but all Moslem social and religious practices were forbidden. In May 1989, the leaders of the Turkish dissident community were forcibly expelled to Turkey, starting a cycle of demonstrations, regime repressions, and further expulsions. By the end of August 1989, over 310,000 Bulgarian Turks had been expelled across the border, creating enormous tensions both regionally and internally.

One of the first steps by the National Assembly following the overthrow of Todor Zhivkov was to restore full rights to the country's 1.5 million ethnic Turks. However, as proof of the continuing popularity of the nationalist appeals that Zhivkov increasingly had used to maintain himself in power, this move was resisted in several large-scale rallies by Bulgarian Slavs.

The electoral defeats and popular demonstrations that rocked the region in 1989 revealed the essential failure of the strategies pursued by these regimes to deal with the key constituencies amongst the youth, the intelligentsia, and the churches. Public-opinion polling, which also reemerged throughout the region during this period, underlined these failures. Poll results and other surveys carried out in the summer and fall of 1989 uniformly showed the ruling communist parties receiving particularly low confidence ratings from young people – the same people who took to the streets to unseat the parties months later.[10] The writing had been on the wall – the regimes simply had chosen not to read it.

The Case of Poland. Regime–society relations in all of these fields took on a different character and intensity in Poland. Church–state relations (as discussed in Chapter 3) were unique because of the numerous cultural, historical, and political factors that made the Church a particularly robust institution and the state a particularly weak one. As a result, the Church was always a force whose power could be ignored by the communist authorities only at their peril. This was discovered in the 1950s, when the imprisonment of Cardinal Stefan Wyszyński produced massive demonstrations for his release, in 1966, when celebrations of the millennium of Catholic Poland produced a major test of will between the two sides, and again in the mid-1970s, when the Church blocked constitutional changes that would have been disadvantageous for landowning peasants, who provided a major pillar of Church strength.

But at no time did the relationship between the state and other societal groups, including the Church, become more strained than in the wake of the 1980–1 crisis over Solidarity. That crisis both set the newly established unofficial trade-union movement against the state and mobilized the Church and the intelligentsia to examine their own relationships to central authority.

Solidarity's refusal to recognize the leading role of the Communist Party within the union and within society as a whole precipitated the imposition of martial law and the mass detention of Solidarity leaders in December 1981. Throughout the crisis, the Church acted as intermediary between Solidarity and the state, trying to avoid an increase in political tension in the country while at the same time promoting the substance of Solidarity's demands.

After 1981, when Solidarity was banned, the Church played an even more important role. It provided a legal channel both to the government and to the people for the promotion of key Solidarity demands, including the release of political prisoners, improvement in living standards, and political reforms that would take non-party interests more fully into account.

The Church clearly benefited from this role. Never before had so many young Polish men studied for the priesthood, with a rise from 20,198 in 1979 to 22,381 in 1985. The *Statistical Yearbook of the Catholic Church* also reveals that Poland had the highest annual percentage increase in the number of priests among European countries; in 1985, the nation accounted for 30 percent of all newly ordained priests on the Continent.

Clearly influenced both by Cardinal Karol Wojtyła's election to the papacy in 1978 and by the Solidarity era, young people flocked to the Church as never before. A survey carried out in

December 1984 for the Public Opinion Research Center in Poland revealed 82.5 percent of all respondents to be religious, with
90 percent of senior high school pupils declaring themselves
believers.[11]

The kidnapping and murder of a pro-Solidarity priest, Father
Jerzy Popiełuszko, by officers of the Polish security police in
October 1984 symbolized the extent to which the battle lines had
been drawn between the state on the one hand and the Church
and Solidarity on the other. At the same time, the trial and
imprisonment of the four security officers found guilty of the
murder symbolized the concern of the Jaruzelski government to
reach a compromise both with indigenous forces and with key
external forces – including the Vatican – as a precursor to Western acceptance of the regime and the lifting of punitive economic sanctions.

Jaruzelski's efforts in 1985 and 1986 were designed to further
promote dialogue with the Church and the intelligentsia, without giving in to the strategic demands of Solidarity, namely, a
trade-union movement independent of party control. Guidelines
for the Polish Party Congress published in March 1986 emphasized the dual need for "constructive development" of Church–
state relations and for a struggle against "militant clericalism."

At the end of 1986, as a result of recommendations made by
Jaruzelski at the June Party Congress, a Consultative Social
Council composed primarily of non-party intellectuals came into
existence. Jaruzelski hailed the body as an "unprecedented ex-
periment" opening the way to "still bolder solutions," and it
seemed clear that he hoped the council would assist in the further stabilization of government authority.

Given the fact that some members used the occasion of the
council's first meeting to call for repeal of the 1982 law banning
Solidarity, it was not clear that Jaruzelski would succeed in de-
taching the intelligentsia from their support for this key demand.
Concessions in other areas, including the release of political
prisoners, won the regime breathing space and much-needed
international recognition, culminating in Jaruzelski's audience
with Pope John Paul II in the Vatican early in 1987 and the visit
by the pope to Poland that summer. After that period, it was
only a matter of time before Solidarity would gain legal recogni-

tion. In the meanwhile, it had been the Church which had promoted the union's core demands.

Economic Issues

East European economies collectively suffered serious shocks in the late 1970s and early 1980s that were brought on by a combination of economic mismanagement, structural problems, Western inflation, oil price rises, and the stagnation of the Soviet economy. Although each country responded differently to these multiple shocks, the situation produced major problems throughout Eastern Europe.

The first was the decline in GNP growth rates, which, as Table 6.1 shows, dipped from an annual average of 4.9 percent for all six East European countries in the period 1970–5 to 2.0 percent in 1975–80 and 1.4 percent in 1980–5. Growth rates in subsequent years continued their steady decline, with the region's poor overall performance buoyed by the relatively good figures reported by the Romanian regime in these years. Even though Ceauşescu was able to achieve a 5.8 percent rate of growth in the GNP of his country in 1986, increased output certainly was not passed on to the Romanian population, whose standard of living fell signifi-

Table 6.1. *Annual percentage rates of growth of GNP, six East European countries, 1970–88 (constant prices)*

Country	1970–5	1975–80	1980–5	1986	1987	1988[a]
Bulgaria	4.5	1.2	0.9	4.8	−0.8	1.8
Czechoslovakia	3.4	2.2	1.4	2.1	1.0	1.4
East Germany	3.5	2.4	1.8	1.5	1.8	1.8
Hungary	3.4	2.3	0.9	2.2	1.0	1.1
Poland	6.6	0.9	1.2	2.7	−1.7	1.9
Romania	6.2	3.9	2.0	5.8	1.1	2.1
Totals	4.9	2.0	1.4	3.0	0.1	1.5

[a] 1988 figures provisional.

Source: Thad Alton, "East European GNP's, Domestic Final Uses of Gross Product, Rates of Growth, and International Comparisons," in 101st Congress, *Joint Economic Committee Pressures for Reform in the East European Economies* (Washington, D.C.: U.S. Government Printing Office, 1989), Vol. 1, p. 81.

cantly during this period. And after 1979, almost every country had at least one year of "negative growth." The only exception was East Germany, which nevertheless showed one year of no growth and managed to achieve that only with a harsh austerity program and significant economic assistance from West Germany.

The situation looks worse if we examine the index for annual rates of growth of GNP *per capita* for the same period, which are presented in Table 6.2. Using this measure, it is clear that even East Germany did not escape years of negative figures regarding growth, with 1988 producing a near catastrophe and clearly foreshadowing the political tumult that followed the next year. The effects in Poland of the crisis which led to the rise of Solidarity are also clear from the figures, with Poland's per capita GNP

Table 6.2. *Indexes of East European real GNP per capita*
at adjusted factor cost, 1970 and 1975–88
(indexed to 1975 = 100)

Year	Bulgaria	Czecho-slovakia	GDR	Hungary	Poland	Romania	Yugoslavia
1970	81.1	87.5	83.4	86.6	76.4	75.9	83.9
1975	100.0	100.0	100.0	100.0	100.0	100.0	100.0
1976	102.6	101.0	102.4	99.8	101.5	109.7	102.1
1977	101.0	104.6	105.6	105.5	102.4	111.4	108.5
1978	103.1	105.5	107.7	107.5	105.1	115.6	113.5
1979	106.9	105.7	110.6	107.7	102.5	118.7	120.2
1980	103.4	107.7	113.0	108.7	99.1	116.1	125.2
1981	105.8	107.2	115.3	109.4	92.9	115.6	126.3
1982	108.9	108.8	115.1	113.4	91.2	117.2	126.4
1983	106.6	110.1	117.4	112.4	94.8	116.9	126.7
1984	109.9	112.5	120.9	115.6	97.4	123.5	128.8
1985	106.6	113.0	124.8	113.0	97.6	124.5	128.7
1986	111.8	115.1	126.8	115.6	99.6	131.2	132.7
1987	110.7	116.0	128.9	117.0	97.3	131.9	131.3
1988[a]	103.0	108.4	98.0	104.1	101.2	126.3	130.7

[a] 1988 data are provisional, based on available incomplete or preliminary data.
Source: Thad Alton, "East European GNP's, Domestic Final Uses of Gross Product, Rates of Growth, and International Comparisons," in 101st Congress, *Joint Economic Committee Pressures for Reform in the East European Economies* (Washington, D.C.: U.S. Government Printing Office, 1989), Vol. 1, p. 82.

falling below 1975 levels practically for the entire decade of the 1980s.

These figures can also be compared with the average annual growth rates for the GNPs of less developed countries (LDCs), the USSR, and the advanced industrial countries which are members of the Organization for Economic Cooperation and Development (OECD). These comparisons are presented in Figure 6.1.

Clearly, no economic grouping was able to continue growth rates in the 1970s and 1980s at the levels achieved in the 1960s. Indeed, during the 1970s, East European economies continued to grow at a faster pace, on average, than their OECD counterparts, giving some credence to the argument of East European central planners that the nature of their systems protected them from some of the worst effects of OPEC (Organization of Petroleum Exporting Countries) oil price increases at the beginning of the decade. Nevertheless, over the three decades 1960–90, East European economies grew at a slower rate than any of their counterparts, including the Soviet Union. Moreover, be-

Figure 6.1. Average annual percentage growth of GNP.
Source: *PlanEcon Report,* Vol. 5, No. 42–3, November 3, 1989, p. 5.

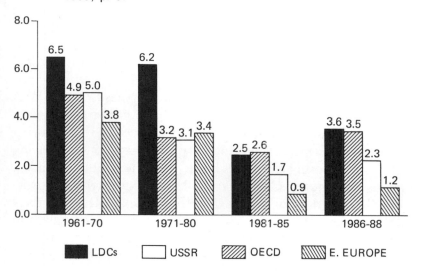

cause these economies were structured to favor heavy industrial production over consumer industries and agriculture, populations in Eastern Europe experienced a much greater decline in living standard than is indicated by gross GNP or GNP per capita figures.

This slowdown in Eastern Europe created enormous economic and political problems. In the early decades, impressive growth levels had been achieved primarily through "extensive" development, that is, through high inputs of capital investment, labor, and natural resources. All these inputs became more scarce in the 1970s and 1980s: Financial reserves shrank, declining birthrates and higher educational attainment reduced the labor pool available for unskilled and semiskilled work, and the poorly endowed East European countries became even more dependent on imported raw materials as existing reserves declined and were squandered by planners whose insensitivity to environmental concerns created an ecological wasteland in Central Europe.

Having squeezed all the potential out of extensive development, planners sought to achieve economic progress through "intensive" growth which would increase the efficiency of production. Planners sought to improve efficiency through the infusion of technology into the production process, and rather than spend decades developing indigenous high-technology industries, it was decided to import this technology directly from the West. In that way it was hoped that a "quick fix" could be achieved, with Western banks providing short-term credits for the purchase of high-technology imports which would be repaid in the long term through export of the products of restructured industries.

That strategy, however, did not work. Imports from the West did increase, but efficiency did not. A huge hard-currency debt was incurred, but because they did not succeed in restructuring the economy to increase productivity, the prospects for repaying it without imposing enormous burdens on the population faded. Figures presented in Chapter 4 (Table 4.1) showed that the gross hard-currency debt of the six East European CMEA members (CMEA-6) increased from $6.1 billion in 1971 to $95.6 billion in 1988. The imports had not been used to restructure the economies. The conclusions of a report from the Joint Economic Committee of the U.S. Congress made it clear:

The strategy did not work in part because of excessive investment in import-intensive industries, neglect of modernizing the agricultural sector, and the use of government subsidies to raise living standards to artificially high levels. Decisions regarding the level and composition of imports were based more on considerations of ideology, political expediency, and excess demand than on cost or efficiency. . . . [T]he opportunities for development were squandered.[12]

As a result, the need to service hard-currency debt became an additional burden on already overloaded and weakened economies. Rather than being able to enter the 1990s with sleeker and more efficient industries, these countries faced the prospect of still having to implement basic economic reforms twenty years after any possibility for sustained growth had been exhausted. Realization of that fact underlay both the apathy of local populations and their growing awareness that in the absence of fundamental political reform, no economic progress could be made. That was why virtually every major demonstration in Eastern Europe in the troubled 1980s called not only for political freedoms but also for thoroughgoing market reforms.

The responses to these problems in individual countries varied, as did the remedies adopted. Differences between the countries resulted not only from varying internal economic conditions but also from the dynamics between political and social forces within each country, as well as their responses to external pressures and opportunities.

Problems and Remedies

East European economies had been interlinked in certain important ways. They had the same legacy of central planning and control imposed on them by the Soviet Union in the late 1940s, a legacy that exerted a major influence on economic activity, even in those countries like Bulgaria, Poland, Hungary, and the GDR that introduced reforms of one or more sectors of their economies beginning in the late 1960s.

Apart from structural similarities and Soviet interest in maintaining them, these countries also were linked by the fact that they were each other's major trading partners. As Figures 6.2

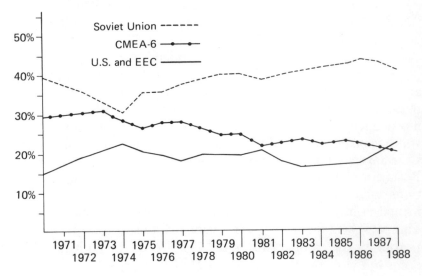

Figure 6.2. Percentages of East European imports by trading partners. Source: *1980 Yearbook of International Trade Statistics* (New York: United Nations, 1981); *Monthly Bulletin of Trade Statistics* (New York: United Nations).

and 6.3 show, although East European trade with non-CMEA countries grew throughout the 1970s and 1980s, total intrabloc trade still accounted for over 50 percent of all East European trade. Of particular importance is the fact that although the Soviet Union's share of East European trade declined in the early and middle 1970s, it was once again on the increase after 1975. However, that increase occurred not at the expense of Eastern Europe's trade with Western countries, which increased over the entire period, but at the expense of intra–East European trade, which declined markedly throughout the period.

After 1986, however, the share of Soviet imports in total CMEA-6 imports declined, as clearly indicated by Figures 6.2 and 6.3. That occurred partially as a result of a deliberate reorientation of trade by the Soviet Union and partially because of a marked drop in world oil prices after 1986. That made the energy that East Europe received from the Soviet Union cheaper and

Figure 6.3. Percentages of East European exports by trading partners. Source: *1980 Yearbook of International Trade Statistics* (New York: United Nations, 1981); *Monthly Bulletin of Trade Statistics* (New York: United Nations).

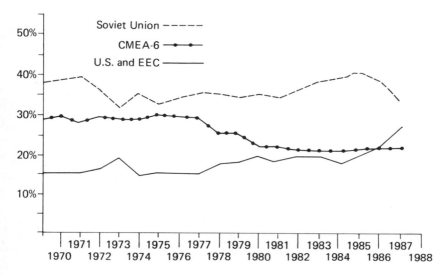

also decreased Soviet imports as a share of total CMEA-6 imports. One effect was that by 1989 Hungary and Czechoslovakia had run up enormous trade surpluses with Moscow, amounting to approximately 1 billion transferable rubles. The USSR did not move quickly to redress that imbalance, both because of continuing low world oil prices and because of energy shortages within the USSR itself during the politically troublesome winter of 1989. As a result, East European interest in looking elsewhere for trade was stimulated, with exports to the USSR also declining in the late 1980s.

These factors increased the likelihood that in the short term, at least, there would continue to be marked shifts in intrabloc trade away from the Soviet Union. Trade among the CMEA-6 was likely to increase, particularly amongst Czechoslovakia, Poland, and Hungary, and overall East European trade with hard-currency markets was also likely to see steady improvement. Such an improvement was, of course, dependent upon overcoming the many structural impediments in both the political and economic realms that continued to plague these countries.

The Case of Hungary. The New Economic Mechanism introduced by Kádár in 1968 was implemented by using economic regulators such as credits, exchange rates, taxes, and prices to supplement production targets as guides to economic activity. Laws were also introduced that allowed enterprises to trade directly with those in other countries. Such measures were designed to diminish inefficiency and shorten the time needed to respond to marketplace demands. While the growth rates achieved by the Hungarians in the 1970s were not as high as in some other CMEA countries, as shown in Tables 6.1 and 6.2, significant improvements were made in the provision of foodstuffs, consumer goods, and services.

One of the problems faced by the Hungarians was that while such reforms helped them trade with Western companies, the same reforms were actually impediments to trade with CMEA counterparts. Up until the end of 1986, when selected reforms were introduced, the ministries of foreign trade in all bloc countries except Hungary exercised total control over all external trading relations. That structural imbalance between a decentralized system in Hungary and a centralized system elsewhere effectively blunted the beneficial effects of the Hungarian reform and put decentralized Hungarian firms at a disadvantage when negotiating with larger and more powerful centralized ministries in other CMEA countries.

But not all of Hungary's problems were imported from abroad. In the early 1970s, the reform came under pressure from conservatives, who feared both the loss of central control and the long-term political effects of the growing differentiation of incomes that was making itself felt in societal relations. The reformers also supported efforts by the government to protect the economy from the oil price rises of 1974 and 1979. As a result, subsidies and price supports were introduced that protected living standards, but also lessened the impact of economic regulators. As a result, growth began to slow, and trade deficits mounted.

In 1985 and 1986, Hungary had two years of zero or even negative growth, which, along with a current-account deficit in 1986 of $1.4 billion, further frustrated efforts to reduce the country's debt burden. Although Hungary's debt was not as high in absolute terms as Poland's, it was higher than Poland's in per capita terms. As Table 6.3 shows, in 1982 the debt represented 15 percent of Hungary's total GNP.

In an effort to reduce its hard-currency debt and eliminate trade deficits, the Hungarian government maintained investments in the profitable and export-oriented agricultural sector. It also decided to protect the living standard of the politically important urban working population, while holding the wages and pensions of other groups at 1980 levels. In industry, investment was reduced, with measures being introduced – including a bankruptcy law and greater foreign investment in chemical, pharmaceutical, and banking sectors – designed to increase enterprise efficiency and provide for imports of foreign technology and investment that the central government otherwise would have to forgo.

Despite these efforts, the seventh Five-Year Plan (1986–91) forecast that real growth would average only 2 percent each year. Some Hungarian economists, however, felt that even that growth rate was unachievable. Looking at the plan gloomily, one predicted that "should the seventh Five-Year Plan be fulfilled the way it has been adopted, it would set our international rating back by 15 to 20 places."[13]

This pessimism was increased by concern that because of the inefficiency of intra-CMEA trade, any increase in such trade, which was being encouraged by Moscow, would only further damage Hungary's economic recovery.[14] Moreover, the Soviets were insisting that the quality of goods imported from Eastern Europe be improved. As a result, Hungarian planners had to take measures to upgrade all exports, not just those designated for export to the West.

Finally, a growing portion of Hungary's trade with the bloc was being designated in hard currency, with 15–20 percent of USSR–Hungarian trade in 1985 conducted in dollars, including vital oil imports from the Soviet Union. The result, as noted by a specialist in Hungarian fiscal policy, was that "the structure of

Table 6.3. *Eastern Europe: debt indicators for 1982 and country rankings*

Country	Net debt in percentage of exports to the West	Per capita net debt (U.S. dollars)	Net debt in percentage of GNP[a]	Short-term liabilities[b] in percentage of exports to the West	Debt ranking[c]	Assets[a] in percentage of imports from the West	Liquidity ranking[c]	Final ranking[c]
Bulgaria	141	199	4.4	85	2	52	1	1
Czechoslovakia	117	212	3.7	32	1	25	4	2
GDR	166	663	8.6	52	3	35	2	3
Hungary	267	657	15.0	85	5	23	5	4
Poland	649	656	21.2	125	6	33	3	6
Romania	268	417	17.2	47	4	18	6	5
Eastern Europe	274	510	12.0	68		31		

[a]GNP according to World Bank *Atlas*; Vienna Institute for Comparative Economic Studies update using net material product growth rates.
[b]Liabilities of up to one year with commercial banks reporting to Bank for International Settlement (maturity distribution end 1982); BIS, 1983.
[c]Best = 1.
[d]Assets with commercial banks reporting to BIS.
Source: Joint Economic Committee, U.S. Congress, *East European Economies: Slow Growth in the 1980s* (Washington, D.C.: U.S. Government Printing Office, 1985), Vol. 1, p. 216.

our foreign trade with the CMEA countries will place increasing burdens on our hard-currency balance of payments in the future."[15]

The situation moving into the 1990s remained bleak. The Hungarians had a huge foreign debt, which, as shown in Figure 6.4 neared $20 billion and imposed the highest per capita burden of any within Eastern Europe, and inflation was projected at 20 percent and rising. Western creditors, led by the International Monetary Fund (IMF), had begun to insist on sharp austerity measures to curb domestic consumption, which nevertheless grew by 4 percent in 1989. Comprehensive economic reforms began to be implemented, including property and enterprise ownership by foreign investors, the selling of unprofitable state-run enterprises, and a 25 percent rise in food prices.

These measures came into effect at the same time that major social and political transitions were under way. In October 1989, a majority of the ruling Hungarian Socialist Workers' Party split off to form a new Hungarian Socialist Party. The old HSWP retained Károly Grósz and János Berecz among its leaders, with Resző Nyers, Imre Pozsgay, and Prime Minister Miklós Németh going over to lead the new HSP. Although the HSP certainly garnered initial popular support, the standing of neither party was high amongst the population, with the HSP being charged with attempting to maintain itself as a ruling party.

This absence of strong national consensus led to a proliferation of groups and parties in the run-up to the national elections held in March 1990. While Hungary's population showed none of the high mobilization characteristics of other bloc states in 1989, many real challenges still faced the country.

The Case of Poland. Polish economic performance during the 1970s and 1980s showed extremely wide variation. The annual rate of growth of GNP, both in total and in per capita terms (as indicated in Tables 6.1 and 6.2), showed Poland to be the fastest-growing economy between 1970 and 1975, but the slowest-growing economy in both 1975–80 and 1980–5. Serious disruptions caused by the debt crisis and the rise of Solidarity in 1979–82 led to further decline in the Polish economy, and despite more favorable growth rates in 1983 and 1984, per capita GNP rose in 1985 only to the level achieved a decade previously.

More than most other East European countries during this period, Poland was faced with very stark conflicting demands on limited resources. In the area of personal consumption, leaders realized the need to protect and raise living standards, both to increase labor productivity and to decrease worker unrest. Food availability above all was crucial in a country where food price increases had sparked repeated riots, including those which had preceded PUWP General Secretary Edward Gierek's downfall and the rise of Solidarity in August 1980. Per capita food consumption declined 15 percent in 1981–3, with meat consumption dropping 23 percent in 1981–4 and recovering only 4 percent in 1985. That decline in food supplies harmed government attempts to reestablish some measure of stability and growth in the country, since their inability to deal with this crucial area not only had a real impact on labor productivity but also led the population to believe that economic growth had not been achieved.

The drop in food supplies unfortunately was not matched by an increase in investment at the end of the 1970s. Poor planning earlier in that decade had resulted in many ill-conceived projects that relied on Western parts and materials that by the early 1980s Poland could no longer afford. The Solidarity crisis exacerbated difficulties because the government could not sufficiently reduce funds devoted to consumption in the 1979–82 period. Thus, the reduction in total productive investment was double the reduction in funds for consumption in this period.

The decline in funds for consumption and investment coincided with a third element in the early 1980s – the enormous debt crisis. As Table 6.3 indicates, Poland's hard-currency debt in 1982 was the highest in Eastern Europe, both as a percentage of exports to the West (649 percent) and as a percentage of GNP (21.2 percent). Poland sought to meet debt repayment schedules by cutting imports, but poor labor productivity rates prevented any major increase in exports. There seemed little hope that Poland would be able to meet all interest payments on its debt, let alone repay any principal. Even if Poland's annual growth rate targets of 3–4 percent were met, Western bankers considered it unlikely that much headway could be made toward debt elimination before the mid-1990s. Nevertheless, Poland continued to import substantial quantities from the West and appeared committed to maintaining the link at all costs.

Poland also developed a significant debt with its CMEA trading partners. At the height of the Polish crisis in 1981, the trade deficit was highest, amounting to 1.8 billion rubles, of which 1.6 billion was with the Soviet Union. Under considerable pressure from other East European countries, Poland reduced the imbalance over the next four years, so that by 1985 its deficit was under 700 million rubles in total. It was the East Europeans and not the Soviets, however, who were the major beneficiaries of Polish efforts, since Moscow continued to provide economic assistance to Poland by allowing Warsaw to run average annual trade deficits of 600 million rubles throughout the 1982–5 period.

The economic problems Poland faced were enormous, and economic reforms were impossible to implement without political reconciliation. Reforms introduced in 1982 to decentralize the economy were implemented in name only, while government efforts in November 1986 to recentralize also brought condemnation from all sides.

The Jaruzelski regime attempted to balance competing demands being made by its own very volatile population, Western creditors, and CMEA partners – all of whom had an interest in preventing the collapse of the Polish economy, but none of whom possessed either the economic capability or the political will to lend the massive further assistance necessary to lift the Polish economy out of stagnation. The further lifting of international economic sanctions and the announcement in mid-October 1987 of sweeping economic decentralization and political reform underlined the efforts being made to restore growth and stability to the Polish economy.

The new Solidarity-led government which took over in September 1989 following popular elections marked a victory for opposition politics both in Poland and in the bloc more generally. Solidarity stood towering over the events of 1989, being both the midwife of those events and the only opposition party to command an overwhelming majority of the electorate in its own country. It took over control of key economic, social, and foreign-affairs ministries, conceding continued control over defense and internal security to the PUWP. Under such circumstances, the PUWP rapidly began to lose authority, with the January 1990 congress its last before the emergence of two rival reformist alternative groupings along the Hungarian model. The Catholic Church was able to reemerge fully into public life, with legislation passed in May 1989 giving it guarantees of independence.

All this served as preparation for the economic shocks imposed by the crash reform program introduced in January 1990. Clearly attempting to maintain its lead within the bloc, the Sejm removed almost all price controls, converted many state-owned companies to private ownership, ended subsidies to unprofitable enterprises, and allowed layoffs and bankruptcies. The plan was widely expected to produce extremely high short-term four-digit inflation and six-figure unemployment.

The use of wage controls to dampen inflationary pressures was particularly sensitive for a government which had criticized communists for never having truly represented workers' interests. The reform package was pushed through by Solidarity economists, who won the argument being waged throughout the Soviet bloc, namely, whether or not piecemeal reform could succeed. Clearly, in Poland, they felt it could not, but the high moral standing of Solidarity and the ethnic and religious homogeneity of Poland made it politically more feasible to introduce harsh measures there than elsewhere.

The Case of Romania. Of all the countries of Eastern Europe, Romania's prospects were the most bleak in the early 1980s. The causes of its problems were familiar ones, but were exacerbated in Romania's case by an overemphasis on heavy industry at the expense of agriculture, a dependence on imported oil at a time of market volatility, and a particularly centralized and inefficient bureaucracy.

All CMEA countries had energy problems in this period, but Romania was particularly hard hit. Previously self-sufficient in oil and natural gas in the 1960s, Romania had built an extensive oil refining and petrochemical industry to meet indigenous and export requirements.

By the mid-1970s, however, oil production had peaked, and by 1980 Romania was producing only 250,000 barrels per day, despite the fact that it had a daily refining capacity of almost 700,000 barrels. The difference was imported, which left the country's key industry (to say nothing of the rest of the economy) open to severe price fluctuations in crude oil and oil products.

A trade surplus in oil products in the early 1970s evaporated under the impact of two successive OPEC price increases – increases that hurt Romania more than other bloc countries because it did not receive large quantities of oil from the USSR at concessionary prices. Thus, Romania showed only a small deficit in petroleum transactions in 1979, importing almost 37 billion lei (the local currency) worth of crude petroleum and exporting 33.5 billion lei of petroleum products; in the following year, however, when the full impact of the second oil price shock was felt, Romania's imports were valued at 68.7 billion lei, while its exports of petroleum products brought only 39.7 billion lei. That differential produced a deficit of $1.5 billion for that year alone.[16]

Ceauşescu financed his continued hard-currency imports with credits throughout the 1970s, and by 1980 the Romanian debt stood in excess of $10 billion. Not as worried about domestic unrest as the Poles or as sensitive to consumer needs as the Hungarians, Ceauşescu implemented a harsh austerity program to reduce domestic consumption in order to service the debt. Particularly in the energy field, household heat and light were strictly rationed in order that energy savings could be exported to reduce the debt. By 1989, Romania had succeeded in paying off its debt altogether.

As the world's largest producer of crude oil, the Soviet Union could have assisted Romania by increasing exports of oil for refining and resale by Romania. Although Soviet exports did increase slightly, they came nowhere near Soviet oil exports to other CMEA countries, apparently reflecting preferential treatment for more loyal allies. Not until after Ceauşescu was overthrown did Soviet oil deliveries improve, with Foreign Minister Shevardnadze emphasizing during his first meeting in Bucharest with the new Iliescu leadership that large-scale emergency supplies of oil would be sent to Romania to prevent a crisis during the winter months. In addition, Romania would no longer be required to export its equally scarce food to the Soviet Union.

Although Ceauşescu succeeded in eliminating the debt burden, he did so at the cost of enormous suffering by his own people. The debt was repaid not by higher Romanian productivity or by efficient garnering of resources, but through sheer exploitation of the population. Moreover, he was able to extract that heavy toll because he systematically destroyed any institutional alternative to his power, including the Romanian Communist Party. In its place, he ruled through the internal security forces, the Securitate, and with the help of a family clique. At the height of his power, he and his wife, Elena, personally controlled the *nomenklatura,* with most top positions going to family members. Thus, Ceauşescu's brothers controlled the armed forces, counterintelligence, and agriculture, with Elena's brother running the trade unions, and their son in charge of the Young Communist League. The family literally considered the country to be their personal property, with millions of dollars spent on their lavish life-style in Romania, and further millions put into Swiss banks. The country also was unusually isolated internationally, with both Eastern and Western leaders holding little sway in Bucharest.

As a result, although the paying off of the foreign debt was considered by some to have been a significant achievement by Ceauşescu, in fact the debt was paid by the Romanian people. The legacy left by Ceauşescu was one of complete excess, rigidity, and insensitivity to the people's suffering. When he was overthrown, and ultimately shot, along with his wife, on December 25, 1989, he left a country without any institutions which had credibility or popular support.

Whereas the process of de-Stalinization had been gradual in most bloc countries, in Romania it was achieved practically overnight. In the first two weeks of the new regime, enormous legal changes were made in the entire structure of state–society relations. Romanians were given the right to organize new political parties, meet with foreigners, attend church services, travel abroad, have abortions, and circulate materials without the approval of the censors and the police. The absence of any democratic tradition in Romania, and the repression of the Ceauşescu years, made it difficult for political leadership to emerge out of the revolutionary events. Enormous suspicion surrounded even those leaders in the National Salvation Front who had risked their lives in overthrowing Ceauşescu. The front operated as an umbrella organization for all political trends until the end of January 1990, when it announced that it would form itself into a political party and run candidates in the elections scheduled for that year. That decision met with resistance from liberal intellectuals and students concerned about the front's grasp on power. Alternative political parties began to appear, and the front agreed to share power even before planned elections. It seemed clear, however, that it would be some time before an efficiently functioning multiparty democracy could be established in the country.

Economic recovery would also take time. Living standards were the lowest in Europe (barring Albania), making it difficult to imagine that the population could shoulder any further sacrifices in the transition to a market economy. Additionally, practically no modernization of industry had been carried out, with Western economists estimating that perhaps 25 percent of the labor force would lose their jobs if unprofitable industries were closed down. However, the country does have greater potential for developing natural resources and agriculture than some of the other East European countries, giving it a good long-term potential.

The Case of Bulgaria. Prior to the communist revolution, Bulgaria was among the least developed states of Europe, with 82 percent of its population still employed in agriculture in 1948. It is still among Europe's poorest countries, although major changes have been made in the economy to bring it up to modern levels.

Rapid industrialization brought high growth rates and shifts in the demographic structure of the working population. By the early 1980s, only 24 percent of the Bulgarian population remained in the agricultural sector. Annual GNP growth rates showed Bulgaria to be less affected by the debt crisis of the early 1980s than were the other bloc countries. Growth rates remained slightly in excess of 4 percent per annum for the 1970–5 period, declined to 1.2 percent for 1975–80, then declined further to 0.9 percent for 1980–5. Despite one good year in 1986, economic performance was lackluster throughout the late 1980s. The per capita growth rates presented in Table 6.2 indicate the same general trend.

Bulgaria was more dependent on trade with the USSR and other CMEA countries than were its bloc allies, and thus it was cushioned to a certain extent from the debt crisis in the late 1970s. The nation also maintained a high trade surplus with developing countries, which offset its own deficit with the West. With a net debt of only $1.8 billion in 1982 (or only 4.4 percent of GNP, compared with 21.2 percent for Poland) and large assets deposited with commercial banks, Bulgaria had the best ranking of all CMEA countries in the early 1980s, as shown in Table 6.3.

Bulgarian economic performance had been assisted by reforms introduced in the 1970s. In the agricultural sector, agro-industrial enterprises were established to eliminate the decline of agriculture, which was the only sector with a negative growth rate in the 1965–80 period.[17]

The reforms were extended in 1982 to other sectors. The basic principles guiding them had become familiar in countries like Hungary and included economic accountability, reduction in centralized planning, enterprise self-sufficiency, and profit sharing by workers. These reforms produced a higher standard of living and improved availability of foodstuffs. Thus, while the Zhivkov regime had hardly been the most dynamic in the bloc, these measures, plus greater emphasis on Bulgarian national culture, contributed to stability.

When Gorbachev came to power, debates about further reform increased. Although the Bulgarian leadership initially resisted calls for more reform, and even withdrew from public debate the draft "Regulations on Economic Activity" in November 1986, by July of the following year, important new measures were approved by the party and government. Among them were a new labor code, a code on economic activity, and a law establishing independently financed trade banks. The implications of the changes were seen as far-reaching, with Zhivkov himself stating that "direct self-management must be introduced in all fields of work" and bluntly warning that "an enterprise that works badly must go bankrupt."[18] If consistently implemented, the reforms would have been among the most radical in the bloc.

Like previous reforms, however, the "July concept" remained largely on paper. By the beginning of 1986, Bulgaria's hard-currency debt had begun to increase, and by the second quarter of 1989 the gross debt was in excess of $7 billion. Along with Hungary and Poland, Bulgaria then had the worst per capita net (gross debt minus reserves) debt burden in Eastern Europe. This is shown in Figure 6.4.

The introduction in January 1989 of another set of poorly prepared decrees had created further chaos in the economy. In an effort to attract foreign investors, the Bulgarian government, in promulgating the famous "Decree No. 56," had announced that self-governing enterprises "might" be transformed into firms, including joint-stock companies. But no clear guidelines were developed, leaving individual units at odds over its interpretation. That decree and others similar to it were abandoned once Zhivkov was overthrown.

Under General Secretary Petar Mladenov and Andrei Lukanov, his deputy for economic and financial matters, early efforts were made to reassure both domestic and foreign audiences that reform efforts would be concerted and serious. A legal framework for democracy was established in December 1989 during meetings of the National Assembly, with the groundwork for a full review of the labor code, and statutes governing property ownership, state and personal finance, and party activity also promised. Continued communist control of all central institutions created suspicion amongst new political groupings, however, with the prospect that economic reforms also would be jeopardized unless national consensus could be achieved. Popular pressure produced a leadership shake-up early in 1990 in which Mladenov and Lukanov resigned their party positions, becoming president and prime minister, respectively. The party, however, still remained entrenched in the country.

The Case of Czechoslovakia. Almost any indicator will show Czechoslovakia to have been one of the best-performing CMEA

Figure 6.4. Soviet and East European gross and net hard-currency debt, totals and per capita, 1988. Source: *PlanEcon Report,* Vol. 6, No. 1–2, January 12, 1990, p. 29.

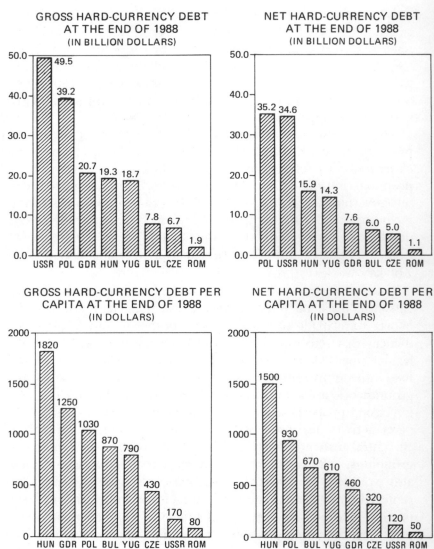

economies in the 1970s and 1980s. Annual rates of growth in GNP, presented in Table 6.1, indicate that Prague maintained an average annual rate slightly below 2 percent for the entire 1970–88 period. Moreover, the debt indicators given in Table 6.3 and Figure 6.4 reveal that using any number of indicators, whether gross or net debt, or per capita debt, the burden of hard-currency debt on Czechoslovakia started out low and has remained low.

The economic aspects of the policy of so-called normalization introduced by Husák after taking power as general secretary in 1969 stressed increasing the standard of living of Czechoslovak citizens and bringing the relatively underdeveloped Slovak region up to the standards of the Czech lands. Both policies met with some success. Czechoslovakia ranked among the leaders in almost every category.

While the economy grew steadily during the 1970s, nevertheless it experienced some of the same stagnation and declining growth rates seen in neighboring economies. Difficulty in transforming the economy from extensive to intensive development remained, despite government recognition of key industries that should be targeted for favored investment treatment.

In particular, Czechoslovak planners emphasized the production of nuclear power to diminish dependence on indigenous coal supplies and imported oil. As in other targeted industries, efforts were hampered by technical supply problems, labor shortages, construction delays, and the central planners' continued emphasis on gross output as the primary indicator of enterprise performance. Thus, despite the fact that the nuclear-power-plant construction program received as much as one-fifth of all capital investment in the early 1980s, the construction of nuclear power plants remained well behind schedule.[19]

Under Husák, the government's response to its economic problems was to emphasize the need to improve central planning, not abandon it. Additional measures introduced in the early 1980s stressed energy efficiency, quality controls, and enterprise rewards for increased output. In external relations, Czechoslovakia's orientation towards intra-CMEA trading was also increased. Clearly, even after Gorbachev came to power, substantial reform of the Czechoslovak system was going to prove difficult, both because of the political resistance offered by the conservative leadership and because of the relative economic success of central planning as practiced in the 1970–85 period.

Czechoslovakia's high standard of living compared with other East European countries, however, ultimately did not cushion its leadership against the pressures for political reform. With the continuing introduction by Gorbachev of plans for further economic decentralization, limited privatization, and political democratization, Poland and Hungary were given the green light to put their own reforms into motion. That put enormous pressure on the Czechoslovak leaders, who knew that it would be politically very costly to be seen to be siding with those regimes in Bucharest, Sofia, and East Berlin that were becoming increasingly unpopular domestically. Leadership changes began in 1988 in an attempt to appease popular pressure without changing the structure, but that palliative was only temporary.

Under the influence of a core group of the same hard-liners who had invited in the Soviet troops in 1968, the decision was made, late in the autumn of 1989, to resist change to the last. Even as thousands of young East Germans sought haven in the West German Embassy in Prague, seeking exit visas to the West, repression against Czechoslovak citizens increased. A full six months after Polish and Hungarian governments had approved plans to decentralize and privatize their economies, Czechoslovak economists were still being obliged to draw up drafts for the next Five-Year Plan. And fully a month after the Berlin Wall had been opened, with East Germans being allowed to join their Hungarian and Polish counterparts in practically unlimited rights to travel abroad, Czechoslovak citizens still had no right to a passport. Instead, the leadership had decided to take the Chinese route – to forcibly put down student democracy demonstrations. Rudolf Hegenbart, a senior party official responsible for state security, stated subsequently that a decision was made to use force against demonstrators, but, crucially, that decision was rescinded under enormous pressure from Soviet diplomatic and military sources.[20] As a result, within one week the entire structure of communist control of Czechoslovakia crumbled.

The entire old guard within the top leadership was forced to resign. Civic Forum was founded, and Václav Havel emerged as its leader; ne was then elected by the Federal Assembly as the interim president of the republic. Reformers who had been purged after

1968 were allowed to return, with former General Secretary Alexander Dubček elected president of the Federal Assembly. The communists' right to exercise a monopoly of power was removed as a provision in the constitution, and a government with a noncommunist majority was named. The whole process had taken less than six weeks.

The reforms of the economy would take longer. But the strength of reform-minded and expert economists in key positions within the new government ensured that a blueprint for the most wide-ranging overhaul of the system would be introduced within the shortest possible time. The intrinsic strength of the economy (despite the catastrophic pollution caused primarily by industrial emission of 3.5 million metric tons of sulfur dioxide per year – twice that of West Germany), the quality of its labor force, the relative absence of social and ethnic tensions within the country, and the history of close relations with Western Europe would stand the economy in good stead in making the core transitions that were planned.

The Case of the GDR. Ever since the failure of the 1968 reform movement in Prague, the East German leadership had prided itself on maintaining steady increases in labor productivity and economic growth without introducing fundamental political reform. The provision of stable prices, relatively good housing, increased wages, and favorable working conditions did much to contribute to East Germany's position as the most developed socialist state.

The economic pressures of the early 1980s were felt in East Germany, too, where the regime introduced an austerity program and a campaign to increase labor productivity 30 percent over five years.[21] The growth in labor productivity was to be achieved both by harder work on the part of the population and by so-called socialist rationalization of the production process. That would entail organizational changes as well as greater energy efficiency and automation in the production process.

Organizational changes played an important part in East German successes and were publicly admired by other bloc leaders, including Gorbachev. At the highest levels, the ministerial structure was considerably streamlined, with economic ministries surrendering much of their power to newly formed combines.

These combines grouped research and development functions directly with production so as to minimize the time lag between technological innovation and industrial infusion. Ministries and combines shared planning functions, and success was determined more by profitability than by production. The regime also allowed some private and collective enterprises in the service, craft, and retail-trade sectors, which helped to ease consumer demand.

Energy conservation also played a part in boosting growth rates. In Czechoslovakia, Hungary, and Poland (data for Bulgaria and Romania are unavailable), the growth in electric power consumption by industry continued to outpace the growth of output. In the GDR, however, that trend had been reversed by 1981, where, for example, the chemical industry's output grew by 3.2 percent between 1975 and 1981, while its use of power grew by only 0.6 percent in the same period. Similar results were achieved in the machinery sector.[22] In the economy as a whole, Wharton Econometrics calculated that the ratio of energy used to national income earned dropped between 1979 and 1982 by 9 percent in East Germany, followed by Bulgaria, Hungary, and Romania with 4–5 percent, and Czechoslovakia with 3–4 percent. In Poland, because of the disastrous collapse in output, the 1982 ratio exceeded the 1979 level by 29 percent.[23] The East German regime was also able to reduce the demand for expensive imported oil by switching to dwindling – and highly polluting – domestic supplies of brown coal, a policy that was meant to tide the country over until more nuclear energy was available. These factors set the GDR economy on a steady course for slow growth.

Automation, robotics, and microelectronics were all important components of the GDR's industrial strategy in the 1980s. East Germany boasted the most advanced computer industry in Eastern Europe (with Hungary the most advanced in computer software), as well as the largest number of robots at work in industry (over 30,000 in 1984, up from 220 in 1974).[24]

East Germany's greater relative success in meeting targets and maintaining slow but steady rates of growth made the leadership extremely confident about the correctness of its economic course. That stood in marked contrast to the self-criticism of the Soviets, the soul-searching of the Hungarians, and the other variations on a theme that existed throughout Eastern Europe.

Honecker's assertion at the SED Central Committee plenum in June 1986 that the GDR was "no field of experimentation" further confirmed that while the East Germans certainly welcomed efforts to reform the Soviet economy, they had no intention of abandoning their own policies.

By the end of 1989, it was clear that such complacency was obviously misplaced: Growth rates had slowed to less than 2 percent; gross hard-currency debt per capita was the second highest in the bloc; and external economic relations with both the West and the Soviet Union were being affected adversely by the SED leadership's resistance to change. Even those poor statistics masked a sharper deterioration in living standards, with domestic debt estimated at 50 percent of national income.

Patience wore thin in both Bonn and Moscow as East German leaders resisted popular demands to change direction. Gorbachev's trip to East Berlin in October 1989 to celebrate the fortieth anniversary of the establishment of the GDR came at a time when record numbers of East German youth were seeking to emigrate to West Germany via Hungary, Czechoslovakia, and Poland. Within days of Gorbachev's departure, Honecker was replaced by Egon Krenz.

But popular demonstrations did not stop. Pressure from virtually every source produced the momentous decision on November 9 to open the Berlin Wall. It was this decision that set the seal on the development of a reform movement in the GDR which would be linked intrinsically with the question of German reunification, making it a qualitatively different process than other changes which took place in the bloc in 1989. All issues relating to future economic reform were related to the question of the form, structure, and intensiveness of West Germany's involvement in East German recovery. But beyond that, the future relations between these two parts of Germany would be of the deepest significance for the West, for international security, and for the Soviet Union. As such, they are considered in greater detail in Chapters 7 and 8.

Prospects

East European leaders may have been reconciled to a further period of reduced growth and political malaise into the 1990s, but their populations were not. The high rates of growth that had been achieved in the 1960s and 1970s as a result of rapid capital accumulation and continued capacity for extensive forms of development simply could not be achieved in the next decade.

All of the major "factors of production" – capital, labor, energy, and materials – were in short supply and were expected to increase only slightly in the late 1980s. Capital investment, which had already come to a virtual halt, was not expected to grow as long as the CMEA countries were grappling with external debt repayments.

Labor productivity declined in every country, with the exception of the GDR, between 1979 and 1984, which combined with a growing labor shortage. Clearly, East European economies were going to have to develop policies that would utilize existing labor more efficiently while introducing further mechanization and providing better incentives to individual workers to improve the quality of their work. Some measures were adopted by different East European countries in the early 1980s, but further attention to this problem would be required.

It was recognized that energy would continue to be a major concern to CMEA countries, all of which were very dependent on external sources of energy, whether they be Soviet and Middle Eastern oil and gas or Soviet electricity through the "Mir" power grid. Conservation had become an increasingly important factor, particularly since the Soviet Union continued to reduce its own deliveries to Eastern Europe while also insisting on payment in hard currency or equivalent commodities. Before the Chernobyl nuclear-power disaster in April 1986, all East European countries were pursuing rapid expansion in nuclear energy, with CMEA planners envisaging that 50 percent of the region's electricity would be generated by nuclear power in the year 2000. Chernobyl obviously set these plans back, both by slowing down the Soviet Union's own research and design program and by creating further domestic resistance to nuclear power.

Possibilities for growth in the East European economies could be realized only through structural reform, in both the USSR and Eastern Europe. First, given the size of the Soviet economy, which has an annual GNP almost triple the combined GNPs of all the East European states, a period of dynamic growth in the Soviet Union obviously would pull the East European economies along in its wake. Revisions in CMEA trading practices and pricing mechanisms would also do much to eliminate inefficiency and inequality in current practices.

All this depended crucially, however, on the success of Gorbachev's agenda for the Soviet Union, as well as on the stability and depth of economic and political changes in Eastern Europe over the next decade. Irrespective of the extent of reformist tendencies in Moscow under Gorbachev, the Soviet Union will continue to exert enormous and decisive influence on events in the bloc. Whether that influence will be positive or negative, however, depends on the reform of the Soviet economy. Recessionary trends throughout the Soviet bloc are to be expected as economies undergo transitions to market systems. It would be catastrophic for the same trends to appear without reforms in place to give hope to desperate populations. For without the feeling that there is light at the end of the tunnel, extremist and separatist tendencies will only be reinforced.

Notes

1 Leonid I. Abalkin, whose statement was made at a symposium in Yugoslavia, quoted in the Yugoslav magazine *Politika* (Belgrade), October 26, 1986, Radio Free Europe (RFE), *Yugoslav Situation Report*, No. 11, November 20, 1986, p. 37.

2 Reuters (Budapest), November 21, 1986.

3 *Scinteia* (Bucharest), August 20, 1989, Foreign Broadcast Information Service, *East European Daily Report (FBIS-EEU)*, August 22, 1989, p. 41; *Washington Post*, January 14, 1990.

4 Two detailed articles on the structure and power of the *nomenklatura* appeared in *Polityka*, September 2, 1989, and *Gazeta Wyborcza*, October 2, 1989, *FBIS-EEU*, October 2, 1989, pp. 57–62.

5 Radio Prague, December 4, 1986, RFE, *Czechoslovak Situation Report*, No. 17, December 22, 1986, p. 17.

6 Speech to the Communist Youth League, *Magyar Ifjúság*, December 6, 1985, Joint Publication Research Service, *East Europe Review* (JPRS, *EER*), March 3, 1986, p. 111.

7 For further details, see Otto Ulc, "Czechoslovakia," in Teresa Rakowska-Harmstone, ed. *Communism in Eastern Europe*, 2nd ed. (Bloomington: Indiana University Press, 1984), pp. 115–37.

8 *Társadalmi Szemle*, March 1976, p. 18, as quoted by Bennett Kovrig, "Hungary," in Rakowska-Harmstone, *op. cit.*, p. 105.

9   *Kritika* (Budapest), September 1983, JPRS, *EER,* November 28, 1983, p. 120.

10 Warsaw PAP (Polska Agencja Prasowa), in English, October 20, 1989, *FBIS-EEU,* November 2, 1989, p. 74; Warsaw Domestic Service, in Polish, *FBIS-EEU,* November 14, 1989, pp. 61–2; *Heti Vilaggazdasag* (Budapest), May 27, 1989, JPRS, *EER,* July 27, 1989, pp. 1–3; *Rudé právo* (Prague), November 9, 1989; *FBIS-EEU,* November 16, 1989, pp. 27–8; East Berlin ADN (Allgemeiner Deutscher Nachrichtendienst), in English, November 14, 1989, *FBIS-EEU,* November 14, 1989, pp. 24–5.

11 RFE, *Background Report,* No. 139, October 1, 1986, p. 45.

12 John P. Hardt and Richard F. Kaufman, "Introduction," 101st Congress, Joint Economic Committee, *Pressures for Reform in the East European Economies* (Washington, D.C.: U.S. Government Printing Office, 1989), Vol. 1, p. xii.

13 Academician József Bognár, director, World Economy Research Institute of the Hungarian Academy of Sciences, in *Külgazdaság,* No. 2, 1986, pp. 2–17, JPRS, *EER,* May 12, 1986, p. 29.

14 Ferenc Vissi, deputy chairman, National Material and Price Office, *ibid.,* p. 37.

15 László Antal, deputy director, Fiscal Research Institute, *ibid.,* p. 23.

16 International Monetary Fund, *International Financial Statistics,* June 1986, p. 404. Most of the statistics in this section are drawn from this source.

17 Thad P. Alton, "East European GNP's: Origins of Product, Final Uses, Rates of Growth, and International Comparison," Joint Economic Committee, U.S. Congress, *East European Economies: Slow Growth in the 1980s* (Washington, D.C.: U.S. Government Printing Office, 1985), Vol. 1, p. 120.

18 *Rabotnichesko delo,* May 1, 1987, *FBIS-EEU,* May 19, 1987, pp. C5, C8.

19 Josef C. Brada and J. Michael Montias, "Industrial Policy in East Europe: A Comparison of Poland, Czechoslovakia, and Hungary," in Joint Economic Committee, *op. cit.,* pp. 198–203.

20 *Washington Post,* January 14, 1990.

21 Arthur M. Hanhardt, Jr., "The German Democratic Republic," in Rakowska-Harmstone, *op. cit.,* p. 152.

22 Alex Wynnyczuk, "Electric Energy in Eastern Europe," in Joint Economic Committee, *op. cit.,* p. 365.

23 *The Economist,* April 20, 1985.

24 *Ibid.*

7

Beyond the Brezhnev Doctrine: Can Moscow Meet the Challenge of a New Europe?

Perestroika should not be blamed for the destruction of the political structure of Europe. It has been destroyed by the will of peoples no longer willing to put up with oppression. The undermining of faith in a Socialism based on suppression and violence began in the 1940s, not in 1985. . . . Today you can hear people say: . . . Why did we not foresee the events in these countries? We did. And that was why, starting in April 1985, we fundamentally restructured the nature of interstate ties with them, abandoned interference in their internal affairs, and stopped imposing solutions. But . . . it is easier to change policy than to change people. Many leaders in these countries were cut from the same cloth. . . . Some of them came to power not without the help of former Soviet leaders, but after April 1985 they could not be removed from power by the current Soviet leadership, since, I repeat, it had forsworn interference in other countries' internal affairs. This was the only correct decision. How many times was the country's image in the eyes of mankind distorted by such interference. Remember the Czechoslovak Spring? Surely the Czechoslovak Spring couldn't be regarded as imperialist intrigue. And how many examples of that kind there are!—Soviet Foreign Minister Eduard Shevardnadze, speaking against charges made by party conservatives that Gorbachev's policies had resulted in the "loss" of Eastern Europe, at the February 1990 plenum of the CPSU Central Committee.[1]

This lengthy but important quotation from Soviet Foreign Minister Shevardnadze sets the context for the enormous development in the Soviet attitude towards change in Eastern Europe which occurred in the years after Gorbachev took power. A major policy shift was achieved against resistance from conservatives both in Eastern Europe and in Moscow, with battles waged as much in Kremlin corridors as in East European streets.

While the upheavals started to flood world television screens only in 1989, the agenda for change began to be drawn up almost as soon as Gorbachev realized that the Europeanization of the Soviet Union could not proceed without the de-Sovietization of Eastern Europe. While this came to be the view of a major sector of the Soviet political elite only gradually, beginning in 1987 and 1988 Gorbachev began to assemble a group of experts who shared his radical vision of the East European future.

Gorbachev's East European Team

It is undoubtedly the case, as has been shown in previous chapters, that the election of Mikhail Gorbachev as general secretary of the CPSU awakened immense expectations in Moscow and throughout the Soviet bloc. Here was an opportunity under new leadership to take a fresh look at accumulated problems, including those affecting relations with Eastern Europe. In particular, what were going to be the limits of political reform in Eastern Europe, and how much uniform adherence to the principle of socialist internationalism were the Soviets going to demand? What progress could be made in solving economic problems facing the bloc, and how many of these problems could be solved through enhanced cooperation within the bloc and with the West?

Issues in these areas had remained unresolved as a combined result of the stagnation of the late 1970s and the Brezhnev, Andropov, and Chernenko succession crises of the early 1980s. Policy towards Eastern Europe also had been allowed to drift because of the deaths of other key leaders involved in formulating policy for Eastern Europe, including Prime Minister Aleksei Kosygin, Defense Minister Dmitrii Ustinov, and Party Secretaries Mikhail Suslov and Arvid Pel'she.

In the year after coming to power, Gorbachev also replaced many key officials formerly involved in decision-making for Eastern Europe, such as Foreign Minister Andrei Gromyko (who was essentially "kicked upstairs" to become the titular head of state before being retired in October 1988), Konstantin Rusakov, secretary of the Central Committee department responsible for liaison with the socialist bloc, and Boris Ponomarev, head of the International Department. Taking charge of relations with Eastern Europe was a whole new generation of Soviet officials. At the top were three new party secretaries – Aleksandr Yakovlev, Anatolii Dobrinin, and Vadim Medvedev – who, while all were given other responsibilities as well, nevertheless were involved both in meetings with East European leaders and in policy formulation for this region. Within the Central Committee departments, while some holdovers from the Brezhnev era remained, new faces emerged, amongst them men like Nikolai Shishlin and Georgii Shakhnazarov, who were on record for their reformist views.

These personnel changes occurred throughout the year following Gorbachev's accession and continued right up to the close of the much-awaited 27th Party Congress in 1986. As a result, the 27th Congress, far from marking the end of the period of reappraisal, appeared to fuel further expectations without providing definite guidelines as to the extent of possible changes in Eastern Europe.

It was only in the three years after the 27th Party Congress that substantial policy shifts towards Eastern Europe were made. Further personnel and organizational decisions served as a precursor to these shifts: Changes in the structure of the Central Committee apparatus reduced the role of this organization as a central player in policy debates about Eastern Europe.

At the end of September 1988, a hastily called session of the CPSU Central Committee approved organizational and leadership changes which weakened the hold of party conservatives on ideological and international issues. A number of leading conservatives were retired, including Andrei Gromyko, whose retirement as chairman of the Presidium of the Supreme Soviet (equivalent to the role of president) cleared the way for Gorbachev's own election to this position. Within the party secretariat, six commissions were established whose membership could include experts drawn from outside the Central Committee apparatus. These commissions included many conservatives, with, for example, Party Secretary Yegor Ligachev and former KGB chief Viktor Chebrikov assuming chairmanships of the commissions on agriculture and legal affairs, respectively. But leading liberals took over key portfolios which would affect relations with Eastern Europe: Aleksandr Yakovlev became secretary in charge of foreign affairs, and Vadim Medvedev assumed the portfolio for ideology. Working with them, formally and informally, were specialists drawn from the USSR Academy of Sciences (USA and Canada Institute director Georgii Arbatov, Institute for World Economy and International Relations Institute director Yevgenii Primakov, Institute for the Economics of the World Socialist System director Oleg Bogomolov, and several of these institutes' specialists), Central Committee workers Shishlin and Shakhnazarov, and Foreign Ministry personnel, including Foreign Minister Eduard Shevardnadze and officials from his new departments responsible for policy assessment and state-to-state relations with socialist countries.

Within the Central Committee *apparat,* the department responsible for liaison with the socialist bloc was abolished, with its functions taken over by the International Department, which itself was reorganized and drastically reduced in size. After the September 1988 plenum, many second-tier conservative *apparatchiks* also lost their positions. The new head of this department, Valentin Falin, himself a former ambassador to West Germany, worked with a group whose interests more closely suited Gorbachev's agenda. As such, specialists in U.S.–Soviet relations, arms control, and Western Europe were enlisted. Relations between the CPSU and socialist countries became the responsibility not of a full department but of a subsector within a department which obviously lacked the clout of its predecessor. The sector on East and West Europe was taken over by the first deputy chief of the International Department, Raphael P. Fyodorov, with the subsector on Eastern Europe headed by Georgii S. Ostroumov.

Several of Gorbachev's closest advisors began to move over to new positions in the Supreme Soviet once it became clear that the new legislative structure was going to emerge both as a serious power base for Gorbachev and as a major focus for policy debates on all issues, including Eastern Europe. Several – like Anatolii Dobrinin, Vadim Zagladin, and former chief of the General Staff Marshal Sergei Akhromeyev – were appointed as official advisors to the chairman of the Presidium of the Supreme Soviet (Gorbachev's formal title as president). Others took up positions within the Supreme Soviet itself, such as Yevgenii Primakov and Georgii Shakhnazarov, who respectively were elected to be chairmen of the Soviet of the Union (one of the two houses of the Supreme Soviet) and the International Affairs Committee of the Supreme Soviet. Primakov, who, along with Yakovlev and Shevardnadze, began to play a key role in providing new thinking in international and ideological issues, was also made a candidate member of the CPSU Politburo in 1989.

As this group came to be assembled, serious reconsideration of key issues began. Contentious debates on the crisis of socialism in Eastern Europe had already started within academic circles in the early and middle 1980s, but with so many of the key academic players rising to policy positions, their views could begin to gain a foothold at the summit of power. What, then, was the background to key debates, and to what extent did the 27th Party Congress and the years following it provide a clear enunciation of policy and principle? In particular, did Gorbachev himself foresee the changes which took place in Eastern Europe in 1989 and encourage them? If so, what were his motives, and what forms are envisaged for a reunified Europe?

The Emerging Debate

In the five-year interval between the 26th and 27th CPSU Congresses, a debate about the principles underlying the construction of socialism emerged in both the USSR and Eastern Europe. At the heart of this debate, which came to be carried on at the highest political level, were such key issues as the applicability and definition of the principle of socialist internationalism, the universal relevance of the Soviet economic model, and the prospects for reform of key political principles – including democratic centralism and the leading role of the party.

The concept of socialist internationalism was enunciated most explicitly by the Soviets in the aftermath of their invasion of Czechoslovakia in 1968. Soviet party theoreticians, in codifying what in the West came to be called the "Brezhnev Doctrine" or the "doctrine of limited sovereignty," pointed out that "every Communist Party is responsible not only to its own people but also to all the socialist countries." They went on to state that "the sovereignty of individual socialist countries cannot be counterposed to the interests of world socialism and the world revolutionary movement."[2]

The communist parties not under Moscow's direct control (i.e., those of Romania, China, Yugoslavia, Albania, and the Eurocommunists) refused to adhere to this principle from the very beginning. The Soviets' subsequent attempt to foist it on them at the 1976 meeting of ruling and non-ruling European communist parties in Berlin was also a failure. By the early 1980s, concomitant both with the downturn of Soviet–American relations and with the growing assertiveness of East European diplomacy in Europe as a result of the Helsinki process, several of the East European states – most notably the GDR, Hungary, Bulgaria, and Romania – openly promoted the state as co-equal to the class in both international and intrabloc relations.

In June 1984, at an economic summit of CMEA heads of state (the first the Soviets had succeeded in convening since 1971), the Soviet delegates and the Soviet press made repeated calls for closer integration of member states. There were even some references to the much criticized line enunciated by Brezhnev in 1976 at the 25th CPSU Congress that the "process of gradual drawing together of socialist countries is now operating quite definitely as an objective law."[3] The East European delegates almost uniformly called for greater attention to national differences, and the total absence from the final statement of any reference to integration as a universal law reflected their ultimate predominance.[4]

The succession from Chernenko to Gorbachev in March 1985 only further stimulated the debate. It appeared also to have been affected by the negotiations for the renewal of the Warsaw Pact Treaty, which culminated in a thirty-year extension signed in April 1985. During this period, István Roska, the Hungarian deputy foreign minister for Soviet-bloc relations, in an article that was reprinted in East Germany, pointedly stated that "the member states are independent and sovereign countries that, without exception, respect the principle of non-interference in each other's internal affairs." He went on to add that "anyone in touch with reality will be cognizant of these differences and not see them as an 'aberration.'"[5]

Even Gorbachev, who was regarded by the East Europeans from the moment of his election as the best hope for reform, conceded little to his bloc partners in his speech on the occasion of the Warsaw Pact Treaty renewal. No mention was made of Soviet adherence to noninterference or the supremacy of state sovereignty over class relations. The new Soviet party chief chose instead to state that "relations are based on the full equality and comradely mutual assistance of sovereign states" who uphold "the principle of socialist internationalism."[6]

In an apparent attempt to limit the possibility of any but the most hard-line interpretation of Gorbachev's rather ambiguous remarks, a pseudonymous *Pravda* article appeared in June 1985. Signed by "O. Vladimirov," it was reliably reported to have been written by Oleg Rakhmanin, the first deputy head of the department for liaison with ruling workers' and communist parties. It was certainly the strongest and most coherent attack on the pro-reform position to appear just prior to the 27th Party Congress.

In a sharp attack on unnamed East European and Soviet theoreticians, the article pointedly noted: "Anti-communist theoreticians and opportunists, slandering proletarian internationalism, declare it to be 'outdated,' and try to pose as trailblazers of some kind of 'new unity.'"[7] But, it warned, "V. I. Lenin demanded that those who only pay lip service to internationalism be exposed," particularly now, "when various kinds of revisionist, nationalistic, and clerical concepts are coming to the surface of ideological life." Claiming that any attempt to appeal to the "specific nature" or "special role" of certain East European countries was playing into imperialism's attempt to "estrange them from the USSR," the article threatened that "we, who are combating imperialism, constitute an alliance that requires close cohesion, and we regard all attempts to disturb this cohesion as a completely impermissible phenomenon and as a betrayal of the interests of the struggle against international imperialism."

Rakhmanin also clearly showed himself to be against any further reforms within the East European states by condemning "national models of socialism" as little more than an attempt to "obtain levers for influencing the policy of one socialist state or another from without and from within." In this regard, "attempts are being made to discredit state ownership and to pit it against other forms of ownership under socialism." While the author paid lip service to the fact that "solutions to urgent problems require maximum consideration both for the common interests of socialism and for the specific tasks of socialist and communist construction in each country," the very next sentence made it clear where his priorities in fact lay:

> The main criterion here is the interests of socialism
> and the observance of the fundamental principles of
> socialist economic management – the planned manage-
> ment of the economy, the priority of socialist goals,
> the strengthening of socialist ownership, and the im-
> provement of its forms.

In apparent response to the "Vladimirov" article, other Soviet analysts became engaged. Writing in the July 1985 issue of the party's preeminent theoretical journal, *Kommunist,* Oleg Bogomolov, the director of the Institute for the Economics of the World Socialist System and already a leading advisor to Gorbachev, countered the Vladimirov article indirectly by saying that only by respecting the differing interests of other states could socialist internationalism ever be a really operative principle:

> Specific national and state interests cannot, of course,
> be ignored. That would not further the realization of
> our common international interests, nor would it
> strengthen the unity of the socialist countries.[8]

In the following month, Nikolai Shishlin, the head of the External Affairs Sector of the Central Committee Propaganda Department (headed at that time by Aleksandr Yakovlev), contributed to the debate on sovereignty versus socialist internationalism by stating that "ruling communist parties must be masters of the art of combining the national and international interests of the socialist countries." The only way to ensure such an approach, he said, was through "absolute respect for each country's sovereignty, looking after each other's interests." Almost as if he suddenly realized the bold implications of his statement, Shishlin then proceeded to qualify it by invoking the principle of socialist internationalism, which might, he continued, require at times "certain sacrifices in the name of duty to one's allies."[9]

A more radical note was struck by Yurii Novopashin, at that time a sector head at the Institute for the Economics of the World Socialist System, when he warned that there was "no magic wand" that could dispose of "national egoism" on the one hand or "great-power ambitions" on the other.[10] Novopashin pointed out that, far from diminishing, the "national and state interests" of individual socialist states were increasingly being expressed and often were "contradictory." As a result, even though the socialist states were by no means equal, they should be treated equally. This would involve a renunciation of "domineering" methods, "great-power ambitions," and "hegemonistic pretensions." Novopashin also decried the notion that democratic centralism – with its subordination of lower bodies to higher bodies – could possibly be an appropriate principle governing relations between the East European countries and the Soviet Union. Within the socialist world, he stated, there could be no question of "hierarchy or subordination," rejecting "attempts to define the essence of socialist internationalism in terms of subordination or to suggest, for example, that, where the socialist countries are concerned, the principle of respect for national sovereignty could be subordinated to some higher principle governing their relations – namely that of unity." In an indication of support for this view at higher levels, Novopashin was later promoted to become deputy director of the Slavonic studies institute of the Academy of Sciences – an institute which previously had been noted for its conservatism.

The definition of socialist internationalism was by no means resolved in the months leading up to the 27th CPSU Congress. At the end of November, Georgii Shakhnazarov, the newly appointed deputy head of the department for liaison with ruling workers' and communist parties, voiced an opinion at odds with his colleague Oleg Rakhmanin. He lamented the fact that "the process of building a new type of international relations [between socialist countries] is far from being completed. . . . It can happen that theory and practice move in parallel directions. They may often diverge, and this does, unfortunately, occur."[11]

The 27th Party Congress

There is no doubt that in comparison with speeches at previous CPSU congresses or with East European expectations, the speech by Gorbachev at the 27th Congress was little short of electrifying. That speech identified him as a person of both vigor and vision. The phrases that appeared in his speech were reminiscent of Khrushchev and even bolder than those used by Bogomolov and Shakhnazarov in their previously mentioned articles.

When Gorbachev told delegates and foreign guests that "radical reform is necessary,"[12] it did not matter that he was talking about the Soviet Union and not Eastern Europe. The East Europeans understood that this simple sentence had enormous implications for their future development, too. Similarly, when he chided another speaker for including too many references to "Mikhail Sergeevich," Gorbachev was making an important statement about the cult of personality and the need to relegate that style of operating firmly to the past. When Boris Nikolayevich Yel'tsin, at that time the first secretary of the Moscow city party committee, asked "Why have we not managed to uproot bureaucratism, social injustice, and abuse from our lives over so many years?"[13] the East European commentators knew that they were witnessing a truly historic event. Not since Khrushchev's speech at the 20th Congress in 1956 had the top Soviet leadership so openly discussed problems and so clearly called for major changes, including new intrabloc relations.

The implications of these statements by Soviet leaders were enormous. In effect, by opening the debate in the Soviet Union about radical reform, the Soviets were implicitly giving, whether they wished to or not, the green light to similar debates and experiments throughout Eastern Europe. By criticizing fundamental aspects of the system of economic management and planning, Moscow was admitting what certain East Europeans had been saying for years – that some aspects of the classic model of Soviet economic development introduced under Stalin were inappropriate for sustaining growth and shifting to the intensive high-technology stage of development.

This impression of a historic shift was supported as much by what Gorbachev did not say as by what he did say about Eastern Europe and the socialist commonwealth. First of all, absent from his speech was any mention of the principle of socialist (or pro-letarian) internationalism, or any euphemism for the same doc-trine. Instead, Gorbachev specifically emphasized "uncondi-tional respect in international practice for the right of every people to choose the paths and forms of its development." Gone, too, were any references to common, scientific principles under-lying socialist construction within socialist states. Rather, in what appeared as almost a *mea culpa* on behalf of past Soviet practices, Gorbachev stated that "unity has nothing in common with uniformity, with a hierarchy." Rather, he emphasized the need to "solve problems," to "avert crisis situations," and to "find mutually acceptable solutions to even the most difficult problems."

Clearly, however, not everyone in the Central Committee agreed with Gorbachev. The new CPSU program, which re-placed the utopian Khrushchevite 1961 version, contained an as-sessment of the parameters of reform in Eastern Europe which was more circumspect than that presented by Gorbachev in his speech.[14] The differences between the two documents, which were marked in some cases, indicated that Gorbachev was con-ceptually out in front of the more conservative Central Commit-tee bureaucracy – with the result that East European conser-vatives could delay reforms in the hope that Gorbachev might yet fail.

"New Thinking" and Eastern Europe

Almost immediately after the 27th Congress, the political de-bates began afresh. The Soviet attitude towards change in East-ern Europe was tied up with two crucial issues which came to the fore soon after the congress: the debate about democratization within the Soviet Union and the debate about military doctrine. If Gorbachev were going to push for democratization within the USSR, then as a matter of principle it seemed unlikely that he could or would prevent it in the bloc. And the likelihood of him moving against East European reforms would be further diminished if Eastern Europe ceased to be considered a vital part of the USSR's national security zone. These debates proceeded in parallel with the rejection of a single model of socialism and the elaboration of a new policy concept towards Europe, embodied in the idea that all of the Continent should be considered as a "common home" for its inhabitants. The resolution of these debates in favor of Gorbachev's position led inexorably towards the formal renunciation of the Brezhnev Doctrine in 1988 and 1989.

Democratization. The January 1987 plenum of the CPSU Central Committee endorsed Gorbachev's proposals for the democratization of public life. Gorbachev later observed that "there was a particular situation before the January plenum, and after it, events went in a completely different direction."[15] Before this date, the watchwords in the new Soviet political lexicon had been *perestroika, glasnost,* and *uskorenie* (acceleration). Now *demokratizatsiya* would be added.

From the beginning, Gorbachev distanced himself from the traditional Soviet definition of the term. He rejected the notion that the political institutions of a state should favor one class over another; rather, the state should serve the needs of all the people, and the institutions of the state should be structured so as to ensure equal access to, and representation in, those institutions. Thus, for example, in a statement that was absolutely startling at the time, Gorbachev claimed in October 1986 that "the interests of societal development and pan-human values take priority over the interests of any particular class."[16] Specifically, as he made clear in an impromptu speech in Krasnodar on September 18, 1986, "the essence of *perestroika* . . . is for people to feel they are the country's master."[17]

Against this backdrop, the January 1987 CPSU Central Committee plenum adopted a number of resolutions which called for ideological and political reforms. It set in motion the process which produced the July 1988 decision of the 19th CPSU Conference to allow multicandidate elections in the USSR for local and national posts and the establishment of the Congress of Peoples' Deputies, which first convened in June 1989.

The issue of democratization produced many contentious debates, all of them ultimately won by Gorbachev, about whether or not his vision of the future was in fact Marxist. He challenged the role of the working class as the favored class in society and criticized the past willingness to deny individual freedom in the interests of ensuring class supremacy as "barracks collectiveness that levels the individual."[18] A group of his aides advised him "to drop the myth of the working class altogether," a view ultimately embodied in the statement rejecting "a simple class approach" of the CPSU draft program unveiled in advance of the 1990 28th Party Congress.[19] Indeed, this appeared to be what Gorbachev had wished to do for some time, judging from his attacks on the concepts of a political vanguard and democratic centralism, which he said had come to be "bureaucratic centralism" without any real democratic essence.[20] He repeatedly spoke against any political arrangement which would prevent the emergence of democracy based on individual rights within a rule-governed society.

To the extent that the CPSU would continue to play a leading role, Gorbachev clearly believed that this role had to be earned. Gorbachev's key advisors concurred. Following the February 1990 plenum, Aleksandr Yakovlev stated that "as a Communist party we are going to fight to remain the ruling party, but through political methods, through Communists in parliaments, in other bodies of government, and so on."[21] Anatolii Lukyanov, the first deputy chairman of the Supreme Soviet, laid out the wording which was likely to be adopted governing the party's future role:

> The CPSU, just like other sociopolitical organizations
> and mass movements, takes part in running state and
> public affairs, and puts forward its representatives to
> soviets of peoples' deputies and other state bodies.
> The party does not take upon itself state commanding
> power. Its role is to be the democratically recognized
> political leader, acting through Communists, not
> claiming advantage and not claiming to have its special
> position written into the Constitution of the USSR.
> In this connection the party considers it essential to
> introduce, as a legislative initiative for examination by
> the Congress of Peoples' Deputies, the proposal for

the corresponding change in Article 6 of the country's basic law.[22]

Such views were incorporated into the draft program for the 28th Party Congress.

Clearly, the Soviet debate on democratization had a major direct and indirect influence on events in Eastern Europe. Soviet pronouncements were followed by communist and noncommunist circles in these countries, with reform leaders able to introduce the same ideas into the public debate in allied capitals without fear of censure from Moscow. And indeed the fact that such debates were taking place in the USSR meant that, in principle, Soviet leaders could not but support similar movements in other countries. As Yakovlev stated in his speech to the February 1990 plenum:

> If we are proclaiming the principle of freedom and democracy in our own country, how can we deny this to others? If we want our republics to be free and autonomous, we ought to approach other countries with the same logic too. If we proclaimed freedom of social choice back in 1985, it is pointless now to invent some kind of magic prescriptions for halting events in these regions, and anyhow this is both impossible and unnecessary.[23]

Both Yakovlev and Shevardnadze, in their speeches cited earlier, noted the important decision taken in April 1985 to allow freedom of choice – that is, the idea that, as Gorbachev stated in his book *Perestroika,* "every nation is entitled to choose its own way of development, to dispose of its fate, its territory, and its human and natural resources."[24] However, as long as Eastern Europe was part of the USSR's national security zone, it was unlikely that Moscow could allow true choice. Indeed, the statements made by Gorbachev at key anniversaries, such as the renewal of the Warsaw Pact (which also took place in April 1985), suggested that until military doctrine was redefined, Eastern Europe would not in fact be entirely free to choose its own path of development.

Military Doctrine. Very soon after the Warsaw Pact renewal, Gorbachev signaled the start of a major debate on military doctrine.

In the fall of 1985, and then again at the 27th Party Congress in 1986, Gorbachev called for "restricting military potential within the bounds of reasonable sufficiency."[25]

Only seven months later, in September 1986, the Stockholm Conference on Disarmament in Europe (CDE) was able to reach agreement following the Soviet decision to allow intrusive verification. The agreement introduced a thirty-five-nation regime allowing challenge inspections, as well as both advance-notification and routine observations of all maneuvers above negotiated levels.

It was not until after the January 1987 Central Committee plenum, however, that the real elaboration of concepts connected with rethinking military doctrine began. It began with Gorbachev's announcement at the end of February that the Soviet Union would negotiate the withdrawal of all intermediate-range nuclear missiles (1,000–3,000 miles) from Europe. Soon after, articles began appearing which began to redefine doctrines governing both strategic and theater conventional forces. On the central front in Europe, analysts began to make proposals which would deny offensive capabilities to either side. In order for such a shift to enhance stability in Europe, Soviet analysts proposed that "the defense capabilities of the Warsaw Pact must substantially exceed the offensive capabilities of NATO and the defensive capabilities of NATO must substantially exceed the offensive capabilities of the Warsaw Pact under lowered levels of military confrontation between the two alliances."[26]

Changes in conventional strategy from offense to defense diminished the need for a forward military presence in Eastern Europe, and successive Soviet proposals for troop withdrawals highlighted this change in emphasis. While several offers were put forward in 1985 and 1986, it was not until May 1987 that the Soviets recognized the need for asymmetrical cuts between the Warsaw Pact and NATO. This requirement was adopted at a Warsaw Pact meeting, as was the need to formulate doctrine with a defensive orientation.

The implications for Eastern Europe of all these changes were obvious. Confidence-building measures agreed on at the CDE talks effectively denied the Soviets a whole range of options for concealing a military buildup during a crisis which might be a prelude to an invasion of an East European country. Indeed, it was estimated by American negotiators to the conference that every military move conducted by the Soviets during the 1980–1 Polish crisis would have violated the CDE agreement had it been in force at that time. The Soviets, therefore, either would have had to risk a challenge inspection by any one of the other thirty-four signatories to the Helsinki Final Act or would have had to configure their forces in a way so as not to be subject to inspection, a move which in itself would have revealed malfeasance.

The announcement by Gorbachev (made in his speech before the United Nations General Assembly in December 1988) that the USSR would withdraw 50,000 Soviet troops and 5,000 tanks from Eastern Europe was made after conservatives within the Warsaw Pact (notably East Germany and Czechoslovakia) had failed to endorse deeper cuts proposed at a pact meeting held in Warsaw in July 1988.[27] Gorbachev pressed ahead nonetheless, and his announcement did nothing to shore up the already tottering political positions of those leaders who had come to power on the backs of Soviet tanks. It also accelerated the reform process in Hungary and Poland, where debates accelerated in 1989 on even more thoroughgoing political, economic, and military reforms, including neutrality – a debate which was stimulated by Soviet analyst Oleg Bogomolov's suggestion that Hungarian neutrality might not undermine Soviet security.

The thoroughgoing revision of core ideological and military doctrines took place at the same time that new bases for Soviet relations with Eastern Europe were being elaborated. Innovations in all these areas were interlinked and mutually reinforcing. Failure to implement one would spill over and inhibit progress in another: Domestic democratization, for example, was seen as a crucial prerequisite for democratization in Eastern Europe, just as success in ameliorating international tensions was sought also as a way of easing the defense burden and changing the psychological mind-set of the Soviet elite. As Soviet Foreign Minister Shevardnadze observed, the "deep-rooted distrust" of the USSR which Gorbachev inherited from his predecessors "preyed not only on the country's foreign policy but on its attitudes to its own citizens." As Shevardnadze asked, "how could anyone fail to be afraid of a state which dealt so severely in its relations with its own people?" Clearly, for Shevardnadze and for the entire Gor-bachev leadership, "it is only through extensive international cooperation that we will be able to solve our most acute domes-tic problems."[28]

With this in mind, Gorbachev also moved to revise key aspects of Soviet relations with Eastern Europe. In particular, these relations were affected by the redefinition of socialism, by the conceptualization of Europe as a "common home," and by the rejection of the use of force to protect socialism.[29]

Many Roads to Socialism. Gorbachev himself set the standard in revising these notions at the 27th Party Congress, when, as al-ready noted, he specifically emphasized "unconditional respect" for the right of all peoples to choose their own paths of develop-ment. He was subsequently to outline in detail the source of many previous problems in Soviet–East European relations:

> In the field of state building, too, the fraternal socialist states largely relied on the Soviet example. To an extent, this was inevitable. Assertions concerning the imposition of the "Soviet model" distort this objective necessity of that time [the immediate post-war period]. . . .
>
> But it was not without losses, and rather serious ones at that. Drawing on the Soviet experience, some countries failed duly to consider their own specifics. Even worse, a stereotyped approach was given an ideological tint by some of our . . . leaders who acted as almost the sole guardians of truth. Without taking into consideration . . . features of different socialist countries, they sometimes displayed suspicion toward those countries' approaches to certain problems.
>
> . . . Furthermore, negative accretions in these rela-tions were not examined with a sufficient degree of frankness, which means that not everything obstruct-ing their development and preventing them from en-tering a new, contemporary stage was identified.[30]

If this was the problem, the solution also appeared clear: Adopt new principles which would eliminate the need for slavish adherence to a single model of socialism. Towards this end, Gorbachev enunciated the need for intrabloc relations to proceed according to principles which have at their root the "absolute independence" of every socialist state. As Gorbachev made clear, "the independence of each Party, its sovereign right to decide the issues facing its country and its responsibility to its nation are the unquestionable principles."[31]

This view came to be shared by other leaders and top advisors. Central Committee Secretary Yegor Ligachev, long considered a conservative opponent of liberalization, was at pains during a trip to Hungary in April 1987 to emphasize his agreement with this new approach. Speaking on Hungarian television, Ligachev stressed that "every country looks for solutions independently, not as in the past. It is not true that Moscow's conductor's baton, or Moscow's hand is in everything . . . every nation has a right to its own way."[32]

Gorbachev and Ligachev were also in agreement during this period that while there might be more models of socialism and more paths to socialism, nevertheless it was the improvement of socialism, not its demise, which was the object of the exercise. Gorbachev was able to tell Western reporters (who had asked his opinion of reforms in Poland following disturbances there in April 1988) that *"perestroika* was born out of our conditions, and we need it . . . but we will not impose it on any other country. Therefore, it is up to the Polish people to decide what they want to do." However, at the same time he expressed confidence that Poland would remain socialist.[33]

The definition of a socialist system undoubtedly had become broad enough to encompass the progressive income tax and stock market of Hungary as well as the continued reliance on state ownership to be found elsewhere. Multicandidate secret elections had become as acceptable as single-candidate public acclamation for the selection of officeholders. Indeed, with every advance in the democratization debate in the USSR, the very definition of socialism was stretched, and many of the key components with which it had previously been identified came under scrutiny: the primacy of the proletariat in a society and world divided into classes; the leading and directing role of the communist party in all aspects of society; the organization of the party according to the principle of democratic centralism, with particular emphasis on centralism at the expense of democracy; and the planning and central control of all aspects of economic activity.

As events in Eastern Europe and the Soviet Union unfurled in 1989, the definition of socialism was stretched, some would say, to the breaking point. At the opening session of the USSR Congress of Peoples' Deputies, the noted writer Chengis Aytmatov tried to break through the conceptual deadlock in the following way:

> While we were surmising, judging, and laying down
> the law as to what socialism must and cannot be, other
> people already have it, have built it, and are enjoying
> its fruits. . . . I have in mind such prosperous, law-
> based societies as Sweden, Austria, Finland, Norway,
> the Netherlands, and finally Spain, Canada across the
> sea, not to mention Switzerland, which is a model. . . .
> We can only dream about the social security and level
> of prosperity enjoyed by workers in those countries.
> [These] countries do not call themselves socialist;
> however, they are none the worse for that.[34]

Flowing from this, the view developed that the deformation of Soviet socialism had exhausted whatever attractiveness it might have had as a model for export. Thus, *Izvestiya* commentator Aleksandr Bovin's analysis reflected emerging sentiment when he stated in 1987 that foreign communist parties had every right to take their own paths to socialism, because "the failures and difficulties along the road of developing real socialism . . . have not attracted people to socialism but rather repelled them."[35]

The failure to improve the Soviet economic situation only increased the conviction among a large section of the Soviet elite that Eastern Europe should be allowed to go its own way. The process of renewal in the Soviet Union clearly had created both great hopes for their own country and a great sense of responsibility for the errors that had been committed in other countries in the name of socialism. As a leading Soviet analyst, Marina Pavlova-Silvanskaya, bluntly stated: "We created an artificial scheme of socialism. . . . We assured mankind that we were building a crystal castle for it. But we dug a pit."[36]

Europe as a "Common Home." Soviet views of Europe are complex and multifaceted. As discussed in Chapter 2, they arose from the historical Russian conflict between, on the one hand, the Slavophile rejection of Western culture's subversive and corrupting nature and, on the other, the Westernizers' embrace of the values of the Enlightenment and the objectives of economic development. These two strains continued into the post-1917 Soviet phase, with Soviet policy towards the West frequently influenced by one or the other of these conflicting views.

The Gorbachev period proved to be no exception. The goals of economic autarky and social isolationism were as alien to Gorbachev's reform plans as they were to the Westernizers who dominated the Russian court under Peter the Great. Gorbachev's conception relied on greater economic, political, and social interaction amongst the socialist and capitalist states of Europe, with the aim of reducing the rigid division of Europe. Some NATO policymakers expressed concern about the impact of such formulations on alliance cohesion. But for East European leaders and populations, Gorbachev's opening to the West was seen as their opening to the West, too, and a golden opportunity to fulfill fundamental aspirations in that direction. To the extent, therefore, that the Soviet conception envisaged a fundamental commitment to significant improvements in intersocietal relations across a divided Europe, East European leaders, virtually without exception, welcomed the Soviet change of heart.

To many in Eastern Europe, Gorbachev appeared sincere when he labeled Europe a "common home" and declared that "Europe's historic chance and its future lies in peaceful cooperation between the states of that continent." This pan-European element of Gorbachev's outlook was developed at the 27th Party Congress and then further elaborated during his 1987 visit to Czechoslovakia and in his book *Perestroika*. There he emphasized the broader philosophical, historical, and cultural underpinnings of this view, stemming from his own belief that "we are Europeans. Old Russia was united with Europe by Christianity. . . . The history of Russia is an organic part of the great European history. . . . Europe 'from the Atlantic to the Urals' is a cultural-historical entity united by the common heritage of the Renaissance and the Enlightenment."[37]

This aspect of new thinking came to be accompanied in the minds of top Soviet officials by the notion that the United States and Canada were also part of Europe. For the Soviets, therefore, the concept no longer involved the splitting of NATO into its European and North American components. On the contrary, a significant segment of Soviet elite opinion supported U.S. and Canadian participation in the pan-European process. And amongst some Soviet analysts, this notion gained in attractiveness after movements towards reunification between East and West Germany gathered momentum in 1990.

"Europe as a common home" was one Soviet policy universally welcomed in Eastern Europe. In reaction to Gorbachev's earliest statements on the subject in 1985, even the most skeptical East European intellectuals like Hungary's George Konrád admitted the possibility of a "gradual, controlled transformation of the Soviet bloc into a looser community of nations capable of interacting with Western Europe on a partnership basis."[38]

Alexander Dubček, the former general secretary of the Czechoslovak Communist Party, who had been in internal exile for almost two decades, gave an illicit interview to the Italian communist newspaper *L'Unita* in January 1988. In it, he emphasized that

> one of the main positive aspects of Gorbachev's visit to
> Prague was the idea of a "new way of thinking" about
> Europe. This idea ought to be consistently affirmed in
> our country, to overcome the burden of the past and
> to set in motion Czechoslovak restructuring. To build
> a united process, we must first restore confidence
> among European nations and states. I see this as the
> only way in which we can have a future, given the
> present conditions.[39]

This policy gained real meaning with the significant erosion of all divisions within Europe after November 1989, the month when unrestricted travel for East Germans who wished to travel to the FRG was introduced. Throughout the entire year, however, it had become increasingly clear that it would be almost impossible to maintain any concept of bloc unity "against" the West. To the extent that existing bloc structures could survive, they would do so only if they were made porous to the widest possible interactions with the international community in general and Western Europe, Japan, and North America in particular. The CMEA summit in January 1990 accepted the need for a complete restructuring of the organization on market principles which would facilitate, not impede, greater interaction with external markets. So, too, with the Helsinki process and arms-control negotiations in Europe. They were both aimed towards massive expansion of all forms of interaction between East and West Europe and equally significant reductions in the levels of military forces. The Vienna seminar on military doctrines, which was held in January 1990 between Warsaw Pact and NATO chiefs of staff, saw an unprecedented exchange of information and opinions between East and West European members of the two pacts about their respective force structures. It is doubtful that the process of change in Eastern Europe would have unfolded the way it did without the early elaboration of the concept of a European common home. The remaining piece of the puzzle was the Soviet renunciation of the right to use force within Eastern Europe.

The Brezhnev Doctrine. That the Soviets, under Gorbachev, have continued to monitor reforms in Eastern Europe and communicate their support or concern about events is incontestable: Gorbachev's call to Polish communists urging them to join a non-communist majority government in August 1989; Soviet diplomatic activity to signal the withdrawal of support for conservative leaders in Czechoslovakia, East Germany, and Bulgaria in November and December 1989; the visit of Soviet Foreign Minister Shevardnadze to Romania immediately after Ceauşescu was overthrown to promise emergency fuel deliveries – all these activities, and others, as discussed elsewhere, were intrinsic to Soviet activism in Eastern Europe in the period after Gorbachev came to power. However, there is a qualitative difference between sending a foreign minister with promises of economic aid and sending a defense minister with threats of military "assistance." That is what had changed in the five years after Gorbachev came to power, but the renunciation of the use of force came only gradually.

The "Brezhnev Doctrine," as it was known in the West, or

"socialist internationalism," as it was sometimes called in the Soviet bloc, had been enunciated after the Soviet invasion of Czechoslovakia in 1968 and was taken to mean that each communist party was responsible not only to its own people but also to all the socialist countries, that the sovereignty of individual socialist countries was of lesser importance than the interests of world socialism, and that it was not only the right but also the positive duty of all socialist countries to come to the aid of any socialist state where socialism was threatened.[40] As discussed in Chapter 4, Soviet insistence that bloc parties adhere to the principle of socialist internationalism had been one of the keys to Soviet ideological control in Eastern Europe.

After coming to power in March 1985, Gorbachev, however, called several times for building intrabloc relations on a new basis. On the whole, he shied away from using the term "socialist internationalism" in his speeches and writings. But, as noted earlier in this chapter, many agreements and party documents, such as the 1985 renewal of the treaty creating the Warsaw Pact, the CPSU program introduced at the 27th Party Congress, and the April 1987 Polish–Soviet "Declaration on Ideology, Science, and Culture" all affirmed continued Soviet support for the principle, even though it ceased to be defined in the same restrictive way.

This duality of approach was illustrated in Gorbachev's speech before the CPSU meeting to celebrate the seventieth anniversary of the Bolshevik Revolution in November 1987. After acknowledging that "unity does not mean being identical or uniform," Gorbachev went on to say that "we also know what damage can be done by weakening the internationalist principle in mutual relations of socialist states, by deviation from the principles of mutual benefit and mutual aid, and by a lack of attention to the general interests of socialism in action on the world arena."[41] Even in his writings, Gorbachev left the door open by continuing to use formulae which emphasized principles other than the complete independence and sovereignty of each party:

> We are also firmly convinced that the socialist community will be successful only if every party and state cares for both its own and common interests, if it respects its friends and allies, heeds their interests and

pays attention to the experience of others. Awareness
of this relationship between domestic issues and the
interests of world socialism is typical of the countries
of the socialist community. We are united, in unity
resides our strength, and from unity we draw our
confidence that we will cope with the issues set forth
by our time.[42]

On the other hand, Gorbachev used other important occasions to emphasize principles which were at odds with socialist
internationalism, principles like the independence and sovereignty of every state, the "inalienable right" of all parties "to
make decisions on the choice of paths of social development,"
and the "impermissibility of interference in internal affairs under
any pretext whatsoever," all of these principles being affirmed in
an important mutual declaration with the Yugoslavs in March
1988.[43] Similar messages were contained in Gorbachev's speech at
the June 1988 19th CPSU Conference and the joint Soviet–Finnish declaration in October 1989. The latter was particularly significant because it occurred after the Polish United Workers'
Party had lost its ruling position. The declaration stated that
"there can be no justification for any use of force: whether by
one military-political alliance against another, or within such
alliances," and that "freedom of sociopolitical choice" should
become a universal norm in interstate relations. As such, it set
the backdrop for the Soviet decision not to interfere to prevent
the virtual collapse of communist party rule in Eastern Europe in
the months that followed.[44]

The only question which remained was whether or not the
collapse of *perestroika* inside the Soviet Union, including potentially the loss of power by Mikhail Gorbachev, could bring about
a reassertion of the Brezhnev Doctrine. Certainly East European
reformers were aware of the need, in the words of a popular
Polish poster, to "forge steel while we have Gorbachev." They
were especially concerned about the growth of a Russian nationalist backlash. However, virtually all the comments about
these events in the USSR, whether from various strata of elite
opinion, from mass media, or from public-opinion findings,
showed that by the beginning of 1990 there was no real popular

constituency left for intervention to save socialism in Eastern Europe. Its passing went virtually unmourned in the Soviet Union, where leaders and public alike were far more concerned to save their own ailing economy. Russian nationalist opinion had always been ambivalent about the benefits of Eastern Europe, and those in the movement who might naturally have allied with ideological conservatives were in any case far too preoccupied with the collapse of the internal empire to worry about saving the remnants of the external empire.

Soviet commentators openly admitted that East European communist parties had lost their leading role, that these countries would now "veer appreciably towards the West," and that there would be a rise in anti-Soviet sentiment throughout the region. But at the same time, analysts continued nonetheless to praise the fact that "people in Eastern Europe already take for granted that the 'Brezhnev doctrine' no longer exists and that the USSR poses no threat to their sovereignty."[45] Moreover, no one seriously believed that even if the Brezhnev Doctrine were revived in the Kremlin, under whatever circumstances, it could be employed in Eastern Europe to save socialism. Events had already gone far beyond the point where violence could effectively restore a political system. Soviet leaders like Yegor Ligachev, Viktor Chebrikov, and Dmitrii Yazov came under such attack in the Soviet parliament for using force against civilians within their own country – in Tbilisi in April 1989 and Baku in December 1989 – that they were hardly likely to propose its use outside the Soviet Union. As Soviet analysts observed: "Nowadays the supporters of violent methods in politics cannot justify the Tbilisi action even before their own parliament. Coping with the whole of Eastern Europe has been beyond them for a long time now, and they are perfectly well aware of this."[46]

With the removal of the CPSU's constitutional protection as the leading force of society, the prospects of gaining any consensus in the future, with or without Gorbachev, for military moves to impose a particular political order anywhere in Eastern Europe have faded even further. By the spring of 1990, not only had the Soviet–East European relationship moved well beyond the Brezhnev Doctrine, but guarantees in the form of new and democratic political structures had begun to come into existence on both sides of the relationship to ensure that it could not be reimposed.

Moscow, the German Question, and a New European Order

Just because the Soviet leaders had denounced the Brezhnev Doctrine did not mean that Moscow had no interest in Eastern Europe or that the USSR did not plan to play a role in shaping its future. In fact, the changes which occurred in the region in 1989 led to a profound debate about those interests, with the debate tending always to come back to one set of issues – the immutability of postwar borders and the future of Germany.

Not everyone in elite and analytical circles agreed with the optimistic forecast of one specialist that the prestige and interests of the Soviet Union "would surely be greatly helped by the prospect of a union of both German states."[47] Indeed, while most were resigned to the inevitability of a closer union, if not total reunification, between the two German states, many, including many liberals, expressed grave reservations.

Soviet policy in the center of Europe has long been dominated by the belief that the splitting of Germany into two German states best served Soviet interests. However, it is only now being recalled that until the incorporation of West Germany into NATO in 1955, Soviet policy had been directed at maintaining German unity on the basis of nonalignment with any military bloc.

The borders of Germany were always less important to the USSR than the military strength and configuration of the German army. As long as forces hostile to the Soviet Union were stationed on German territory, Moscow would hold half of Germany hostage and array counterforces. But with the advancement of the view in Moscow that the division of Europe into rival military blocs should be overcome, the Soviet rationale for maintaining the division of Germany was deprived of its foundations.

What is more, with the pursuit of a vigorous policy of expanding contacts in Western Europe, it was clear that the FRG, which was by far the dominant economic power on the Continent,

would exclude the USSR unless incremental moves towards unification were allowed. In other words, Bonn made it clear that
Gorbachev's policy of Europe as a common home would not
succeed unless the core feature of Bonn's policy of *Ostpolitik* was
also promoted.

The acceptance of this view at the highest levels of the Soviet
leadership was gradual, but was well under way by the time the
Berlin Wall was opened on November 9, 1989, thereby explaining
why the reaction to that event was not more alarmist in Moscow.
To the extent that Soviet leaders were concerned about these
events, they focused on key issues: that the Soviet Union continue to be a co-guarantor of the European order, that military
forces arrayed against the Soviet Union continue to diminish,
that the policy of military containment not be replaced by a
policy of economic containment, and that any breaking down of
barriers between the two Germanys should take place within the
context of, not instead of, the broader elimination of other trade,
cultural, political, and military divisions on the Continent. In
this way, the reunification of the two Germanys was seen in
Moscow as a vehicle for accelerating the reentry of the Soviet
Union into the mainstream of West European and Western political and economic life.

This view, held by Gorbachev and some top Soviet officials,
was not universally shared. The memories of the war, the legacy
of fascism, and the prospect of the absorption of a socialist state
by a capitalist state created a critical mass of fundamentally
important and emotionally explosive issues which had to be resolved all at the same time. For many Soviets in all walks of life,
the "German question" had been settled once and for all at the
battle of Stalingrad. To reopen it at a time when the Soviet
economy seemed to be foundering and military cutbacks were
being announced practically weekly bolstered the impression
amongst some that Gorbachev was negotiating this crucial issue
from a position of weakness.

Those conservatives who had been seeking to find his Achilles'
heel lost no time. Speaking at the February 1990 CPSU Central
Committee plenum, Yegor Ligachev described German reunification as a "danger" and warned that "it would be un-
forgivably shortsighted and mistaken not to see that a Germany

with vast economic and military potential has begun to loom on the world horizon." He stated that it was not too late to prevent another "Munich" and urged a countrywide campaign to "tell the party and the people about it at the top of our voices."[48]

Gorbachev and his advisors quickly moved to defuse such criticisms. They did so by trying to control the debate and prevent the conservatives from co-opting it (Yakovlev insisted that the German question had not been on the official agenda for the February 1990 plenum, so that all the considerable discussion of the issue that occurred had in fact been unplanned[49]). They also expressed equal concern, as did Foreign Minister Shevardnadze on several important occasions, about the difficulty of controlling events and about the danger that German reunification could turn at some point against Soviet interests. As he stated at the plenum, "negative factors are clearly visible in the positive dynamism. The spector of revanchism is stalking Europe in an embrace with the ideas of unity and unification, and the craving for justice is tainted by a craving for political vengeance. The new status of the German question has awakened dangerous hopes of a revision of borders."[50]

As with domestic *perestroika,* the considerable revision of ideological tenets governing Soviet foreign policy in Eastern Europe had stimulated changes with both great promise and great risks for long-term Soviet interests. The extent to which stabilization, economic progress, military disarmament, and greater political interaction would increasingly characterize Soviet relations with both Eastern and Western Europe in the future was no longer dependent on Moscow's wishes alone. Increasingly, Western responses would shape East European futures – but whether the West was itself sufficiently united or far-sighted to take advantage of the opportunities and responsibilities at hand remained to be seen.

Notes

1 *Pravda,* February 8, 1990.
2 *Pravda,* September 26, 1968.
3 L. I. Brezhnev, *Report of the CPSU Central Committee and the Immediate Tasks of the Party in Home and Foreign Policy* (Moscow: Novosti Press Agency Publishing House, 1976), p. 9.
4 *Pravda,* June 16, 1984.

5 István Roska, writing in *Népszava*, as reprinted in *Neues Deutschland*, March 4, 1985.

6 *Pravda*, April 28, 1985.

7 O. Vladimirov, *Pravda*, June 21, 1985.

8 O. Bogomolov, "Soglasovaniye ekonomicheskikh interesov i politiki pri sotsializme," *Kommunist*, No. 10, July 1985, p. 91.

9 Nikolai Shishlin, "Top-Priority Task," *New Times*, No. 35, 1985, pp. 9–10.

10 Yurii Novopashin, "Politicheskie otnosheniya stran sotsializma," *Rabochii klass i sovremennii mir*, No. 5, September 1985, pp. 55–65.

11 Moscow Television Service, November 16, 1985, as quoted in Radio Liberty Research 4/86, December 20, 1985.

12 "Political Report of the CPSU Central Committee Delivered February 25, 1986, by M. S. Gorbachev, General Secretary of the CPSU Central Committee, to the 27th CPSU Congress," Moscow Television Service, in Russian, February 25, 1986, Foreign Broadcast Information Service, *Soviet Daily Report (FBIS-SOV)*, February 26, 1986, pp. 01–042, *passim*.

13 Moscow Television Service, in Russian, February 26, 1986, *FBIS-SOV*, March 3, 1986, p. 01.

14 "CPSU Program, New Edition Adopted by the 27th CPSU Congress," *Pravda*, March 7, 1986, *FBIS-SOV*, March 10, 1986, in four parts.

15 *Pravda*, July 15, 1987. I am grateful to Michael MccGwire of the Brookings Institution for pointing out the interconnectedness of the debates on democracy and national security, which is a major theme of his forthcoming book *Perestroika and Soviet National Security*.

16 *Literaturnaya gazeta*, November 5, 1986.

17 *Pravda*, September 25, 1986, *FBIS-SOV*, September 25, 1986, p. R10.

18 Mikhail Gorbachev, "The Socialist Idea and Revolutionary *Perestroika*," *Pravda*, November 26, 1989.

19 According to a "political note" drafted by "Gorbachev's close aides" and leaked to *Le Monde*, January 31, 1990; "Towards a Humane, Democratic Socialism," draft program of the Communist Party of the Soviet Union, issued by TASS, February 12, 1990, *Washington Post*, February 13, 1990.

20 *Pravda*, November 26, 1989.

21 News conference on the results of the CPSU Central Committee plenum, February 7, 1990, *FBIS-SOV*, February 8, 1990, p. 52.

22 News conference on the results of the Central Committee plenum, Moscow Domestic Service, in Russian, *FBIS-SOV*, February 8, 1990, p. 49.

23 *Pravda*, February 8, 1990.

24 Mikhail Gorbachev, *Perestroika* (New York: Harper & Row, 1987), p. 177.

25 M. S. Gorbachev, "Political Report of the CPSU Central Committee to the 27th Congress of the CPSU," *Pravda*, February 26, 1986.

26 Andrei Kokoshin, "The Development of Military Affairs and Reduction of Armed Forces and Conventional Arms," *Mirovaya ekonomika i mezhdunarodniye otnosheniya* (hereafter *MEiMO*), No. 1, January 1988, p. 32. Other key writings began to appear even earlier: R. Sagdeev, A.

Kokoshin, et al., *Strategic Stability Under the Conditions of Radical Nuclear Arms Reductions* (Moscow: Committee of Soviet Scientists for Peace and Against the Nuclear Threat, April 1987); A. Kokoshin and V. Larionov, "The Battle of Kursk from the Standpoint of Defensive Doctrine," *MEiMO*, No. 8, 1987, pp. 32–40; V. V. Zhurkin, S. A. Karaganov, and A. V. Kortunov, "Reasonable Sufficiency – Or How to Break the Vicious Circle," *New Times*, No. 40, October 12, 1987, pp. 13–15.

27 According to data leaked to the *Baltimore Sun*, July 17, 1988.

28 Speech by Foreign Minister Eduard Shevardnadze, Central Committee plenum, February 6, 1990, *Pravda*, February 8, 1990.

29 Some of the following analysis draws on an earlier policy paper written by the author with Lincoln Gordon and John W. Kiser III, *Change in Eastern Europe: Soviet Interests and Western Opportunities* (Washington, D.C.: The Atlantic Council of the United States, April 1989).

30 Gorbachev, *Perestroika*, pp. 162–164.

31 *Ibid.*, p. 165.

32 Budapest Television Service, in Hungarian, April 26, 1987, Foreign Broadcast Information Service, *East European Daily Report (FBIS-EEU)*, April 27, 1987, p. F6.

33 *Washington Post*, May 22, 1988.

34 Moscow Television Service, in Russian, June 2, 1989, *FBIS-SOV*, June 5, 1989, p. 13.

35 "On the Threshold of a New Century, Dialogue between A. Ye. Bovin and V. P. Lukin," *MEiMO*, No. 12, December 1987, p. 55.

36 Interview with M. P. Pavlova-Silvanskaya, *Komsomol'skaya pravda*, January 3, 1990.

37 Gorbachev, *Perestroika*, pp. 191–197, *passim*.

38 George Konrád, interviewed by Richard Falk and Mary Kaldor, "The Post-Yalta Debate," *World Policy Journal*, Vol. 2, No. 3, Summer 1985, p. 461.

39 *L'Unita*, January 10, 1988, *FBIS-EEU*, January 19, 1988, p. 18.

40 As stated most succinctly in *Pravda*, September 26, 1968.

41 *Pravda*, November 3, 1987.

42 Gorbachev, *Perestroika*, p. 165.

43 *Pravda*, March 19, 1988.

44 *Pravda*, October 27, 1989.

45 Marina Pavlova-Silvanskaya, "Eastern Europe: A Painful Step Forward," *Moscow News*, No. 1, January 7, 1990. Also see the interview with Yurii Novopashin, *Komsomol'skaya pravda*, December 6, 1989, and the article by Aleksandr Drozdov, "Last Day of the Month: January Is Hard Going," *Komsomol'skaya pravda*, January 31, 1990, in which the latter states that "the regeneration of political power in East European states as classical social democracy is changing not only the nature of relations among the members of the socialist community but also the situation in Europe and throughout the world. Our allies are concertedly and decisively taking

their leave of Stalinism and returning to panhuman values, to national political and religious traditions."

46 *Komsomol'skaya pravda,* January 3, 1990.
47 Marina Pavlova-Silvanskaya, *Moscow News,* No. 1, January 7, 1990.
48 *Pravda,* February 7, 1990.
49 News conference, Moscow Domestic Service, in Russian, February 7, 1990, *FBIS-SOV,* February 8, 1990, p. 50.
50 *Pravda,* February 8, 1990.

8

Epilogue: Can, or Should, Europe Overcome Its Division?

In 1748, the French philosopher Charles-Louis de Secondat, Baron de Montesquieu, wrote the following prescient description of the situation in Europe:

> A new [disease] has spread itself over Europe; it has infected our princes and induces them to keep an exorbitant number of troops. It . . . of necessity becomes contagious. For as soon as one prince augments what he calls his troops, the rest of course do the same; so that nothing is gained thereby but the public ruin. Each monarch keeps mobilized all the divisions he would need if his subjects were threatened with extermination; and they gave the name of "peace" to this general effort of all against all.[1]

Using Montesquieu's definition, "peace" reigned in Europe for more than forty-five years. But it was a peace defined as the absence of war, marked by crises and tensions, as borders, agreements, and regimes were challenged by restless populations and revisionist leaders on both sides of the central divide.

Beginning in the 1970s, however, détente began to take root in Europe. It was marked by specific agreements regularizing both relations and borders and also by an evolving process of transactions and contacts between Eastern and Western Europe. Détente took hold on several levels, leading not only to burgeoning high-level political and economic relations but also to vastly increased low-level contacts in the fields of tourism, cultural exchanges, and family visits. This combination of state-to-state and people-to-people exchanges opened up the prospect that the physical and psychological walls that had divided Europe since Yalta were beginning to crumble from both above and below.

This is not to imply that détente totally eliminated the cyclical pattern of East European reform, Western support, Soviet repression, Western challenge, and mutual military buildup that had typified crises in past decades. On the contrary, the 1970s and early 1980s were marked by major upheavals as governments strove to cope with the repercussions of crises in Poland, the deployment of additional short- and medium-range nuclear weapons in Europe, and widespread economic downturn throughout the Continent. What distinguished this phase from previous cycles, however, was the mutual concern of East and West Europeans alike to build an oasis of détente that would nourish and repair relations once negative trends had abated.

This new and quite significant development was symptomatic of the stability in Europe that emerged following the normalization of inter-German relations beginning in 1970. Clearly, détente between Eastern and Western Europe could not have proceeded without the recognition by both blocs of the existence of two Germanys. While the quest for improved inter-German relations became an increasingly strong, if still sometimes discordant, component of this chorus, it was by no means the solo voice. All the East European countries sought improved relations with Western Europe and made substantial progress in this sphere throughout the 1970s and early 1980s.

With the inter-European dialogue came debate about whether détente signified the final stabilization of a permanently divided Europe or presaged the ending of that very division. It was unclear whether the crises of the 1945–70 period had been the inevitable result of the destabilizing division of Europe or the labor pains in the birth of an intrinsically stable order – a permanently divided Europe. Divergent views also emerged on the relation between inter-German détente and inter-European détente, with forward movement in the former not always seen as supporting progress in the latter. At the heart of the debate were strongly held beliefs for and against the view that both the division of Germany and the division of Europe were somehow "unnatural" and therefore intrinsically unstable. Some thought that the process of détente would put an end to this division and lead to the "Europeanization" of Europe. Others adamantly rejected the necessity or advisability of reunifying

Germany, arguing that the formula of "two Germanies, one Europe" would satisfy the aspirations of Germans and Europeans alike.[2]

There were no true answers to these questions, only opinions, preferences, and imposed solutions, of which the latter prevailed. The dream of reclaiming Europe for the Europeans had long cast its shadow over the legitimacy of both the Warsaw Pact and NATO. In the Western alliance, challenges came from the general climate of anti-Americanism in Europe and isolationism in the United States. They led to various conceptions by specific leaders and opinion-makers, such as French President Charles de Gaulle's concept of Europe from the Atlantic to the Urals (incorporating, somehow, only the European portion of Russia), or German writer Peter Bender's notion that Europeanization was emerging out of the end of the age of ideology.[3] In the United States, policymakers at very different ends of the political spectrum once again began to address the question of a U.S. withdrawal from Europe. Some proposed the idea as a reprisal against perceived West European ingratitude for increased U.S. defense spending; others favored a cutback of American troops in Europe so that more funds would be available for development of the expensive technology for the strategic defense initiative (SDI). Still others, such as former national security advisor Zbigniew Brzezinski, supported U.S. withdrawals as a way of defusing the military confrontation with the Soviets in Central Europe and thereby increasing East European autonomy.[4]

In Eastern Europe, the entire debate on Europeanization was even more explicit than in the West. There, the idea took hold among leading political and intellectual circles that the small and medium powers in Europe could and should act as a bridge between the superpowers. A bloc system which had as its "price" the suppression of human rights could not be stabilized; there was a deep hope that the accession of Mikhail Gorbachev would provide new opportunities both for the democratization of East European society and for the pursuit of increased contacts with Western Europe. Gorbachev himself promoted and fostered such hopes. During his April 1987 trip to Czechoslovakia, he developed his views on Europe at some length:

> Europe from the Atlantic to the Urals is also an
> historical and cultural category in a high, spiritual

sense. Here world civilization has been enriched with
the ideas of the Renaissance and the Enlightenment.
The humanitarian tradition and the doctrine of socialism have been strongly developed. By the efforts of
geniuses of all the European nations, a priceless fund
has been created in all branches of scientific knowledge
and of artistic comprehension of the world. So, instead
of a nuclear crematorium for Europe, we propose the
peaceful development of European culture, which has
many faces, yet forms a single entity.[5]

Gorbachev's frequent expressions of concern for Europe as "our
common home," as described in Chapter 7, showed his own nonclass approach to such issues, his interest in Europe, and his
political acumen regarding this growing trend in inter-European
public opinion.

Reforms in the USSR and Eastern Europe portended erosion
of the mistrust that previously had appeared to cement the division of Europe and had served as the basis for the policy of
containment. In retrospect, some may eventually wonder if it
was in either the West's or the Soviet Union's interest to encourage such erosion if the costs to the cohesion of one's own alliance
ultimately outweighed the benefits in diminishing the unity of
the adversary's alliance. In particular, the extent to which new
security arrangements can, or will, replace existing military structures is of the utmost importance, particularly as Eastern Europe
and Germany seek new roles in the heart of the Continent.

Western Policy: Its Origins and Limitations

Examining the total devastation of victors and vanquished alike
across the entire Eurasian continent in the aftermath of World
War II, statesmen attributed much of the cause for the outbreak
of the war to the failure of diplomacy as an instrument and the
European balance of power as a system. Leaders in Moscow,
Washington, London, and Paris vowed that diplomacy, not only
having failed to prevent the aggrandizement of Hitler's territorial ambitions but also having appeased his early assaults on
the peace of Europe, would henceforth be no substitute for
military preparedness in vigilance against foreign encroachment.
The first victim of this brutal lesson was Germany itself, with the

Four Powers agreeing that once and for all they must put an end to the prospect of renewed German strength in the center of Europe. But the idea of containment of German power soon gave way to mutual suspicion, and in the years following the war, it became clear that both the United States and the Soviet Union were committed to the maintenance of a strong military presence in the center of Europe. With the defeat of Germany and the division of Europe, the dominance of power flowed from the European heartland to the global periphery. Europe had, in its division, become the object, rather than the subject, of global competition, and so it was likely to remain as long as mistrust forced diplomacy to give way to deterrence.

Fully one month before the Potsdam Conference in 1945, Konrad Adenauer, who was to become the first chancellor of the Federal Republic of Germany, warned that an "iron curtain" was descending on Europe, ending any hopes for postwar cooperation and reunification. In February 1946, George Kennan, second in command at the U.S. Embassy in Moscow, sent home his famous "long telegram." A revised version of this telegram appeared under the title "The Sources of Soviet Conduct," signed only by "X," in *Foreign Affairs* in July 1947. Like former British prime minister Winston Churchill in his famous 1946 speech at Fulton, Missouri, Kennan warned that the West might yet be defeated even in the absence of war if it failed to recognize the threat to Western values, interests, and, ultimately, Western territory posed by the Soviet Union's subversive intent, the phalanx-like purposiveness of its internal order, and the expansionist aspirations inherent in its ideology.

In the Soviet Union, meanwhile, Party Secretary Andrei Zhdanov enunciated the "two-camp" theory, dividing the world into implacably opposed ideological blocs.[6] And in the same issue of *Foreign Affairs* that contained Kennan's "X" article, the noted Soviet economist Evgeni Varga published an article that forecast the further demise of European, and particularly British, influence over world affairs, leaving a vacuum in Europe and elsewhere that he felt would be filled by the United States.[7] By the beginning of 1948, therefore, each side saw the other as its primary opponent in the next phase of global struggle.

This struggle initially manifested itself in the consolidation of

Soviet and American power – defined and exercised quite differently – within their respective spheres of influence. The United States concentrated on economic recovery through the Marshall Plan, the implantation of democratic systems of government in the former Axis states, and the construction of NATO, which was established in 1949. The Soviet Union built up an extensive network of control through military, intelligence, and political officers that systematically placed pro-Moscow communists in positions of power and purged leaders of rival parties or tendencies.

Only when some measure of stability was achieved in the consolidation of the bloc systems did the United States turn actively to the question of an East European policy. In December 1949, a secret directive, NSC 58/2 (subsequently declassified), established American policy towards Eastern Europe. Taking as its starting point the fact that "substantial strides" had been made "in developing Western Europe as a counterforce to communism," the document recommended measures designed to "cause the elimination or at least the reduction of predominant Soviet influence in the satellite states of Eastern Europe." It sought "to foster a heretical drifting away process" such as was currently being witnessed in Yugoslavia, but it also emphasized that "the satellite question is a function of our main problem – relations with the Soviet Union."[8]

So from the very beginning, even in this most offensive phase of "rolling back" communism in Eastern Europe, American objectives towards this region nevertheless were shaped and determined by the apparently higher priorities of relations with Western Europe on the one hand and the Soviet Union on the other. They were also functions of the substantial changes in international relations wrought by the advent of "nuclear diplomacy."

The fear of a third world war that would be nuclear had a salutary effect on international relations even in the late 1940s, when, at the height of the Berlin blockade in 1948–9, American statesmen acted forcefully to demonstrate commitment to existing alliance arrangements while avoiding direct challenges to Soviet authority over Eastern Europe.[9] The prevention of nuclear war thereby became a much higher goal than the liberation of Eastern Europe, even in the period of massive American nuclear preeminence. Because the fear of a nuclear war was paramount, efforts to deter it also predominated. And given the collapse of trust between the two blocks, the militarization of interbloc relations was to be expected. As a result, statesmen who in 1946 had hoped for a restoration of the balance of power and had advocated a multidimensional policy of containment to meet the challenge of Soviet expansion saw instead the birth of the balance of terror. The transformation of the international system by nuclear weapons was complete: Not only did these arms revolutionize the waging of war, but they also transformed the waging of peace.

Nowhere did the effects of this transformation in the technology of war intermingle with mutual suspicion more than in Eastern Europe. By 1955, NATO and Warsaw Pact states had already begun a deterrence-oriented process of rearmament and military buildup. The two Germanys were incorporated into rival military blocs, and hundreds of thousands of U.S. and Soviet forces faced each other in the center of Europe.

Even as early as 1948, many in the West had serious reservations about the wisdom of both the division of Germany and the creation of rival military blocs in Europe. George Kennan warned, for example, "from such a trend of developments, it would be hard . . . to find 'the road back' to a united and free Europe."[10] As he was to observe in his memoirs, the major difficulty posed by the creation of NATO and the Warsaw Pact was that although both pacts were formed as *instruments* of policy, they inexorably became *ends* of policy, with questions of alliance cohesion and military preparedness taking precedence over reunification and genuine security in Europe. He regarded the stationing of Soviet and American forces in Europe as unnatural, and he hoped it would be temporary.[11]

It seemed that these hopes could not be realized. Not only was the division of Europe maintained, but the deployment of Soviet and American intermediate-range nuclear weapons in Europe at the end of the 1970s increased doubts in Europe that the division could ever be overcome. At the same time, general resistance to "bloc thinking" increased throughout Europe. Many challenged the raison d'être of the bloc system in Europe, maintaining that the division of Europe was both artificial and dangerous: Far from guaranteeing continued security, Europe's division was seen as a major source of insecurity. The overreliance on military solutions, it was argued, had created an unnecessary intrusion of security interests into political and economic debates. This intrusion occurred to some extent in Western Europe (as in American concerns over the security implications of socialist or communist party electoral victories in Italy or France), but it took on a sharper and qualitatively different significance in Eastern Europe. There, local regimes struggled to increase the viability of their own rule against the backdrop of widespread unpopularity brought about largely by the universal perception that local leaders served Moscow's interests, particularly in the security field. The difficulty for local groups or leaders who sought to attune themselves to indigenous needs was that unless they defied the USSR in the military-security field as well, the West was unlikely to devote significant resources to support them.

Western leaders certainly faced the charge that overreliance on military competition blinded them to the particular needs and aspirations of East European nations. The problem for the West was that because of the clash between Soviet and Western military interests in Eastern Europe, the West was constrained from openly supporting measures that might improve living conditions in Eastern Europe but that at the same time might enhance the strength of the Warsaw Pact.

A more fundamental problem of shaping policy for the West in general and for the United States in particular was that while Western interests collided with the USSR's in Eastern Europe, the fate of this region (except for that of Germany) was not considered to be a *casus belli* for the West.

At the root of Western attitudes towards Eastern Europe was an absence of focus and a lack of passion about what was at stake there. To be sure, there was a general Western awareness that Eastern Europe's fate was linked to the West's through centuries of crossing paths – of migrations, expulsions, conquests, and colonization. At the same time, studies of these connections revealed a millennium-old pattern of Western perceptions of Slavic inferiority, beginning with the "civilizing" mission of the Teutonic Knights in the Baltic lands and continuing with the spread of Western languages, with Latin, German, or French serving as the *lingua franca* binding Eastern Europe to what was seen as the Western mainstream. Emerging as largely peripheral to the concerns of Western civilization, Eastern Europe was too often described as the set of countries where talented Germans and Jews resided and produced great works among generally backward and illiterate native populations. Although this false characterization pertained mainly to the Slavs, the Magyars and Romanians fared little better in the history books.

The prejudice, however, was nothing new to the West. For example, it had always been the prospect of the defeat of Vienna, rather than the fall of Hungary, that mobilized the faithful. Describing the fourteenth-century push by Ottoman armies toward Vienna, Barbara Tuchman provided an analysis which may have been a distant mirror but was nonetheless a clear reflection of the West's own dilemma over how to deal with the Soviet presence in Eastern Europe. Describing a Hungary weakened by conflicts with Poland and Lithuania to the north and receiving no support from hostile neighbors to the south, she noted that the West was alarmed by the fall of Hungary, not out of great concern for the fate of the Hungarians but because it anticipated the imminence of Western collapse:

> While not oblivious to the Turkish advance, the West, having no great attachment to Constantinople, paid little serious attention to the danger until it reached Hungary. Every Pope in the last forty years had, it is true, called for crusade against the approaching infidel, some with real fervor, but the fervor was more for invigoration of the Faith than from a realistic appreciation of the danger. Such enterprises as were launched against the Turks were narrow in scope and motivated by special interests.[12]

How portentous such perceptions were for Western policy in the postwar era. And the same held true for virtually every major European power, as well as for the United States. Even in West Germany, the easing of Soviet influence over East Germany arguably had a lower priority, at least up to the end of 1989, than did the strengthening of relations with Europe and the United States. Indeed, in the decades following World War II, the price paid for the considerable stability achieved in Europe and between NATO and the Warsaw Pact was the de facto acceptance of illegitimate and repressive East European regimes. The dilemma faced by American and Western leaders, therefore, was to frame policies which would maintain and enhance the achievement of higher-priority goals without appearing to endorse the negative aspects of these regimes. Optimally, it was hoped that such policies would promote positive and constructive change inside Eastern Europe without putting European stability at risk.

The formulation of such policies was made all the more difficult because although Eastern Europe was not considered a geographical region over which most Americans would be willing to go to war, it nevertheless proved to be one of the most volatile and sensitive regions on the globe. Western leaders were aware that crises could easily escalate to envelop Germany and the rest of the NATO alliance and threaten nuclear conflagration. They saw the need, therefore, to balance their interest in the promotion of constructive change inside Eastern Europe against the equal, if not greater, need to maintain regional stability.

The West's apparent preference for stability over change arose not from a callous disregard for the moral imperative of pursuing policies in Eastern Europe that would give greater attention to human rights and democratic freedoms. Rather, it was based on previous experience which indicated that the Soviet Union and local regimes could not be "forced" by the West to provide such rights and freedoms. Promoting crises through intrusive diplomatic and military policies of "roll-back," "bridge building," or "decoupling" in Eastern Europe all too often backfired.

The challenge for the West always was to channel the growing demands for greater diversity in Eastern Europe along paths favorable to Western interests without so alarming Moscow as to provoke a crisis, thereby ending any incipient reforms and producing a threat to European security as well. No policy towards Eastern Europe was likely to succeed unless it recognized, without promoting, the Soviet Union's security interests in Eastern Europe. Nor would any policy have succeeded which assumed that the Soviet bloc was just another empire (i.e., an empire composed of European "colonies," of which the Soviet Union could be persuaded to divest itself if the costs became too high).

According to Alexander Haig, this view was promoted at the height of the Polish crisis by "hard-liners" within the Reagan administration who thought that the Soviet Union could be "brought to its knees" if the West would abet the development of ever more costly cycles of collapse, crisis, and oppression in Eastern Europe.[13]

Repeated crises in Eastern Europe showed that no member of the Western alliance, including the United States, had either the political will or the military capability (short of nuclear war) to take the kinds of actions required to challenge Soviet hegemony in Eastern Europe directly. A grain embargo, the withholding of most-favored-nation trading status, and a ban on European exportation of parts for the Soviet Union's gas pipeline were reasonably useful for censuring specific Soviet actions, but were insufficient to achieve fundamental redefinition of Soviet aims and interests in Eastern Europe. Such measures were skillfully employed in situations short of a major crisis in Eastern Europe to achieve important changes at the margins (such as the release of political prisoners in Poland), but were less successful in achieving major breakthroughs. Rather, it was the steady and purposeful engagement of the Soviet bloc by the West which over time increased East European determination to pursue such links and decreased Soviet concern. This is why the rush towards the West which occurred in 1989 was so effortless: The majority of the distance had been run, and most of the hurdles had either been jumped or removed by Moscow in the preceding months and years. Only the sprint to the finish remained.

Alliance Cohesion: At What Cost?

The careful and patient construction of formal and informal networks of relationships that crisscrossed and thereby gradually bound Europe more closely together was an aspiration shared by many Europeans, both East and West. It was espoused, too, by many American and Soviet policymakers, past and present.

To the extent, however, that stability in Europe increased in the decades following the establishment of NATO and the Warsaw Pact, this was because the policies of the two blocs were designed to ameliorate the consequences of the military division of Europe rather than to remove that division. Security in Europe came to be synonymous with the stability between the two blocs. And this stability was itself often seen as resulting at least as much from the internal cohesion of each bloc as from the lack of open tension between them.

Both Soviet and American leaders promoted the ideal of European unity, as with the commitment by successive U.S. presidents to German unity and as with Gorbachev's references to Europe as "our common home"; but in the past both sides were willing to foster that idea only to the extent that it weakened the cohesion of the opposing bloc without in any way diminishing the unity of their own. The point here is simply that for both the United States and the Soviet Union, the cohesion of NATO and the Warsaw Pact alliances, respectively, was a higher goal than inter-alliance links.

Many felt that these two goals were not always or necessarily incompatible, and during tranquil periods they were pursued simultaneously. But in times of crisis or poor superpower relations, the requirement for cohesion often led to demands for severance of inter-alliance links. Indeed, the greater were these links, the less successful leaders were in fostering cohesion. This appeared in part to be because the dehumanization of the enemy required to maintain bloc unity was undermined by the cross-cultural humanization which occurred because of people-to-people contacts. Put another way, the more that West European youths traveled as tourists in the Soviet bloc, the less East Europeans could envisage the same people returning in tanks. Soviet appeals for increased defense preparedness against the enemy not only fell on deaf ears but also came to be regarded in Eastern Europe as little more than a mechanism for justifying the Soviet presence. While the American presence in Europe always had more intrinsic legitimacy, and certainly Soviet actions more than convinced most West European populations that there really was a Soviet threat, nevertheless many specific decisions by American administrations in the late 1970s and early 1980s (like the stationing of cruise missiles in Europe) were interpreted by European public opinion as efforts by the United States artificially to main-

tain a Cold War psychology. Cultural contacts thus worked to
deprive military and political leaders on both sides of the most
important element of alliance cohesion – fear of the enemy.

There were, and remain, of course, qualitative differences in
the bases for cohesion of the two alliances. The Warsaw Pact was
no more united after the invasion of Czechoslovakia in 1968
(despite the fact that this action convinced the Czechoslovaks
and others that they had to sever their links with the West) than
NATO was incohesive after the United States failed to impose a
pipeline embargo. That is to say, no amount of superficial uniformity in external bloc relations would produce cohesion if it did
not already exist on a more substantial basis; conversely, if an
alliance enjoyed real cohesion based on the unified pursuit of
core systemic goals, diverse external actions could be taken without undermining that cohesion.

Gorbachev, at a very early stage, acknowledged that the entire
basis of unity within the socialist bloc had been imposed. This
was clear from his remarks on this subject at the 27th Party
Congress:

> We consider that the variety of our movement is not
> a synonym for disjointedness, just as unity has nothing
> in common with uniformity, with a hierarchy, with
> interference by some parties in the affairs of others,
> with an aspiration by any party for a monopoly of
> truth. . . . That is how the CPSU understands unity
> and it intends to foster it in every way.[14]

Such remarks supported the subsequent tolerance of reformist
trends in Eastern Europe, although the limits of Moscow's tolerance of bloc challenges to core Soviet security interests were
largely untested until the end of 1989, when the Warsaw Pact
began to unravel, while NATO remained in place. However, by
that time, core changes in Soviet military doctrine, as discussed
in Chapter 7, had essentially removed Eastern Europe from the
Soviet Union's zone of vital national security. As a result, while
the move to reunify Germany within the context of continued
German membership in NATO raised many serious political issues, it was accepted in Moscow because inter-European ties had
virtually replaced alliance cohesion as the best guarantor of Sovi-

et security, as long as the trend towards demilitarization of international relations and arms reductions continued.

Fostering a European Identity

The buildup of conventional and nuclear forces in Europe into the 1970s and 1980s produced the growing feeling that a continuing arms race in Europe, far from alleviating tensions, actually diminished security. The historical record had further indicated that no change was likely in Eastern Europe as long as tensions between Eastern and Western Europe remained acute. The prospect of further arms reductions opened up by the December 1987 signing by Reagan and Gorbachev of the INF agreement eliminating intermediate-range nuclear forces from Central Europe held out the promise of a significant reduction of tensions in Central Europe.

Thoroughgoing arms reductions had increasingly been proposed as a way to promote the quest for common or equal security as a *modus operandi* in inter-European relations. The concept came into political usage with the report called *Common Security,* produced by the Independent Commission on Disarmament and Security Issues. The commission was headed by Sweden's former prime minister, the late Olaf Palme, and consisted of sixteen commissioners from various states, including former U.S. Secretary of State Cyrus Vance, former British Foreign Secretary David Owen, and the Kremlin's chief specialist on the United States, Georgii Arbatov. In their 200-page report, published in 1982, they concluded:

> States can no longer seek security at each other's expense; it can be attained only through cooperative undertakings. Security in the nuclear age means common security. Even ideological opponents and political rivals have a shared interest in survival. There must be a partnership in the struggle against war itself. The search for arms control and disarmament is the pursuit of common gains, not unilateral advantage. *A doctrine of common security must replace the present expedient of deterrence through armaments. International peace must*

*rest on a commitment to joint survival rather than a
threat of mutual destruction.*[15]

Arms reductions, however, constituted only the first step toward achieving the goal of common security. Long-term security
in Europe depended on the achievement of two no less difficult
tasks. The first was the fundamental transformation of the Soviet–
East European relationship along the lines suggested in previous
chapters. Elimination of the Stalinist legacy from the relationship
began to occur in East European countries in 1989, even though in
the process the future of both socialism and the Warsaw Pact was
challenged. At the same time, the changes reduced the internal
sources of crisis within these systems.

Was the way finally open, therefore, for Eastern Europe to
reclaim its place in Europe? The answer suggested throughout
this book is the one provided by the East Europeans themselves:
They are a definite part of Europe, as socialists, social democrats,
nationalists, Christian democrats, and even Eurocommunists. To
the considerable extent that all sectors of opinion seek to move
closer to Europe, they aim to do so without eliciting a backlash
from the USSR. And they believe this to be possible only if the
current debate in the Soviet Union deepens and is resolved in
favor of domestic transformation, reduced military expenditures, and the fundamental opening of the system to more diverse internal and external influences, including those from Europe. For this reason, most believe that given the Soviet Union's
geo-political position, any attempt to isolate it would diminish
the ability of Eastern Europe to reestablish links with the West.

To many in Eastern Europe, Gorbachev appeared sincere
when he declared that "Europe's historic chance and its future
lies in peaceful cooperation between the states of that continent." He has sought to implement the vision he outlined in a
speech before the 27th Party Congress: "it is important . . . to
move forward from the initial phase of détente to a more stable,
mature détente; then to the creation of reliable security on the
basis of the Helsinki process and radical cuts in nuclear and
conventional arms."[16]

Such transformations appear realizable, but will make as many
demands on the West as they will provide opportunities. The
first demand will be in the area of arms reductions. Reflecting on

the reasons for the West's failure to prevent the division of Europe, George Kennan concluded, some twenty years after the "X" article, that responsibility lay not in the injustice of Western ideals but in the overwhelming and therefore self-defeating American reliance on the military instrument to achieve Western goals. To the extent that containment had failed, he wrote, "the failure consisted in the fact that our own government, finding it difficult to deal with it [the Soviet threat] in other than military terms, . . . exerted itself, in its military preoccupations, to seal and to perpetuate the very division of Europe which it should have been concerned to remove."[17] Continued acceptance of the need to reduce both conventional and nuclear arsenals, as supported by both sides since the December 1987 Reagan–Gorbachev summit, would go far to end the preeminence of the military instrument in interbloc policy. The removal of existing divisions between East and West will serve as the prelude to an era of peace on the Continent, however, only if the general trend towards arms reduction and the elimination of military blocs continues. In particular, to work towards the strengthening of a NATO which includes a united and militarily powerful Germany will only sow the seeds for the next round of East–West enmity.

In attempting to formulate a policy that will promote transformation and continue the trend towards arms reductions, greater attention also needs to be focused on the absolutely crucial role of cultural relations in spawning ties that will draw Eastern and Western Europe closer together. In promoting such ties, the West needs to examine its own culpability for failing to appreciate and develop the rich cultural heritage these states offer. The truth is that it was not just the position of Soviet troops in 1945 that determined the fate of Eastern Europe. It was also the centuries-old perception that the non-Germanic countries of Central Europe were peripheral to "the West" and its future. And this perception was translated in the postwar period into the enduring notion that Eastern Europe was little more than a pawn in the superpower game, a "target in search of a policy."[18]

The East European conviction that they could make a unique contribution was summed up by the great Hungarian poet Gyula Illyés, who wrote:

> The sons of great nations most often know only their
> own literature, believing it is so great it can answer all
> their questions. It is great, but it is still not the world.
> The world is known to him impelled to be on the
> move.[19]

Those nations which had been on the move for forty years were finally able to regain their place in Europe only because they had maintained their moral compass. Certainly, East European intellectuals and leaders sought, and seek, Western standards of consumer welfare. To achieve it they will need enormous levels of economic assistance. But they hope to enrich the West as much as they seek to be enriched by it. As Václav Havel, Czechoslovakia's acting president, said in his New Year address to the nation:

> Our state should never again be a burden or a poor
> relation to anyone else. Although we have to take a
> great many things and learn many things from others,
> we must do this, after a long period of time, as equal
> partners who also have something to offer. . . . We are
> a small country, but nonetheless we were once the
> spiritual crossroads of Europe. Is there any reason why
> we should not be so again? Would this not be another
> contribution through which we could pay others back
> for the help we will need from them?[20]

Eastern Europe has much to offer the West, but it also challenges the West to recognize its own cultural needs.

Changes in Eastern Europe also challenge the West to recognize that genuine reform can strengthen security by ameliorating those sources of instability in Eastern Europe and Germany that have rocked the postwar world. Western leaders also need to accept the possibility that while Soviet–American rivalry is deep, fundamental, and systemic to both societies, it may be possible, given sufficient reform in the Soviet Union, to channel that rivalry along lines that will allow the considerable progress already made in inter-European relations to flourish. Recognition of the vast potential offered by current trends for enhanced stability and security in Europe will ensure that the 1990s will not become another decade of missed opportunities for eliminating the more negative consequences of the division of Europe, including its military division.

The enormous changes which took place in Eastern Europe will also continue to present challenges to the Soviet Union. There is first of all the personal position of Gorbachev, which some conservatives have sought to undermine by attacking him as being "soft" on the German question. While it appeared to many in the West that the movement towards unification was unstoppable, many in the East continued to doubt this, with some, like Yegor Ligachev, arguing before the CPSU leadership that "it is not too late" to prevent East Germany from being swallowed up by the West. Broad opposition in the USSR to unity on such terms could become a rallying cry for anti-Gorbachev forces. If Lenin could come to power through Germany, after all, Gorbachev could leave it the same way.

And then there is the entire structure of the Soviet–East European relationship which is going to have to be rebuilt on a completely new basis. CMEA and the Warsaw Pact will have to take on new roles if they are to survive scrutiny from democratically elected noncommunist governments. CMEA will have to become a vehicle for the integration of market-based economies into the international system, rather than an impediment to this process. The Warsaw Pact can only survive as a multilateral adjunct to the Helsinki process, responsible for coordinating verification and confidence-building measures. Its ability to make such a transition smoothly will be affected by the enormous potential for friction between East European governments that wish to drop out of the pact altogether and Soviet concern to maintain its military presence in Central Europe as a united Germany moves back onto the world stage, potentially as a part of NATO.

Finally, there is the internal cohesion of the Soviet Union itself, which threatens to dissolve under the burden of economic collapse, ethnic strife, and rival nationalisms. These processes are accelerated by the events in Eastern Europe. Nationalities draw inspiration from the ease of the transformations in East Germany, Bulgaria, and Czechoslovakia, where almost overnight mass demonstrations effected a transfer of power. At the same time, the incredible vilification in the Soviet mass media of Ceauşescu – frequently called "Dracula-Ceauşescu" – for the cold-blooded killing of peaceful demonstrators has put enormous additional constraints on the use of force by Soviet leaders

who want to avoid being tarred with the same brush. And the
sharp worsening of the standards of living in Hungary and Poland, involving inflation, unemployment, and wage freezes imposed during the transition to a market economy, is seen
amongst some Soviet citizens as a bleak harbinger.

Many in the USSR who were alarmed by the events in Eastern
Europe blamed Gorbachev's policy of *perestroika* for the changes
and saw in that policy the seeds for the destruction of even the
USSR. As one young party member lamented:

> The year 1989 will go down in history as the year that
> the world socialist system collapsed. . . . It is very
> likely that the very concept of the "Union of Soviet
> Socialist Republics" will disappear from the political
> map of the world in 1990. . . . Our faith has been
> taken away and we do not have the will to live or
> work.[21]

Given the outright rejection of socialism which occurred
throughout much of Eastern Europe, it became more difficult
for Gorbachev to convince the CPSU that his plan to introduce
"humane, democratic socialism," the program title for the 28th
Party Congress, would not inevitably lead to capitalism. And
considering the apparent alacrity with which the Soviet military
agreed to withdraw from parts of Eastern Europe, it was not
difficult to understand why the Baltic states also sought a withdrawal of Russian troops. The events in Eastern Europe opened
up possibilities for the Soviet Union to improve its position in
Europe and the world, but there were challenges still to be
overcome.

All of these challenges, however, faded in comparison with
the opportunities presented for all parties by the changes which
occurred in Eastern Europe. While a few in the Soviet Union
may have mourned the passing of empire, and while many feared
the reemergence of a Germany united, armed, and untethered,
most Soviets shared with the peoples and leaders of the West and
Eastern Europe enormous hopes for the future growth and prosperity of this region – a prosperity which they could contribute
to and benefit from.

This new Eastern Europe would no longer be the bridgehead
in Soviet military plans, but would become the political bridge
between East and West. It would cease fulfilling the role of the

ideological vanguard and would resume its role as the cultural avant-garde. It could stop pretending to be a developed socialist society, and start developing. It could give up the facade of democratic centralism, and discover democracy.

Seven decades earlier, Lenin had predicted that the lava from revolutionary eruptions in the East would flow to engulf the West. Now, in a clear reversal of the Leninist prediction, the lava is flowing from West to East, bringing with it the triumph of democratic ideals. It is not primarily the triumph of one bloc over another. It is finally the victory of people's desires to govern themselves in decency and peace. Whether this victory will be recorded in history books as permanent or temporary will depend above all, however, on Mikhail Gorbachev's success in transforming the USSR from a totalitarian regime into an open society. When Václav Havel told the U.S. Congress that the best guarantee of Czechoslovakia's independence was Soviet democracy, he spoke with the historical knowledge that fledgling states in Central Europe cannot easily survive when tyranny reigns on their borders. How to democratize the USSR without unleashing anarchy, and with it a simultaneous authoritarian backlash, will, however, present a major challenge.

The peoples of Eastern Europe know that their independence cannot be purchased with the continued denial of the same rights to the peoples of the USSR. Just as Western Europe was threatened as long as Eastern Europe was occupied, so now Eastern Europe cannot be truly secure as long as the USSR is unstable. To live in decency and peace may indeed be a basic human right, but historically it has existed more in aspiration than in practice. To establish it in Eastern Europe — at the crossroads of cultures, religions, nationalities, and armies — may be possible, but it will demand great skill, enormous effort, and fabulous good fortune.

Notes

1 Charles-Louis de Secondat, Baron de Montesquieu, *The Spirit of Laws* (Berkeley: University of California Press, 1977), p. 237.

2 For an interesting analysis of these trends, see Michael Stürmer, "Germany, East and West: Prospects for a Divided Nation in Europe," in N. Edwina Moreton, ed., *Germany Between East and West* (Cambridge University Press, 1987).

3   Peter Bender, *Das Ende des ideologischen Zeitalters* (Berlin: Severin & Siedler, 1981).

4   Zbigniew Brzezinski, "The Future of Yalta," *Foreign Affairs,* Winter 1984–5, pp. 279–302.

5   Gorbachev speech at Czechoslovak–Soviet Friendship Rally, Prague, April 10, 1987, *Pravda,* April 11, 1987.

6   The two-camp theory had its roots in party resolutions and articles by Zhdanov on "survivals of bourgeois ideology" amongst those Soviet intellectuals who supposedly expressed "servility" towards the West while ignoring the decisive role of Russian ideas. See, for example, his sharp denunciation of G. F. Aleksandrov's book, *History of West European Philosophy,* in *Bol'shevik,* No. 16, August 1947, p. 22. Aleksandrov at that time was the head of the Propaganda Department of the CPSU Central Committee.

7   E. Varga, "Anglo-American Rivalry and Partnership: A Marxist View," *Foreign Affairs,* Vol. 25, No. 4, July 1947, pp. 583–596.

8   NSC 58/2, *A Report to the President by the National Security Council on United States Policy Toward the Soviet Satellite States in Eastern Europe,* December 8, 1949, 14pp., Top Secret (declassified), as quoted by Raymond L. Garthoff, "Eastern Europe in the Context of U.S.–Soviet Relations," in Sarah Meiklejohn Terry, ed., *Soviet Policy in Eastern Europe* (New Haven, Conn.: Yale University Press, 1984), p. 318.

9   See Avi Shlaim, *The United States and the Berlin Blockade, 1948–49* (Berkeley: University of California Press, 1983).

10 *PPS 37,* "Policy Questions Concerning a Possible German Settlement," August 12, 1948, FR: 1948, II, 1287–1297, quoted in John Lewis Gaddis, *Strategies of Containment: A Critical Appraisal of Postwar American National Security Policy* (Oxford University Press, 1982), p. 75.

11 George Kennan, *Memoirs, 1925–1950* (New York: Bantam, 1967), pp. 477–481.

12 Barbara Tuchman, *A Distant Mirror: The Calamitous 14th Century* (New York: Knopf, 1978), pp. 542–543.

13 Alexander Haig, in his memoirs, as excerpted in *Time,* April 9, 1984, recounts that while administration hard-liners did not seek military confrontation, they did believe that the United States could "control Soviet behavior toward Poland . . . through the application of economic or trade sanctions that would 'bring her to her knees.'" Haig believed such views to be totally fallacious.

14 Gorbachev speech to the 27th Party Congress, *op. cit.,* p. 33.

15 The Independent Commission on Disarmament and Security Issues, *Common Security, A Blueprint for Survival* (New York: Simon & Schuster, 1982), p. 139 (italics in original).

16 Gorbachev speech to the 27th Party Congress, *op. cit.,* p. 31.

17 Kennan, *Memoirs,* p. 385.

18 Bennett Kovrig, "The United States: 'Peaceful Engagement' Revisited," in Charles Gati, ed., *The International Politics of Eastern Europe* (New York: Praeger, 1976), p. 143.

19 Gyula Illyés, quoted in János Kádár, "Hungary and Peace in Europe," *New Hungarian Quarterly,* Vol. 26, No. 100, Winter 1985, p. 9.
20 Prague Television Service, in Czech, January 1, 1990, Foreign Broadcast Information Service, *East European Daily Report,* January 2, 1990, p. 10.
21 S. Stolbun, "Ideas Must Conquer," *Komsomol'skaya pravda,* January 17, 1990.

APPENDIX I

Chronology of East European Events

February

At Yalta, the Allies agree to allow the Soviets to maintain positions in Eastern Europe.

March

Under pressure from the National Democratic Front (NDF), the Rădescu government resigns in Romania, and a new administration is formed under Petru Groza of Ploughman's Front (part of the NDF).

April

A twenty-year treaty of friendship and mutual assistance is signed between Yugoslavia and Soviet Union.

July

At Potsdam, the Polish Provisional Government is recognized by the Allies; reparations and the future disposition of defeated Germany are discussed.

August

Polish–Soviet agreements are reached on the Oder-Neisse line and the supply of Polish coal to the Soviet Union.

October

Opposition leaders resign from the Yugoslav cabinet, leaving it Communist-dominated.

November

With 90 percent of the vote, Josip Broz Tito's National Front wins an election boycotted by opposition parties; Yugoslavia is declared a republic. In Hungary, Zoltán Tildy of the Smallholders' Party forms a government after winning National Assembly elections. The Communist Party receives only 17 percent of the vote.

December

U.S. and Soviet troops begin the evacuation of Czechoslovakia.

1946

January

The Allied Control Commission from Great Britain, the United States, and the Soviet Union visits Bucharest for talks to broaden the Groza government. Albania is proclaimed a republic under Enver Hoxha; the return of King Zog is forbidden.

February

Hungary is declared a republic after abolition of the monarchy.

March

The Georgiev cabinet in Bulgaria resigns and is reconvened under the heavily communist Fatherland Front. In the United States, Winston Churchill's speech in Fulton, Missouri, warning of Soviet expansionism in Eastern Europe marks the de facto end of the wartime Anglo-American alliance with the USSR.

May

The Communist Party in Czechoslovakia polls 38 percent of the vote in elections. At the Paris Peace Conference, the Council of Foreign Ministers agrees on disposition of Romanian territory: Transylvania remains with Romania, southern Dobruja is retained by Bulgaria, Bessarabia and North Bukovina are given to the USSR. This arrangement, along with reparations, is confirmed by a peace treaty in July.

June

Reports surface in Czechoslovakia of 100,000 Ukrainians and thousands of Jews fleeing Carpatho-Ukraine.

July

In Czechoslovakia, Klement Gottwald calls for a new constitution, with provisions for the nationalization of large industries.

August

Gustáv Husák heads a new Slovakian cabinet. The Soviet Union signs trade agreements with East European states.

September

Bulgaria overwhelmingly rejects the monarchy in a plebiscite and is proclaimed a "People's Republic."

October

The Fatherland Front wins a majority in the Bulgarian National Assembly elections; a Communist-dominated cabinet under Georgii Dimitrov soon takes power.

November

In the Romanian general elections, the National Democratic Front gains 68 percent of the vote amid accusations of heavy discrimination against opposition parties; the election is followed by arrests of opposition members.

1947

January

The Communist Party under Bolesław Bierut and Władysław Gomułka wins elections in Poland.

February

In Hungary, allegations against the Smallholders' Party by Communist-controlled security forces culminate in the arrest of Smallholders' General Secretary Béla Kovács. A peace treaty with Hungary is signed in Paris, in which Hungary loses all territory gained during World War II.

March

The Marshall Plan is announced.

May

Ferenc Nagy resigns as Hungarian prime minister while in Switzerland; this is accompanied by arrests and defections of ruling Smallholders' Party leaders.

July

Czechoslovakia and Poland initially accept the Marshall Plan, but refuse it two days later under Soviet pressure.

August

In Hungary, elections give the Communist-dominated leftist block 46 percent of the vote. Communists now dominate the National Assembly and all key government posts.

September

Cominform is established. Andrei Zhdanov gives his "two-camps" speech.

October

In Romania, Communist and Social Democrat parties begin the merger to become the Romanian Workers' Party.

December

In accordance with the peace treaty, the Soviets begin an evacuation of all forces from Bulgaria. The Romanian monarchy is abolished.

1948

February

Tensions increase in Czechoslovakia over Communist nationalization policies and efforts to replace security personnel; twelve non-Communist ministers resign, and Gottwald forms a new Communist-dominated cabinet.

March

The death (officially by suicide) of Czechoslovakia's last remaining non-Communist leader, Foreign Minister Jan Masaryk. Gottwald outlines nationalization measures. The Soviets walk out of the Allied Control Commission, accusing the Allies of undermining quadripartite control. The Soviet–Yugoslav dispute erupts, and continues with increasing tensions through the spring.

April

The Social Democrats merge with the Communists in Czechoslovakia. The Soviets impose stringent controls on access to Berlin.

May

The Communist-dominated National Front wins an electoral victory in Czechoslovakia. Edward Beneš resigns the presidency in June.

June

At a Cominform conference in Budapest, Tito is denounced for nationalist deviation. Soviets begin blockade of Berlin, and Allies respond with airlift.

September

"Nationalist deviationists" are purged in Poland; Gomułka is ousted as general secretary.

December

The Polish United Workers' Party (PUWP) is created from the merger of the Socialist and Communist parties; the party leadership calls for collectivization and industrialization, with heavy state participation. Dimitrov enunciates the "People's Democracy" theory, which soon is adopted by other East European leaders.

1949

January

The Council for Mutual Economic Assistance (CMEA) is created in response to the Marshall Plan. Former German territories are officially incorporated into Poland.

April

Vice-Premier Kostov is removed from the Bulgarian Politburo for nationalist deviation by an "inner cabinet" of Kolarov, Traikov, and Yugov while Dimitrov is in the USSR for health reasons. NATO is founded.

May

The Berlin blockade ends.

June

László Rajk, Hungarian foreign minister, is arrested on charges of high treason and conspiracy with Tito and the West. He is subsequently executed, signaling the beginning of purges in Hungary.

September

The Soviets denounce a friendship treaty with Yugoslavia; other East European countries soon follow suit.

October

The German Democratic Republic (GDR) is established under Walter Ulbricht. Yugoslavia alleges a border incident committed by Hungary. Widespread arrests begin in Czechoslovakia, signaling the purging of "bourgeois elements."

November

Gomułka is ousted from the PUWP Central Committee, along with Marian Spychalski and Zenon Kliszko. Soviet Marshal Rokossovski becomes Polish minister of defense and Politburo member.

December

Anti-Tito purges are reported in Albania. Kostov, with nine other former officials, is tried in Bulgaria for plotting with Yugoslavia, then is hanged.

1950

February

The GDR's Ministry of State Security is created.

March

A continuing Church–government conflict in Czechoslovakia culminates in espionage and treason trials for leading religious figures. A mass expulsion of Germans from Polish territory to the Federal Republic of Germany (FRG) takes place (125,000 Germans were estimated to have been in Poland).

June

GDR and Czechoslovakia accept the finality of the expulsion of Sudeten Germans (most of whom went to the FRG) and territorial changes; the GDR signs economic and cultural agreements with Poland and accepts the Oder-Neisse line. Yugoslav Workers' Councils in industry are established.

June–July

Purges in Hungarian cabinet and campaign against "rightist Social-Democrats" and trade unionists take place. Romania announces that 192,000 have been purged from the party since 1948.

July–October

Border incidents occur between Yugoslavia and Bulgaria.

July

At the Socialist Unity Party (SED) 3rd Congress in Berlin, a new constitution modeled on that of the Soviet Union is adopted, as is a Five-Year Plan. Christian Democrats, Liberal Democrats, and other opposition parties face mounting pressure.

August

Bulgaria commences the expulsion of more than 250,000 Turkish Moslems.

September

Six leading members of the SED are expelled for alleged espionage contacts. Further expulsions of CDU and Liberal Democrats take place; some flee to West Berlin.

October

Purges of officials and cabinet members begin in Bulgaria and continue into 1951. In Czechoslovakia, the number of political trials increases, and they continue through March 1951. Klementis is arrested. Cominform meets in Prague and urges the reunification of Germany, a peace treaty, and the prevention of German remilitarization.

November

Soviet nationals in Bulgaria are granted the same rights as Bulgarian citizens.

1951

January

"Emergency" speed-up of industrialization is demanded in Hungary, followed by rationing of food and gas in February. Rákosi calls collectivization the most important task.

March

An abortive deputy foreign ministers' meeting in Paris is intended as a prelude to Four Powers Conference. The Soviet Union stresses the need to fulfill the Potsdam agreement.

April

In decentralization of Yugoslav government, among other steps taken, the number of ministries is reduced to 19 from 34.

May

Compulsory food deliveries in Yugoslavia are abolished, and farmers are allowed to sell on the free market. Tito warns against farmers leaving collectives. In Hungary, Foreign Minister Gyula Kállai and Interior Minister János Kádár are among those arrested.

August

In a trial of four generals and five other officers in Poland, all receive long prison terms for espionage.

September

In Romania, ten Roman Catholic priests on trial for espionage and anti-state activity receive long prison terms. In a Czechoslovak cabinet shake-up, Svoboda is ousted, Slánský is demoted, and Gottwald assumes general secretary functions.

1952

March

A new Soviet proposal for a German peace treaty is endorsed by the GDR's Parliament; it calls for reunification and accepts German national defense force.

May–June

In Romanian cabinet purge, Interior Minister Georgescu is removed; Foreign Minister Ana Pauker is ousted from the Politburo.

July

At SED congress in Berlin, Ulbricht promulgates an economic plan emphasizing heavy industry and imposes administrative centralization and travel restrictions. Ties between East and West German churches are severed.

August

Rákosi "elected" prime minister by Hungarian National Assembly.

November

In Czechoslovakia, Slánský, who was arrested in November 1951, is tried along with thirteen high Communist officials; eleven are executed, and three receive sentences of life imprisonment. Eleven of the fourteen are Jewish.

1953–1955

The period of Georgii Malenkov's "New Course" in the bloc produces collective leaderships, amnesties for political prisoners, and improvements in living standards.

1953

March

Stalin dies. Gottwald warns about Czechoslovak economic difficulties and underfulfillment and institutes government reorganization. Food rationing is introduced. Gottwald dies.

May

Soviet control of the German zone is reorganized: The Control Commission is abolished and is succeeded by a Soviet high commissioner (Vladimir Semenov).

June

An increase in working norms leads to riots in Berlin. Protests spread to other cities before being suppressed by Soviet forces.

July

Lavrenti Beria is executed, and the Soviet secret police apparatus in Eastern Europe is reorganized. At Soviet insistence, Imre Nagy becomes prime minister in Hungary, while Rákosi remains party head; enforced collectivization and liberalization measures are abandoned.

August

Gheorghe Gheorghiu-Dej calls industrialization efforts excessive and announces increases in the food supply and in consumer goods.

September

In Czechoslovakia, following the death of Gottwald, the government and party are reorganized, the Presidium is abolished, and ministries are merged; economic planning shifts to favor consumer goods. Starting in fall 1953 and continuing through the following spring, leading Romanian Jews are arrested and tried on charges of Zionism.

November

The first Yugoslav ambassadors return to Bulgaria and Hungary since Yugoslavia's break with the Cominform.

December

Yugoslav relations are reestablished with Albania, and measures are taken to avoid further border incidents.

1954

January–December

The Soviet Union dissolves joint-stock companies throughout Eastern Europe.

January–February

The Berlin Conference of Foreign Ministers fails to reach an accord over the reunification of Germany.

March

Following the Bulgarian Communist Party 6th Congress, Vulko Chervenkov announces the release of former opposition members, creates a secretaryship separate from the premiership to be taken over by Todor Zhivkov, and announces that Bulgaria's rate of collectivization is highest among the satellites. Following the PUWP 2nd Congress, Poland adopts a collective leadership similar to that of the post-Stalin Soviet Union.

April

Accused of Slovakian separatism, Gustáv Husák is sentenced to life imprisonment, while three other former members of the Slovak Board of Commissioners receive long sentences; other religious and political trials take place.

June

Diplomatic relations between Yugoslavia and Romania are resumed.

July

The Albanian Workers' Party is reorganized along Soviet lines.

August

Yugoslavia joins the Balkan Pact with Greece and Turkey.

November

At the Moscow conference of East European states (excluding Yugoslavia), the Paris agreement on the remilitarization of Germany is denounced, and collective countermeasures in the event of ratification are threatened.

1955

March–May

Rákosi makes comeback; Imre Nagy loses all party and government positions and is denounced for "rightist deviations." Rákosi appoints András Hegedüs as prime minister, while keeping real power for himself.

May

The FRG enters NATO; one week later, the Warsaw Pact (WTO) is created. A Soviet peace treaty with Austria is signed. Nikita Khrushchev visits Belgrade, a sign of the beginning of Soviet–Yugoslav rapprochement.

June

The Soviet Union and Yugoslavia mark the formal end of their feud by signing a joint agreement advocating various measures for international peace.

September

The Soviet Union and the GDR sign a treaty recognizing East German sovereignty; the Soviet High Commission is abolished.

December

The Soviet Union reaffirms GDR control of East Berlin, the perimeter and border with West Berlin, and the border with the FRG.

1956

January

A National People's Army is created in the GDR; Grotewohl still suggests efforts at collaboration with the FRG.

February

At the 20th Party Congress in the Soviet Union, de-Stalinization begins and produces a reaction throughout the bloc: Gomułka is released from prison, with many others, and Rajk (Hungary) and Kostov (Bulgaria) are rehabilitated; the reaction is more cautious in Czechoslovakia. Over 1.5 million Germans are reported to have fled to the FRG.

March

Edward Ochab succeeds Bierut as head of the PUWP.

April

The Cominform is dissolved.

June

Strikes break out in Poznań, Poland. Relations between the CPSU and the League of Communists of Yugoslavia are reestablished.

July

Liberalization efforts in Poland serve as beacon for similar movements throughout the bloc, and especially in Hungary, where debating societies formed by reform-minded intellectuals are condemned by the Central Committee. Under public pressure, Rákosi is dismissed as general secretary, but is succeeded by another "Stalinist," Ernö Gerö.

October

Gomułka is reinstated as general secretary of the PUWP, and Rokossovski is dismissed, thereby avoiding a Soviet invasion of Poland. In Hungary, Nagy becomes prime minister; the first Soviet invasion occurs, ending when Mikoyan and Mikhail Suslov accept Nagy's regime and replace Gerö with Kádár. Nagy announces democratic reforms. The Soviet Union announces equality of rights between socialist countries. On October 31, Nagy announces Hungary's withdrawal from the WTO.

November

The Soviet Union invades Hungary a second time; Nagy is replaced by János Kádár.

1957

January

In a speech, Kádár expresses a hard-line, conservative policy by asserting a return to the "dictatorship of the proletariat"; sporadic work stoppages and strikes continue in Hungary.

February

In Bulgaria, more than 1,500 student sympathizers of the Hungarian revolt are expelled from Sofia University, and 200 are arrested.

May

Soviet–Hungarian agreement is reached on "temporary stationing" of Russian troops in Hungary.

July

In cabinet shake-ups in Bulgaria, Politburo and Central Committee members said to be advocates of closer ties with Yugoslavia are ousted.

October

Following the publication of his book *The New Class* in August, Milovan Djilas is sentenced to seven years in prison in Yugoslavia for propaganda.

November

Yugoslavia does not attend the Moscow meeting that produces the Declaration by Twelve Communist and Workers' Parties.

1958

April

A new Yugoslav party program is promulgated and is later attacked by the Soviets as revisionist.

June

Nagy is executed in Hungary; the first period of East European revisionism ends.

July

Soviet troops are withdrawn from Romania.

November

Khrushchev proposes transferring control of Berlin to the GDR, thus setting off a second Berlin crisis.

1959

January

In Bulgaria, Zhivkov puts forward plans for the full collectivization of agriculture and decentralization of some industrial ministries.

April

It is officially announced in the GDR that collectivization is completed.

May

The conference of foreign ministers meets in Geneva to resolve the Berlin crisis, but adjourns without success in August.

July

Albania signs trade and economic agreements with the Soviet Union.

November

In the first Hungarian party congress since the uprising, Kádár blames Rákosi and Nagy for problems and says that Soviet troops will remain for "international reasons."

December

The CMEA charter is promulgated.

1960

January

A reported secret meeting in Poland between Cardinal Wyszyński and Gomułka leads to a Church–state accord.

February

The Warsaw Pact Political Consultative Committee (PCC) threatens separate East European peace treaties with the GDR and calls for a Berlin settlement.

April

Rioting is reported in Nowa Huta, Poland, over the removal of a cross from a Church site.

May

The failure of the Paris summit as a result of a U-2 spy-plane incident leaves the Berlin crisis unresolved.

June

Gomułka announces an economic speed-up and more investment in heavy industry.

1961

February

During its 4th Party Congress, Albania denigrates the peaceful coexistence policy, thus supporting China in the Sino–Soviet dispute.

May

Eight Soviet subs leave Vlora, Albania. Vice Admiral Temp Sejku, a leader of the pro-Soviet faction in the Albanian military forces, is arrested and executed, and 60 others are arrested in anti-Soviet purges.

June

At a Vienna summit, Khrushchev gives President John F. Kennedy an aide-mémoire on Berlin, reiterating his threats.

July

In an economic crisis in the GDR, ministries are reorganized.

August

The Berlin Wall is erected. The Polish education ministry eases restrictions somewhat on teaching Catholicism.

October

Albania is denounced at the CPSU 22nd Party Congress and leaves the CMEA.

November

East European ambassadors are withdrawn from Albania; Hoxha blames the rift on Khrushchev.

December

A socialist division of labor is proposed for the CMEA. The Soviet Union and Albania close their respective embassies; Albania says that the Soviet Union initiated the break.

1962

March

Romania opposes the CMEA division of labor.

June

The CMEA countries agree to substantial economic integration and soon establish an Executive Committee.

November

In a struggle over anti-Stalinist policies in Bulgaria, Zhivkov ousts Yugov, Chervenkov, and others from party and government positions.

December

The CMEA establishes a development bank and payment system, replacing the voluntary cooperation plan of the late 1950s.

1963

March

An amnesty in Hungary releases nearly all political prisoners.

April

A new Yugoslav constitution replaces the 1946 constitution.

May

Centralization of industry, agriculture, and party agencies is announced in Bulgaria.

June

The rehabilitation of Klementis is announced in Czechoslovakia; in August, Slánský and other executed leaders are cleared of crimes.

September

In Czechoslovakia, Viliam Široký, along with other pro-Stalinists, is ousted by Antonín Novotný for past political mistakes related to the Klementis and Slánský trials.

1964

March

Most-favored-nation (MFN) trading status, which the United States had suspended in 1962, is returned to Poland and Yugoslavia.

April

Romania offers to mediate the Sino–Soviet dispute.

May

A Romanian–U.S. joint trade agreement is announced.

June

Romania announces the release of practically all political prisoners imprisoned during the past three years.

September

In Hungary, an accord with the Church allows for the establishment of a Roman Catholic hierarchy.

October

Khrushchev is ousted and replaced as CPSU general secretary by Leonid Brezhnev.

1965

April

A plot against Zhivkov by liberals seeking less reliance on Soviet Union and involving Central Committee members and the Sofia military district commander is reported.

July

A new party statute and constitution adopted at the Romanian Party Congress assert an increasingly independent Romanian position with the bloc. The new Five-Year Plan emphasizes industrial development to assure independence.

November

A party document from the Czechoslovak 13th Party Congress admits serious errors in economic management and introduces incentives to spur production.

December

An economic agreement between the GDR and the Soviet Union is announced; in the FRG, it is reported that highly advantageous terms of trade for the Soviet Union prompted GDR Deputy Premier Erich Apel to commit suicide.

1966

February

Hungary announces that an undisclosed number of people associated with the 1956 opposition took part in a conspiracy against the regime.

March

Following the CPSU 23rd Party Congress, Eastern-bloc leaders assert unity with the Soviet Union against China; the notable exception is Romania, which offers to mediate.

May

In his strongest assertion of independence, Nicolae Ceauşescu attacks the Soviet seizure of Bukovina and assails the existence of blocs. Soviet General Secretary Leonid Brezhnev pays a surprise visit to Bucharest.

June

During a visit to Bucharest, Chou En-Lai is prevented from making an anti-Soviet speech; he later visits Albania and attacks Romanian neutrality.

July

Yugoslav Interior Minister Alexander Ranković, the expected successor of Tito, is purged along with other members of his faction; the purge continues for several weeks.

October

A major reorganization of the Yugoslav League of Communists is announced.

November

A law enacted in Hungary allows more than one candidate on the election list, but all candidates still are chosen by the Patriotic Front.

1967

January

Romania establishes relations with the FRG, becoming the first East European state to do so. The FRG's attempt at better East European relations spurs a renewal of friendship and cooperation treaties signed in the late 1940s between the Soviet Union and bloc allies, except Romania. The existing Soviet–Romanian treaty nevertheless remains in force.

April

Twenty-four European communist parties meet at Karlovy Vary, Czechoslovakia, and propose the abandonment of the bloc system and the establishment of a joint European security system. In Yugoslavia, an almost complete change of cabinet personnel follows a plan for lessening the party's leading role.

June

At a Writers' Union Congress in Czechoslovakia, substantial criticism of the party and government is expressed.

August

The FRG and Czechoslovakia reach a trade agreement.

December

Novotný is almost ousted by the Presidium at the start of a Czechoslovak leadership crisis; Brezhnev flies to Prague, but declines to intercede on his behalf.

1968

January

The New Economic Mechanism is introduced in Hungary. Alexander Dubček replaces Novotný as head of the Czechoslovak Communist Party (CPCz), marking the beginning of the Prague Spring.

March

Ludvík Svoboda replaces Novotný as president of Czechoslovakia. The WTO meeting in Dresden expresses concern over the situation in Czechoslovakia.

April

An Action Program for thoroughgoing political and economic reform in Czechoslovakia is promulgated.

June

WTO maneuvers begin in Czechoslovakia. The "Two Thousand Words" statement by leading intellectuals seeks greater liberalization in Czechoslovakia.

July

The WTO "Warsaw Letter" warns Czechoslovakia against excessive liberalization. A meeting of Soviet and Czechoslovak leaders in Čierna reaches a short-lived accord.

August

The WTO meets in Bratislava, Czechoslovakia, followed by a WTO invasion. Dubček is reinstated after the Soviet Union fails to form a government.

September

In a major *Pravda* article on the "international obligations" of socialist countries, the Soviets assert the doctrine of limited sovereignty, thus emphasizing the wider consequences of the Czechoslovak invasion.

October

A treaty is signed between the USSR and Czechoslovakia on the "temporary" stationing of troops.

November

Brezhnev endorses concept of limited sovereignty of socialist states at PUWP 5th Congress.

1969

January

A CMEA meeting in Berlin is stalemated over currency and trade issues. Two thousand protesting students issue the "Prague Manifesto," condemning the Soviet occupation, after the self-immolation of Jan Palach on Wenceslas Square.

March

After violent anti-Soviet protests in Prague, visiting Defense Minister A. A. Grechko threatens the use of Soviet forces. Husák replaces Dubček in Czechoslovakia. In its first meeting since the invasion, the WTO in Budapest adopts a joint command structure, acceding to Romanian and other members' demands for a greater voice. Bloc states renew their call for a European Security Conference. Bulgarian officials warn against deviationism and Western influences in the arts.

May

The Czechoslovak Central Committee adopts a resolution on party goals reasserting "democratic centralism"; two progressive weeklies, along with three other periodicals, are banned. Recognition of the GDR by Iraq and the establishment of relations with Cambodia mark the effective end of the FRG's Hallstein Doctrine.

June

At a world conference of communist parties held in Moscow, Romania dissents over the Brezhnev Doctrine.

August

The anniversary of the 1968 invasion is marked by three days of unrest and clashes with police in Czechoslovakia. Bulgaria and Turkey agree on the repatriation of ethnic Turks from Bulgaria. Massive crowds greet Richard Nixon on his visit to Romania; measures to increase relations between the United States and Romania are agreed upon.

September

At a plenary meeting of the Czechoslovak Central Committee, the long-expected purge of reformers begins. A more conservative cabinet is formed, and the purge continues for several months.

1970

January

Husák cautions against extreme antireformism in a *Rudé právo* interview, but purges in Czech unions and universities continue.

March

Willi Brandt and Willi Stoph meet to discuss normalization of relations between the FRG and GDR. A second meeting in May leads to the FRG's recognition of the GDR and to an agreement on access to Berlin; concurrently, four-power talks on Berlin resume for the first time since 1959.

May

The CMEA establishes an investment bank. Poland adopts economic incentive measures to increase productivity.

June

The WTO foreign ministers' meeting issues a call for a European security conference, and for the first time accepts the presence of the United States and Canada. Dubček is expelled from the Czechoslovak Communist Party, which is seen as a victory for conservatives.

August

The Moscow Treaty between the FRG and the Soviet Union, recognizing postwar borders, is signed.

December

The Warsaw Treaty between the FRG and Poland is signed; as in the Moscow Treaty, the FRG explicitly recognizes the Oder-Neisse line. Riots and strikes occur in Polish coastal cities in response to price increases and economic reforms; 300 are reported killed. Gomułka is replaced by Edward Gierek, with changes in the Politburo and cabinet. In Czechoslovakia, centralization measures are enacted, reducing the authority of the Czech and Slovak regional governments; in a final report on a loyalty drive, Husák reports that 326,817 have been expelled from the party's membership of 1.5 million.

1971

February

In Poland, changes occur in cabinet and party personnel stemming from December riots, and continue through June.

April

Two Croatian nationalists assassinate the Yugoslav ambassador to Sweden.

May

Ulbricht is succeeded by Erich Honecker in the GDR. The 14th Party Congress in Czechoslovakia approves changes resulting from the Soviet invasion. A new Five-Year Plan calls for increased production for trade. Novotný is readmitted to the party.

July

The CMEA announces a comprehensive plan for greater economic integration.

September

Four-Power Agreement governing status of Berlin is signed.

November

During a Central Committee plenary session, Ceauşescu calls for the role of the party to be strengthened, to combat liberalizing trends in cultural and artistic areas.

December

Reconfirming his policy since the riots of the previous year, at the PUWP 6th Party Congress Gierek stresses improvement of living standards as the "supreme goal" of the party; further changes in the hierarchy occur. In

Zagreb, Yugoslavia, four nights of rioting involving Croatian nationalists lead to the resignation of top Croatian leaders.

1972

February

In a concession to the Church, the Polish government no longer demands to see the Church's financial records. It is reported that a Romanian general, Ion Serb, was executed for passing military secrets to the Soviet Union.

March

In the first student demonstration since 1956, students march through Budapest commemorating the revolt of 1848.

May

A treaty is concluded between the GDR and FRG regulating traffic between the two countries; the FRG also ratifies the Moscow and Warsaw treaties.

June

The final protocol to the Four-Power Agreement is signed, ending tension over Berlin.

July

In Czechoslovakia, trials start of 46 Dubček supporters – some former Central Committee members – on charges of subversive activity.

November

The GDR begins to release political prisoners, and the amnesty eventually frees 30,000. A draft treaty between the FRG and GDR begins normalization of relations, but does not institute full diplomatic ties.

December

The treaty between the FRG and GDR is signed. Yugoslavs purge Croatian nationalists from posts in the party and government; the purge continues through 1973 against the Serbian party organization.

1973

January

WTO foreign ministers meet in Warsaw to prepare a joint strategy for upcoming European security conferences.

February

The fourth Yugoslav constitution adopted since World War II grants greater power to workers through factory councils. Czechoslovak President Svoboda declares amnesty for those who fled during the 1968 crisis. The GDR gains diplomatic recognition from Britain and France.

March

Permanent diplomatic missions are agreed to by the GDR and FRG.

April

During a visit by Brandt, Yugoslavia drops its remuneration claims against the FRG and reaches an agreement on economic cooperation.

June

On a five-day visit, Ceaușescu becomes the first East European head of state to visit the FRG.

July

The Conference on Security and Cooperation in Europe (CSCE) opens in Helsinki.

October

During a visit to Yugoslavia, Soviet Prime Minister Aleksei Kosygin and Yugoslav Prime Minister Djemal Bijedić agree to noninterference in internal affairs, industrial cooperation, and better understanding. The Soviet Union opens a natural-gas pipeline to the FRG.

December

The Moscow Conference of Nine Ruling Communist Parties is held; it stresses that détente and peaceful coexistence do not apply to the ideological sphere. In Prague, Brandt signs a treaty formalizing relations with Czechoslovakia, thus voiding the Munich Agreement of 1938. FRG representatives in Bulgaria sign preliminary documents normalizing relations.

1974

March

The Hungarian Socialist Workers' Party slows down economic reform and reasserts the "primacy of politics." Widespread purges are reported in Albania; they are believed to have followed from Hoxha's denunciation of superpower détente.

April

While the WTO renews its alliance at a PCC meeting in Warsaw, Romania dissents over a Soviet proposal for a world meeting of communist parties.

June

The CMEA charter is amended.

July

Romania receives a World Bank loan, but also announces greater control of economic investment and foreign trade. A new law is enacted in Czechoslovakia which, in reference to the 1968 crisis, gives extended powers to security forces in overriding civil rights.

August

In a massive purge of libraries in Czechoslovakia, 300 Czech writers, along with many foreign writers, are said to be on a list of banned authors compiled by the Culture Ministry.

September

Albanian Defense Minister Beqir Balluku is executed in connection with a purge of pro-Soviet party members. The GDR and the United States establish relations.

December

Renewed attacks against Dubček in *Rudé právo* reaffirm the hard-line policies adopted by the Czechoslovak regime.

1975

May

Increased administrative centralization in Poland through the reorganization of provincial governments makes challenges to Gierek's authority more difficult.

June

At the 29th CMEA session, measures are agreed upon enhancing economic integration; the construction of a new gas pipeline to Eastern Europe is proposed.

August

The Final Act of the CSCE is signed in Helsinki.

November

Zhivkov visits the FRG and signs a trade and economic agreement.

December

In Czechoslovakia, regulations are promulgated allowing representation of foreign firms for the first time since 1948.

1976

February

In Yugoslavia, 31 ethnic Albanians are convicted of "irredentist" activities.

April

Purges occur in Albania of anti-Chinese factions within the leadership, including the ministers of agriculture and of education and culture.

June

Food price riots occur in Poland. At the conference of Soviet bloc and

European communist parties in East Berlin, Eurocommunists assert independence from the Soviet model. Tito attends, marking the end of his 19-year boycott of Communist Party conferences.

July

Polish price increases are reduced, then deferred, in the wake of riots; rationing is instituted instead.

October

An increase in the cost of Soviet crude oil, coupled with a sharp economic reduction projected through 1980, prompts major conservation efforts in Czechoslovakia. A continuing increase in the price of Soviet oil is also reported in Hungary.

1977

January

Czechoslovakia's "Charter 77" on nonobservance of human rights is published and signed by 240 Czech intellectuals. Tito rejects Brezhnev's attempts at closer military cooperation.

February

Poland is forced to increase its costly grain imports. Poland's debt is reported to have grown, with exports increasing at only half of the planned rate.

March

Jan Patočka, a leading Charter 77 spokesman, dies in a hospital after being admitted for a heart ailment following several days of police detention. In Yugoslavia, a new foreign-trade law will give factory organizations control over the foreign-currency earnings of their enterprises.

August

Romanian miners in the Jiu River valley, Romania's main coal-producing area, strike over living standards and pension cuts.

1978

January

The United States returns the Crown of St. Stephen to Hungary.

March

Hungary gains MFN status in a trade agreement with the United States. The Belgrade CSCE meeting (which opened in 1977) closes without adoption of any new proposals.

May

The Yugoslav 11th Party Congress decides on collective leadership, and Tito accuses the superpowers of interference in the Third World. Vietnam becomes the 10th full CMEA member.

July

China ends technical and economic aid to Albania.

October

Polish Cardinal Karol Wojtyła is elected pope, taking the name John Paul II.

November

At a WTO PCC meeting, Romania refuses to increase its contributions beyond its current $923 million appropriation or to sign a pro-Arab declaration.

December

U.S. Treasury Secretary Michael Blumenthal visits Romania and reaffirms the importance to the United States of Romanian friendship and independence.

1979

January

Romania and Yugoslavia criticize the Vietnamese invasion of China.

June

Pope John Paul II visits Poland.

October

Charter 77 dissidents in Czechoslovakia are imprisoned.

1980

February

Polish Prime Minister Piotr Jaroszewicz is dismissed over economic policies.

March

Romania criticizes the USSR's invasion of Afghanistan in a joint statement with Great Britain.

April

Yugoslavia signs a new preferential trade and cooperation agreement with the European Economic Community (EEC). Czechoslovakia announces a new austerity budget. A five-year transport accord is signed between the GDR and FRG.

May

The WTO celebrates its 25th anniversary at a Warsaw meeting and emphasizes the need to protect détente.

June

Bulgaria enacts laws allowing joint ventures with noncommunist foreign enterprises and companies; similar laws already exist in Romania, Hungary, and Poland. Fifteen members of Charter 77 are arrested in Prague.

July

Increased meat prices in Poland spur worker protests and pay-raise demands; protests spread to Lublin, where 800,000 workers strike. Widespread strikes across Poland soon follow.

August

Eighty thousand workers take over the Lenin Shipyard in Gdańsk, Poland. An interfactory strike committee demands the right to form free trade unions, the abolition of censorship, and the right to strike. Gierek resigns, and a major purge of leadership begins. Negotiations take place, and Soviet comments call the situation a "completely internal affair." Agreement is reached on the right to strike and the right to independent trade unions and is approved by the PUWP Central Committee.

September

An accord is reached with striking Silesian workers. Stanisław Kania, the new PUWP general secretary, calls strikes legitimate responses to the party's mistakes; Politburo hard-liner Zdzisław Grodzien is ousted in response to strike demand. The first live broadcast of a Catholic mass in Poland takes place. Solidarity forms as an independent trade union. The WTO ends four days of maneuvers.

October

The PUWP Central Committee purges eight members and backs Gdańsk agreements. A Warsaw court legalizes Solidarity, on the condition that it recognizes the leading role of the party. Kania and Prime Minister Józef Pińkowski meet with Brezhnev in Moscow. WTO defense ministers meet in Prague.

November

WTO troops concentrate near the Polish border. In a compromise, a Warsaw court legalizes Solidarity, with acknowledgment of the party's role in an annex to charter.

December

The border zone between the GDR and Poland is closed to Western journalists by the Soviet Union. A surprise WTO summit is held in Moscow; GDR and Czechoslovak military commanders are recalled, and reserves are activated in these countries. Fearing invasion, Solidarity calls off planned strike. A memorial to Polish workers killed in 1970 protests is unveiled in the Lenin Shipyard. (This was one of the first demands of the Gdańsk strikers.) The first meat rationing in Poland since World War II is instituted, and an austerity budget is announced.

1981

January

Solidarity and the government are unable to agree on a five-day work week; most factory workers start taking Saturdays off, and an accord on a 40-hour week is reached in 1982. WTO Commander-in-Chief Kulikov confers with Polish General Wojciech Jaruzelski and Pińkowski. Sit-ins and warning strikes occur across Poland.

February

Jaruzelski replaces Pińkowski as prime minister, while retaining his position as defense minister. After a strike at Łódź University, students win the right to form a union and other concessions. The Polish Supreme Court rules against a farmers' union. Soviet–East German military exercises begin in the GDR.

March

Polish and Soviet leaderships hold a meeting in Moscow and agree that the defense of communism concerns the entire bloc. "Soyuz '81" WTO maneuvers take place around Poland, headed by Marshal Kulikov instead of the host-country defense minister; these maneuvers are extended at the end of the month. Kania meets with Kádár in Hungary. Three die from beatings after Polish riot police break up a Bydgoszcz farmers' sit-in; strikes erupt in four cities in protest, and Solidarity calls a strike alert. The Politburo meets in an emergency session, blames extremists for spreading unrest, and labels union actions as political. A strike called for March 31 is cancelled after an accord is reached between Solidarity and the government, although it falls short of union demands. The EEC warns the Soviet Union and offers economic aid to Poland. A U.S. Senate resolution says that the United States cannot "be indifferent" to Soviet intervention; throughout most of the year, the Polish government seeks extensive rescheduling of its hard-currency debt. In Yugoslavia, a state of emergency is declared in Kosovo; measures taken against the province's Albanian population continue through May.

April

Extensive food rationing begins in Poland. Politburo member Mieczysław Jagielski visits Washington, and the United States gives $70 million in surplus food. *Pravda* criticizes Kania's handling of the crisis; Brezhnev attends the Czechoslovak 16th Party Congress, during which Husák likens the crisis to the 1968 intervention and restates the Brezhnev Doctrine. *Pravda* continues its criticisms. The 10th SED Party Congress voices qualified support

for the PUWP; TASS calls unnamed PUWP members "revisionists."
Yugoslav troops put down Albanian separatist riots in Kosovo; the official
toll is 11 dead, 57 wounded, 22 arrested.

May

Former Czech Foreign Minister Jiří Hájek and 19 activists are arrested in an
ongoing crackdown. A Warsaw court grants legal recognition to the Polish
farmers' union. Cardinal Stefan Wyszyński, Primate of Poland, dies. The
Yugoslav embassy in Tirana is bombed.

June

Jaruzelski replaces five cabinet ministers, orders a crackdown on anti-Soviet
activity, and stresses the seriousness of the economic situation. Solidarity
votes for, then postpones, a strike over delay of punishment of aides responsible for the March Bydgoszcz violence.

July

The Czechs warn the Poles about the PUWP being taken over by counter-
revolutionaries. At the 35th CMEA session, Romania requests hard-currency credit; no aid is offered to Poland. Andrei Gromyko visits Poland, talks
with Kania and Foreign Minister Józef Czyrek and, in a joint communiqué,
in effect restates the Brezhnev Doctrine. Pope John Paul II appoints Bishop
Józef Glemp as Primate of Poland. Strikes continue throughout Poland in
July and August.

August

A meeting is reported to have taken place between Kulikov and Jaruzelski
without Kania. Kania warns of national tragedy and asks for an end to food
protests (an action also urged by Solidarity until its convention). Joint
Polish–East German maneuvers in northwest Poland are extended, as are
Soviet maneuvers in Byelorussia. Kania and Jaruzelski meet with Brezhnev
in the Crimea, and a conciliatory communiqué pledges more economic aid.
A U.S.–Polish accord defers $380 million debt for 5–8 years. The Yugoslav
press announces the first Albanian purge in six years to be under way.

September

At Solidarity's national convention, Solidarity leader Lech Wałęsa appeals
for unity; the government releases a harsh Soviet letter of September 17
calling for a crackdown and warning of danger to the Polish state. The U.S.
State Department calls the letter meddling. A letter from Soviet workers to
Polish workers invokes their WTO obligations to the socialist system; *Pravda* prints a reminder of the Hungarian and Czechoslovak crises. A
crackdown on anti-Soviet action takes place in Poland.

October

Wildcat strikes occur in three Polish cities over food shortages. Jaruzelski
replaces Kania. By October 22, strikes and strike threats spread to 28

provinces; Solidarity asks an end to uncontrolled strikes. The army is deployed in small units to help resolve "local disputes."

November

Jaruzelski, Wałęsa, and Glemp meet for the first time and agree on forming a body to end the crisis. Over 200,000 Poles end 22 wildcat strikes; the Polish army announces a pullback of troops deployed in October. Solidarity and the government open their first negotiations since August; a Central Committee meeting backs "extraordinary" steps, banning strikes and curbing rights. A U.S.–Czechoslovak accord is signed in Prague on the return of 18.4 tons of gold seized by the Nazis, in return for the settlement of $81.5 million in American claims. The Albanian 8th Party Congress discusses Kosovo unrest.

December

Police backed by the army break up a sit-in at Warsaw fire cadets academy, which is protested by Solidarity. Poland and Western banks agree on a $2.4 billion debt rescheduling. Solidarity discusses a new series of demands, including free national elections, access to the media, and joint union–party control of the economy; the union also calls for a referendum on the future of Poland's socialist government if their demands are not met. Wałęsa declares that Solidarity cannot "retreat any longer." TASS says that the Polish crisis directly affects Soviet security and condemns the Church's role. Jaruzelski declares martial law, suspends civil rights and union operations, and announces the formation of the Military Council for National Salvation. Union extremists, Gierek, and 26 other former leaders are arrested; Wałęsa is flown to Warsaw; widespread strikes are crushed in major Polish cities as the United States suspends all pending aid. TASS calls the events an "internal matter"; the United States outlines sanctions. Albanian Prime Minister Mehmet Shehu dies.

1982

February

The East German news agency ADN reports a minor relaxation of regulations governing family visits by East Berliners and East Germans to the FRG.

March

Jaruzelski visits Brezhnev; he also visits the GDR, Czechoslovakia, Hungary, and Bulgaria in subsequent months. WTO maneuvers take place in Poland.

April

Gromyko visits Yugoslavia, the first high-level visit in two years.

May

Thirty thousand Poles march in Warsaw to protest martial law.

June

The 36th CMEA session discusses economic developments resulting from the Polish crisis.

July

The Polish government postpones the visit of Pope John Paul II to Poland.

August

Jaruzelski holds talks with Brezhnev in the Crimea. Two people are killed in three days of violent protest against martial law in Lublin.

October

New union laws enacted in Poland are intended to dismantle Solidarity. The United States suspends Poland's MFN status in protest of the new laws.

November

Wałęsa is released and returns to Gdańsk. *Izvestiya* publishes an article concerned with improving Albanian relations; but the USSR is rebuffed by Albania. Brezhnev dies, is succeeded by Yurii Andropov.

December

The Polish Council of State announces that martial law will be formally suspended by December 31.

1983

January

Officially sanctioned trade unions come into existence in Poland, replacing the banned Solidarity union. WTO PCC meeting in Prague introduces joint resolution on drafting of nonaggression pact with NATO, renouncing first use of nuclear weapons, presenting disarmament proposals, and strengthening the role of the United Nations. Relations between Albania and Yugoslavia continue to be strained over treatment of Albanians in the Yugoslavian province of Kosovo.

February

A campaign against corruption begins in the USSR. A follow-up CSCE conference convenes in Madrid.

May

Nationwide demonstrations occur in Poland on behalf of Solidarity.

June

Pope John Paul II visits Poland, meets with Jaruzelski and Wałęsa, and is extremely critical of the Polish situation. A major antigovernment protest rally in Prague is broken up by police.

July

Martial law is lifted in Poland, and a limited amnesty is declared for political and other offenders.

October

Wałęsa wins Nobel Peace Prize. The 37th session of the CMEA, held in East Berlin, addresses Polish and Romanian debt rescheduling. Butter and margarine rationing is reinstituted in Poland.

1984

February

Andropov dies, and he is succeeded by Konstantin Chernenko.

June

Bodgan Lis, fugitive Solidarity leader, is arrested in Poland. The first CMEA summit held in Moscow in 15 years adopts political declaration and statement of guidelines for future economic, scientific, and technical cooperation.

July

Poland announces amnesty that could lead to the release of 660 political prisoners and 35,000 common criminal offenders; the United States praises the action, but refuses to lift economic sanctions.

September

Honecker postpones visit to the FRG under Soviet pressure. Zhivkov cancels a scheduled visit to the FRG as well.

October

Father Jerzy Popiełuszko, a leading supporter of the banned Solidarity union, is murdered by members of the Polish security forces.

December

WTO foreign ministers meet in East Berlin and call for negotiations, with clearly defined goals on a range of arms issues, including medium-range missiles in Europe and antiballistic missile systems in space.

1985

January

The Reagan administration lifts some sanctions on Poland, citing a "general improvement" in the internal situation. A Greek–Albanian economic cooperation agreement is signed in Athens.

February

Four officers of the Polish security services are sentenced for their role in the Popiełuszko murder.

March

Chernenko dies, is succeeded by Mikhail Sergeevich Gorbachev. A U.S. military liaison officer in the GDR is shot by Soviet guards for allegedly being in a restricted military area northwest of Berlin. At the 13th National Congress of the Hungarian Socialist Workers' Party, Kádár is reelected as general secretary; for the first time, however, a deputy general secretary – Károly Németh – is elected.

April

Hoxha, general secretary of the Albanian Party of Labor, dies and is succeeded on April 13 by Ramiz Alia, president of the Presidium of the People's Assembly (head of state). At a summit meeting of the WTO, the East European military treaty is renewed for another 20 years, with provisions for a 10-year extension.

May

Romanian President Ceauşescu proposes a freeze on military expenditures at the 1985 level, to be reduced by 5–10 percent annually.

June

Relations are established between the EEC European Commission and the CMEA.

October

The Executive Political Committee of the Romanian Communist Party declares a state of emergency in the energy sector.

November

Polish Foreign Minister Stefan Olszowski resigns from the PUWP. Herbert Haber and Konrad Naumann are removed from the Politburo of the SED. Naumann is replaced as SED first secretary for Berlin by Gunther Schabowski.

December

At the 41st session of the CMEA, which met in Moscow at the prime-ministerial level to discuss the Comprehensive Program until the year 2000, CMEA partners sign a 15-year agreement on scientific and technological cooperation. Poland announces the release of all but seven detainees held under martial law.

1986

January

Czechoslovakia and the Soviet Union reach agreement on the former's participation in the construction of a pipeline from the Yamburg gas field in western Siberia to Eastern Europe.

February

Figures are released showing that key targets set out in the latest Hungarian Five-Year Plan, which ended in December, were not met. The Soviet 27th Communist Party Congress opens in Moscow; Gorbachev proposes "radical reform" of economic and political life.

March

The 17th Czechoslovak Communist Party Congress, held in Prague, offers evidence that the conservative CPCz is resisting the prompting of Gorbachev in relation to reforms.

April

The 11th Party Congress of the SED is held in East Berlin, marking the first visit of Gorbachev to the GDR since taking power in March 1985. Gorbachev avoids Honecker's proposal to be the first East German leader to visit the FRG; Moscow had forced Honecker to cancel such a trip in 1984. West European countries ban imports of food from East Europe because of radiation levels after the Chernobyl nuclear accident.

May

Zbigniew Bujak, underground Solidarity leader and head of its Provisional Coordinating Committee, is arrested.

June

In a crackdown against Solidarity, Polish police arrest about thirty activists. Poland's entry into the IMF is approved. At the Budapest summit, the WTO proposes large reductions in conventional forces in Europe. Gorbachev has a lengthy meeting with Kádár. At the PUWP 10th Congress, Jaruzelski is seen to consolidate power.

July

Bogdan Lis and Adam Michnik are released from prison in Poland as part of an amnesty.

September

The remaining political prisoners in Poland receive amnesty; Jaruzelski asks for conciliation, as well as normalization of ties with the United States. In Czechoslovakia, members of a cultural dissident group, the Jazz Section, are arrested as part of a general crackdown. Bulgaria and Greece sign a nonaggression treaty; the Helsinki Watch reports the killings of ethnic Turks in Bulgaria during a campaign to make them adopt Slavic names.

October

The Polish government bans the Provisional Council of Solidarity, which was founded as a replacement for the Provisional Coordinating Committee in an effort to establish dialogue with the government.

November

The Hungarian government, stressing the official version of events, quietly marks the 30th anniversary of the 1956 uprising; 122 leading dissidents from throughout Eastern Europe sign a document remembering Hungarian and other uprisings. At a hastily called CMEA summit (the first since 1984), Gorbachev presses for economic reform and arms control. At the CMEA annual meeting in Bucharest, Ryzhkov calls for higher-quality goods and cites a need for expansion of the nuclear power industry in Eastern Europe.

December

An austerity plan is adopted in Poland. Jaruzelski forms a consultative council to advise the government; the council includes party representatives, lay Catholic activists, and three former Solidarity members.

1987

January

Jaruzelski visits Italy. The Czechoslovak government announces that state-owned companies will receive greater independence, although it avoids using the word "reform."

February

Vasil Bil'ak criticizes those who try to apply Gorbachev's reform program to Czechoslovakia; he asserts that Czechoslovakia must "respect its own experience." President Reagan lifts U.S. sanctions against Poland imposed in 1981 and 1982.

March

Fifteen hundred people march in Budapest calling for liberalization. Poland announces a price increase on consumer goods. Husák publicly backs Gorbachev's reforms in a speech to the Central Committee.

April

After a delay of three days, Gorbachev arrives in Prague for a visit and is greeted by cheering crowds; "frank" discussions with Husák are reported. Speaking at a trade-union fair, Honecker strongly rejects the GDR's emulation of Soviet reform. A joint "Declaration on Soviet–Polish Cooperation in Ideology, Science, and Culture" is signed by Jaruzelski and Gorbachev, calling for the elimination of "blank spots" in the treatment of Soviet–Polish relations.

May

In Prague, five members of the Jazz Section are convicted on charges related to unauthorized publications on jazz and receive short jail sentences. Gorbachev visits Romania. Coal miners end a 33-day strike in Yugoslavia when the government agrees to wage increases and management changes. The GDR cancels an invitation to West Berlin's mayor to visit during the city's 750th anniversary, citing his "slanderous attacks." In Bulgaria, Zhivkov pushes broad reforms, attacks the party in his plenum speech, and proposes reducing the government's role in the economy.

June

The pope makes his third visit to Poland. In East Berlin, three nights of clashes occur between police and youths who had gathered near the Wall to hear a West German outdoor rock concert. President Reagan notifies Congress that MFN trading status will be given to Hungary and Romania. GDR party-to-party ties with China, suspended in 1963, are restored.

July

A political amnesty is announced in the GDR; Western estimates of the number of political prisoners run as high as 5,000.

September

The Polish government announces the planned release of nine "political terrorists," claimed by Solidarity to be political detainees. The Hungarian Parliament approves harsh austerity measures and the bloc's first personal income and value-added tax code. Honecker makes his long-postponed trip to the FRG.

October

An extensive package of political and economic reforms is introduced in Poland. The CMEA prime ministers' meeting in Moscow adopts a long-range plan for reform of the intrabloc trading system.

December

Riots of 10,000 Romanian citizens in Braşov challenge the stability of the Ceauşescu regime. In Czechoslovakia, Husák is replaced by Miloš Jakeš as general secretary.

1988

February

Conference of Balkan foreign ministers in Belgrade is attended by Yugoslavia, Romania, Bulgaria, Greece, Turkey, and Albania. Limited multi-candidate elections take place in Bulgaria.

March

The infamous "Nina Andreeva" letter is published in the conservative newspaper *Sovetskaya Rossiya*, sending a signal to fellow conservatives in Eastern Europe that *perestroika*'s opponents are numerous and powerful. The letter receives widespread publicity in Eastern Europe as the local conservative leaderships attempt to slow the reform process.

April

On his return to Moscow, Gorbachev rallies the liberals, arranges criticism of the Andreeva letter in *Pravda,* and forces *Sovetskaya Rossiya* to print a

retraction. Strikes at Poland's Nowa Huta steelworks are put down forcefully by police antiterrorist brigades.

May

János Kádár is removed after thirty-two years as HSWP general secretary and is replaced by a four-member Presidium, with Reszö Nyers as its
president.

July

CMEA member countries, with Romania abstaining, announce plans to
establish a unified market.

August

Throughout the fall, Hungarian–Romanian relations worsen over the issue
of the latter's treatment of its Hungarian minority. In Poland, more strikes
take place, this time to demand restoration of Solidarity. Interior Minister
Kiszczak proposes "round-table" talks with the opposition.

October

In a major shake-up of the top echelons of the Soviet leadership and the
CSPU *apparat,* the Central Committee department responsible for bloc
relations is merged with and subordinated to the International Department.
Striking workers protest for four days in Montenegro, forcing resignation
of the republic's leadership.

November

At the United Nations, Gorbachev announces unilateral cuts in the size of
the Soviet armed forces and the withdrawal of 50,000 troops from the
GDR, Czechoslovakia, and Hungary.

1989

January

Dissident playwright Václav Havel and more than 800 others are arrested
after human-rights protests in Czechoslovakia.

February

In Poland, round-table talks between opposition and government leaders
begin. In Czechoslovakia, Havel is sentenced to nine months in jail.

March

More than 75,000 march in Budapest on the anniversary of the 1848 revolution, calling for withdrawal of Soviet troops and free elections, under a law
passed earlier in the year permitting freedom of assembly and association.

April

Solidarity and the Polish government reach agreement in their round-table
talks; 35 percent of the seats in the Sejm and all 100 seats in the Senate are to
be contested.

May

More forced assimilation of Bulgaria's Turkish minority takes place in the process of reform of the passport system. In late May and early June, thousands of ethnic Turks are forced to leave the country, choking border crossings and straining relations with Turkey. János Kádár is removed from the post of head of state, which had become only ceremonial, and Hungary begins dismantling its portion of the iron curtain along its border with Austria. Havel is released from prison on parole in Czechoslovakia.

June

The PUWP is roundly defeated in elections under the round-table agreement worked out earlier in the year. Solidarity and independent candidates win 99 of 100 seats in the Senate, and all 161 seats in the Sejm for which they are allowed to compete. In Hungary, János Kádár dies one week before the reburial of former prime minister Imre Nagy and four associates with state honors. In a process of "national reconciliation" a sixth casket is included in the ceremony, left empty to symbolize all those who died in 1956.

July

Wojciech Jaruzelski resigns his post as PUWP first secretary to become president. After reports in June that Romania had begun construction of a barbed-wire fence along its border with Hungary, officials from both countries meet to discuss the treatment of the former's ethnic Hungarians. The fence is dismantled after criticism from Great Britain and the Soviet Union.

August

The PUWP ceases efforts to form a government and hands the task to Solidarity. The PUWP retains the ministerial portfolios of interior and defense in the government headed by Prime Minister Tadeusz Mazowiecki. Almost 400 are arrested in Prague after demonstrations marking the anniversary of the 1968 invasion.

September

An independent Polish newspaper publishes an exchange of telegrams between the Romanian and Polish parties from August, in which the Romanians expressed their concern over the imminent formation of a Solidarity-led government and urged "joint action" with other socialist countries to prevent it. The Polish party responds with a harshly worded statement. Hungary opens its border with Austria for more than 13,000 East Germans, while another 17,000 leave via the West German embassies in Warsaw and Prague. Agreement is reached between the Hungarian government and opposition parties on creation of a multiparty system in 1990.

October

In East Germany, Erich Honecker is removed as party leader and head of state in the face of widespread public demonstrations for democracy and continuing emigration of the country's youth and professionals. On the thirty-third anniversary of the 1956 uprising, Hungary declares itself a "republic" in which bourgeois democracy and democratic socialism will apply, rather than a "people's republic." Earlier in the month, the HSWP had renamed itself the Hungarian Socialist Party (HSP) and abandoned Leninism as its ideology. In Czechoslovakia, a demonstration by more than 10,000 is broken up by club-wielding riot police.

November

The GDR announces an end to travel restrictions for its citizens, throwing open its borders and allowing emigration directly to the West. Millions of East Germans pour across the border into the FRG and West Berlin to purchase consumer goods scarce in their own country; only a few thousand do not return. The entire Politburo and government resign, replaced by streamlined bodies. Plans for political and economic reform are introduced. In Bulgaria, the veteran BCP leader and president, Todor Zhivkov, retires and is replaced by a considerably younger Petar Mladenov, former foreign minister, who immediately promises political reforms designed to develop a "socialist pluralism." One week later, 50,000 demonstrate in Sofia to press for further reform, criticizing Zhivkov. At the Romanian Communist Party's 14th Congress, Ceauşescu continues to resist any suggestion that reform is necessary. In Czechoslovakia, meanwhile, the authorities also resist growing popular pressure for reform, despite almost daily demonstrations of over 150,000 in Prague. One week of such protests, however, results in the downfall of the government and party leadership, followed by a two-hour general strike, which the next day leads to renunciation of the leading role for the Communist Party.

December

In the GDR, at an SED Central Committee plenum, the entire party leadership resigns, and here, too, the party's leading role is scrapped. Later in the month the SED changes its name to Socialist Unity Party of Germany–Party of Democratic Socialism (SED-PDS). In Czechoslovakia, President Husák resigns immediately after swearing in the country's first majority noncommunist government since 1948. The end of the month sees the election of Havel as president and Prague Spring leader Alexander Dubček as president of the Federal Assembly. Mass demonstrations of over 50,000 in Sofia are met with proposals for free elections and an end to the party's monopoly on power. In Romania, however, the government's attempt to seize a priest who defended the rights of ethnic Hungarians prompts massive demonstrations, which quickly turn into antigovernment protests. Security and army troops open fire on crowds in the western city of Timisoara and in Bucharest. The defense minister is executed for refusing to cooperate in further repression, the army joins the demonstrators, and the government falls. A brief and bloody civil war is ended only with the capture, trial, and summary execution of Nicolae and Elena Ceauşescu.

1990

January

In Czechoslovakia and Hungary, government leaders call for rapid withdrawal of Soviet troops from their countries, and Soviet–Czechoslovak negotiations begin against the backdrop of continuing ethnic unrest and
violence in the Soviet Union. At an extraordinary Bulgarian Communist
Party Congress, orthodox conservatives are roundly defeated; the Central
Committee and Politburo are abolished and replaced with a 153-member
Supreme Council and seventeen-member Presidium. In East Germany, at an
emergency meeting of the Socialist Unity Party of Germany–Party of Democratic Socialism, the party's name is officially changed to the Party of
Democratic Socialism. The mass exodus of East Germans to the West continues, and by the end of the month more than 4,000 per day are leaving the
country, straining the East German infrastructure and the West German
ability to absorb them. Reunification is increasingly seen as a solution to the
problem. In Poland, meanwhile, Solidarity leader Lech Wałęsa also calls for
the withdrawal of Soviet troops, but is rebuffed by Prime Minister
Mazowiecki and President Jaruzelski. The Solidarity government's economic program takes effect and immediately results in price rises for many
basic foodstuffs. The PUWP splits into two social-democratic groups. Continuing protests in Romania force the ruling National Salvation Front to
rethink its intent to stand in the coming elections as a political party. The
front is forced as well into a coalition Council of National Unity with other
parties which is to govern until the spring elections.

February

A deepening crisis in East Germany lends further impetus to the push for
reunification. After visits to Moscow by both Prime Minister Modrow and
PDS leader Gysi, the Soviet Union accepts what appears inevitable, despite
continuing resistance from some leaders to the notion of a reunified Germany remaining in NATO. After Modrow's visit to West Germany, a merger
of the East and West German currencies is announced, with no clear timeta-
ble. At the Open Skies conference in Canada, agreement is reached among
the USSR, the United States, Great Britain, and France to schedule a "two-
plus-four" conference (the two Germanys plus the allies) to address external
(security) aspects of German reunification. In Bucharest, hundreds of angry
Romanians storm and briefly occupy the National Salvation Front headquarters, charging that the front has not distanced itself from the excesses
and policies of the Ceaușescu period. Almost four thousand coal miners
stage a counterdemonstration the next day in support of the front.

March

In the bloc's first free elections, East Germans give a 49 percent plurality to
the conservative Alliance for Germany, which is closely tied to the FRG's
Christian Democrats and promises quick reunification. In the first round of

voting the next week, Hungarians apparently give 24 percent to the Hungarian Democratic Front, 20 percent to the Alliance of Free Democrats, and about 10 percent to the Socialists, the former communist party. The strongly nationalistic appeal of the HDF was helped by Eastern Europe's first flare-up of ethnic violence in neighboring Romania, as clashes between hundreds of Hungarians and Romanians resulted in six Hungarian deaths and dozens of injuries. Footage of the fighting, which broke out in response to calls for Hungarian-language schools and institutes, was televised in Hungary in the middle of the election campaign and strained relations between the two countries. In the first of what may become increasingly common revelations as to the foreign policy activity of Eastern Europe's communist regimes, Czechoslovakia's President Havel revealed that the Husák government had sold thousands of pounds of the plastic explosive Syntex to Libya.

April

In Hungary, the Hungarian Democratic Front wins 43 percent of the votes in the final round of elections and begins negotiations to form a government. In East Germany, Lothar de Maiziere forms the country's first noncommunist government. In the USSR, the Soviet government finally admits responsibility for the execution of 15,000 Polish officers at Katyn in 1940.

APPENDIX II

Soviet and East European Leadership Successions, 1945–1990 (Current to April 15, 1990)

GENERAL SECRETARY

Albania

Hoxha, Enver until 1985
Alia, Ramiz 1985–

Bulgaria

Kostov, Traicho until 1948
Dimitrov, Georgii 1948–1949
Chervenkov, Vulko 1949–1954
Zhivkov, Todor 1954–1989
Mladenov, Petar 1989–1990
Lilov, Aleksandr 1990–

Czechoslovakia

Slánský, Rudolf until 1951
Gottwald, Klement 1951–1953
Novotný, Antonín 1953–1968
Dubček, Alexander 1968–1969
Husák, Gustáv 1969–1987
Jakeš, Miloš 1987–1989
Urbánek, Karel 1989
Adamec, Ladislav 1989–

German Democratic Republic (GDR)

Ulbricht, Walter until 1971
Honecker, Erich 1971–1989
Krenz, Egon 1989
Gysi, Gregor 1989–

Hungary

Rákosi, Mátyás until 1956
Gerő, Ernő 1956
Kádár, János 1956–1988
Grósz, Károly 1988–1989
Nyers, Resző 1989–

Poland

Gomułka, Władysław until 1948
Bierut, Bolesław 1948–1956
Ochab, Edward 1956
Gomułka, Władysław 1956–1970
Gierek, Edward 1970–1980
Kania, Stanisław 1980–1981
Jaruzelski, Wojciech 1981–1989
Rakowski, Mieczysław 1989–90

Romania

Gheorghiu-Dej, Gheorghe until 1965
Ceauşescu, Nicolae 1965–1989

USSR

Stalin, Josef until 1953
Malenkov, Georgii 1953
Khrushchev, Nikita 1953–1964
Brezhnev, Leonid 1964–1982

290

Andropov, Yurii 1982–1984
Chernenko, Konstantin 1984–1985
Gorbachev, Mikhail 1985–

Yugoslavia

Tito, Josip Broz until 1980
Doronjski, Stevan 1980
Mojsov, Lazar 1980–1981
Dragosavac, Dusan 1981–1982
Ribičič, Mitja 1982–1983
Marković, Dragoslav 1983–1985
Žarković, Vidoje 1985–1986
Renovica, Milanko 1986–1987
Krunić, Boško 1987–1988
Šuvar, Stipe 1988–1989
Pančevski, Milan 1989–

PRESIDENT (HEAD OF STATE)

Albania

King Zog until 1946
Nishani, Omer 1946–1953
Lleshi, Haxhi 1953–1982
Alia, Ramiz 1982–

Bulgaria

Regency for King Simeon until
    1946
Kolarev, V. 1946–1950
Neichev, Mincho 1950–1954
Damianov, Georgi 1954–1957
Ganev, Dimiter 1957–1964
Traikov, Georgi 1964–1971
Zhivkov, Todor 1971–1989
Mladenov, Petar 1989–

Czechoslovakia

Beneš, Edward until 1948
Gottwald, Klement 1948–1953
Zápotocký, Antonín 1953–1957
Novotný, Antonín 1957–1968
Svoboda, Ludvík 1968–1975

Husák, Gustáv 1975–1989
Havel, Václav 1989–

GDR

Pieck, Wilhelm 1949–1960
Ulbricht, Walter 1960–1973
Stoph, Willi 1973–1976
Honecker, Erich 1976–1989
Krenz, Egon 1989
Gerlach, Manfred 1989–

Hungary

Horthy, Miklós Nagybányai until
    1945
Regency Council 1945–1946
Tildy, Zoltán 1946–1948
Szakasits, Árpád 1948–1950
Rónai, Sándor 1950–1952
Dobi, István 1952–1967
Losonczi, Pál 1967–1988
Straub, Brunó 1988–1989
Szürös, Mátyás 1989–

Poland

Bierut, Bolesław 1945–1952
Zawadzki, Aleksander 1952–1964
Ochab, Edward 1964–1968
Spychalski, Marian 1968–1970
Cyrankiewicz, Józef 1970–1972
Jabłoński, Henryk 1972–1985
Jaruzelski, Wojciech 1985–

Romania

King Michael until 1947
Parhon, Constantin 1947–1952
Groza, Petru 1952–1958
Maurer, Ion Gheorghe 1958–1961
Gheorghiu-Dej, Gheorghe 1961–
    1965
Stoica, Chivu 1965–1967
Ceauşescu, Nicolae 1967–1989
Iliescu, Ion 1989–

USSR

Kalinin, Mikhail until 1946
Shvernik, Nikolai 1946–1953
Voroshilov, Klement 1953–1960
Brezhnev, Leonid 1960–1964
Mikoyan, Anastas 1964–1965
Podgorny, Nikolai 1965–1977
Brezhnev, Leonid 1977–1983
Andropov, Yurii 1983–1984
Chernenko, Konstantin 1984–1985
Gromyko, Andrei 1985–1988
Gorbachev, Mikhail 1988–

Yugoslavia

King Peter until 1945
Ribar, Ivan 1945–1953
Tito, Josip Broz 1953–1980
Koliševski, Lazar 1980
Mijatović, Cvijetin 1980–1981
Krajger, Sergej 1981–1982
Stambolić, Petar 1982–1983
Špiljak, Mika 1983–1984
Djuranović, Veselin 1984–1985
Vlajković, Radovan 1985–1986
Hasani, Sinan 1986–1987
Mojsov, Lazar 1987–1988
Dizdarević, Raif 1988–1989
Drnovšek, Janez 1989–

PRIME MINISTER

Albania

Hoxha, Enver 1945–1954
Shehu, Mehmet 1954–1982
Çarçani, Adil 1982–

Bulgaria

Georgiev, Kimon until 1946
Dimitrov, Georgii 1946–1949
Kolarov, Vasil 1949–1950
Chervenkov, Vulko 1950–1956
Yugov, Anton 1956–1962

Zhivkov, Todor 1962–1971
Todorov, Stanko 1971–1981
Filipov, Grisha 1981–1985
Atanasov, Georgi 1985–1990
Lukanov, Andrei 1990–

Czechoslovakia

Fierlinger, Zdeněk 1945–1946
Gottwald, Klement 1946–1948
Zápotocký, Antonín 1948–1953
Široký, Viliam 1953–1963
Lenárt, Józef 1963–1968
Černík, Oldřich 1968–1970
Štrougal, Lubomír 1970–1988
Adamec, Ladislav 1988–1989
Čalfa, Marián 1989–

GDR

Grotewohl, Otto 1949–1964
Stoph, Willi 1964–1973
Sindermann, Horst 1973–1976
Stoph, Willi 1976–1989
Modrow, Hans 1989–1990
De Maiziere, Lothar 1990–

Hungary

Miklós, Béla until 1945
Tildy, Zoltán 1945–1946
Nagy, Ferenc 1946–1947
Dinnyés, Lajos 1947–1948
Dobi, István 1948–1952
Rákosi, Mátyás 1952–1953
Nagy, Imre 1953–1955
Hegedüs, András 1955–1956
Nagy, Imre 1956
Kádár, János 1956–1958
Münnich, Ferenc 1958–1961
Kádár, János 1961–1965
Kállai, Gyula 1965–1967
Fock, Jenö 1967–1975
Lázár, György 1975–1987
Grósz, Károly 1987–1988
Németh, Miklós 1988–

Poland

Osóbka-Morawski, Edward 1945–1947
Cyrankiewicz, Józef 1947–1952
Bierut, Bolesław 1952–1954
Cyrankiewicz, Józef 1954–1970
Jaroszewicz, Piotr 1970–1980
Babiuch, Edward 1980
Pińkowski, Józef 1980–1981
Jaruzelski, Wojciech 1981–1984
Messner, Zbigniew 1984–1988
Rakowski, Mieczysław 1988–1989
Mazowiecki, Tadeusz 1989–

Romania

Groza, Petru 1945–1952
Gheorghiu-Dej, Gheorghe 1952–1955
Stoica, Chivu 1955–1961
Maurer, Ion Gheorghe 1961–1974
Manescu, Manea 1974–1979
Verdet, Ilie 1979–1982
Dăscălescu, Constantin 1982–1989
Roman, Petre 1989–

USSR

Stalin, Josef until 1953
Malenkov, Georgii 1953–1955
Bulganin, Nikolai 1955–1958
Khrushchev, Nikita 1958–1964
Kosygin, Aleksei 1964–1980
Tikhonov, Nikolai 1980–1985
Ryzhkov, Nikolai 1985–

Yugoslavia

Tito, Josip Broz, until 1963
Stambolić, Petar 1963–1967
Špiljak, Mika 1967–1969
Ribičič, Mitja 1969–1971
Bijedić, Djemal 1971–1977
Djuranović, Veselin 1977–1982
Planinc, Milka 1982–1986
Mikulić, Branko 1986–1989
Marković, Ante 1989–

FOREIGN MINISTER

Albania

Miskane, N. 1945–1946
Hoxha, Enver 1946–1950
Shehu, Mehmet 1950–1953
Shtylla, Behar 1953–1966
Nase, Nesti 1966–1982
Malile, Reiz 1982–

Bulgaria

Stainov, P. until 1946
Kulishev, G. 1946
Georgiev, Kimon 1946–1947
Kolarov, Vasil 1947–1949
Poptomov, Vladimir 1949–1950
Neichev, Mincho 1950–1956
Lukanov, Karlo 1956–1962
Bashev, Ivan 1962–1971
Mladenov, Petar 1971–1989
Dimitrov, Boyko 1989–

Czechoslovakia

Masaryk, Jan until 1948
Klementis, Vladimir 1948–1950
Široký, Viliam 1950–1953
David, Václav 1953–1968
Hájek, Jiří 1968
Černík, Oldřich, 1968–1969
Marko, Jan 1969–1972
Chnoupek, Bohuslav 1972–1988
Johanes, Jaromír 1988–1989
Dienstbier, Jiří 1989–

GDR

Dertinger, Georg 1949–1953
Ackermann, Anton 1953
Bolz, Lothar 1953–1965
Winzer, Otto 1965–1975
Fischer, Oskar 1975–1990
Fleck, Werner 1990
Meckel, Marcus 1990–

Hungary

Gyöngyösi, János until 1947
Mihályfi, Ernő 1947
Molnár, Erík 1947–1948
Rajk, László 1948–1949
Kállai, Gyula 1949–1951
Kiss, Károly 1951–1952
Molnár, Erík 1952–1953
Boldoczky, János 1953–1956
Horváth, Imre 1956–1958
Sík, Endre 1958–1961
Péter, János 1961–1973
Puja, Frigyes 1973–1983
Várkonyi, Péter 1983–1989
Horn, Gyula 1989–

Poland

Rzymowski, Wincenty 1945–1947
Modzelewski, Zygmunt 1947–1951
Skrzeszewski, Stanisław 1951–1956
Rapacki, Adam 1956–1968
Jedrychowski, Stefan 1968–1971
Olszowski, Stefan 1971–1976
Wojtaszek, Emil 1976–1980
Czyrek, Józef 1980–1982
Olszowski, Stefan 1982–1985
Orzechowski, Marian 1985–1988
Olechowski, Tadeusz 1988–1989
Skubiszewski, Krzysztof 1989–

Romania

Tatarescu, Gheorghe 1945–1947
Pauker, Ana 1947–1952
Bughici, Simion 1952–1955
Preoteasa, Grigore 1955–1957
Maurer, Ion Gheorghe 1957–1958
Bunaciu, Avram 1958–1961
Manescu, Corneliu 1961–1972
Macovescu, Gheorghe 1972–1978
Andrei, Stefan 1978–1985
Vaduva, Ilie 1985–1986
Totu, Ioan 1986–89
Celac, Sergiu 1989–

USSR

Molotov, Vyacheslav until 1949
Vyshinskii, Andrei 1949–1953
Molotov, Vyacheslav 1953–1956
Shepilov, Dmitrii 1956–1957
Gromyko, Andrei 1957–1985
Shevardnadze, Eduard 1985–

Yugoslavia

Šubasić, Ivan 1945–1946
Simić, Stanoje 1946–1948
Kardelj, Edvard 1948–1953
Popović, Koča 1953–1965
Nikezić, Marko 1965–1969
Tepavac, Mirko 1969–1972
Petrić, Jakša 1972
Minić, Miloš 1972–1978
Vrhovec, Josip 1978–1982
Mojsov, Lazar 1982–1985
Dizdarević, Raif 1985–1989
Lončar, Budimir 1989–

DEFENSE MINISTER

Albania

Shehu, Mehmet until 1953
Hoxha, Enver 1953–1954
Balluku, Beqir 1954–1974
Shehu, Mehmet 1974–1981
Hazbiu, Kadri 1981–1984
Murra, Prokop 1984–

Bulgaria

Velchev, D. until 1947
Damianov, G. 1947–1949
Panchevsky, Petur 1949–1959
Mihailov, Ivan 1959–1963
Dzhurov, Dobri 1963–

Czechoslovakia

Svoboda, Ludvík 1945–1950
Čepička, Alexej 1950–1956

Lomský, Bohumír 1956–1968
Dzúr, Martin 1968–1985
Václavík, Milán 1985–1989
Vacek, Karol 1989–

GDR

Stoph, Willi 1956–1960
Hoffmann, Heinz 1960–1985
Kessler, Heinz 1985–1989
Hoffmann, Theodor 1989–1990
Eppman, Rainer 1990–

Hungary

Vörös, János until 1947
Veres, Péter 1947–1948
Farkas, Mihály 1948–1954
Bata, István 1954–1956
Maléter, Pál 1956
Révész, Géza 1956–1961
Czinege, Lajos 1961–1986
Kárpati, Ferenc 1986–

Poland

Żymierski, Michał Rola 1945–1949
Rokossovski, Konstanty 1949–1956
Spychalski, Marian 1956–1969
Jaruzelski, Wojciech 1969–1983
Siwicki, Florian 1983–

Romania

Rascanu, Vasiliu until 1946
Lascar, Mihail 1946–1948
Bodnaras, Emil 1948–1957
Salajan, Leontin 1957–1966
Ionita, Ion 1966–1977
Coman, Ion 1977–1981
Olteanu, Constantin 1981–1985
Milea, Vasile 1985–1989
Militaru, Nicolae 1989–1990
Stanculescu, Anastase 1990–

USSR

Stalin, Josef until 1947
Bulganin, Nikolai 1947–1949
Vasilevsky, A. M. 1949–1953
Bulganin, Nikolai, 1953–1955
Zhukov, Georgii 1955–1957
Malinovsky, Rodion 1957–1967
Grechko, Andrei 1967–1976
Ustinov, Dmitrii 1976–1984
Sokolov, Sergei 1984–1987
Yazov, Dmitrii 1987–

Yugoslavia

Tito, Josip Broz until 1951
Gošnjak, Ivan 1951–1967
Ljubičič, Nikola 1967–1982
Mamula, Branko 1982–1988
Kadijević, Veljko 1988–

APPENDIX III

East European Communist Parties, Their Successors, Leaders, and Memberships (as of April 15, 1990)
by Jonathan Valdez

Country	Ruling party	Membership, mid-1980s	Successor party or parties	Leaders, March 1990	Approximate membership, March 1990
Bulgaria	Bulgarian Communist Party (BCP)	932,055 (Apr. 88)	(no change)	Aleksandr Lilov	900,000
Czechoslovakia	Czechoslovak Communist Party (CPCz)	1,705,490 (Sept. 88)	(no change)	Ladislav Adamec	1,100,000
East Germany	Socialist Unity Party of Germany (SED)	2,324,386 (July 88)	Party of Democratic Socialism (PDS)	Gregor Gysi	1,200,000
Hungary	Hungarian Socialist Workers' Party (HSWP)	870,992 (Jan. 85)	Hungarian Socialist Party (HSP)	Resző Nyers, Imre Pozsgay	50–60,000
			HSWP	Károly Grósz, János Berecz	20,000
Poland	Polish United Workers' Party (PUWP)	2,129,002 (1986)	Party of Social Democracy (PSD)	Aleksander Kwaśniewski	47,000
			Social Democratic Union (SDU)	Tadeusz Fiszbach	1000
Romania	Romanian Communist Party (RCP)	3,640,000 (Dec. 86)	(The National Salvation Front explicitly denies any connection to the RCP, although several of its members in fact held leadership positions before falling out of favor with Ceauşescu; similarly, many former communists held their posts in the bureaucracy after the revolution.)		

East European Elections and Major Contenders, 1990 by Jonathan Valdez

A bewildering array of parties sprang up in Eastern Europe in 1989 – over fifty in Hungary, and more than three dozen in Romania, for example. This appendix includes what were considered in early 1990 to be the major contenders for power in the elections scheduled for later that year, with other possible coalition partners and minor parties listed separately. In those cases where party leadership is exercised collectively, the most prominent figures have been listed as leaders.

Country	Date	Parties	Leaders
Bulgaria	June 10	Bulgarian Communist Party (BCP)	A. Lilov
		Bulgarian Agricultural National Union (BZNS)	A. Dimitrov
		Social Democratic Party	P. Dertliev
		Union of Democratic Forces (UDF)	Z. Zhelev

The UDF includes groups such as the Green Party and the independent labor federation *Podkrepa* ("Support"). The Nikola Petkov Agrarian Union, led by Milan Drenchev, has tried (so far unsuccessfully) to resurrect itself, and to gain legitimacy has taken on the name of the former leader who was hanged by the communists in 1947. Liberal as well as conservative factions exist within the BCP; representative of the former are the "Bulgarian Road to Europe" and the Alternative Socialist Union.

Czechoslovakia	June 8	Czechoslovak Communist Party	L. Adamec
		Green Alternative Party	M. Machovec
		Czechoslovak Social Democracy	S. Klaban
		Czechoslovak Agrarian Party	P. Deling
		Czechoslovak Democratic Initiative	E. Mandler
		Christian Democratic Party	V. Benda
		Czechoslovak People's Party	J. Bartončík
		Czechoslovak Socialist Party	J. Škoda
		Agrarian Cooperative Party	F. Trnka

Country	Date	Parties	Leaders

There are several smaller groups in addition to those listed here, and Civic Forum has attempted to maintain itself as an umbrella group rather than a political party, but may participate in elections.

East Germany	March 18	Party of Democratic Social-ism (PDS, the former SED)	G. Gysi
		Neue Forum	J. Reiche, B. Bohley
		Social Democratic Party	I. Böhme
		Green Party	H. Schramm, C. Weiske
		National Democratic Party	G. Hartmann
		Democratic Peasants' Party	G. Maleuda
		Christian Democratic Union	L. de Maiziere
		Liberal Democratic Party	M. Gerlach

The Christian Democratic Union and its conservative allies won 49 percent of the March vote, while the Social Democrats gained 22 percent. The PDS did surprisingly well with sixteen percent.

Hungary	March/April	Hungarian Socialist Party (MSzP)	R. Nyers
		Hungarian Democratic Front (MDF)	J. Antall
		Alliance of Free Democrats (SzDSz)	J. Kis
		Federation of Young Demo-crats (FIDESZ)	T. Deutsch, G. Fodor
		Independent Smallholders' Party	V. Vörös
		Hungarian Socialist Workers' Party (HSWP)	K. Grósz, J. Berecz

In addition to these major parties, some HSWP members joined two small conservative groups: the Ferenc Münnich Society and the János Kádár Society (reportedly inactive in early 1990). Noncommunist parties which may play a role in future coalition governments include the Social Democrats and the Greens. Elections in April resulted in the MDF receiving 43 percent of the vote, SzDSz 24 percent, and the MSzP 8.3 percent.

Country	Date	Parties	Leaders
Poland	April	Solidarity	L. Wałęsa
		Rural Solidarity	G. Janowski
		Party of Social Democracy of the Republic of Poland (SDRP)	A. Kwaśniewski
		Social Democratic Union	T. Fiszbach
		Polish Peasant Party	F. Kamiński
		Polish Peasant Party "Renewal"	K. Olesiak
		Confederation of Independent Poland	L. Moczulski

In addition to these parties, over eighty smaller parties existed representing all political persuasions.

Country	Date	Parties	Leaders
Romania	May 20	National Salvation Front	I. Iliescu
		National Christian Peasants' Party	C. Coposu
		National Liberal Party	S. Botez
		Social Democratic Party	S. Cunescu

In addition to these main parties, more than thirty parties came into existence after the revolution and were incorporated into the Council of National Unity interim government formed in February 1990. Among them are the National Democratic Party, the Democratic Union of Hungarians in Romania (A. Gurvat), a strongly anti-communist student group, the League of Students, and two environmental groups with platforms similar to those of the European Green parties.

Index

Ackermann, Anton, 293
Adamec, Ladislav, 136, 290, 292, 295, 296
Adenauer, Konrad, on "iron curtain," 232
Afanas'yev, Yurii, 38n
Afghanistan
    and CMEA, 116
    nonaligned status of, 28–9
    war in, 1, 10, 23, 274
Agrarian Cooperative Party, 297
Akhromeyev, Marshal Sergei, 201
Albania
    and China, 263, 274
    chronology of events (1945–90, in, 251–88
    communist party in, 41, 127, 259
    declared republic, 252
    ethnic unrest in, 278, 279
    and Greece, 280
    leadership successions (1945–90) in, 290–4
    and leading role of communist party, 91
    legitimacy of regime in, 139
    and military, 100
    purges in, 255, 263, 271, 272, 277
    and socialist internationalism, 86, 87, 202
    and ties with West, 32–3
    and USSR, 121, 262, 263, 279
    and Yugoslavia, 258, 279
Albanian Workers' Party, 259
Alia, Ramiz, 281, 290, 291
Alliance of Free Democrats (Hungary), 298
Allied Control Commission, 252, 254
Alternative Socialist Union, 297
Alton, Thad, 78–9n32
Andreeva, Nina, 23, 37n22, 38n25, 284
Andrei, Stefan, 294
Andropov, Yurii, 27, 153, 198, 279, 280, 291, 292

Antall, J., 298
anti-Semitism, 26
    and Poland, 18, 162
anti-Sovietism
    in bloc armies, 98
    in Bulgaria, 51
    in Czechoslovakia, 62–3
    in Eastern Europe, 1, 3, 33, 143, 144, 221
    in Hungary, 62
    and nationalism, 142
    and Poland, 62, 113, 131, 277
    see also Russophobia
Apel, Erich, 265
Arbatov, Georgii, 200
    on common security, 241–2
arms control, see Gorbachev, military doctrine of
Atanasov, Georgi, 291
Ausgleich, 57
Austro-Hungarian Empire, 52
Aytmatov, Chengis, on socialism, 215

Babiuch, Edward, 293
Baku, 221
Bakunin, Mikhail, and Polish independence, 13
Balluku, Beqir, 272, 294
Baltic states
    and "Eurocommunism," 29
    and military, 246
    and West, 27
Bartončík, J., 297
Bashev, Ivan, 293
Bata, István, 295
Bayer, Josef, on legitimacy of regimes, 140
BCP, see Bulgarian Communist Party
Benda, V., 297
Bender, Peter, on Europeanization, 230

Beneš, Edward, 254, 291
Benin, 156
Berecz, János, 154, 179, 296, 298
    on Hungarian–Soviet friendship, 161
    on 1956 uprising, 136
Beria, Lavrenti, 258
Berlin, 65, 260
    blockade of (1948), 34, 233, 254
    and FRG, 278
    Four-Power Agreement on, 65, 268,
        269, 270
    and Khrushchev, 261, 262, 263
    riots in, 258, 284
    see also Berlin Wall
Berlin Wall, 82, 145, 163, 190
    erected (1961), 34, 263
    opened (1989), 36, 67, 193, 223, 287
Berman, Jakub, and "two-camp"
        doctrine, 18–19
Bessarabia
    annexed by USSR, 51
    given to USSR, 252
Bierut, Bolesław, 253, 260, 289, 291, 293
Bijedić, Djemal, 271, 293
Bil'ak, Vasil, 162, 283
Bismarck, Otto von, 65
Black Madonna, 161
Blumenthal, Michael, 274
Bodnaras, Emil, 295
Bogomolov, Oleg, 200, 206
    on Hungarian neutrality, 212
    on socialism in Eastern Europe, 76n5
    on socialist internationalism, 204
Bohemia, 61
    and fascism, 17
    and West, 27
Bohley, B., 298
Böhme, I., 298
Boldoczky, János, 294
Bolz, Lothar, 293
Bondarev, Yurii, 24, 38n28
Botez, S., 299
Bovin, Aleksandr, 31
    on socialism, 215
Brandt, Willi, 268, 271
Brezhnev, Leonid, 198, 264, 279, 290, 292
    on communist party in intrabloc
        relations, 86
    and Czechoslovakia, 9, 33–4, 63, 93,
        266
    on economy of East European bloc,
        115–16
    and interparty relations, 98, 202
    and Kania, 130
    and limited sovereignty, 267, *see also*
        Brezhnev Doctrine

longevity of, 132
    on *nomenklatura*, 93
    and Poland, 130, 275, 276, 277, 278, 279
    and Romania, 265
    on *sblizhenie*, 115
    and Yugoslavia, 273
Brezhnev Doctrine, 86, 88, 202, 268, 276,
        277
    under Gorbachev, 218–22
    see also socialist internationalism
Brus, Włodzimierz, 82
    on economic reform, 114–15
Brzezinski, Zbigniew, on U.S.
        withdrawals from Europe, 230
Budapest Cultural Forum, 165
Bughici, Simion, 294
Bujak, Zbigniew, 282
Bukovina, 265
    annexed by USSR, 51
    given to USSR, 252
Bulganin, Nikolai, 293, 295
Bulgaria
    and attempted assassination of pope,
        26
    chronology of events (1945–90) in,
        251–88
    communist party in, 50, 87, 88, 90–1,
        153, 187, 218, 252, 259, 261, 263, 265,
        287, 288, 296, 297
    and Czechoslovakia, 63
    debt of, 118, 121, 178, 186, 187, 188
    democratization of, 187
    demonstrations in, 245, 261, 287
    and economy, 118, 169, 170, 173, 178,
        185–7, 188, 262, 264, 275, 283–4
    ethnic unrest in, 51, 256, 282, 286
    and fascism, 17
    FRG and, 271, 272
    GNP growth rate of, 169, 170, 185–6,
        192
    Greece and, 282
    Hungary and, 261
    intelligentsia of, 158, 165–6
    and intrabloc trade, 186
    leadership successions (1945–90) in,
        290–94
    and Macedonia, 48–9
    multicandidate elections in, 284
    and nationalism, 48, 49, 50, 51, 165–6
    and *nomenklatura*, 93–4, 96
    purges in, 256
    and socialist internationalism, 87, 88, 202
    and trade with USSR, 119, 186
    Turkey and, 51, 268, 286
    USSR and, 25, 48–50, 51, 119, 186, 218,
        253

Bulgaria (*cont.*).
  and Warsaw Pact, 10
  and West, 32–3, 40
  Yugoslavia and, 256, 258, 261
Bulgarian Agricultural National Union, 297
Bulgarian Communist Party, 50, 90–1, 187, 252, 259, 261, 263, 265, 287, 288, 296, 297
"Bulgarian Road to Europe," 297
Bunaciu, Avram, 294
Bur'latskii, Fyodor, 38n22
Byelorussia, 277
BZNS, *see* Bulgarian Agricultural National Union

Čalfa, Marián, 153, 292
Cambodia and GDR, 268
capitalism in Europe, 14, 15
Çarçani, Adil, 291
Catherine the Great, 70
Catholic Church
  and coexistence, 163–4
  co-optation of, 164–6
  in Czechoslovakia, 48, 162–3
  in Eastern Europe, 30, 31, 161–9
  in Hungary, 164–5, 264
  in Poland, 13, 26, 48, 70, 72–3, 74, 166–9, 182, 262, 263, 270, 274, 275, 277, 278, 279, 284
  in Romania, 53, 163
  suppression and confrontation of, 162–3
  and USSR, 37n6
CDE, *see* Stockholm Conference on Disarmament in Europe
Ceauşescu, Elena, 129, 184, 287
Ceauşescu, Nicolae, 154, 218, 291
  and Catholic Church, 163
  and communist party, 269
  corruption of regime of, 55
  and cult of personality, 94, 164
  and debt, 183, 184
  durability of, 129–30
  fall of, 95, 149, 284, 287, 290
  and FRG, 271
  and German reunification, 66
  and GNP growth rate, 169–70
  and Hungarian minority, 58, 59, 138
  and military, 101, 103, 281
  and National Salvation Front, 185
  and *nomenklatura*, 184
  and USSR, 96, 114, 245, 265
  and West, 54–5
Celac, Sergiu, 294
Central Europe, *see* Eastern Europe
Čepička, Alexej, 294

Černík, Oldřich, 291, 293
Charlemagne, 53
Charles IV (King of Czechoslovakia), 60
Charter 77, 135, 159, 273, 274, 275
Chebrikov, Viktor, 200
  and Tbilisi and Baku, 221
Chernenko, Konstantin, 153, 198, 202, 280, 281, 291, 292
Chernobyl, 282
Chernyshevsky, Nikolai, 17
Chervenkov, Vulko, 259, 263, 290, 292
China
  Albania and, 274
  GDR and, 284
  and socialist internationalism, 86, 202
  USSR and, 10, 263, 265
Chnoupek, Bohuslav, 293
Chou En-Lai, 265
Christian Democratic Party (Czechoslovakia), 297
Christian Democratic Union (GDR), 298
chronology (1945–90) of East European events, 251–88
Churchill, Winston
  on Soviet threat in Europe, 232, 252
  and Stalin in Eastern Europe, 25
Civic Forum (Czechoslovakia), 298
  and Charter 77, 159
  on communist party, 135
  founding of, 190
  pro-European platform of, 95
CMEA, *see* Council for Mutual Economic Assistance
Coman, Ion, 295
Comecon, *see* Council for Mutual Economic Assistance
Cominform, 256, 258
  dissolved, 85, 260
  established, 84, 253
Comintern and democratic centralism, 89
Committee for State Security, *see* KGB
Common Market, 144
Common Security, 241
communism
  in Eastern Europe, 2, 221
  Russian hegemony and, 15
  Stalinism and, 121n1
  and unity of eastern bloc, 11–12
  see also communist parties listed under individual countries
Communist International, *see* Comintern and democratic centralism
Communist Manifesto (Marx and Engels), 13, 16
communist parties, East European (1990), 296

Communist Party of Czechoslovakia
(CPCz)
  and Catholic Church, 162–3
  chronology of events in, 252–88
  conservatism of, 62, 63
  intelligentsia and, 158–9, 161
  and invasion of Czechoslovakia, 134–6
  and Masaryk, 60, 61
  in 1946, 41, 252
  in 1989–90, 90, 91, 135–6, 190–1, 296,
    297–8
  and *nomenklatura*, 129
Communist Party of the Soviet Union
(CPSU)
  and cells within nonparty
    organizations, 97–8
  Central Committee of, 199–200, 207,
    208, 285
  and democratic centralism, 89, 91, 97,
    98
  and intrabloc relations, 85–99
  and leading role of communist party,
    76, 89–98, 108, 201, 209–10, 221
  nomenklatura system of, 91–7, 98
  parallel party bureaucracy of, 91, 98
  and socialist internationalism, 86–9, 98
  27th Party Congress of, 11, 199, 201,
    206–7, 219, 246, 282
Conference on Security and Cooperation
  in Europe (CSCE) (*see also* Helsinki
  Final Act), 34, 271, 272, 273, 279
Congress of Peoples' Deputies,
  establishment of, 208
Coposu, C., 299
"cosmopolitanism," 18
Council for Mutual Economic Assistance
  (CMEA), 115, 119, 264, 267, 268,
    269, 271, 272
  Albania and, 263
  created, 84, 254, 262
  debt of, 118, 172–3
  and de-Stalinization, 85
  future of, 245
  GNP growth rate of, 79n32
  Gorbachev and, 283
  and imports from USSR, 174–5
  and intrabloc trade, 173–5, 284
  1984 economic summit meeting of,
    116–18, 202
  and oil, 111, 114, 183
  Poland and, 279, 280
  restructuring of (1990), 218
  Romania and, 277, 280, 285
  and subsidies (Soviet) and trade
    surpluses, 111–14
  and trade with West, 112, 118
  Vietnam and, 274

Council of National Unity (Romania),
  299
Counter-Reformation, 48, 53
CPCz, *see* Communist Party of
  Czechoslovakia
CPSU, *see* Communist Party of the
  Soviet Union
Croatia, 17
Crusades, 53
CSCE, *see* Conference on Security and
  Cooperation in Europe
Cserhat, Bishop, 165
Cuba, 10
  economic aid and, 116
  socialism and, 28
cult of personality, 81, 82, 83, 84
  and Ceauşescu, 94, 164
  Gorbachev on, 206
Cunescu, S., 299
Cyrankiewicz, Józef, 291, 293
Czechoslovak Agrarian Party, 297
Czechoslovak Democratic Initiative, 297
Czechoslovak People's Party, 297
Czechoslovak Social Democracy, 297
Czechoslovak Socialist Party, 297
Czechoslovak Writers' Union, 266
  purge of, 162
Czechoslovakia
  anti-Sovietism in, 62–3
  Catholic Church in, 48, 162–3, 255
  chronology of events in (1945–90),
    251–88
  civil rights in, 271
  communist party of, 41, 60, 61, 62, 63,
    90–1, 129, 134–5, 136, 158–9, 161,
    162–3, 190–1, 252, 253–4, 258, 265,
    266, 268, 269, 270, 272, 282, 287,
    296, 297–8
  Czech and Slovak rivalries in, 26
  debt of, 118, 178, 188
  defense industry in, 104
  democratic traditions and, 43
  and democratization, 155
  demonstrations in, 245, 286, 287
  de-Stalinization in, 264
  and economy, 113, 187, 189–91, 258,
    274, 283
  and First Republic, 59, 60, 61–2
  FRG and, 266, 271
  GDR and, 193, 286
  and Germans, 255, 260
  GNP growth rate of, 141, 169, 170,
    189, 192
  intelligentsia of, 162, 267, 273, 274,
    275, 282, 285
  and intrabloc trade, 175, 189
  invasion of, 9, 30, 33–4, 45, 47, 60, 61,

Czechoslovakia (*cont.*)
  62–3, 82, 86, 92, 93, 102, 106–7,
  113, 134, 136, 190, 202, 219, 240,
  267, 268, 269, 271, 286
and Jews, 252, 257
leadership successions in (1945–90),
  290–5
and Little Entente, 54
and military (indigenous), 102, 105–6,
  106–7
and military (Soviet), 102, 103, 107–8,
  143
and military doctrine (post-1985), 212
in 1989–90, 90, 91, 135–6, 190–1, 296,
  297–8
and *nomenklatura*, 94, 95, 96, 128, 153,
  218
and normalization, 134, 135, 189
and nuclear power, 189
and oil, 189
Poland and, 130, 275, 277
political issues facing, 158–9
pollution in, 191
and Prague Spring, 1–2, 26, 60, 102,
  134, 136, 141, 266
purges in, 255, 256, 268, 272
and Slavophiles, 12
and Slovaks, 26, 60–1
and socialism, 29
and socialist internationalism, 86, 87, 88
and Stalinism, 62
and trade with USSR, 119, 175
Ukrainians and, 252
U.S. and, 251, 278
USSR and, 25, 113, 119, 175, 251, 267,
  273, 281, 288
viability of regime in, 134–6
and Warsaw Pact, 10
and West, 32–3, 40, 62
World War II and, 62, 251
and Writers' Union, 162, 266
Czinege, Lajos, 295
Czyrek, József, 277, 294

Danianov, Georgi, 291, 294
Danubian Principalities, *see* Romania
Dăscălescu, Constantin, 293
David, Vaclav, 293
Davies, Norman, 67
"Declaration on Soviet–Polish
  Cooperation," 283
Deling, P., 297
democracy
  and Czechoslovakia, 43
  in Poland, 43, 132
democratic centralism, 97, 268
  defined, 89

in Eastern Europe, 247
Gorbachev on, 209
in intrabloc relations, 89
Novopashin on, 205
in USSR, 91
Democratic Forum (Hungary), and pro-
  European platform, 95
Democratic Party (Poland), 299
Democratic Peasants' Party (GDR), 298
Democratic Union of Hungarians
  (Romania), 299
democratization
  in Eastern Europe, 154–5
  and national security, 225
  in USSR, 208–10, 212, 247
demokratizatsiya, see democratization
Dertinger, Georg, 293
Dertliev, P., 297
de-Stalinization, 85, 260
  in GDR, 92
  and KGB, 102
  in Romania, 184
détente, 1, 271, 275
  described, 228–9
  Eastern Europe and, 159–60
  FRG and, 92
  GDR and, 144, 145
  Honecker and, 58, 145
  Kádár and, 58
Deutsch, T., 298
Dienstbier, Jiří, 107, 293
Dimitrov, A., 297
Dimitrov, Boyko, 293
Dimitrov, Georgii, 252, 254, 290, 292
Dinnyés, Lajos, 292
disarmament, 211–12
Dizdarević, Raif, 292, 294
Djilas, Milovan, 261
Djuranović, Veselin, 292, 293
Dobi, István, 291, 292
Dobrinin, Anatolii, and East European
  policy, 199, 201
Dobruja and Bulgaria, 252
dolg, 19
Doronjski, Stevan, 291
Dragosavac, Dusan, 291
Drenchev, Milan, 297
Drnovšek, Janez, 292
Dubček, Alexander, 270, 272, 290
  and Communist Party of
    Czechoslovakia, 92, 93, 102, 266,
    267, 268
  on Europe as "common home," 217
  on German reunification, 66
  and invasion of Czechoslovakia, 62, 63
  and Prague Spring, 63, 102, 266
  return of, 94, 135–6, 191, 287

durability of East European regimes,
127–32
Dzhurov, Dobri, 294
Dzúr, Martin, 294

East Berlin, *see* Berlin
"East European five"
defined, 87
East Germany, *see* German Democratic
Republic
Eastern Europe
anti-Sovietism in, 1, 3, 221
and arms reductions, 241–2
and autocracy, 42–4
and Brezhnev Doctrine, 218–22
Catholic Church in, 30, 31, 161–9
chronology of events in (1945–90),
251–88
communist parties in, 85–99, 108, 221,
296
and conservation, 194
and debt, 118, 121, 178, 194
and defense industries, 104–5
democratic centralism in, 247
democratization of, 154–5, 212
and détente, 228–9
and economy, 4, 23, 43, 109–21, 133,
141, 169–95
elections in (1990), 297–9
and energy, 194
and Europe as "common home," 21,
22–3, 216–18, 223, 239
and Europeanization, 230
and foreign investment, 24
generational change in, 159–61
GNP growth rate of, 105, 109, 169–72,
193–4
governance issues in, 155–8
intelligentsia in, 161–6
intrabloc trade of, 173–5
leadership successions in (1945–90),
290–5
leading role of communist party in,
210
and Lenin, 15
and military and security cooperation
with USSR, 3, 10–11, 99–109,
246
and military doctrine (post-1985),
210–13
and nationalism, 3, 26–7, 31–3, 35, 42,
43, 47–8, 142, 203–5, 226–7n45
and *nomenklatura* systems, 156–7
and oil, 111, 114, 115, 171, 183, 194
and peace movements, 34
political issues facing, 4, 152–9
political parties of (1990), 297–8

and political ties with USSR, 3, 25–9,
45–7
and reforms under Gorbachev, 21
regimes of, 44, 45, 46–7, 48
reunification of Germany and, 66
and security, 33–6, 44–6
social issues facing, 159–69
and socialism, 27–9, 32–3, 214–15, 221,
242, 246
Soviet conceptions of, 11–24
Soviet subsidies of, 110–14
and Stalinism, 242
and subversion, 30
succession issues in, 153–4
and trade with USSR, 118, 119–21,
174–5
and trade with West, 112, 118, 172, 174,
175
and ultranationalism, 16
and USSR, 1, 3, 4, 9–11, 11–24, 25–9,
30, 44–7, 99–109, 109–21, 246
and West, 1, 2, 3, 6, 27, 30, 40–1, 159,
161, 163, 224, 233–8, 243–4, 267
and World War II, 19–20
see also entries for individual countries
Eastern Orthodox Church
in Bulgaria, 48
and Poland, 70
in Romania, 53, 163
Eberstadt, Nicholas, 76n
EEC, *see* European Economic
Community
elections (1990), East European, 297–9
Engels, Friedrich, 15, 16, 18
and Europe as home of socialism,
13–14
Enlightenment, 216
Estonia annexed by USSR, 52
Ethiopia and CMEA, 116
"Eurocommunism" and USSR, 29
Europe
as "common home," 21, 22–3, 216–18,
223, 239
détente in, 228–9
divided, 5, 228–31, 231–2, 234–5
Europeanization of, 229–31, 241–7
and fascism, 16–17
Lenin and, 15
NATO and Warsaw Pact states and,
238–41
reunification of, 229–31, 241–7
and security, 33–6, 241–2
and West, 231–8
see also Eastern Europe
European Economic Community (EEC)
and CMEA, 281
and Poland, 276

European Economic Community (EEC)
(*cont.*)
Yugoslavia and, 274

Falin, Valentin, 200
Farkas, Mihály, 295
fascism
and communism, 16–17
and socialism, 41
and USSR, 23
Fatherland Front, 252
Federal Republic of Germany (FRG)
and Bulgaria, 271, 272
and Czechoslovakia, 266, 271
and détente, 92
economic success of, 64
and GDR, 64, 65, 66, 144–6, 147,
151n43, 193, 229, 236, 268, 270, 271,
274, 278, 283, 288
Germans flee to, 255
and NATO, 222, 259
and Poland, 269
and reunification, 67, 193, 217
and Romania, 266
and USSR, 268, 271
and West, 222–3, 236
see also Germany
Federation of Young Democrats
(Hungary), 298
Fekete, Sándor, and reform, 136–7
FIDESZ, *see* Federation of Young
Democrats
Fierlinger, Zdeněk, 292
Filipov, Grisha, 292
Finland, 66
First Republic, *see* Czechoslovakia
Fischer, Oskar, 293
Fiszbach, Tadeusz, 296, 298
Fleck, Werner, 293
Fock, Jenö, 292
Fodor, G., 298
Four Powers Agreement (1971), 65, 269,
270
Four Powers and division of Germany,
232
Four Powers Conference (1951), 256
Francis Joseph I, 56
Frederick the Great, 65, 147
FRG, *see* Federal Republic of Germany
"Front to Defend Real Socialism and
Perestroika," 297
Fyodorov, Raphael P., 200

Ganev, Dimiter, 291
Gaulle, Charles de, on Europe, 230
GDR, *see* German Democratic Republic

generational change in Eastern Europe,
159–61
Georgescu, Interior Minister, 257
Georgiev, Kimon, 292, 293
Gerlach, Manfred, 291, 298
German Democratic Republic, 153
and amnesty, 284
and army, 260
Britain and France and, 270
Cambodia and, 268
China and, 284
chronology of events (1945–90) in,
251–88
communist party of, 64, 67, 90–1,
256, 257, 276–7, 281, 282, 287, 296,
298
Czechoslovakia and, 63
and debt, 118, 121, 178, 188, 193
and defense, 104, 105
democratization in, 155
demonstrations in, 286
and de-Stalinization, 92
and economy, 64–5, 66, 78–9n32, 147,
173, 191–3, 262, 263
exodus of East Germans from, 286,
287, 288
FRG and, 64, 65, 66, 144–6, 147,
151n43, 217, 229, 236, 268, 270, 271,
274, 283, 288
GNP growth rate of, 169, 170, 192, 193
intelligentsia of, 158, 163–4
Iraq and, 268
leadership successions (1945–90) in,
290–95
and legitimacy and viability of
regimes in, 65, 134, 144–8
Lutheran Church in, 147–8
military doctrine (post-1985) of, 212
and nationalism, 144
1953 uprising in, 33, 144
and *nomenklatura*, 95–6, 218
and oil, 192
Poland and, 130, 275, 276, 277
political reform in, 287, 288
and reunification, 67, 193, 217, 222–4,
229–30, 240–1, 257, 258, 288
and socialism, 29
and socialist internationalism, 87, 88,
202
and Soviet military, 103
and Sudeten Germans, 255
and trade with USSR, 119–21, 193
and U.S., 272
and USSR, 119–20, 193, 259, 260, 265
and West, 32–3, 40, 65, 67, 193
see also Germany

Germany
  division of, 44, 63, 65, 228–31, 231–2,
    234, 251
  and fascism, 16–17
  Hitler and, 62–3, 66
  NATO and, 237, 243, 245
  Protestant Church in, 48
  remilitarization of, 259
  reunification of, 36, 66, 67, 193, 217,
    222–4, 229–30, 240–1, 245, 257,
    258, 288
  ultranationalism of, 16
  USSR and, 25
  Warsaw Pact and, 10
  and World War II, 20
  see also Federal Republic of Germany;
    German Democratic Republic
Gerő Ernő, 92, 260, 290
Gheorghiu-Dej, Gheorghe, 54, 258, 290,
  291, 293
Gierek, Edward, 92, 141, 180, 269, 272,
  275, 278, 290
glasnost, 3, 24, 36n3, 152, 208
Glemp, Bishop Józef, 277, 278
Goldstücker, Edward, 61
Gomułka, Władysław, 289
  Catholic Church and, 262
  communist party and, 253, 254, 255
  on cult of personality, 83
  election of, 93, 100, 128
  Gierek and, 92, 269
  and Stalinism, 82
Gorbachev, Mikhail Sergeevich, 11, 13, 29,
  33, 82, 127, 153, 291, 292
  accession of, 1, 281
  on arms control, 107, 210–13, 241–3,
    283, 285
  and Baltic secession, 143
  and Bulgaria, 50
  Catholic Church and, 37n6, 164
  communist party and, 86, 88–9, 206–
    7, 218, 246, 282
  conceptions of Eastern Europe under,
    20–4
  on cult of personality, 206
  on democratic centralism, 209
  and democratization, 148, 154, 155, 190,
    208–9, 210
  on détente, 242
  and East European advisors, 198–201
  on East European leaders, 4
  and East European policy, 1–6, 47, 66
  and economy of Eastern Europe, 59,
    117, 118–19, 189
  and economy of USSR, 24, 38n28,
    118–19

on Europe as "common home," 22–3,
  216–18, 223, 231, 239, 242
on Europeanization, 230–1
GDR and, 191, 193
Honecker and, 146, 148
Husák and, 283
and INF agreement, 241, 243
Jaruzelski and, 75, 283
Khrushchev and, 87
on leading role of communist party,
  209–10
and liberals, 284–5
military doctrine of, 107, 210–13, 241–
  3, 283, 285
and nationalism, 22–4, 164
and *nomenklatura*, 94, 95–6, 97
and political independence of East-
  bloc states, 35, 75–6, 87–9, 98–9,
  144
and reform, 1–6, 36, 135, 152, 186, 195,
  205–7
and reunification of Europe, 5, 230–1
and reunification of Germany, 223,
  224, 245
Romania and, 55, 283
on Russophobia, 142–3
and socialism, 1–2, 26, 28, 31–2, 132,
  140, 213–15
and socialist internationalism, 87–8,
  202, 203, 219–22
and succession issues in Eastern
  Europe, 154
and 27th Party Congress, 206–7, 282
and 28th Party Congress, 246
on Warsaw Pact states, 240
Gošnjak, Ivan, 295
Gottwald, Klement, 252, 254, 257–8, 290,
  291, 292
Gottwald Military Academy, 106
governance in Eastern Europe, 155–8
Grabski, Tadeusz, 130
Grechko, Andrei, 267, 295
Green Alternative Party
  (Czechoslovakia), 297
Green Party (Bulgaria), 297
Green Party (GDR), 298
Green Party (Hungary), 298
Grodzien, Zdzisław, 275
Gromyko, Andrei, 199, 278, 292, 294
  and Brezhnev Doctrine, 277
  on reunification of Germany, 146
Grósz, Károly, 153, 179, 290, 292, 296, 298
Grotewohl, Otto, 260, 292
Groza, Petru, 251, 252, 291, 293
Gurvat, A., 299
Gyöngyösi, János, 293

Gysi, Gregor, 96, 153, 288, 290, 296, 298
and dissidents, 94–5, 164

Haber, Herbert, 281
Habsburg Empire, 56
Hager, Kurt, 96
Haig, Alexander, on Eastern Europe, 238,
248n13
Hájek, Jiří, 277, 293
Hallstein Doctrine, 268
Hartmann, G., 298
Hasani, Sinan, 292
Havel, Václav, 155, 247, 285, 286, 291
and Charter 77, 159
and Civic Forum, 159, 190
on Czechoslovakia, 244
elected president, 96, 287
Hazbiu, Kadri, 294
Hegedüs, András, 259, 292
Hegenbart, Rudolf, 190
Helsinki Final Act (*see also* Conference
on Security and Cooperation in
Europe), 34, 135, 212, 218
Helsinki Watch, 282
Herzen, Alexander, 14
on partition of Poland, 30
and Polish independence, 13
Hitler, Adolf, 63–4, 231
and Czechoslovakia, 62
and Poland, 71
and Russia, 16–17
Hoffmann, Heinz, 295
Hoffmann, Theodor, 295
Honecker, Erich, 149, 154, 290, 291
accession of, 269
and détente, 58
on economy, 193
and intelligentsia, 163–4
legitimacy of regime of, 144–7
and reform, 283
removal of, 95–6, 193, 286
West Germany and, 144–6, 280, 282,
284
Horn, Gyula, 293
Horthy, Miklós Nagybányai, 290
Horváth, Imre, 293
Howe, Sir Geoffrey, 50
Hoxha, Enver, 41, 252, 263, 271, 281, 289,
291, 292, 293
HSP, *see* Hungarian Socialist Party
HSWP, *see* Hungarian Socialist Workers'
Party
Hungarian Democratic Front, 290, 298
Hungarian Socialist Party (HSP), 59, 96,
155, 179, 287
in 1990, 296, 298

Hungarian Socialist Workers' Party
(HSWP), 58, 59, 90–1, 96, 155, 179,
296, 298
chronology of events in, 253, 262, 287
and economic reform, 271
and Kádár, 281, 285
and Németh, 281
and Nyers, 285
and political reassessment, 136–8
USSR and, 161
"Hungaricus," 134
Hungary
amnesty in, 264
and anti-Sovietism, 62
Austria and, 56, 57
Catholic Church in, 164–5, 264
chronology of events (1945–90) in,
251–88
communist party in, 15, 58, 59, 90–1,
96, 136–8, 155, 161, 179, 251, 253, 262,
271, 281, 285, 287, 296, 298
Czechoslovakia and, 58, 63, 135
and debt, 118, 121, 177, 178, 179, 187, 188
defense industry in, 104
and democratization, 154, 155
and economy, 58–9, 118, 119, 173, 175,
176–9, 187, 188, 190, 256, 258, 266,
275, 282, 283, 284
and fascism, 17
foreign domination of, 56, 58, 59
in fourteenth century, 236
and FRG, 193
GDR and, 286
and *glasnost,* 36n3
GNP growth rate of, 169, 170, 176,
177, 192
governance issues in, 157
and Hungarian diaspora, 58, 59
intelligentsia of, 134, 162, 165, 260, 265,
270
and intrabloc trade, 175, 176, 177, 179
leadership successions in (1945–90),
290–95
legitimacy of regime in, 129, 140
and military (indigenous), 100
and military (Soviet), 108, 143, 261
and military ties with USSR, 138–9
multicandidate elections in, 266
multiparty system in, 286
and nationalism, 58, 59, 138
and neutrality, 212
in 1956, 1, 30, 33, 34, 56, 57, 58, 82, 100,
136, 137, 138, 260, 283
and *nomenklatura,* 96
purges in, 255
Romania and, 26, 52, 58, 285, 286

and Slavophiles, 12
and socialism, 29, 149, 214
and socialist internationalism, 87, 202
succession issues in, 153
and trade with USSR, 119, 175
and trade with West, 176, 177
unrest in, 261, 285, 286
U.S. and, 273, 284
USSR and, 25, 56–7, 138–9, 273, 288
viability of regime in, 133, 134, 136–9
and Warsaw Pact, 10, 58, 260
and West, 32–3, 40, 56, 58, 59, 176, 177
in World War II, 56
and Yugoslavia, 255, 258
Huns, 52
Hus, Jan, 60, 161
Husák, Gustáv, 95, 162, 287, 290, 291
and antireformism, 268
and Bohemia and Moravia, 61
Brezhnev Doctrine and, 276
communist party and, 269, 283
Dubček and, 267
durability of regime of, 129
Gorbachev and, 283
and intelligentsia, 162
Jakeš and, 94, 284
and normalization, 134–5, 189
Slovakia and, 252, 259, 269
Hussite rebellion, 30

Ignotus, Paul, 148
Iliescu, Ion, 153, 183, 291, 299
communist party and, 55, 95, 157
and governance issues, 157
and *nomenklatura*, 96
Illyés, Gyula
on Eastern Europe, 243–4
IMF, *see* International Monetary Fund
*Imperialism, The Highest Stage of
    Capitalism* (Lenin), 14
Independent Smallholders' Party
    (Hungary), 298
INF agreement, 241, 243
intelligentsia
in Bulgaria, 158, 165–6
and coexistence, 163–4
and co-optation, 164–6
in Czechoslovakia, 162, 273, 274, 275,
    282, 285
in Eastern Europe, 161–9
in GDR, 158, 163–4
in Hungary, 134, 162, 165, 260, 265, 270
in Poland, 162
in Romania, 158, 162, 164
suppression and confrontation of,
    162–3

International Monetary Fund (IMF) and
    Hungary's debt, 179
internationalism, *see* socialist
    internationalism
Ionita, Ion, 295
Iraq and GDR, 268

Jabłoński, Henryk, 291
Jagielski, Mieczysław, 276
Jakeš, Miloš, 149, 290
and communist party, 134, 135
and Husák, 94, 284
interim leadership of, 95, 96
and normalization, 135
Janowski, G., 298
Jaroszewicz, Piotr, 274, 293
Jaruzelski, Wojciech, 290, 291, 293, 295
on alliance with USSR, 70, 74
and anti-Sovietism, 277
and Catholic Church, 37n6, 168
on Eastern Europe as Trojan horse,
    30
and economy, 181, 283
Gorbachev and, 75, 283
John Paul II and, 168, 279
Kania and, 128, 277
on *liberum veto*, 69
and military (Soviet), 288
and 1981 crisis, 276, 277, 278
and Pinkowski, 276
as president, 286, 288
and U.S., 282
on Warsaw Pact, 107
Jazz Section, 282, 283
Jedrychowski, Stefan, 294
Jews
and Czechoslovakia, 252, 257
and Hitler, 64
as non-Russians, 23
and Poland, 18, 162
in Romania, 53–4, 258
as subverters of Russian culture, 24
Johanes, Jaromir, 293
John Paul II, Pope, 274, 277, 279, 284
attempted assassination of, 26
and Jaruzelski, 168, 279
see also Wojtyła, Cardinal Karol

Kádár, János, 154, 257, 261, 276, 286, 289,
    291
on Catholic Church, 165
and communist party, 92, 262, 281, 285
and détente, 58
and economy, 58–9
Gerő and, 260
Gorbachev and, 282

Kádár, János (*cont.*)
  and "Hungaricus," 134
  indigenous base of support of, 129
  and military (Soviet), 262
  and New Economic Mechanism, 176
  ouster of, 137, 153, 285
  on socialism and reform, 140
Kádár, János, Society, 298
Kadijević, Veljko, 295
Kalinin, Mikhail, 292
Kállai, Gyula, 257, 292, 294
Kamiński, F., 298
Kania, Stanisław, 94, 290
  Jaruzelski and, 128
  and 1980–1 crisis, 275, 276, 277
  nomenklatura and, 128, 130
Kardelj, Edvard, 294
Kárpati, Ferenc, 295
Kennan, George
  on division of Europe, 243
  on military blocs in Europe, 234
  on Soviet threat in Europe, 232
Kennedy, John F., 263
Kessler, Heinz, 295
KGB
  and de-Stalinization, 102
  and East European security, 101
  and Lyudmila Zhivkova, 94
  and 1989 changes, 103
Khrushchev, Nikita, 62, 206, 290, 293
  and Berlin, 34, 261, 263
  Gomułka and, 128
  and Hungarian uprising, 1
  and intrabloc relations, 85
  and *nomenklatura*, 93
  ousted, 264
  on revolution, 45
  on socialism, 1, 87
  Yugoslavia and, 259
Kiss, Károly, 294, 298
Kiszczak, Czesław, 285
Klaban, S., 297
Klementis, Vladimir, 256, 257, 264, 293
Kliszko, Zenon, 255
Kohl, Helmut, Chancellor, 145
Koivisto, Mauno (President of Finland), 9
Kolarov, Vasil, 254, 291, 292, 293
Koliševski, Lazar, 292
Konrád, George, 45
  on Europe as "common home," 217
  on Hungary and USSR, 56
Korniyenko, Georgii, 88
Kostov, Traicho, 254, 255, 260, 290
Kosygin, Aleksei, 198, 271, 293
Kovács, Béla, 253
Kozhinov, V., 38n25

Krajger, Sergej, 292
Krasnaya zvezda, 23
Krenz, Egon, 149, 290, 291
  Gysi and, 95, 96, 164
  Honecker and, 96, 193
Krunić, Boško, 291
Kulikov, WTO Commander-in-Chief, 276, 277
Kulishev, G., 293
Kundera, Milan
  on Europe, 40
  on Germany, 66
Kwaśniewski, Aleksander, 296, 298

Lascar, Mihail, 295
Latvia annexed by USSR, 52
Lázár, György, 292
leadership successions (1945–90), Soviet
  and East European, 153–4, 290–95
leading role of the communist party, 89–
  98, 108, 201, 209–10, 221
League of Students (Romania), 299
legitimacy of regimes
  Albania and, 139
  in Eastern Europe, 44, 45, 139–49
  GDR and, 65, 134, 144–8
  Hungary and, 29, 140
  Poland and, 74
  USSR and, 29
  in West, 139, 148–9
Lékai, László, 164
Lenárt, József, 291
Lenin, Vladimir I., 11, 17
  and democratic centralism, 89
  Germany and, 245
  and imperialism, 109–10
  Poland and, 70
  and socialism, 14–15, 63, 247
Lenin Shipyard, 275, 276
Liberal Democratic Party (GDR), 298
liberum veto, 67, 68, 69
Ligachev, Yegor, 200
  and Gorbachev, 38n28
  and political independence of East-
    bloc states, 99
  on reunification of Germany, 223–4,
    245
  on socialism, 214
  and Tbilisi and Baku, 221
Likhachev, Dmitrii, 22
Lilov, Aleksandr, 290, 296, 297
limited sovereignty (*see also* Brezhnev
  Doctrine; socialist
  internationalism), doctrine of, 86,
  88, 202, 267
Lis, Bogdan, 280, 282

Lithuania
  annexed by USSR, 52
  Hungary and, 236
  Poland and, 26, 70
Little Entente, the, 54
Ljubičič, Nikola, 295
Lleshi, Haxhi, 291
Lomský, Bohumír, 294
Lončar, Budimir, 294
Losonczi, Pál, 291
Lublin Committee, 71
Lukanov, Andrei, 187, 292
Lukanov, Karlo, 293
Lukin, Vladimir, 22
Lukyanov, Anatolii, on leading role of
  communist party, 209–10
Luther, Martin, 65, 147, 161
Lutheran Church in East Germany,
  147–8

Macartney, C. A., 55
Macedonia
  and Bulgaria, 48–9
  and Yugoslavia, 49
Machovec, M., 297
Macovescu, Gheorghe, 294
Magyars
  Hungary and, 55–6, 138
  Romania and, 52
  and Slovaks, 61
  Western attitudes toward, 236
Main Political Administration (MPA), 98
Maiziere, Lothar de, 290, 292, 298
Malenkov, Georgii, 290, 293
  and intrabloc relations, 85
  and "New Course," 257
Maléter, Pál, 295
Maleuda, G., 298
Malile, Reiz, 293
Malinovsky, Rodion, 295
Mamula, Branko, 295
Mandler, E., 297
Manescu, Corneliu, 294
Manescu, Manea, 293
Marer, Paul
  on East European products, 112
  and GNP of CMEA members, 78–
    9n32
  on postwar reparations of Eastern
    Europe, 110
Marko, Jan, 293
Marković, Ante, 293
Marković, Dragoslav, 291
Marshall Plan, 110, 233
  announced, 253
  and CMEA, 84, 254

and Czechoslovakia and Poland, 253
Marx, Karl, 15, 16, 17, 18
  and Europe as home of socialism,
    13–14
Marxism-Leninism
  as alien ideology, 24
  in Eastern Europe, 31, 41–2
  and Europe vs. Russia, 13–15
  and Poland, 70–1, 72, 73
  scientific nature of, 29
  in USSR, 31
Masaryk, Jan, 254, 293
Masaryk, Tomáš, 59, 60
  and communism, 61
  and support for anti-Leninists, 25
Maurer, Ion Gheorghe, 291, 293, 294
Mayer, Kurt, 148
Mazowiecki, Tadeusz, 155, 286, 288, 293
MDF, *see* Hungarian Democratic Front
Meckel, Marcus, 294
Medvedev, Roy, on socialism, 82
Medvedev, Vadim, 135
  and Czechoslovakia, 135
  and East European policy, 99, 199,
    200
Messner, Zbigniew, 293
Michael, King, 291
Michnik, Adam, 282
Mihailov, Ivan, 294
Mihályfi, Ernő, 294
Mijatović, Cvijetin, 292
Miklós, Béla, 292
Mikoyan, Anastas, 92, 260, 292
Mikulić, Branko, 293
Milea, Vasile, 295
Militaru, Nicolae, 295
Military Council for National Salvation,
    278
military doctrine (post-1985) of USSR,
    210–13
Miliukov, Paul, and Polish nationalists, 13
Miłosz, Czesław, on Russophobia, 142
Mindszenty, József, 164
Minić, Miloš, 294
Miskane, N., 293
Mladenov, Petar, 153, 287, 290, 291, 293
  and economy, 187
  and *nomenklatura*, 96
Mlynář, Zdeněk, 9
Moczar, Mieczysław, 93
Modrow, Hans, 288, 292
Modzelewski, Zygmunt, 294
Mojsov, Lazar, 291, 292, 294
Moldavia, 52, 53
Molnár, Erík, 294
Molotov, Vyacheslav, 294

Mongolia and economic aid, 116
Montenegro, 53, 285
Montesquieu, 68, 228
Moravia
  and fascism, 17
  Husák and, 61
Moscow Conference of Nine Ruling
    Communist Parties, 271
Moscow Protocol, 92
Moscow Treaty, 269, 270
MPA and the military, 103–4
MSzP, *see* Hungarian Socialist Party
Munich Agreement (1938), 59, 62, 271
Münnich, Ferenc, 292
Münnich, Ferenc, Society, 298
Murra, Prokop, 294

Nagy, Ferenc, 253, 292
Nagy, Imre, 262, 286, 292
  and communist party, 258, 259
  executed, 261
  legacy of, 137
  and 1956 crisis, 260
  and *nomenklatura*, 258
  and reunification of Germany, 66
Napoleon, 16
Nase, Nesti, 293
"national Bolshevism," 17
National Christian Peasants' Party
    (Romania), 299
National Democratic Front (Romania),
    251, 252–3
National Democratic Party (GDR), 298
National Democratic Party (Romania),
    299
National Liberal Party (Romania), 299
National Salvation Front (Romania)
  and Ceauşescu, 185
  and governance issues, 157
  in 1990, 288, 296, 299
  and *nomenklatura*, 96
  and pro-European platform, 95
  and socialism, 55
  and Warsaw Pact, 55
nationalism
  and anti-Sovietism, 142
  in Bulgaria, 48–51, 165–6
  in Eastern Europe, 3, 26–7, 31–3, 35,
    42, 43, 47–8, 142, 203–5, 226–7n45
  in GDR, 144
  Gorbachev and, 22–4
  and Hungary, 58, 59, 138
  and legitimacy of regimes, 142
  in Poland, 69–70, 71–4, 113, 131
  and Romania, 54, 55
  and Russophobia, 142

  in USSR, 220
  and West, 3
NATO, *see* North Atlantic Treaty
    Organization
Naumann, Konrad, 281
Nazi–Soviet Pact of 1939, 17
NDF, *see* National Democratic Front
Neichev, Mincho, 291, 293
Németh, Károly, 153, 281
Németh, Miklós, 179, 292
Neue Forum (GDR), 298
New Class, The (Djilas), 261
"New Course," 257
New Economic Mechanism, 58, 176, 266
Nicholas I (Tsar) and Hungary, 56
Nikezić, Marko, 294
Nikola Petrov Agrarian Union, 297
Nishani, Omer, 291
Nixon, Richard, 268
nomenklatura system, 91–7
  in Bulgaria, 93–4, 96
  in Czechoslovakia, 94, 95, 96, 128, 153,
    218
  in Eastern Europe, 156–7
  in GDR, 95–6
  in Hungary, 96
  and military, 103
  in Poland, 95, 97, 156–7
  in Romania, 94, 96, 184
"normalization," 47
  in Czechoslovakia, 134, 135, 189
North Atlantic Treaty Organization
    (NATO), 33, 233, 254
  and arms deployment, 145, 234–5
  and burden sharing, 105
  cohesion of, 216, 238–41
  and disarmament, 279
  and East European regimes, 237
  FRG and, 222, 259
  future of, 243
  Germany and, 245, 288
  Gorbachev's military doctrine and,
    211, 217, 218
  military and security threat to, 100,
    101, 104
  and reunification of Europe, 230
  USSR and Eastern Europe alliance
    against, 46
North Bukovina, *see* Bukovina
Novopashin, Yurii, on socialist
    internationalism, 205
Novotný, Antonín, 266, 290, 291
  and Brezhnev, 93
  and de-Stalinization, 62
  and Siroky, 264
  and stagnation, 134

NSF, *see* National Salvation Front
nuclear diplomacy, 233–4
Nyers, Resző, 108, 153, 179, 285, 290, 296,
    298

obshchina and socialism, 13
Ochab, Edward, 84, 260, 290, 291
OECD, *see* Organization for Economic
    Cooperation and Development
Olechowski, Tadeusz, 294
Olesiak, 298
Olszowski, Stefan, 130, 281, 294
Olteanu, Constantin, 295
"On the Article of Engels: 'The External
    Policy of Russian Tsarism'"
    (Stalin), 17–18
OPEC, *see* Organization of Petroleum
    Exporting Countries
Open Skies conference, 288
openness, *see glasnost*
Organization for Economic Cooperation
    and Development (OECD)
    GNP growth rate of, 171
Organization of Petroleum Exporting
    Countries (OPEC), 171, 183
Orzechowski, Marian, 294
Osóbka-Morawski, Edward, 293
Ostroumov, Georgii S., 200
Ottoman Empire, 48, 51
    and Romania, 53, 56
Owen, David, on common security, 241–2

Palach, Jan, 267
Palme, Olaf, on common security, 241–2
Palmer, Alan, 67
Pančevski, Milan, 291
Panchevsky, Petur, 294
Parhon, Constantin, 291
Paris Peace Conference, 252
Party of Democratic Socialism (GDR),
    288, 296, 298
Party of Social Democracy of the
    Republic of Poland, 298
Party of Social Democracy (Poland), 296
Paskievich (Russian commander), 56
Patočka, Jan, 273
Patriotic Front (Hungary), 266
Pauker, Ana, 257, 294
Pavel, Josef, 102
Pavlova-Silvanskaya, Marina, on
    socialism, 215
PDS, *see* Party of Democratic Socialism
Petkov, Nikola, 297
Pel'she, Arvid, 198
perestroika, 23, 24, 32, 37n22, 96, 143, 197,
    208, 220, 224, 246, 284

Péter, János, 294
Peter, King, 292
Peter the Great, 70, 216
Petrić, Jakša, 294
Pieck, Wilhelm, 291
Pínkowski, Józef, 275, 276, 293
Pius IX, Pope, 73
Planinc, Milka, 293
Ploughman's Front (Romania), 251
pluralism, 24
Podgorny, Nikolai, 292
Podkrepa, 297
Poland, 149, 153, 159, 229, 251
    and anarchy, 68–9
    and anti-Sovietism, 62, 113, 131, 141,
        277
    Catholic Church and, 13, 26, 48, 70,
        72–3, 74, 166–9, 182, 262, 263, 270,
        274, 275, 277, 278, 279, 284
    chronology of events in (1945–90),
        251–88
    civil rights and amnesty in, 278, 279,
        280, 281, 282, 284
    communist party in, 18, 47, 69, 75, 82,
        88, 90–1, 95, 97, 106, 130, 141, 154–
        5, 160, 162, 167, 168, 218, 220, 253,
        254, 259, 260, 267, 269, 272, 275,
        276, 277, 278, 282, 285, 286, 288,
        290, 296, 298–9
    and "cosmopolitanism," 18
    Czechoslovakia and, 63, 135
    and debt, 118, 121, 177, 178, 180–1, 187,
        188
    defense industry in, 104
    and democracy, 43, 132
    and democratization, 154–5
    and de-Stalinization, 92
    durability of regime in, 130–2
    and economy, 26, 113–14, 118, 173, 177,
        178, 179–82, 187, 188, 190, 245, 254,
        268, 269, 273, 275, 276, 277, 280,
        282, 283, 284, 288
    espionage trials in, 257
    and Europe as common home, 162
    expulsion of Germans from, 255
    and former German territories, 254
    FRG and, 193, 269
    GDR and, 275, 277, 286
    GNP growth rate of, 169, 170–1, 179–
        80, 192
    Hungary and, 236
    and intelligentsia, 162
    and intrabloc trade, 175, 181
    and Jews, 162
    leadership successions in (1945–90),
        290–95

Poland (*cont.*)
    legitimacy of regime in, 74, 140, 141
    Lenin and, 15
    and *liberum veto*, 67–8, 69
    and Lublin Committee, 71
    and Marxism-Leninism, 70–1, 72, 73
    and military (indigenous), 100, 106
    and military (Soviet), 102, 106, 108,
        143
    nationalism in, 69–70, 71–4, 113, 131
    1956 crisis in, 93, 100
    1980–1 crisis in, 30–1, 33, 34, 102–3,
        106, 113–14, 127, 130–2, 141, 167,
        212, 238
    nomenklatura system and, 95, 97, 128,
        156–7
    and partition, 30, 68, 69, 71
    purges in, 254, 275
    and reform, 212
    riots and strikes in, 260, 269, 272–3,
        275, 276, 277–8, 279, 285, *see also*
        Solidarity
    Romania and, 286
    and Russophobia, 70–1, 75
    Slavophiles vs. Westernizers and, 13
    and socialism, 29, 70, 71, 214
    and socialist internationalism, 87
    and Stalinism, 84
    and *szlachta*, 68
    and trade unions, 275, 277, 279
    and trade with USSR, 119, 181
    and trade with West, 180, 181
    U.S. and, 264, 276, 277, 278, 279, 280,
        282
    USSR and, 15, 25, 56, 69–70, 74–5,
        113–14, 119, 181, 251, 276, 278, 288
    viability of regime in, 133
    Warsaw Pact and, 10
    and West, 27, 32–3, 40, 72, 73–4, 75
    and World War II, 71
    see also Solidarity
Polish United Workers' Party, 18, 69, 220,
    259, 260, 267, 269, 282, 290, 296,
    299
    Brezhnev and, 267
    created, 254
    Czechoslovakia and, 277
    and durability of regime, 130
    and excesses and corruption, 141
    and Gomułka, 82
    Gorbachev and, 218
    and intelligentsia, 162
    and military (Soviet), 106
    in 1990, 288, 296
    and *nomenklatura*, 97
    and Solidarity, 47, 75, 95, 97, 154–5,

    160, 167, 168–9, 182, 275, 276, 277,
    278, 282, 285, 286, 288
Ponomarev, Boris, 199
Popiełuszko, Father Jerzy, 168, 280
Popov, Gavril, 38n22
Popović, Koča, 294
Poptomov, Vladimir, 293
Potsdam, 20, 33, 232, 251
Pozsgay, Imre, 96, 138, 179, 296
"Prague Manifesto," 267
Prague Spring (*see also* Czechoslovakia,
    invasion of), 1–2, 26, 60, 102, 134,
    136, 141, 266
Preoteasa, Grigore, 294
Primakov, Yevgenii, and East European
    policy, 200, 201
"Principles of Perestroika" (Yakovlev),
    37n22
Protestant Church in Germany, 48, 147–8
PSD, *see* Party of Social Democracy
Puja, Frigyes, 294
PUWP, *see* Polish United Workers' Party

Rădescu, Nicolae, 251
Rajk, László, 255, 260, 294
Rakhmanin, Oleg, 205
    on socialist internationalism, 203–4
Rákosi, Mátyás, 92, 256, 257, 258, 259,
    260, 262, 290, 292
Rakowski, Mieczysław, 95, 96, 290, 293
Rand Corporation on Soviet subsidies,
    111
Ranković, Alexander, 265
Rapacki, Adam, 294
Rascanu, Vasiliu, 295
Rasputin, Valentin, 24
RCP, *see* Romanian Communist Party
Reagan, Ronald, 283, 284
    and INF agreement, 241, 243
Reformation, 30, 48, 53
regimes, East European
    durability of, 127–32
    legitimacy of, 139–49
    and *nomenklatura*, 128
    viability of, 132–9
Reiche, J., 298
Renovica, Milanko, 291
reunification
    of Europe, 229–31
    of Germany, 67, 193, 217, 222–4, 229–
        30, 240–1, 257, 258, 288
Révész, Géza, 295
"revolution from above," 83, 84
Ribar, Ivan, 292
Ribbentrop–Molotov pact (1939), 71
Ribičič, Mitja, 291, 293

Rokossovski, Konstanty, 255, 260, 295
Roman, Petre, 293
Romania, 6, 153
  Bessarabia and, 51, 54
  and Brezhnev Doctrine, 268
  Catholic Church in, 53, 163
  chronology of events (1945–90) in,
    251–88
  and CMEA, 263, 277, 285
  communist party and, 90–1, 184. 253,
    265, 269, 287, 296, 299
  and debt, 118, 178, 183, 184, 188
  and democratization, 155
  and de-Stalinization, 184
  durability of regime in, 129–30
  and economy, 112, 114, 118, 178, 182–5,
    188, 271, 275, 277, 281
  espionage trials in, 257
  ethnic unrest in, 285, 286, 287
  and fascism, 17
  FRG and, 266
  GNP growth rate of, 169–70, 192
  governance issues in, 157
  Hungary and, 26, 52, 138, 285, 286
  intelligentsia of, 158, 162, 164
  and Jews, 258
  leadership successions in (1945–90),
    290–95
  and Little Entente, 54
  and military, 100–1, 103, 104, 105,
    106
  and National Democratic Front, 251,
    252–3
  and National Salvation Front, 55, 95,
    96, 157, 185, 288, 296, 299
  and nationalism, 54, 55
  nomenklatura system in, 94, 96, 184
  and oil, 182–4
  and Ottoman Empire, 53, 56
  and Paris Peace Conference, 252
  Poland and, 155, 286
  purges in, 255, 257
  and Slavophiles, 12
  and socialist internationalism, 86, 87,
    202
  strikes and riots in, 95, 273, 284, 287,
    288
  and trade with USSR, 112, 114, 119,
    183–4
  Transylvania and, 52, 54
  U.S. and, 268, 274, 284
  USSR and, 25, 51, 112, 114, 119, 183–4,
    261, 264, 265, 266, 271, 274, 286
  Vietnam and, 274
  Wallachia and Moldavia and, 52, 53
  and Warsaw Pact, 10, 108–9, 274
  and West, 32–3, 40, 52–3, 54–5, 236
  Yugoslavia and, 259
Romanian Communist Party, 265, 296
  Ceauşescu and, 184, 269, 287
  see also Romanian Workers' Party
Romanian Workers' Party, 90–1, 253
Rónai, Sándor, 291
Roska, István, on noninterference in
  Eastern Europe, 202–3
Rousseau, Jean-Jacques, 68
Rural Solidarity (Poland), 298
Rusakov, Konstantin, 199
Russian Revolution, 41, 61
Russophobia
  and nationalism, 142
  in Poland, 70–1, 75
  see also anti-Sovietism
Ryzhkov, Nikolai, 283, 293
Rzymowski, Wincenty, 294

St. Methodius, 163
St. Stephen (King of Hungary), 58
St. Wenceslas, 60
Sakharaov, Andrei, 38n22
Salajan, Leontin, 295
San Stefano Treaty, 48–9
Saxony, 30
sblizhenie, 116
  defined, 115
Schabowski, Gunther, 281
Schöpflin, George, 57
Schramm, H., 298
SDI, *see* strategic defense initiative
SDRP, *see* Party of Social Democracy of
  the Republic of Poland
SED, *see* Socialist Unity Party
Sejku, Vice Admiral Temp, 263
Semenov, Vladimir, 258
Serb, Ion, 270
Seton-Watson, Hugh, 43, 48
Shafarevich, Igor, 23, 38n25
Shakhnazarov, Georgii, 206
  and East European policy, 199, 200,
    201
  on socialist internationalism, 205
Shehu, Mehmet, 278, 292, 293, 294
Shepilov, Dmitrii, 294
Shevardnadze, Eduard, 99, 294
  and East European policy, 200, 201,
    210, 213
  on Eastern Europe, 197, 198
  on reunification of Germany, 224
  and Romania, 183–4, 218
Shishlin, Nikolai
  on Brezhnev Doctrine, 88
  and East European policy, 199, 200

Shishlin, Nikolai (*cont.*)
  on military, 122n13
  on socialist internationalism, 204–5
Shteppa, Konstantin F., and new
  Slavophilism, 17
Shtylla, Behar, 293
Shvernik, Nikolai, 292
Sík, Endre, 294
Simeon, King, 291
Simić, Stanoje, 294
Sindermann, Horst, 292
Široký, Viliam, 264, 292, 293
Siwicki, Florian, 295
Škoda, J., 297
Skrzeszewski, Stanisław, 294
Skubiszewski, Krzysztof, 294
Slánský, Rudolf, 257, 264, 290
Slavophiles vs. Westernizers, 12–13, 16
Slavs, 52
  and Hitler, 64
  Western attitudes toward, 236
Slovakia, 60, 163
  and fascism, 17
  and USSR, 25
Slovaks, 61–2
  and Slavophiles, 12
Smallholders' Party, 251, 253
Sobieski, Jan, 68
Social Democratic Party (Bulgaria), 297
Social Democratic Party (GDR), 298
Social Democratic Party (Hungary), 298
Social Democratic Party (Romania), 299
Social Democratic Union (Poland), 298
socialism
  and democratic centralism, 205
  in Eastern Europe, 25, 28–9, 32–3, 41–
    4, 149, 221, 242, 246
  Europe as home of, 13–15
  and fascism, 41
  German roots of, 65
  in Hungary, 214
  and Khrushchev, 1
  in Poland, 70, 71, 214
  redefined, 213–15
  and reform, 1–2, 5, 6, 21, 27–8
  and Romania in 1989, 55
  separate paths to, 1
  and socialist internationalism, 201–6,
    207, 219
  and unity of bloc members, 46
socialist internationalism, 198, 207
  debate on, 201–6
  defined, 219
  under Gorbachev, 218–22
  and nationalism, 86–7

  and political independence of East-
    bloc states, 87–9
  and unity of alliance, 87
  see also Brezhnev Doctrine; limited
    sovereignty, doctrine of
Socialist Party (Poland), 299
Socialist Unity Party of Germany–Party
  of Democratic Socialism (SED–
  PDS), 94–5, 287, 288
Socialist Unity Party (SED), 64, 67, 256,
  257, 276–7, 281, 282, 287, 296, 298
Sokol movement, 60
Sokolov, Sergei, 295
Solidarity, 279, 282, 284, 298
  and anarchy, 69, 79–80n42
  Catholic Church and, 73, 74, 167,
    168–9, 182, 280
  and economy, 170, 179, 180, 288
  in 1980–1, 26, 69, 73, 160, 167, 179,
    180, 275–6, 277–8
  in 1988–90, 75, 95, 97, 154–5, 181–2,
    285, 286, 288
  pro-Europe platform of, 95
  PUWP and, 47, 75, 95, 97, 154–5, 160,
    167, 168–9, 182, 275, 276, 277, 278,
    282, 285, 286, 288
Soviet–Finnish declaration (1989), 220
Soviet Ministry of Defense, 98
Soviet Union, *see* Union of Soviet
  Socialist Republics
Špiljak, Mika, 292, 293
Spychalski, Marian, 255, 291, 295
Stainov, P., 293
Stalin, Josef, 257, 290, 293, 295
  Bulgaria and, 49
  and Catholic Church, 162
  Czechoslovakia and, 25
  and economy, 206
  and intelligentsia, 162
  and internationalism, 82–5, 86
  and interparty relations, 98
  on Marx and Engels, 18, 37n14
  and "national Bolshevism," 17–18
  and Poland, 25, 71
  and purges, 45
  and Slavophilism, 14, 16, 17
  and Stalinism, 15–19, 81–5
  and "two-camp" doctrine, 18–19
  and World War II, 19–20
  and Yalta, 43
Stalingrad, battle of, 223
Stalinism
  and communism, 121n1
  and cult of personality, 81, 82, 83, 84
  in Eastern Europe, 81–5

in international relations, 82–4
and Russian socialism, 15–19
Stambolić, Petar, 292, 293
Stanculescu, Anastase, 295
Staniszkis, Jadwiga, 80
Stockholm Conference on Disarmament
in Europe (CDE), 211–12
Stoica, Chivu, 291, 293
Stoph, Willi, 268, 291, 292, 295
strategic defense initiative, 230
Straub, Brunó, 291
Štrougal, Lubomír, 292
Šubašić, Ivan, 294
successions, leadership, Soviet and East
European, 153–4, 290–95
Sudeten Germans, 62, 255
"Support," 297
Suslov, Mikhail, 198, 260
Šuvar, Stipe, 291
Svoboda, Ludvík, 257, 266, 270, 291, 294
Szakasits, Árpád, 291
SzDSz, *see* Alliance of Free Democrats
szlachta, 68
Szürös, Mátyás, 138, 291

Tatarescu, Gheorghe, 294
Tatars, 52
Tbilisi, 221
Tepavac, Mirko, 294
Third International, *see* Comintern and
democratic centralism
Tikhonov, Nikolai, 293
Tildy, Zoltán, 251, 291, 292
Tito, Josip Broz, 251, 291, 292, 293, 295
and economy, 256
and German reunification, 66
and indigenous support, 129
and nationalism, 254
and purges, 255, 265
and Stalinism, 82
Third World and, 274
USSR and, 41, 49, 273
Tiutchev, Fyodor, 13
Todorov, Stanko, 292
Totu, Ioan, 294
Traikov, Georgi, 254, 291
Transylvania, 52–3, 54
and Hungarians, 58
Romania and, 252
Trnka, F., 297
Tuchman, Barbara, on Western attitude
toward Eastern Europe, 236
Turkey
and Bulgaria, 268

and Bulgarian Turks, 51, 166, 256, 268,
286
"two-camp" doctrine, 18, 19
roots of, 248n6
"two-check employees," 102
"Two Thousand Words," 267

UDF, *see* Union of Democratic Forces
Ukraine
and Eurocommunism, 29
nationalism in, 26
Ulbricht, Walter, 92, 144, 163, 255, 257,
269, 290, 291
Union for Social Democracy (Poland),
296
Union of Democratic Forces (Bulgaria),
297
Union of Soviet Socialist Republics
Albania and, 262, 263, 279
and arms buildup, 1
Austria and, 259
Bulgaria and, 25, 48–50, 51, 119, 186,
218, 253
Catholic Church and, 13, 37n6
cohesion of, 245–6
communist party of, 11, 85–99, 108,
199–201, 206–7, 208, 209–10, 219,
221, 246, 260, 263, 265, 282, 285, *see*
also Communist Party of the
Soviet Union
and conceptions of Eastern Europe,
11–24
and Congress of Peoples' Deputies,
208
Czechoslovakia and, 25, 62–3, 113, 119,
175, 251, 267, 273, 281, 288
debt of, 188
and defense industries, 104–5
and democratization, 66, 208–10, 212,
214
and economic interest in Eastern
Europe, 2–3, 4, 23, 109–21
and economy, 1, 2–3, 4, 23, 24, 38n28,
66, 109–21, 245–6, 110–18, 119–21,
174–5, 183–4, 188, 252
ethnic unrest in, 220, 245–6, 288
and fascism, 23
and foreign investment, 24, 38n28
FRG and, 269, 271, 286
GDR and, 119–20, 193, 259, 260, 265
GNP growth rate of, 105, 109, 111, 171,
194–5
Hungary and, 25, 56–7, 138–9, 273, 288
importance of Eastern Europe to,
9–11

Union of Soviet Socialist Republics (*cont.*)
and internationalists, 22–4
and isolationism, 23–4
leadership successions (1945–90) in,
290–5
legitimacy of regime in, 29
Marxism-Leninism in Eastern Europe
and, 42
and military and security presence in
Europe, 3–4, 5, 10–11, 29–36, 44–
5, 46, 99–109, 232, 234–5
military doctrine (post-1985) of, 107,
210–13, 222, 241–3, 283, 285
and multicandidate elections, 208
and "national Bolshevism," 17
and nationalism in Eastern Europe,
26–7
and nuclear diplomacy, 233–4
and oil, 111, 114, 117
Poland and, 15, 25, 56, 69–70, 74–5,
113–14, 119, 181, 251, 276, 277, 278,
288
and political interest in Eastern
Europe, 3–4, 25–9
and reunification of Germany, 66,
222–4, 240–1, 246
Romania and, 25, 51, 112, 114, 119, 183–
4, 261, 264, 265, 266, 271, 274, 286
and socialism, 26, 27–9, 213–15
as stabilizer in Eastern Europe, 25
and trade with Eastern Europe, 110–
14, 119–21, 174–5, 252
and trade with West, 112, 118
Warsaw Pact and, 238–41
and West, 23, 112, 118, 216–18, 222–3, 224
and World War II, 19–20
and xenophobia, 22–4
Yugoslavia and, 251, 254, 255, 259, 261,
271
see also Warsaw Pact
United States
and arms reductions, 242–3
Czechoslovakia and, 251, 278
and deployment of arms in Europe,
232, 239–40
and European policy (postwar), 231–8
GDR and, 272
Hungary and, 273, 284
and NATO, 238–41
and nuclear diplomacy, 233–4
Poland and, 264, 276, 277, 278, 279,
280, 282
and reunification of Germany, 239
Romania and, 268, 274, 284
Urbánek, Karel, 136, 290
USD, *see* Union for Social Democracy

uskorenie, 208
USSR, *see* Union of Soviet Socialist
Republics
Ustinov, Dmitrii, 198, 295
U-2 incident, 262

Vacek, Karol, 295
Václavík, Milán, 295
Vaduva, Ilie, 294
Vance, Cyrus, on common security,
241–2
Varga, Evgeni, on U.S. threat in Europe,
232
Várkonyi, Péter, 294
Vasilevsky, A. M., 295
Velchev, D., 294
Verdet, Ilie, 293
Veres, Péter, 295
viability and legitimacy of East European
regimes, 4, 132–49
Vietnam, 10
China and, 274
and economic aid, 116
and socialism, 28
Vlad the Impaler, 101
Vladimirov, O., *see* Rakhmanin, Oleg
Vlajković, Radovan, 292
Vörös, János, 295
Vörös, V., 298
Voroshilov, Klement, 292
Vrhovec, Josip, 294
vyravnivanie, 116
Vyshinskii, Andrei, 83, 294

Wałęsa, Lech, 155, 277, 278, 279, 280, 288,
298
Wallachia, 52, 53
"Warsaw Letter," 267
Warsaw Pact, 81, 270, 271
and arms reductions, 279, 280, 282
cohesion of, 238–41
created, 259
Czechoslovakia and, 266, 267
and deployment of nuclear weapons,
234–5
de-Stalinization and, 85
and détente, 275
and East European armies, 100, 101,
104–5, 106
and Europeanization, 230
and future, 242, 245
GDR and, 262
Hungary and, 58, 100, 108, 260
members of, 10
and peace in Europe, 33, 237
Poland and, 100, 108, 276, 277, 278

and policy (post-1985) of USSR, 97,
107, 108, 210, 211, 212, 218
renewed, 281
Romania and, 54, 55, 274
and socialist internationalism, 202–3,
210, 219
U.S. and, 268
USSR and, 6, 31, 97
Warsaw Treaty, 269, 270
Warsaw Treaty Organization, *see* Warsaw
Pact
Weiske, C., 298
Weizsaecker, Richard von, 67
West Berlin, *see* Berlin
West Germany, *see* Federal Republic of
Germany (FRG)
Western Europe
and arms reductions, 241–3
and détente, 228–9
peace movements in, 34
as source of democracy, 27
and ties with Eastern Europe, 243–4
Westernizers
and pan-European community, 21–2
vs. Slavophiles, 12–13, 16
What Is To Be Done? (Lenin), 14
Winzer, Otto, 293
Wojtaszek, Emil, 294
Wojtyła, Cardinal Karol, 167, 274
on communism, 72
see also John Paul II, Pope
World War II, 231
impact of, on USSR, 19–20
Writers' Union (Czechoslovakia), 162, 266
WTO, *see* Warsaw Pact
Wyszyński, Cardinal Stefan, 72, 167, 262,
277

Yakovlev, Aleksandr, 37n22, 200, 204
and East European policy, 99, 199, 201
on leading role of communist party,
209, 210
on reunification of Germany, 224
Yalta, 20, 25, 33, 43, 228, 251
Yazov, Dmitrii, 295
and Tbilisi and Baku, 221
Yel'tsin, Boris Nikolayevich, at 27th Party
Congress, 206
Yepishev, General Aleksei
on communist party in intrabloc
relations, 85–6
on socialist internationalism, 98
Yugoslavia, 66, 127, 264

Albania and, 258, 279
Balkan Pact and, 259
Bulgaria and, 255, 256, 258, 261
chronology of events (1945–90) in,
251–88
and Cominform, 84
communist party in, 41, 91, 251, 252,
260, 261, 266, 274
debt of, 121, 188
economy of, 129, 188, 256, 273, 274, 283
ethnic unrest in, 269, 270, 276, 277,
279
FRG and, 271
GNP growth rate of, 170
Hungary and, 258
legitimacy of regime in, 129, 139
and Little Entente, 54
Macedonia and, 49
and military, 100
purges in, 270, 272
Romania and, 259
and socialist internationalism, 87, 202,
220
U.S. and, 233, 264
USSR and, 51, 129, 220, 251, 254, 255,
259, 261, 271
Vietnam and, 274
and West, 32–3
Yugov, Anton, 254, 263, 292

Zagladin, Vadim, 201
Zápotocký, Antonín, 291, 292
Žarković, Vidoje, 291
Zawadzki, Aleksander, 291
Zhdanov, Andrei
and "two-camp" doctrine, 18, 19, 232,
248n6, 253
Zhelev, Z., 296
Zhivkov, Todor, 96, 149, 154, 287, 290,
291, 292
and communist party, 259, 263, 265,
283–4
and economy, 186, 259, 262, 283–4
FRG and, 272, 280
and nationalism, 49, 50, 51, 166
and USSR, 50
Zhivkova, Lyudmila
and intelligentsia, 165–6
and nationalism, 49
and Politburo, 94
Zhukov, Georgii, 295
Zog, King, 252, 291
Żymierski, Michał Rola, 295